FOUNDATIONS OF THE MARKET-PRICE SYSTEM

Milton M. Shapiro

UNIVERSITY
PRESS OF
AMERICA

LANHAM • NEW YORK • LONDON

Library of Congress Cataloging in Publication Data

Shipiro, Milton M.
    Foundations of the market-price system.

    Bibliography: p.
    Includes index.
    1. Microeconomics. I. Title.
HB172.S49   1985   338.5   84-29077
ISBN 0-8191-4542-4 (alk. paper)
ISBN 0-8191-4543-2 (pbk. : alk. paper)

All University Press of America books are produced on acid-free
paper which exceeds the minimum standards set by the National
Historical Publications and Records Commission.

TO MY PARENTS

Baruch and Rivkah,
who gave me life

and

TO MY FAMILY

Jeanne, Johanna and Arthur,
who fulfill that life.

ACKNOWLEDGMENTS

First, intellectual debts. The greatest of them, and most gratefully acknowledged, are to those thinkers who helped create, shape, and nourish the Austrian tradition in economics. Chief among these men are Ludwig von Mises and Friedrich A. Hayek--who never lost sight of the bridges linking economics with the other sciences of human action--and Murray N. Rothbard and Israel M. Kirzner, current regenerators of the tradition and innovators on their own. The Austrians have taught us to view man as a whole person and not as mere "economic man" geared to a materialist calculus, nor as a figment of abstract mechanical constructs--that is, man in his total reality instead of the fore-shortened reality viewed through the prism of mathematical models. Thus they have treated economics as but one facet of the general science of human action.

In this connection I must also mention the late Professor Clyde W. Phelps, who fortunately turned me on to the Austrians in the first place during the final years of my graduate studies, and Henry Hazlitt, whose works feature tributes to the Austrians. Also, like an oasis in the desert was the Foundation for Economic Education, Irvington-on-Hudson, N.Y., whose monthly The Freeman has featured works by the Austrians and on the free-market system, and whose inspired president, the late Leonard E. Read, made sure there was always enough water to refresh the "remnants."

Other intellectual debts are no less noteworthy. Important insights were provided by Armen A. Alchian and William R. Allen in their pathbreaking texts, University Economics and Exchange and Production. Other of these debts are expressed in my references throughout these pages, while still other debts may regretfully go without specific acknowledgement owing to infirmities of memory.

Gratitude of another sort is extended to those who took time out to review early drafts, particularly Professors Rothbard, Alchian, and Ludwig M. Lachmann. Needless to say, none of the above can be held responsible for any misinterpretation or misuse of their work on my part.

On a more practical level, this book would not have been possible without creative and Sabbatical leaves granted by the California State Polytechnic University, Pomona, nor without fellowships and grants from the Institute for Humane Studies, Menlo Park. At the Institute it was my good fortune to receive from the outset the personal encouragement of the late Floyd A. Harper, as well as Kenneth S. Templeton, Jr., both of them dedicated spokesmen for liberty and property rights in a humane society, as well as promoters of research and writing on the free market.

In a similar vein, I am most grateful to the directors of the University Press of America reprint program for their recognition of this book's merits and for this opportunity to reach a much wider audience.

Finally, but no less deserving of recognition are Karen Meade, for her typing skills and editorial acumen, and Robert M. Marvos, for his bold graphics.

CONTENTS

TABLES AND FIGURES

Figures (continued)

x

PREFACE

This book on introductory micro-economics was forged as a by-product of some 20 years' teaching of university economics. Earlier editions appeared under the title The Common Sense of Economics. From its inception in 1974 it has been used as a text in my classes.

Nevertheless, it was also conceived to appeal to the "common sense" of the general audience, as well as to the practical-minded business school student. Indeed, the original title, inspired by Philip Wicksteed's The Common Sense of Political Economy (1910, 1946), was meant to reflect the book's underlying methodology as much as to pay homage to that great writer.

Last but not least: This book, being of convenient length, can also serve as a suitable companion to other texts. Although it treats of the standard material, it does so in a truly alternative and complementary fashion, and is only minimally duplicative. Furthermore, it is thoroughly devoid of mathematical impedimenta.

This new edition incorporates extensive editorial changes and the addition of appendixes to Chapters VIII and X, a vastly expanded introduction and other front matter, an index, and a reading list. Thus, it was also a fitting occasion for the change in title to one that is more descriptive of the book's substance.

Although this is primarily a textbook in the principles of micro-economics, my desire is to give it relevance to a wider audience. Thus, I have reached out beyond the traditional confines of other texts to include non-technical elements which I believe are required for two purposes: to elucidate the ultimate foundations of the subject, and to create links or bridges between human action in the realm of economics and human action in general, particularly in the dimension of subjective motivation and decision-making.

In this connection it is pertinent to note that an ironic strain is intermittently played in this book, starting in Chapter I, precisely because it is so

xi

instructive. The irony involves playing off the primitive Robinson Crusoe (the wilderness man of economics),
who lives so grimly alone in the bosom of nature,
against modern man who lives so much more richly at ease
in the advanced modern division of labor. Specifically,
the irony is based on the following elements. On the
one hand, with respect to the relevance of the basic
economic principles of survival and prosperity there is
no essential difference between the case of Crusoe and
that of modern man (see especially Chapter IV).
However, when it comes to being directly aware of the
basic natural laws of existence, it is Crusoe who has it
over modern man.

The reason is that man living alone in nature's
wilderness learns soon enough the lessons that nature
implies for him: the need to work and produce and live
by his wits; the need to assume the natural right to do
all of these things as well as the right to keep and
cherish the fruit of his labors; and, above all, the
need to assume the burdens of self-responsibility. It
is very much otherwise in the case of modern man
ensconced in polities concerned for his cradle-to-grave
needs. (On this see Chapter I.)

In virtually every dimension of modern existence, the complexities and sophistication required to
sustain and advance civilization have removed man so far
from wilderness existence that the direct, clear dic-
tates of nature are obscured from his view. Thus, while
we unquestionably live so much better than our primitive
ancestors (see Chapter III), too often we don't really
know why! I'm reminded of the very apt line from the
poet Goethe:

Ein jeder lebt's, nicht vielen ist's bekannt.

(We are all doing it; very few of us understand what we are doing.)

Add to this the obfuscations, deliberate or
inadvertent, of those messianic types who would deliver
us from all our travails by imposing their illusions,
myths and utopian visions on the rest of us--and it
follows that the task of discerning and explaining the

true nature of economic existence becomes so much more difficult.[1]

I have also opted to avoid the tendency of texts to become encyclopedic, overloaded with topics and applications at the expense of in-depth treatment of fundamentals. Instead, the present work restricts itself mainly to topics required to understand the workings of the market-price mechanism; it also provides an in-depth treatment of these same topics, reaching down to the irreducible levels of fundamentals.

For the rest, for the purpose of greater illustration and application of analysis to public issues and policies, I defer for the most part to the numerous useful works devoted especially to this purpose.[2] These works, including books of readings, provide ample supplementary materials that illustrate at length how economic theory or principles manifest themselves in practice and how economic analysis can be applied to practical problems.

Before proceeding to the chapter-by-chapter introductions, it is necessary to point out that economic tracts--mainly because of materialist bias--usually omit the very important moral dimension, a dimension that is nevertheless relevant to economic reality--to economics in practice.[3] First of all, economics as a social science is fundamentally concerned with exchange-- "interpersonal transactions." Exchange is inherent in

---

[1]See Thomas Sowell, Knowledge and Decisions (New York: Basic Books, Inc., 1980) for an elaborate analysis of how--despite the complex structures and environments of the modern division of labor--the free society and its market-price system generate, transmit, and apply "authentic" knowledge in the realms of economics, law, and politics. For an earlier treatment, see Friedrich A. Hayek, The Constitution of Liberty (Chicago: University of Chicago Press, 1960).

[2]Excellent examples of this type of supplementary work are John C. Goodman and Edwin G. Dolan, Economics of Public Policy: The Micro View (2nd ed., St. Paul: West Publishing Co., 1982), and Walter E. Williams, America: A Minority Viewpoint (Stanford: Hoover Institution Press, 1982).

[3]A notable exception is the above-mentioned text by Goodman and Dolan which analyzes public issues in terms of moral, political and economic criteria.

every production and trade activity. Thus, the market-
price system may be regarded as comprising multitudinous
exchange transactions.   Since exchange also infuses
every interpersonal transaction in society at large, it
also constitutes the basic coordinating mechanism of
that most complex network of interrelationships called
"society."

     Exchange transactions regarded as interpersonal
activity necessarily involve the elementary moral question: by what moral principle should exchange between
party A and party B be governed? [4]   Here only two basic
principles are relevant: either the principle of non-
violence (non-aggression) or its opposite, violence
(aggression). Violence and aggression can be identified
simply by such acts as theft, killing and fraud.

     From this perspective, the voluntary nature of
market   exchange transactions precludes violence or
aggression, otherwise free exchange or trade would presumably not take place. Voluntary or non-violent mutual
exchange respects the right of any party to a potential
exchange (say, party A) not to be aggressed against,
that is, not to be mugged, slain, or defrauded simply
because someone else (say, party B) covets what A possesses.   Thus, it is not to be taken for granted that
free trade and interpersonal exchange will automatically
occur without mutual respect for the moral precept of
non-violence.   Therefore, any sanction of violence and
aggression in interpersonal relations would not only
preclude real exchange possibilities but would give free
rein to the law of the jungle and barbarism. [5]

     Thus, in this perspective, the study of the
social economy and the market-price mechanism involves
the moral dimension as well as the economic one.   For
the purpose of this book it suffices simply to call
attention to the matter--to the fact that the omni-
present but taken-for-granted act of voluntary exchange
constitutes a moral premise for the free economy and the
free society.

---

[4]For a philosophical treatment of morality in interpersonal
relations, see John Hospers' Human Conduct (2nd ed., New York:
Harcourt Brace Jovanovich, Inc., 1982).

[5]For a detailed study of these and related issues, see Murray
N. Rothbard,   The Ethics of Liberty (Atlantic Highlands, N.J.:
Humanities Press, 1982).

Ultimately, all theoretical economic systems boil down in principle to only two: the <u>free-market</u> society and <u>socialism</u>. In that perspective, the present work on the free market-price system may also be regarded as a contribution, albeit introductory, to the study of comparative economic systems.6

<hr />

[6]For a well-rounded "pluralist" approach to the capitalist system that includes analysis of its "moral-cultural" dimensions, as well as the political and economic, see Michael Novak, <u>The Spirit of Democratic Capitalism</u> (New York: Simon and Schuster, 1982).

INTRODUCTIONS TO CHAPTERS

Following is an outline of the main features and perspectives of each chapter and what I believe are their respective special qualities.

Chapter I

The primary purpose of this chapter is to prepare the reader for the concept of scarcity to be analyzed in the next chapter. Scarcity is the fundamental problem to which economics is addressed. However, the concept of scarcity requires advance preparation since it tends to strike the untutored as too abstract or ideological (e.g., a "bourgeois" rationalization).

Scarcity is the basic reason that man must engage in productive work, yet the institutions of modern complex society (e.g., the elaborate network of transfers and welfare programs) are ironically able to disguise the underlying reality of scarcity. Incidentally, this chapter also introduces Robinson Crusoe, that model of isolated man from whose bare and lonely existence in the bosom of nature we can learn so many of the fundamental concepts of economics.[1]

Also noteworthy is the fundamental categorical distinction between "economic means" and "political means," the analysis of which enables us to argue the primacy of economic production as compared with the principle of governmental political power.[2]

---

[1]An excellent example of the many fundamental concepts that we can learn in "Crusoe economics" are the first 62 pages in Murray N. Rothbard, Man, Economy, and State, 2 vols. (Princeton: D. Van Nostrand Co., 1962).

[2]A noteworthy attempt to apply the distinction between "economic means" and "political means" to the analysis of contemporary domestic issues is by James D. Davidson, The Squeeze (New York: Summit Books, 1980).

Chapter II

        This chapter is concerned not only with
scarcity, the fundamental and unique problem of interest
to economics, but it also establishes a conceptual
framework for most of the remainder of the book (as
illustrated in Figure 5).

        Scarcity is analyzed primarily in terms of the
wants-means connection (i.e., the ends-means connection)
which comprises the twin aspects of the fundamental
condition of human existence. In the first go-around we
see how scarcity implies the necessity of production, an
implication that is drawn both for (a) the case of
Robinson Crusoe and other direct-use models of economy,
and (b) the market mode of economy based on the social
division of labor (Chapters II - IV). In contrast to
the social or "macro" perspective of the latter is the
fundamental individualist perspective (in Chapters V -
VII) which draws out the implications of scarcity for
individual choice or decision-making.

        Economics remains the only social science pre-
occupied with scarcity and its implications. Nevertheless, the other social sciences can surely learn from
the economists' preoccupations. The analysis of
decision-making in Chapter V is but one example. Even
more significant is the variety of bold contributions
being made by economists to the understanding of
decision-making in traditionally non-economic areas,
such as politics and social problems, under the heading
of public-choice theory. 3

Chapter III

        Although this chapter assumes a historical
approach, its purpose is analytical: to explain some
important things that are too often taken for granted.
Thus it tries to fathom the implicit rationality of the
historical evolution of specialization, the social
division of labor, and the invention of money. A social
science like economics is necessarily concerned with the
study of the fundamental elements that induce the

        3A good example of this fruitful work is Richard B. McKenzie
and Gordon Tullock, The New World of Economics (3rd ed., Homewood,
Ill.: Richard D. Irwin, Inc., 1981).

interpersonal relations and transactions (i.e., exchange, trade) that underlie all market-place activity. Coincidentally, the analysis of <u>money</u> is unique since it is a topic usually treated only in macro-economic texts.

Chapter IV

On the one hand this chapter is concerned with the key concept of <u>production</u> and how it is immediately implied as the only relevant human response to unsatisfied wants. Thus it necessarily embraces the analysis of productivity, innovation, technological progress, and capital accumulation.

On the other hand, in the context of the social division of labor, production is necessarily centered in <u>firms</u>, those social-economic units that specialize in playing the role of <u>intermediary</u> between people as consumers and people as resource-owners (i.e., workers, savers, investors). This is a role that necessarily calls for <u>entrepreneurship</u>--decision-making in the face of uncertain market conditions. In this respect the chapter lays groundwork for Chapter IX, on the profit margin, and Chapter X, on consumers' sovereignty.

It is this focus on the <u>centrality of the firm</u>-- as producer and entrepreneurial intermediary--which alone enables us to appreciate how the so-called "impersonal" or "automatic" forces of market supply and demand operate not only to determine prices but also to coordinate the whole range of market-oriented decisions of households and firms. Chapters VI through X analyze in detail how profit-motivated firms provide the market its inherent tendency to relative stability.

A fruitful by-product of this analysis is the realization that,in the social division of labor, it is <u>investment by firms</u> that is the primary source of income earned by resource-owners. Contrary to prevailing orthodoxy, the primary generator of income in the modern economy is the investment by firms in production and employment of resources--not the Keynesians' aggregate demand which, after all, is an abstract, synoptic concept.

Last but not least, this chapter introduces us to the nature of the "consumers' sovereignty" problem, which receives its deserved full-length treatment in Chapter X. 4

Chapter V

Superficially this chapter brings together a string of standard economic concepts that are all relevant to individual decision-making. On a more fundamental level, however, it seeks to connect those concepts in a logical chain whose links are systematically derived from the underlying premise of scarcity. It culminates in an elaborate treatment of both the maximization priniciple and the axiom of self-interest.

Original in the treatment of the maximization principle is the attempt to apply it to all cases, without exception, of decision-making. Treatment of self-interest is likewise unconventional in its argument that maximization and self-interest are, without exception, the sole and fundamental principles of motivation in human action. These constructions should broaden our appreciation of the unitary connection between so-called economic principles and human action in general, by helping to end the misconception that economics is narrowly confined to that phantom called "economic man," and by showing that "economizing" behavior is intimately related to universally maximizing behavior.

In preparing this material the author found no little inspiration in the seminal but sadly neglected works of Ludwig von Mises and Philip H. Wicksteed. 5 A brief passage from Wicksteed suffices to illustrate the perspective:

It follows that the general principles which regulate our conduct in business are identical with those which regulate our deliberations, our selections between alternatives, and our decisions in all other branches of of life. And this is why we not only may,

---

[4]The author is indebted to Israel M. Kirzner, Market Theory and the Price System (Princeton: D. Van Nostrand Co., 1963) for insights developed in this and the next chapter.

[5]Ludwig von Mises, Human Action (New Haven: Yale University Press, 1949); Philip H. Wicksteed, The Common Sense of Political Economy, 2 vols. (London: Routledge & Sons, 1946).

but must, take our <u>ordinary</u> <u>experiences</u> as the starting point for approaching economic problems. We must regard industrial and commercial life, not as a separate and detached region of activity, but as an <u>organic part</u> of our whole personal and social life; and we shall find the clue to the conduct of men in their commercial relations, not in the first instance amongst those characteristics wherein our pursuit of industrial objects <u>differs</u> from our own pursuit of pleasure or of learning, or our efforts for some political and social ideal, but rather amongst those underlying principles of conduct and selection wherein they all <u>resemble</u> each other...[6] (underlinings mine).

Thus the analysis proceeds from the premise of a common or unitary motivational principle in all human action--the "economic" as well as the "non-economic"-- in which so-called <u>economic</u> action is regarded as a special case of human action in general, and whose motivations are consistent with those of human action in general.

In this connection the concept of <u>subjective value</u> is developed as the basic force that <u>determines</u> the degree of importance that we attach to our <u>goals</u> and <u>purposes</u>, on the one hand, and to the <u>means</u> of achieving them, on the other. Explored are two dimensions of influence on subjective value: preference-scale rankings and the supply of means (law of marginal utility); later, Chapter IX explores the third dimension of influence, people's time-preference. In general, subjective value and its primary role in human action are sadly neglected topics in standard texts.

Chapters VI - VIII

This trio of chapters constitute the traditional core of technical analysis of <u>the market</u>--on how the "interplay" of demand and supply determines <u>market prices</u>. The market is the central nexus of the social division of labor; intertwined networks of markets

---

[6]Philip H. Wicksteed, <u>The Common Sense of Political Economy</u>, Vol. I, p. 3.

comprise the market-price system; the latter in turn represents in principle the heart of so-called capitalism as well as the focus of this book. Although the three chapters run to about 120 pages, they are surely less than the subject deserves. However, compared with other introductory treatments, they are truly very ample.

One of the reasons for the elaborate analysis in this work is to counteract the tendency of texts to treat the market process of price determination somewhat mechanically, as though the market operates "automatically" and "impersonally"--a thoroughly illegitimate assumption. Real markets consist of blood-and-flesh human beings, not artificial constructs like "economic man," and therefore behave neither automatically nor predictably. Analysis must take this realism into account, as this book attempts throughout.

There is also the need to amply demonstrate the centrality of the firm in the workings of the market process. This centrality was initially asserted in Chapters II and IV. Then in Chapters VI and VII, market demand is analyzed at sufficient length to comprehend all those relevant dimensions of demand (e.g., income, taste and preference, price elasticity) about which the firm must become informed. Mainly through market research and related studies, as well as through trial and error, can firms gain the knowledge needed to reduce the probability of error in its estimates and forecasts of market demand. [7]

In Chapter VIII, which ostensibly shows how the market determines prices, the analysis attempts to demonstrate that in reality it is not so much the "market" per se that establishes prices but rather it is the firm which sets them at all times. It is the firm that sets prices initially, and it is the firm that later adjusts prices (and quantities) in response to the market feedback of surplus or shortage. Even more significant, it is the firm, in its efforts to maximize profits (or minimize losses), that makes the price and quantity adjustments required to avoid disequilibria

---

[7]On the centrality of the firm and entrepreneurship in the market process see Israel M. Kirzner, Competition and Entrepreneurship (Chicago: University of Chicago Press, 1973) and his Perception, Opportunity, and Profit (Chicago: University of Chicago Press, 1979).

(surpluses, shortages), and thereby creates the market's tendency toward stability of output and prices. The implication is clear: If the market process is shaped by a force that inheres toward stability, then the alleged "instability" and "anarchy" so glibly blamed on the market must be located elsewhere, in non-market sources.[8]

More specifically, Chapters VI and VII, on the demand side of the market, focus on two things: (a) those elements that determine the shape and location of demand, and (b) the ways in which the behavior of these elements can be made known to the firm (especially via the concept of elasticity of demand). It is precisely the economist's task to isolate and describe those determinants of market demand whose impacts are discernable and knowable by the firm.

The text also assists the reader in understanding the partial-analysis method used by economists (e.g. the ceteris paribus proviso) as the necessary first step in unraveling the complex manifestations of reality. Also, Chapter VI offers an alternative explanation of why the demand curve slopes the way it does, and why the law of demand brooks of no exceptions, alleged or otherwise.

Noteworthy also is the lengthy Chapter VII on the elasticity of demand, which makes this significant concept realistic and practical, and avoids the mathematical ("percentage") approach so typical of other texts. Thus it demonstrates that the law of demand (Chapter VI) is not enough, surely not for the firm; indeed, mere reliance on the law of demand can prove disastrous for the firm when it seeks to initiate a price raise or price cut. Thus, there are cases where a raise of price which, under the law of demand, would induce a drop in purchases, may actually result in increased dollar receipts for the firm! Conversely, there are cases where a cut in price which would induce

---

[8]On the market's inherent tendency toward avoiding disequilibria and achieving stability, as well as the role of government interventions and war as major destabilizing factors, see Gerald Sirkin, "Business Cycles Aren't What They Used to Be-- and Never Were," Lloyd's Bank Review (April 1972), pp. 20-34; Murray N. Rothbard, Man, Economy, and State (Princeton: D. Van Nostrand Co., 1962), pp. 661-890, and his America's Great Depression (3rd ed., Kansas City: Sheed and Ward, 1975).

increased purchases, may actually result in a drop in the firm's dollar receipts! These perverse outcomes-- perverse in the context of the law of demand--can only be understood by appeal to the concept of elasticity of demand. Throughout the chapter the treatment neces- sarily relies on the method of partial analysis noted above.

The exceptionally detailed treatment of elasticity of demand is also prompted by the desire to analyze the subject from the practical point of view of the firm, for whom the outcome of its decisions is measured in dollar terms. For this reason, the concept of elasticity of demand is analyzed exclusively in terms of the TR (total receipts) dollar dimension rather than in terms of the mathematical (percentage) approach of other texts. The analysis also avoids the customary treatment of elasticity in terms of whole demand curves (and their overall slopes); instead, it applies the more realistic "marginal" or incremental approach.

Chapter IX

Formally this chapter develops material outlined in Chapter IV and ostensibly seeks to justify the profit margin.[9] In the ensuing analysis the following concepts play a fruitful role: the fact that production takes time and the firm must wait to sell its product before it can earn any profit; the realization that time preference (and the pure interest rate) become relevant as the basic component of the gross-profit margin; and the fact that the firm "works back from price" (see Chapter IV) by discounting the future expected selling price. This not only makes the firm a discounter of future values, but also means that "prices determine costs" rather than costs determine prices.

The analysis is then extended in order (a) to show the broad relevance of "imputation" processes to, for example, capital values and share prices, and (b) to provide a critique of both the Classical cost-of- production theory of pricing and the Marxian labor theory of value. There is a further implication,

---

[9]This chapter owes much to insights provided by Rothbard, Man, Economy, and State, Chapters 6-8, and Raymond J. Chambers, Accounting, Evaluation and Economic Behavior (Englewood Cliffs: Prentice-Hall, Inc., 1966), passim.

however, not developed in this book: the standard notion of the so-called <u>normal</u> <u>rate</u> <u>of</u> <u>return</u> on capital, which is usually treated as a cost, should be treated instead as an earning--as part of the gross profit margin.

Chapter X

This chapter pays homage to the fact that we are <u>all</u> consumers--every last one of us--and shows why this basic fact is far from being a trivial one. When Adam Smith, in his <u>Wealth of Nations</u>, declared that "consumption is the sole and end purpose of production," he unwittingly pronounced the genesis of the <u>consumers'</u> <u>sovereignty</u> <u>problem</u>. The emphasis is on the word "problem," initially introduced in Chapter IV and now analyzed in this chapter. From the political-economic viewpoint, consumers' sovereignty is arguably one of the most central issues facing the individual in the modern social division of labor.

If and when it ever comes up, the consumers' sovereignty issue tends to be treated as an <u>empirical</u> question: To what extent is the consumer <u>actually</u> "sovereign" in the market place? In contrast, this chapter focuses on the practical question: If we assume that consumers should be sovereign, how can this sovereignty be <u>optimally</u> <u>implemented</u>?

In the ensuing analysis the workings of laissez-faire, free competition, and property rights in the means of production take on an integral unity of purpose, all in the service of consumers' sovereignty and the free-market system. The analysis also serves to explode the perennially fallacious dichotomy of <u>property</u> <u>rights</u> versus <u>human</u> <u>rights</u>; it is argued that property rights in the means of production are not only a basic human right on its own merit but is, indeed, the prerequisite for other human rights.

In this perspective socialism is seen to be an essentially restrictive principle of economic organiza-tion and human rights, based as it is on the abolition of property rights in the means of production, and therefore destroys the basis of human rights in general. On the level of pure principle, it can be argued that those who believe socialism can in any way improve on free-market capitalism in the area of human rights are tragically under the spell of a chimerical vision.

Clearly, socialism in practice does lose a great deal in the translation from vision to reality.

A note about the Appendix to this chapter. The argument that, on empirical grounds, the consumer is not at all sovereign in the market place was in recent decades spearheaded by John Kenneth Galbraith. It was his theory of the "dependence effect" that stimulated and nourished the widespread attack on advertising as a "waste," and on the "excesses" of "consumerism," if not on the very essence of market capitalism itself. The Appendix shows why the "dependence effect" is basically a fallacious--and insidious--concept.

Chapter XI

Every chapter but this last one is integrally related to the analytical framework outlined in Chapter II. This last chapter on the abstract model of "perfect competition" is the exception. Thematically this chapter is an odd-man-out as far as this book is concerned, but is being included for two reasons.

For one thing, the theory of perfect competition is a centerpiece in practically every textbook, so its omission might be too glaring. The decisive reason, however, is the smoldering need to subject this concept to extensive critical scrutiny. This chapter argues that perfect competition theory is a terribly flawed area of economics and without practical relevance to industrial capitalism; yet it remains a hallowed pillar of the intellectual edifice. Although economists have pecked away much of this pillar, it is long past time for a systematic dissection. Hence the chapter.[10]

---

[10] Key inspirations for this chapter, in addition to Rothbard's Man, Economy, and State, were Joseph A. Schumpeter, Capitalism, Socialism, and Democracy, Part II (3rd ed., New York: Harper and Brothers, 1950), and Friedrich A. Hayek, "The Meaning of Competition," in his Individualism and Economic Order (London: Routledge and Kegan Paul, Ltd., 1949), pp. 92-106.

CHAPTER I

HOW CAN PEOPLE GET BY?

Imagine, if you will, a community without a
government--a stateless society--in which no group has
the legitimate power to coerce other individuals or
interfere into peaceful, voluntary exchange. In other
words, imagine a world without taxation, without conscription, without government regulation of prices,
rents and wages, without government regulation of production and trade, without government redistribution of
income and wealth, and so on. In this imaginary world
let us raise the basic question: "How can a person get
by?" That is, how can a person acquire the material
goods and services that he or she wants--the goods that
enable a person to survive and prosper?

I. How Individuals Get By

The simplest way to answer the question "How can
a person get by?" is to imagine each of us is a Robinson
Crusoe, that is, an isolated person living and working
alone in the bosom of nature. For Crusoe it is obvious
that his ability to enjoy the world's goods--to consume
its fruits, vegetables, grains and other goods made from
its resources--depends primarily on his own productive
efforts. Clearly, Crusoe's fortunes depend on his own
efforts and ingenuity in exploiting the resources of
nature; he cannot depend on anyone else but himself--
there is no one else from whom he could beg, borrow, or
steal in time of need. If he ever falls upon bad times,
for reasons of poor health or bad weather, he would have
no one but himself to depend on.

How Crusoe Gets By

Initially, of course, Crusoe could get by simply
by scavenging the resources of nature--gathering wild
fruit and grain, hunting wild animals, catching fish.
To increase his productivity as a scavenger, he would
have to create and use simple or crude hand-made tools
and weapons. After a while, having exhausted the resources of a given locale, he would have to move on to
search for new fruitful locales. If he ever runs out of

exploitable locales or decides to give up his migrations and settle down in a given locale, he would have to learn how to cultivate artificially what nature produces naturally.

Thus, for Crusoe it is clear that as scavenger, hunter, or farmer, he can get by only through his own work or productive efforts. Now, how does this imaginary Crusoe model apply to the real world--a world in which people live not as isolated individuals but as members of society in which multitudes of individuals cooperate in production and trade in one way or another? How does a person get by in the context of society? How would Crusoe himself get by if, in his migrations, he stumbles upon a strange community? How would Crusoe's options be affected? Would he still have to rely purely on his own labor? What alternatives would he have to working and producing for himself the goods he wants? What if, for some reason, he couldn't work or didn't want to work?

Getting By In Society

Initially, of course, Crusoe in society could continue to work out of habit ingrained during his existence in isolation. However, in society he would discover opportunities to specialize--to concentrate on the production of a single product or service--rather than pursue his Jack-of-all-trades role of the past, when he himself had to produce the many different things he wanted. Now he finds he can concentrate on being only a farmer, a carpenter, builder, or fisherman, and live as well as, if not better than, formerly in his days of isolation when he was a Jack-of-all-trades. (The advantages of living and working in the social economy, based on specialization and the division of labor, are detailed in Chapter III).

In time, however, Crusoe would begin to discover that his new social existence as a member of society affords him new opportunities of getting by--opportunities that were not available to him in his days of isolation. For one thing, he would observe that some people, in times of personal distress or enhanced need, were able to get by through begging for handouts or charity from others, or by receiving gifts or inheritances. Still others, he would notice, were able to get by through borrowing money from money-lenders or banks. And finally, he would also discover that some

2

people were getting by on theft--by forcibly taking from
others. Most important of all, Crusoe would realize
that all these new opportunities to get by, through
begging, borrowing, and stealing, were all the consequence of the fact that, in society, a person is no
longer a "Crusoe," having to get by purely on his own
resources.

Beg, Borrow or Steal

        This brings us back to the original question:
"How can a person get by"? In the case of isolated
Crusoe it is clear that the only ultimate principle of
getting by is the principle of work and production. In
isolation, Crusoe has no one else but himself to depend
on to make the things he wants--whether he is in health
and strength or whether he is in distress and weakness.
But in society it is a very different matter: the individual can at times resort to other ways of getting by,
such as receiving gifts or handouts, borrowing money or
other goods, or stealing from others. Obviously, none
of these recourses are available to Crusoe living in
isolation. Such are the advantages of living in society:
it becomes possible to depend on others in order to get
by.

        Thus, at first glance, it seems that the answer
to our original question--that a person must work and
produce in order to get by--no longer applies when a
person lives in society. But this would be a rash
conclusion based on the fallacy of composition: the
notion that what is true for the individual would also
be true for society as a whole.

Fallacy of Composition

        It is true that, in society, some people can
occasionally resort to the principle of beg, borrow, or
steal in order to get by. But in no way can a society
as a whole--each and every one of us--resort to the
principle of beg, borrow, or steal at all times, without
anyone engaging in production. That is, it should be
self-evident that, unless some people do the work that
yields useful goods and services, it is impossible for
anyone else to do any begging, borrowing, or stealing!

        This truism can be easily spelled out. Someone
must have produced the goods and wealth that others

3

are able to receive as personal gifts, charity, or donations. Even the sons or daughters who inherit a fortune from rich parents--and therefore do not have to work the rest of their lives--are merely the benefactors of wealth produced by their parents or ancestors. Similarly in the case of borrowing. Borrowing is possible only as long as there are lenders who themselves must have worked and saved to accumulate the funds they lend to borrowers. The only thing different here is that the borrower will also have to work in order to pay back his loan.

Work, Production and Exchange

The same reasoning applies to the principle of getting by on stealing. Clearly there is no future for the thief or robber if there are no victims to steal from--that is, if there are no goods or wealth produced by others which he can covet and forcibly seize from their productive and rightful owners. Indeed, in all of these cases--in receiving gifts, borrowing, and stealing --the great extent to which people have utilized these resources is eloquent testimony to the great amount of income and wealth that others have produced and made available for charity and lending (fortunately) as well as for theft and robbery (unfortunately).

Economics therefore concludes that the only basic principle by which a community or society can get by is the principle of productive work. The more economically productive is a community, the more it is able to sustain those individuals who occasionally resort to the principle of beg, borrow, or steal.

Related to the principle of production, however, is the principle of free and voluntary exchange which is characteristically relevant to the social economy, in contrast to the isolated-man Crusoe economy. As we will see in Chapters III and IV, production in the modern social economy involves a highly developed system of specialization and division of labor, on the one hand, and free trade and exchange, on the other hand. In the present context it is correct to say that, in the social economy, free and voluntary exchange is as important a way of getting by as is production. This principle of getting by on production and voluntary exchange has been dubbed by the German sociologist Franz Oppenheimer as the economic means.

4

Digression on Theft and Counterfeiting

Before we proceed, let us clarify some questions that might have occurred to the reader. The above analysis may give the impression that stealing itself involves no "work." Strictly speaking, we should have used only the word "production" and avoided the word "work," which we used loosely and interchangeably with the word "production." In economics, production refers specifically to the creation of useful goods and services, whereas work is used in the more general sense of "activity." (See Chapter IV for more details on production.) By these definitions, the thief clearly engages in work but in no sense is he an economically productive agent--the creator of the goods he has stolen.

Nor is the person who gets by as a counterfeiter of money in any sense a productive agent. To be sure, there is no little work involved in counterfeiting Uncle Sam's crisp greenbacks, but in no way can such creation be regarded the same as creating the bread, cloth, or machinery that arise from "productive" activities. Furthermore, counterfeiting cannot serve as a universal principle of getting by: if all of us worked at creating and passing out phoney money, and no one worked at producing the goods and services to be purchased with this money, there would be nothing to buy with the phoney money and hence no point to counterfeiting in the first place.

Indeed, what makes counterfeiting sensible and successful is the ability to carry off the deception involved--to make producers and retailers unaware of the counterfeit nature of the money received and therefore deceive them into believing that all dollars in circulation are exactly alike in legitimacy. That is, if sellers of goods and services knew in advance that money was counterfeit, they would refuse to accept it.

II. How Does Government Get By?

Let us now leave our imaginary stateless society--a world without government--and see what difference the existence of government makes, at least as far as economic production and exchange are concerned. Admittedly, a full-length detailed analysis of government and its role in the economy transcends the scope of this introductory book. Instead, we will confine our

analysis to essentials. Since these essentials are
relatively few and well-known, we can proceed to analyze
the role of government in the economy within the same
fundamental framework that we used in the preceding
discussion.

Thus we can start with our basic simple
question: How do governments get by? How do elected
politicians and appointed government officials secure
the "public" goods and services that they provide the
citizens? How do they obtain the resources required to
provide the public with education, defense, police,
welfare, and other services? If we apply the same
framework of analysis that was applied above to Crusoe
and other individuals, it is not difficult to come up
with pertinent answers.

Legal Monopoly of Coercion

First and foremost, governments throughout history have all had the same unique privilege: the legal
monopoly power to exercize physical force or coercion
over the individual. Under this monopoly privilege of
coercive powers, governments have been able to implement
systems of taxation, conscription, expropriation, and
eminent domain as prime means of obtaining command over
resources and wealth. Although under these monopoly
powers governments also exercize controls over production and trade (by means of quotas, licensing, and
prohibitions) and redistribute income and wealth by
taxation and subsidies (transfer payments), it is primarily the power to tax, conscript, and expropriate that
has enabled governments to get by.

The legal power to coerce citizens in these ways
is truly a monopoly privilege that has been arrogated by
all governments and denied to the individual. In
society, no private individual can legally acquire goods
or wealth from others except by voluntary exchange of
goods produced by him or received by him as a gift or in
a prior exchange transaction. That is, it would be
illegal (criminal) for a person to directly seize
another person's property by force, against his voluntary consent. Not so in the case of governments: they
can do legally what, for the individual, would be
illegal (criminal). Specifically and to the point,
governments can command resources for disposal by means
of such forcible actions as taxation, conscription, and
expropriation. And Franz Oppenheimer gave a name to

6

this special way of getting by: he called it the
political means, in contrast to the "economic means" of
free production and exchange. For Oppenheimer, the
economic means and the political means have been the
only basic principles of getting by in all of human
history.[1]

Political Means vs. Economic Means

All of this brings us to a crucial question: Is
it possible for society to survive and prosper purely by
the governmental principle of political means? Clearly,
the answer is, "No." Governments can get by only by
forcibly appropriating the resources and productivity
provided by the social economy under the principle of
economic means. All the tax powers in the world would
not enable any government to exist if there were no
private income and wealth to tax away--income and wealth
earned through the economic means of production and
exchange. The conclusion is obvious: as a principle of
getting by, the economic means is prior, and therefore
superior, to the principle of political means.

A brief digression. The reader may have noticed
an important omission in our catalog of political means.
Governments today get by not only by taxation but also
by deficit financing--by borrowing from the public and
the banks in order to finance expenditures in excess of
tax revenues. Clearly such deficit financing has become
a hallmark of advanced countries throughout the world--a
basic method of getting by for government. Nevertheless, government's ability to borrow from the public and
banks in order to finance deficits is vitally related to
its power to tax. On the one hand, government can
borrow from lenders only so long as it is able to pay
them interest on the securities (debt) it sells them.
On the other hand, government is able to pay interest on
its debt simply by taxing the public to finance these
interest payments. It follows, therefore, that government's ability to finance deficits is vitally dependent
on its power to tax.

---

[1]Franz Oppenheimer, The State (New York: Free Life Editions,
1975).

III. <u>Conclusion</u>

The purpose of this chapter has been primarily introductory. The basic conclusion is that man must work and produce in order to create the goods and services that can satisfy his wants. In essence, however, there is nothing novel here; we knew this at the very start. Nevertheless, the discussion has cleared away some underbrush that enables us to get to the ultimately basic question in economics: <u>Why</u> does man have to work and produce in the first place? <u>Why</u> can't man find the things he wants ready-made, without having to produce them? The answer to this central question is the subject of the next chapter on scarcity, the basic economic problem.

CHAPTER II

SCARCITY--THE BASIC ECONOMIC PROBLEM

As far as economics is concerned, the Bible could just as well have begun with the following words: "In the beginning there was scarcity. . . ." And there still is "scarcity"; its existence is a fundamental premise of economics, the belief that all of human existence and activity is characterized by this basic condition of scarcity.

I. The Meaning of Scarcity

To fully understand the concept of scarcity, let us first regard its opposite, the concept of absolute abundance. Imagine a world in which nature provides the means or goods capable of satisfying our every desire or want in such plentiful supply that man would not have to sacrifice an iota of time and effort to obtain them--a world in which man would not have to sacrifice any leisure time and expend labor effort to produce the things he wanted. Imagine that nature already has supplied desired goods in unlimited supply (i.e., absolute abundance), so that life could then be replete with pure leisure. As Li'l Abner's girlfriend Daisy Mae once put it to him, when Dogpatch was faced with the prospect of just such a world of absolute abundance and pure leisure --a veritable Garden of Eden: "Then yo'll have plenty o'time fo' love!"[1] In stark contrast to the imaginary world of absolute abundance and pure leisure, our own very real earth is saddled with a condition economists refer to as "scarcity."

The Meaning of "Scarcity" in Economics

Economists use the term "scarcity" to epitomize two fundamental conditions of human existence: while on the one hand man is prone to "unlimited" wants, he is also confounded by the fact that the resources or means required to satisfy his wants are relatively "limited."

---

[1] Al Capp, The Life and Times of THE SHMOO (New York: Simon and Schuster, 1948), p. 22.

The fact that mankind in general has "unlimited wants" implies that there is no conceivable limit to the level, quality, or variety of man's desires, wants, satisfactions, or "consumption goals." On the other hand, wanting man is opposed by the fact that the natural and human resources available to him for realizing his goals --primarily natural resources and labor power--are relatively limited in amount or are inappropriate in their given forms; that is, they are "scarce."

To put it another way, from the individual's point of view: at any given moment a person has a whole array of wants he would like to satisfy, but he is stymied by the fact that his personal means of satisfying these wants--his labor power or personal wealth-- are inadequate to the task; that is, no person can get all he wants. It follows that, at each and every moment, a person has to decide (a) what is the relative importance to him of each separately held want or consumptive goal; (b) to what degree does he want to realize these different goals at any given moment; (c) how should he act to realize all these goals, given the constraint that his means or capabilities are insufficient. Thus it is that at any given moment only some of a person's goals (the more important ones) may be satisfied in varying degrees, while other goals (the less important ones) must be postponed. (These and related problems are analyzed in detail in Chapter V.)

Some Comments on "Wants" and "Consumption"

The wants people seek to satisfy include anything and everything one can think of, from the most materialistic to the most spiritual or non-material, including pure leisure. Man truly does not live by bread alone. However, some of his wants can be satisfied more easily than others. The desire for leisure, for instance, can be almost instantaneously satisfied: one needs only to stop doing any work. Leisure is any period of time in which a person is not working.

Unfortunately, most of our wants are not so readily satisfied as the desire for leisure. For example, food, clothing, shelter, and transportation are not so readily available as leisure; if we want them, we have to scrounge for means of obtaining them--usually by working for the money with which to buy them. This is true for most people, and therefore for the community in general, even though there are some who are physically unable to work, or who simply prefer not to work for temporary periods (e.g., the unemployed): for them, purchasing power is obtainable in the form of private charity or government handouts.

In contrast to the concept of wants, "consumption" in economics signifies the actual or direct act of satisfying a want by means of a good or service. It can take the familiar tangible forms of, say, eating food, wearing clothing, and driving a car, but it can also take such intangible forms as listening to music, enjoying a lecture, reading a book, or simply singing in a chorus. Thus, consumption is by no means confined to the enjoyment of "material" or physical objects. Any act in which a person experiences the satisfaction of a want or a goal can be regarded as an act of consumption. In this sense, therefore, the primarily vital function of man is "consumption," since man must satisfy his wants or goals in order to survive and prosper.

On "Production" and the Use of Means

Realistically, practically all goal-satisfaction requires an act of production, that is, the use of labor power, materials, tools, machines, and working space and buildings. About the only exception (besides leisure) is the desire for fresh air; however, fresh air may itself not be readily available due to pollution. Furthermore, man not only has to produce the immediate things he wants, but he must also produce the means or resources required to make these things.

To be sure, the earth is endowed with a variety of (albeit limited) amounts of natural resources or "land"--cultivatable land, forests, mineral deposits, powerful and navigable rivers, and water-bodies of fish. As a rule, however, man has to work them ("mix his labor" with them, as John Locke put it) in order to obtain his clothing, shelter, etc. In this production process, man may require tools, machines, and buildings, that is, means of production, which clearly do not grow on trees but must themselves be produced, primarily by combining his labor power with natural resources. The latter two, labor and "land," constitute the two ultimate or original means at man's disposal. Anything else that he needs to carry on the technical process of production must be man-made as a means of furthering his production goals. (The concept of production is examined in detail in Chapter IV.)

11

The Way Out: Abundance vs. Asceticism

Throughout history man has tried to escape the specter of scarcity by considering two extreme alternatives. One alternative is to dream of a Utopia or Garden of Eden, in which the curse of limited resources is simply wished away by the assumption that resources are somehow "plentiful," absolutely abundant. The other way out involves an ascetic, belt-tightening solution to scarcity: this calls for restriction of people's wants, either by persuasion or physical coercion. In consequence, these extreme alternatives imply either (1) an abundance solution--a magical release of man from the real-world constraints of limited means, by assuming that means are somehow made abundant; or (2) an ascetic solution which involves a drastic reduction of man's scale and variety of wants (i.e., "tighten the belt") in order to "tailor the suit to fit the cloth," so to speak.

Abundance: Absolute vs. Relative

So far, it is clear that the abundance solution has remained beyond man's practical reach, and may never be realized in the absolute sense. In the real world, about the most that can be expected is relative abundance--an increase in the level of living or consumption significantly above the poverty levels that had plagued man until the Industrial Revolution of 1750-1850. To be sure, relative abundance does not in itself abolish the basic condition of scarcity; it can only reduce or modify it.

By a combination of efforts--intellectual as well as physical--man can increase the availability of resources, improve their quality, or increase the efficiency with which they are used, and thereby increase the supply of materials, machines, and buildings required to produce rising levels of consumption. His evident achievements over the past two hundred years, especially in Western economies, is eloquent testimony to this. As a result, Western man has been able to enjoy the "best of both worlds," so to speak: an increase in material living standards, on the one hand, and an increase in leisure on the other, a unique combination of achievements that has become the envy of the rest of the world. (Detailed analysis of this process of production and economic growth is presented in Chapter IV.)

Concerning the opposite alternative, the ascetic
solution, mankind does not on the whole seem to be
sympathetic to it. There are few signs that people will
voluntarily opt for reduced or stagnant levels of
material wealth and/or leisure, that is, to go from
"riches to rags." In totalitarian systems such as the
Soviet Union and China, where patterns of production and
consumption are totally determined by coercive, centralized government, it is not the people but the party
rulers and planning bureaucrats who are opting for the
"ascetic" solution: in their allocation of resources,
these monopolistic states give overwhelming priority to
political, military, and statist economic objectives at
the expense of higher consumption levels for the masses
of people. As for the rest of the world, it remains to
be seen whether governmental policies affecting the
world's resources--e. g., petroleum, grains, strategic
minerals--will lead to "abundant" or "ascetic"
consequences.

Emphasis on Resources and Production

It is important to stress that the scarcity
problem is relative, not absolute. Economics cannot
assume that there are absolutely no means or resources
at man's disposal, that is, that scarcity is "absolute."
Rather, it assumes that such resources as are available
at any given moment are insufficient or inadequate, that
is, means are scarce relative to wants. As a consequence, man is constrained either (a) to tailor his
wants to fit the means at his disposal, or (b) to
increase the resources available to him by a variety of
devices, or (c) to resort to a combination of these two
approaches.

In man's unavoidable wrestling with scarcity, it
appears that he has preferred to amplify resources--to
increase the quantity, quality, and efficiency of
productive means--rather than to restrict wants or consumption. This view is overwhelmingly supported by the
experience of the past two hundred years. On the one
hand, there is the tremendous growth of productive capacity and standards of living in the West, as a consequence of the great Industrial Revolution. On the other
hand, it is precisely in the economically "under-
developed" countries of the world--where productive
capacity is small and masses of people live in poverty
and misery--that the problem of scarcity is most acute.

13

Implication of Scarcity: "Production"

We now illustrate the preceding analysis by means of the diagram in Figure 1. Scarcity is seen here as comprising the basic conditions of both (a) unlimited wants and goals of all types, and (b) the constraint of relatively limited resources or means.

It is precisely at this point that we see the first major implication of scarcity for mankind as a whole--the concept of production. Only by engaging in productive activities can man expect to reduce or modify the condition of scarcity. The concept of production, which will be analyzed in detail in Chapter IV, encompasses all human activities designed to provide the very goods and services that can satisfy man's multifarious wants.

II. Two Modes of Production

If we look back into history, two main modes of production can be discerned. One is the relatively primitive direct-use or self-subsistence mode of production, in which production is undertaken by people for their own direct satisfaction. The other mode is the market division of labor--based on production for the market, specialization, exchange and money--under which increasing numbers of people on the five continents have been living. [2]

Direct-Use Production

Direct-use modes of production can be found mainly in the less industrialized, so-called Third World economies, while the market division of labor (hereafter referred to simply as the market DOL) is predominant in the highly industrialized economies. ("Barter" economy is here regarded as a transitional mode between direct-use production and the market DOL, and will be discussed in Chapter III.)

---

[2] I am indebted to Paul Craig Roberts and Matthew A. Stephenson, Marx's Theory of Exchange, Alienation and Crisis (Stanford, California: Hoover Institution Press, 1973) for the distinction of direct-use versus market modes of production organization.

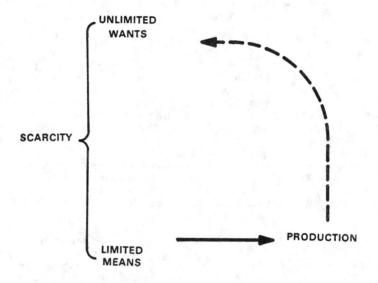

FIGURE 1:
SCARCITY IMPLIES PRODUCTION.

Direct-use production can take place in a wide variety of human contexts. At one extreme is the single isolated person living all to himself, in separation from others and working only for his own direct satisfaction--the so-called Robinson Crusoe model familiar to economists. At the other extreme we find the tribe, consisting of numerous individuals and families, in which production, although organized on a social basis, is still directed towards the tribe's own desires and satisfactions.

In between these two extremes are the individual family unit and the small-scale communal group.

Common to all of these direct-use forms of production is the direct connection or correspondence between (a) what people want to consume and (b) the things that get produced. For example, if people want grain or vegetables, they themselves--singly or cooperatively--proceed to produce the grains and vegetables for their own consumption. The individual's very survival and prosperity depends directly on his own ability and willingness to harness resources--labor power, land and water, tools--and apply them in appropriate technical combinations capable of yielding the desired product. Those who are not able to work or produce--infants, the diseased, and the infirm--are necessarily taken care of by their relatives. In Robinson Crusoe's case, he has no one but himself to rely on.

Furthermore, the goods and services produced for direct-use are absorbed entirely by the producers themselves--none of it is supposed to be allocated for sale in the market place. Thus, the direct-use type of economy is, by definition, characterized by (a) self-subsistence production and (b) absence of production for exchange in the market.

Social Division of Labor

In contrast to the direct-use mode, the market division of labor (DOL) is oriented toward a radically different purpose. Remember: under the direct-use mode, the same person or group is simultaneously responsible for both production and consumption. For example, if person A or tribe A wants to consume fish, he or they must themselves undertake the catching ("production") of the fish. In this way, one and the same person or group undertakes both functions of producing goods and

16

consuming them. In other words, the household unit is the one and only center of both production and con-sumption activities.

Under the market DOL, however, the household unit is no longer the center of both production and consumption. Instead, production is relegated to and centered within a new social-economic unit called the firm. Although members of households continue to own and provide the means of production (especially labor power) which are required and employed by the firm, it is the firm--be it in the form of a factory, large-scale farm, retail department store, or service agency--that provides the predominant share of goods and services produced for ultimate consumption by members of house-holds. (The nature and significance of the transition from direct-use production to the market DOL are analyzed in Chapter III.)

In this connection, one other difference between production under the direct-use mode and in the market DOL is noteworthy. It would be misleading to imply there is no specialization and division of labor under the direct-use mode. Indeed there is, but on a rela-tively narrow domestic basis: individuals may be assigned specific tasks or products within the family or tribe. But as a rule, the individual will have to be a Jack-of-all-trades, capable of handling a variety of tasks. Even more important, however, individual house-hold units are characteristically self-sufficient and not dependent on production-for-exchange in the market.

In contrast, under the market DOL, the orienta-tion of domestic production toward the market--toward exchange with producers in other household units, near and far--generated increasingly larger scale of produc-tion and greater sophistication in technological change. These changes eventually gave birth to the factory-scale output that became characteristic of the Industrial Revolution. This breakthrough in large-scale industry induced, in turn, the further expansion of markets for new goods throughout the world.

Firms Depend on Households

The radically new forms of social interdepen-dence and interrelationship that emerged in the market DOL are outlined in Figure 2. Note, first of all, that production has shifted from the context of the household

17

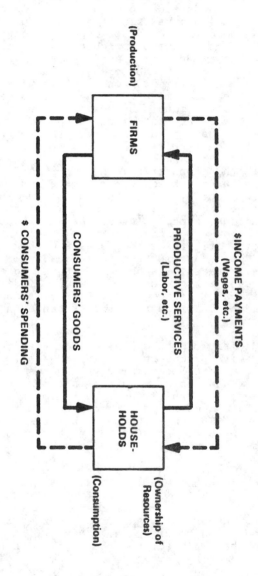

FIGURE 2:
RELATIONS BETWEEN HOUSEHOLDS AND FIRMS.

18

to the firm; the firm is now virtually the center of all productive activity. Nevertheless, the firm remains dependent on the households in two crucial respects. On the one hand, the firm must look to households as the ultimate market for the goods it produces, especially consumers' goods (see heavy line called "consumers' goods"). This follows from the fact that households encompass everyone in the community, including single individuals or bachelors, and this makes everyone a "consumer." Obviously, unless firms succeed in selling their product to consumers, they cannot remain in business. This raises the crucial question: How do households acquire the purchasing power (e.g., money) to buy up the firm's output?

The answer to this crucial question brings us to the second basic dependence relation. The firm must depend on householders to provide the required productive resources (means of production). (See heavy line called "productive resources.") For one thing, the firm has to hire householders to provide labor power. Thus, householders as workers will receive, in return for their labor services, payment in the form of wages and salaries. Furthermore, firms may have to borrow money to finance their purchases of capital goods (tools, machines, land, materials, etc.), but the people owning such loanable funds (in the form of savings that are made available to firms via savings institutions and stock and bond markets) are themselves members of households. (It should also be noted that commercial banks provide "new money" to firms in the form of commercial loans and the creation of check deposits.) In return for their loans and investments, householders receive interest and dividend payments. Finally, firms may also have to rent or lease space (land, factory, office) but the owners of these resources, too, are ultimately members of households, and the payment they receive in return for the use of these resources is called rent.

Firm as Generator of Income

Thus, by making their varied resources available to firms, households in the modern DOL--although no longer the center of production--are able to earn the purchasing power needed to buy the goods produced by firms. That is, by cooperating with firms in the production function, householders are able to earn a variety of income payments--wages and salaries, rents, interest, and profits--which in the aggregate are termed the

19

national income. (See dashed line called "income payments" in Figure 2 and the "production-income" link in
Figure 3). The income generated by firms thus becomes
the prime source of the purchasing power that enables
householders, as consumers, to buy up the firm's output.
(See dashed line called "consumers' spending" in Figure
2).

These vital relationships between households and
firms can be visualized alternatively, as in Figure 4
(parts A and B), which focuses on the firm in the role
of intermediary. In part A of Figure 4, we see the firm
as intermediary between household members as "consumers," on the one hand, and household members as
"owners of means of production," on the other hand. In
part B, we see (a) how the firm depends on consumers'
demand for its product and, in turn, (b) how this consumers' demand determines the firm's demand for labor
and other productive resources, as filtered through the
firm's decision-making process.

In passing we should note something about the
"production-income" link: it is also relevant to self-
employed people such as farmers and professionals.
Although these people depend primarily on their own (and
not on any employer's) ability to sell their products or
services, this should not disguise the fact that
the self-employed are merely a special type of firm
whose "employees" are self-provided for the purposes of
production and marketing.

Only Production is the Source of Income

Although the production-income link is explored
in greater detail in Chapters IV and IX, it is useful to
note here the following two important aspects. First,
economics maintains that the only source of earned
money-income is production. Use of the word "income"
should refer solely to money-payments earned by people
participating in production. This goes for the wages
and salaries received by sellers of labor services as
well as for the rent earned by people who rent or lease
their property to others, the interest earned by people
who lend money, and the profits received by enterprising
owners of firms. The grand total of all such incomes
is, as noted, the national income.

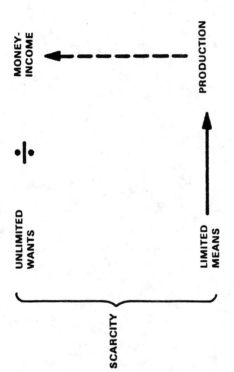

FIGURE 3:
PRODUCTION IS THE SOURCE OF INCOME.

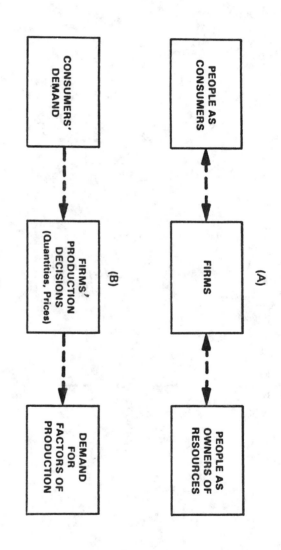

FIGURE 4:
THE FIRM AS INTERMEDIARY.

(A)

PEOPLE AS
CONSUMERS

FIRMS

PEOPLE AS
OWNERS OF
RESOURCES

(B)

CONSUMERS'
DEMAND

FIRMS'
PRODUCTION
DECISIONS
(Quantities, Prices)

DEMAND
FOR
FACTORS OF
PRODUCTION

22

Second, because of the advanced stage of the division-of-labor in the modern economy, we find not only widespread occupational specialization but also an apparent functional specialization with regard to consumption versus production. For convenience, economics often refers to "consumers" as a group separate from "producers," the former belonging to households, the latter comprising the production units called firms. This usage, however, causes a serious confusion. In practice, everyone is a "consumer," including the owners and heads of firms; and every wage-earner or salaried employee, who as a member of a household sells his services to firms, is himself as much a "producer" as any head of a firm. Nevertheless, in our present context it is convenient to associate the functions of consumption with "consumers" and production with "firms" or "producers." This facilitates references to the characteristic dependence of householders on firms not only for (a) the supply of goods they wish to consume, but also for (b) the income to be earned by their offering labor services or other resources.

Production is the Source of "Supply"

Now, there is another vital aspect to production in the modern economy: production is not only the source of income earned by factor-owners, but is also the source of physical supply of goods and services. This is the "supply" which firms offer for sale on the market, and is, therefore, available for purchase by the very same people who have earned income. This brings us to the "production-supply" link (see Figure 5) that is economically associated with the above production-income link.

In connection with supply it is important to note that the quantities supplied are always offered to the market at a price. The firm sets a price that it expects the market will approve and thereby compensate it for two reasons: (1) to recoup the income payments already made to wage-earners and other factor-owners, and (2) to yield a margin of profit on each unit of product. Only if market demand validates the firm's expectations as to quantities offered, prices asked, and expected profit-rate will the firm be able to stay in production and generate income. Whether actual consumer demand in the market will validate all of the firm's expectations as to sales and profits is, at any time, really a big "if." In a truly free market, sales

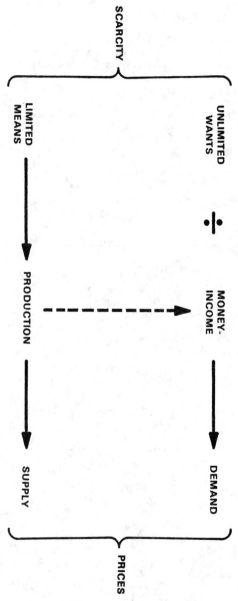

FIGURE 5:
BASIC ELEMENTS OF THE MARKET-PRICE SYSTEM.

24

success is always an <u>uncertainty</u>: truly free markets imply open and unrestricted competition and an absence of governmental protection of profits (e.g., by tariffs or subsidies). (More on this in Chapters VI-XI.)

Thus, even if a given firm enjoys success in its sales objectives at any time, this by no means assures <u>continued</u> profitable sales. No free market can guarantee sales so long as consumer demand is uncertain--so long as consumers can change their minds in unpredictable fashion. As soon as any firm experiences disappointing sales, it must decide whether and to what extent it should lower its price, curtail its supply, or do a combination of both.

Income, Transfers, and Demand

This brings us to another important link in the market economy: the "income-demand" link (Figure 5) in which market <u>demand</u> is presumed to derive entirely from the incomes <u>earned</u> in production. In practice, of course, market demand, although mostly based on earned income, also includes <u>non-income</u> sources of purchasing power. One such non-income source of money is government subsidies, technically referred to as <u>transfer payments</u>, such as old-age benefits, unemployment and other relief, bonuses, etc. (See Figure 6.)

<u>Transfers</u> typically go to people who, for one reason or another, are not working or whose incomes the government wishes to supplement. On the other hand, transfer payments are financed by <u>taxation</u> of the income of the rest of the community. Since these governmental transfers do not derive from the recipient's own income earnings, it must be referred to as a <u>non-income</u> source of purchasing power. (It should be noted that in recent years, total government transfer payments have exceeded $400 billion, far more than the relatively small amounts of private transfers that are voluntarily channeled through charity.)

Inflation of the Money Supply

Another <u>non-income</u> source of market demand--also shown in Figure 6--is the "new money" associated with loans made by the <u>commercial banking system</u>, with the support of the Federal Reserve Banks. This type of purchasing power is typically borrowed from the banking

25

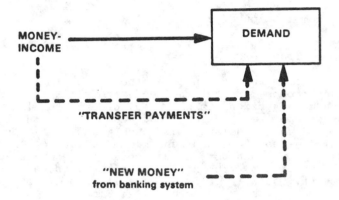

FIGURE 6:
"NON-INCOME" SOURCES OF PURCHASING POWER
(Transfers; New Money)

system, which creates it literally "out of thin air."
The puzzling expression "out of thin air" aptly reflects
the fact that the new bank money--in the form of artificially created check deposits--is not directly derived
or channelled from anyone else's income but is merely
created by a bookkeeping entry by the banks. Firms
usually obtain "new money" in the form of commercial
bank loans for production purposes, while the federal
government also obtains it to cover its budget deficits.

        In recent decades, the "new money" created by
the banking system has enabled the dollar-value of market demand to increase faster than the physical supply
of goods and services, thereby becoming the crucial
basis of price inflation. At this point it suffices to
note that new bank money is not only funnelled to firms
in the form of commercial loans but also to the federal
government, to finance part of its transfer payments; in
this way, the total of government handouts can exceed
the amounts financed by taxation. (Details on bank
creation of new money can be found in any textbook on
money and banking.)

"Demand" vs. "Wants"

        To avoid a possible confusion, note the distinc-
tion between wants and demand. The layman tends to use
these terms interchangeably, but in economics they mean
very different things. "Wants," in their original and
basic sense, are truly limitless: there is no conceivable limit to the quantity and variety of satisfactions
human beings will want to enjoy. "Demand," on the other
hand, relates to the fact that in practice there is a
limit to a person's ability to satisfy his wants. Thus,
while one may "want" pie in the sky, scarcity requires
that one's "demand" be tailored to one's purchasing
power. Such purchasing power typically depends on income earned, although it may also be supplemented by
one's own accumulated savings, or by borrowing, or by
sale of one's wealth assets, such as a car or house.

        Also note that demand is exercised not only by
"consumers" but also by firms as producers. People
exercize demand not only for consumer goods, for their
own direct consumption, but also exert a demand for
productive resources (labor, etc.) to be used in
production. The latter type of demand reflects the fact
that some people--indeed, only a relative few--enter
into the production process as heads of firms and

"entrepreneurs" rather than as employees, albeit a riskier way of earning income. Thus, firms must rely primarily on their own income (i.e., profits) in order to finance their demand for factors of production. Typically, however, profits are not enough, and have to be supplemented by borrowing from the banks and other financial institutions.

The Role of Market Prices

We are now ready for the final leg of our survey of the basic social implications of scarcity: the central role of market prices both as (a) the resultant of the forces of supply and demand, and as (b) the fulcrum on which consumers and firms base their decisions to buy and sell. (See the extreme right-side of Figure 5.) From one perspective, market prices may be viewed as a resultant of supply (S) and demand (D) in the sense that prices will change according to changes in S and D. As will be seen in Chapter VIII, prices would be expected to increase whenever D increases, S decreases, or a combination of both occurs. Conversely, prices would be expected to decrease whenever D decreases, S increases, or a combination of both occurs.

In this connection, a glance at Figure 5 reveals that supply and demand are themselves resultants of more fundamental underlying forces. Thus, reading along the bottom line in Figure 5, we can see that market supply will increase or decrease according to the levels of production. Production itself will, in turn, vary according to the supply of means, the efficiency with which means are used, and the willingness of factor-owners to participate in production for the market. (More on this in Chapter IV.) Similarly in the case of market demand: D will be expected to vary according to (a) the level of income or other purchasing power, as well as (b) the character of people's wants--their tastes and preferences and the intensity of their desires. (More on this in Chapter VI.)

On the other hand, market prices are the fulcrum of information on which buyers and sellers peg their respective buying and selling decisions. Higher prices tend to deter buyers from buying or reduce their rate of purchase, whereas they tend to induce producers and sellers to increase the rate of production and offer greater quantities. Lower prices tend to exert opposite effects: they induce buyers to increase their rate of

purchase, but induce sellers and producers to reduce
their rate of supply. (More details on this in Chapter
VIII.)

Market Demand, the Ultimate Test

Thus there is a vital interdependence between
the underlying forces of supply and demand, on the one
hand, and market prices on the other. Chapter VIII will
explore this interdependence in great detail. At this
point it suffices to expand on a basic fact noted above:
the marketplace constitutes the ultimate testing ground
of the firm's sales and profit expectations. In the
marketplace, it is the actual state of demand--not the
hoped-for or anticipated demand--which ultimately determines the fate of the firm's profit expectations. (More
on profits in Chapter IX.)

Furthermore, only if firms earn profits will
they be willing to hire and purchase factors of production and thereby continue to generate incomes such as
wages and salaries, rent, and interest. Indeed, directly or indirectly, the marketplace ultimately judges the
income fate of all participants in the production process. Whether one participates as a wage-earner, a
professional, or a head of a firm, everyone is in the
same boat: all must await the final, albeit unpredictable, verdict of the market to see whether it ratifies
or vetoes respective income expectations.

Market Demand and Uncertainty

On top of all this, not only is market demand
the ultimate arbiter of the firm's sales and profits,
but it remains ever beclouded in uncertainty. For one
thing, consumers' tastes or preferences are subject to
constant, unpredictable change, and thereby affect the
quantities purchased or the selling prices finally
negotiated. This in turn affects the profits actually
realized. Add to this the ever-present threat of competition from rival firms at home and abroad. Nevertheless, despite these uncertainties, firms must somehow
decide how much to supply and what prices to ask. Only
the final showdown between suppliers and demanders in
the marketplace determines whether firms will have
guessed right or wrong, and, therefore, whether they
will earn profits or incur losses.

29

In the last resort, if a firm guesses wrong as to quantity and price, it will have to adjust to its disappointment. It could slash its prices in order to move unsold goods. If it becomes pessimistic about the state of demand--believing that its disappointing sales are not merely temporary--it could reduce its rate of output. Over the long run, however, the firm cannot escape the market's ever-present uncertainty and the consequent need to make adjustments in quantity produced, costs, and selling prices. Only the firm's ability fo <u>forecast</u> business conditions more successfully, or to make <u>adjustments</u> when its forecasts prove incorrect, can enable the firm to survive and prosper.

III. <u>Conclusion</u>

One final perspective: the validity of this analysis of the basic implications of scarcity is reflected by the polar concepts of <u>scarcity</u> and <u>prices</u> depicted in Figure 5. Given the underlying human condition of scarcity, on the one hand, and the market-price system (further analyzed in Chapters VIII-XI), on the other, our diagram indicates that prices and scarcity are ultimately <u>interrelated</u> and <u>interdependent</u>: prices serve as the "reflector" of scarcity--they are expected to rise when scarcity conditions worsen and fall when scarcity conditions ease up.

A significant segment of economics is concerned not only with demonstrating that market prices are able to reflect scarcity conditions but, indeed, that the market-price system is the only economic mechanism capable of rendering this vital service. Chapter X will explore in detail the nature of the market-price system, based on consumer's sovereignty, individual property rights, and voluntary exchange. [3]

---

[3]This is not the place to analyze how a socialist society, in comparison to a free-market society, would try to solve the problems of <u>coordinating</u> the activities of households and firms-- problems that are inherent in every modern industrial economy, be it capitalist, socialist, or communist. For a perceptive and provocative analysis of Marx's concept of socialism as a reincarnation of the direct-use mode under modern industrial conditions, see P. C. Roberts and M. S. Stephenson, <u>Marx's Theory of Exchange, Alienation and Crisis</u> (Stanford: Hoover Institution Press, 1973).

CHAPTER III

DIVISION OF LABOR AND THE ORIGIN OF MONEY

Let us take a long look back into history and quote from what is probably the first astute analysis of specialization and division of labor (DOL). In his book called Cyropaedia, written by the ancient Greek writer Xenophon (430-355 B.C.), we find the following illuminating passage:

> For just as all other arts are developed to superior excellence in large cities, in that same way the food at the king's palace is also elaborately prepared with superior excellence. For in small towns the same workman makes chairs and doors and ploughs and tables, and often this same artisan builds houses, and even so he is thankful if he can only find (enough) employment to support him. And it is, of course, impossible for a man of many trades to be proficient in all of them. In large cities, on the other hand, inasmuch as many people have demands to make upon each branch of industry, one trade alone, and very often even less than a whole trade, is enough to support a man: one man, for instance, makes shoes for men, and another for women; and there are places even where one man earns a living by only stitching shoes, another by cutting them out, another by sewing the uppers together, while there is another who performs none of these operations but only assembles the parts. It follows, therefore, as a matter of course, that he who devotes himself to a very specialized line of work is bound to do it in the best possible manner.. Exactly the same thing holds true in reference to the kitchen. . . (bracket and underlining mine).[1]

---

[1] Quoted in Alexander Gray, The Development of Economic Doctrine (London: Longmans, Green and Co., 1933), p. 32.

Divison of Labor Signifies Productivity

As far as essentials go, there is little to add: Xenophon practically said it all. He put his finger on a fundamental fact: specialization, because it enables individual improvement in skill and aptitude, tends to be the "best possible" (that is, the most productive) approach to the overall problem of production. But he also notes: the advantages of specialization accrue mainly where there are sufficiently large markets (in "large cities"). These advantages are not to be found in small markets ("small towns") where employment opportunities are barely sufficient for the Jack-of-all-trades (the "man of many trades") who simply cannot be "proficient in all of them." [2]

Twenty centuries after Xenophon, the classical economist Adam Smith celebrated the phenomena of specialization and exchange in the DOL by devoting Chapter I of his famous The Wealth of Nations (1776) to this subject. And he did it for essentially the same reason given by Xenophon. Says Smith: "The greatest improvement in the productive powers of labor, and the greater part of the skill, dexterity, and judgment with which it is anywhere directed or applied, seem to have been the effects of the division of labor." But the illustration Smith used--the manufacture of pins--helped create the misleading impression that the DOL was strictly a modern result of the Industrial Revolution (1750-1850) and factory production. In essence, however, the principle dates back to ancient times.

How do economists explain the fact that, in time, man increasingly resorted to specialization and market exchange as the main principles underlying social cooperation? By and large, the economic explanation has been: the DOL tends to be more productive than the direct-use mode of production. And since man presumably prefers greater output and consumption to lesser (other things being equal), he will discover that specialization is more productive than being a Jack-of-all-trades.

---

[2] Probably the best single work on the history and nature of the market division of labor, which traces it back to earliest recorded times, is Jane Jacobs' The Economy of Cities (New York: Vintage Books, 1970). Although Jacobs' main focus is on the city as the vital center of civilization throughout history, she also analyzes the impact of trade and specialization on the world division of labor.

Conversely, had the DOL been less productive than the direct-use mode, man would surely have turned his back on it. Clearly, the power of the DOL to increase productivity must have attracted growing numbers of people to embrace it. They must have perceived the mutual nature of the beneficial link that formed between (a) the enhanced productivity made possible by the DOL and (b) the gains that accrued to those who participated in it by specialization and exchange in the market.

Montaigne Dogma Under Attack

However, the relentless growth of the market economy over the centuries is significant for more than the economic gains it promised. Eventually the expansion of markets threatened to shatter one of the most widespread but pernicious notions. This notion, ancient in origin, has been dubbed the Montaigne dogma, after the 16th century French writer. In essence, it maintains that exchange and trade in the market cannot be mutually beneficial; one party gains only at the expense of the other's loss. The Montaigne dogma has been extended to the idea that self-interest causes irreconcilable conflict or antagonism between the interests of different groups, classes and nations. [3]

However, by the 18th and 19th centuries, new winds were blowing in Western Europe, especially in England and Holland. These winds blasted away at tradition with revolutionary impact: trade and commerce exploded to open up uncharted worlds; feudal relations in agriculture were transformed by increased market orientation and commercialization; science and technology were swept radically into commercial, agricultural and industrial application; most of all, a school of Liberal thinkers emerged who, like Bernard de Mandeville, Adam Smith and Frederic Bastiat, emphasized with great confidence and persuasiveness the mutually beneficial side of market transactions and relations. Instead of the alleged conflict and antagonism imbedded in the Montaigne dogma, Liberals stressed the mutuality of interests and harmony that resulted from voluntary exchange in the market.

---

[3] On the Montaigne dogma see Ludwig von Mises, Human Action (New Haven: Yale University Press, 1949), Chapter XXIV.

A note on the term "Liberal." As used in the present context, the term "Liberal" (with a capital "L") is sharply distinct from more recent usage of the term. The present-day "liberal" (with a small" l") stands for a principle totally opposite to the original "classical" meaning: modern "liberal" usually means that government should increase its intervention into man's economic and social affairs. In contrast, the classical "Liberal" stood for radical opposition to and break-up of the prevailing mercantilist system--which features strong state initiatives in and paternalistic control of all human affairs--which he sought to replace with a system of free, unhampered trade and production based on protection of the individual's natural rights to life and property as the primary principle of social-political cooperation. As against this, the modern-day liberal tends to subordinate the individual's interests to that of the State in the name of serving "society," the "public good," or "public interest."

Self-Interest as the Invisible Hand

At the core of the Liberal outlook was the premise that self-interest, not altruism or self-sacrifice, was man's primary motivation. (More on the concept of self-interest in Chapter V.) When self-interest is appropriately harnessed to a system of (a) production for the market and (b) exchange on a peaceful, voluntary basis, the result would redound not only to the benefit of the individual but also society as a whole. Irony of ironies: the Liberal took the traditional animus against self-interest and stood it on its head. The true fount of economic productivity, mutual benefit, and general prosperity lay in selfishness and gainseeking (not in purely altruistic service for "the good of others")--albeit only when practiced in a social-political context of peace and non-violence.

In other words, so long as man is willing to achieve gain or profit by producing useful goods for others, so long will it be feasible to harmonize his own self-interest with that of the rest of society. Thus, under the peculiar auspices of the free-market economy, man's social interrelations would turn away from antagonism and violence toward peace and harmony. Only in this light is it possible to appreciate the deservedly famous passage from Adam Smith's Wealth of Nations on the workings of the "invisible hand" of self-interest:

34

(Man's) study of his own advantage naturally, or rather necessarily, leads him to prefer that employment which is most advantageous to the society . . . and by directing that indus-try in such a manner as its produce may be of greatest value (to society) he intends only his own gain, and he is in this, as in many other cases, led by an invisible hand to pro-mote an end which was no part of his intention . . . (i.e.) the public good. (Brackets and underlinings mine.)[4]

The Liberal Social Vision

To Adam Smith and the Liberal writers who rhapsodized about the promise and achievement of the free-market society, it appeared possible that man, for the first time in history, would be able to base social existence on foundations of mutually increasing productivity--achieved by specialization and division of labor--rather than on the prevalent dogma which held that one man's gain can come only at the expense of another's loss. Such a principle of violence implied gain by fraud, theft, plunder, killing or other forms of dominion--with survival assured only to the "fittest." In place of violence and its one-sided benefits, classi-cal Liberalism offered the principle of peaceful social cooperation based on the fruitful division of labor, because it uniquely enabled mutually beneficial rela-tions via voluntary exchange. It made no difference whether the exchange involved goods for money, or labor services for money; so long as exchange was transacted at mutually agreeable terms or prices, both parties would stand to benefit.

In rejecting the "dog-eat-dog" way of life, classical Liberalism was also rejecting prevalent romantic and Utopian notions of a return to a magical, blissful "state of nature" wherein man would presumably be happier than under the emerging Industrial Revolution. To those who yearned for the bygone past, Liberals were saying in effect: life in a pure state of nature would only oppress man with its scarcity of means and its fixed personal horizons, and therefore drive people toward irreconcilable conflict rather than toward

---

[4]Adam Smith, The Wealth of Nations (New York: Modern Library edition, 1937), p. 423.

an expanding social division of labor and a perception of the mutual gains made possible thereby.

What Makes the DOL Feasible?

So far, we have seen only that side of the market DOL that made it increasingly desirable or attractive--the higher standards of living made possible by specialization, mutual exchange, and increased productivity. However, there is the other, even more important side that made the elaborate market DOL feasible in the first place.

It stands to reason that if everyone in the world was equally endowed by nature--with equal personal capabilities or talents and with equal access to the world's natural riches--people would clearly have no need to seek each other out for exchange or trade. Since all persons would be equally capable of taking care of their wants or needs, person A would not need to exchange with person B, and vice versa. In reality, of course, people are not equally endowed by nature. At the root of man's need to engage in interpersonal social-economic transactions, in all their forms, is the universal fact of man's natural condition of personal inequality characterized by differentiation or variation in personal capability and geographical surrounding.

It is precisely these variegated aspects of human existence that prompts each of us to seek each other out for the twin purposes of: (a) obtaining from each other those desirable goods and services we do not produce for ourselves, or alternatively (b) providing others with the things they apparently lack and want. To put it another way: it is the universal fact of individual inadequacy in some respects ("comparative disadvantage"), or, conversely, individual superiority ("comparative advantage") in other respects. It is this personal disparity which explains why human beings are driven, sooner or later, to seek each other out in the hope of discovering opportunities for mutually satisfying interpersonal transactions--transactions in which people either (a) exchange goods and services, or (b) cooperate in joint efforts to produce goods and services for the market.

36

Human and Geographic Variation

Thus it is people's discovery and awareness of how they advantageously complement each other, in personal or material resources, which induces them to <u>specialize</u> in doing what they are most suited for--to "put their best foot forward," so to speak--as the basis for their participating in the social division of labor. In this connection, we must note that specialization in human resources has its counterpart in the specialization of <u>geographic regions</u> via the development of their respectively peculiar natural resources, be they agricultural, mineral, or climatic.

Human variation in personal and material assets is reflected in the equally significant differentiation of people's <u>subjective tastes and preferences</u>. (More on this in Chapter V.) Different individuals have different preference scales--they do not attach the same subjective (personal) value to the same objects of desire. For example, one need only observe an auctioneer at work--trying to sell a set of old books, a rare landscape painting, or set of royal silverware--to see how very <u>different</u> are the values attached to the same object by different bidders.

The Basis of Exchange and Trade

It is precisely these differences in personal valuations which help explain why two parties, willing to engage in exchange (e.g., buy and sell), are actually attaching <u>different</u> (not identical) valuations to the same object. Consider a case of <u>barter trade</u> in which Mr. A exchanges two units of his product X for Mr. B's one unit of product Y. This clearly indicates that A attaches a lower value to his two units of X than to the one unit of Y (or, conversely, he attaches a greater value to one unit of Y than two units of X). Furthermore, similar reasoning applies in the case of trading <u>money for goods</u> ("indirect exchange"). For example, if Mr. C offers two dollars for Mr. D's desk lamp, he is simply revealing that he values his two dollars less than Mr. D's lamp (or, conversely, he attaches a greater value to D's lamp than to his own two dollars). From the other side of the transactions it can be said that, in the first case (barter trade), Mr. B values his one unit of Y less than two units of good X; and in the second case, Mr. D values his lamp less than the two dollars offered for it. In both cases,

37

trade would <u>not</u> be expected to occur if both parties attached the <u>same</u> value to the objects of trade.

In summary, it is the inherent variation of human and geographic conditions, as well as the differentiation of individual tastes and valuations, that gives rise to spontaneous <u>interpersonal exchange</u> as the natural medium of social relationship. The universality of <u>exchange</u> activities, in turn, reflects the fact that <u>individuals</u> seek primarily to exchange less preferred (or less satisfactory) states of affairs for more preferred (or more satisfactory) ones. Thus, when people engage in exchange transactions on a voluntary basis, it is evident that <u>both</u> parties expect to benefit from the exchange. Otherwise, they would not agree to exchange. (More on the nature of exchange in Chapter V.)

The Emergence of Money

We now come to the crucial "lubricant" in the market economy based on the division of labor--the element of <u>money</u>. As desirable as the DOL may have been to those who participated in it, it could not have progressed beyond barter exchange were it not for one of man's great inventions: money. Out of the welter of commodities or goods that man produced and exchanged, there emerged repeatedly a special type of commodity--a "money" commodity--one that had acquired the widest degree of exchangeability, convertibility or marketability. It was this special "money" commodity that induced people to eventually abandon pure barter, and for a paradoxical reason: the barter economy (<u>direct</u> exchange of goods for goods) proved to be more cumbersome than the "money" economy which eventually replaced it, even though the latter involved an <u>indirect</u> or roundabout exchange of goods-for-money-for-goods!

Curiously, in the whole field of economics, the subject of money is one of the least understood by the layman. This lack of understanding is paradoxical: practically everyone knows that money is for spending, and has had first-hand experience at using it. Yet a fundamental understanding of the nature of money beyond the familiar aspect eludes the ken of all but the specialist. How much does the average person know about the "quantity theory"--the relation between money and prices? How much does he know about the "demand for money" and its relation to the value (or purchasing

38

power) of money? About the origins of money and its later development from gold to modern fiat paper issued by government?

Commodity Nature of Money

The mystery of money may be due simply to widespread ignorance of its origins and development. For one thing, practically nothing is taught in school about the history of money. For another, even textbooks on money and banking are, with few exceptions, devoid of significant historical treatment.[5] Yet it is impossible to fully understand the nature and function of money without knowledge of its origins as commodity money.

The forms of money we use today do not tell us enough about money--about its antecedents, its true nature. From his daily experience with money, the average person today knows only that money consists of (1) currency issued by government in the form of coins and paper bills, and (2) demand deposits, or checking accounts, which are the product of commercial banks under control and regulation by government. But it would be erroneous for him to infer from this that money was always like this, or that the government's monopoly of money has any necessary connection with the origin or nature of money. As a matter of fact, modern forms of money are unique; and the historical origins of money tell us more about its proper nature than the fact that today, throughout the world, money is a monopoly of government.

Of greatest importance is the fact that money, in its earliest forms, was essentially a commodity like all other commodities except, of course, in those crucial respects that differentiated it from all other commodities. Gold and silver are probably the most

---

[5]Some notable exceptions to the historical blackout on the history of money are: Elgin Groseclose, Money and Man (4th ed., Norman: University of Oklahoma Press, 1976); Walter W. Haines, Money, Prices and Policy (2nd ed., New York: McGraw-Hill Book Co., 1966), especially Chapters 2 through 5; Murray N. Rothbard, What Has Government Done to Our Money? (2nd ed., Santa Ana: Rampart College Publications, 1974) and The Mystery of Banking (New York: Richardson & Snyder, 1983).

famous of the commodity moneys. But history reveals a
fascinating array of other commodities that served, at
various times and in various places, as money: e.g.,
fishhooks, nails, axes, copper and other metals, shells,
beads, skins, cattle, grain, rice, salt, sugar, tea, and
tobacco. Each of these commodities possessed the
primary characteristic of money: the ability to serve
as a common medium of exchange or means of payment.

Medium of Exchange

Out of the welter of commodities that traders
exchanged in the primitive world of barter, it was the
"money" commodity alone which was selected to serve in a
special new role--in addition to its traditional role as
a consumers' good (e.g., grain, salt) or as a producers'
good (e.g., fishhooks, nails); this was the role of
medium of exchange (MOE hereafter). That is, traders
were willing to accept these special "money" commodities
in direct payment for goods offered in exchange, even
though these "money" goods were not necessarily desired
for their usefulness as a consumers' good or producers'
good. [6]

Why were the "money" goods acceptable to traders
as a means of payment, even though they were not desired
for their own usefulness? Because the trader could turn
around and offer them to other traders as a means of
payment for other goods which they really desired for
their usefulness. Thus, "money" goods were not only
acceptable to traders but were also marketable (i.e.,
exchangeable for other goods). The relevant question
now is: What caused these special commodities to be
singled out as the general money commodity or MOE?

The Burdens of Barter

To answer this crucial question we must take a
brief look at the world of barter trade--the direct
exchange of commodities for commodities. It is
reasonable to conclude that in the early stages of
barter there existed no special "money" commodity.

----

[6] See the classic article by R. A. Radford, "The Economic
Organization of a P. O. W. Camp," in Economica (November 1945), on
how cigarettes became the monetary commodity in a World War II
prisoner-of-war camp.

Traders simply traded with each other only for those goods which they desired for their direct usefulness as a consumers' or producers' good--hence the name "direct exchange." And yet we know that somehow and somewhere there emerged a special commodity which acquired an additional role as MOE.

Economists have concluded that barter trade simply proved too costly a method of exchange--too cumbersome and frustrating--to serve the expanding desires of people whose appetites were being whetted by growing population and variety of tastes. What made barter so cumbersome and traders so willing to adopt alternative methods of exchange?

Double Coincidence of Wants

The primary difficulty with barter exchange was probably the elusive double coincidence of wants--the difficulty a given trader A would have in finding another trader B who possessed precisely both of the following attributes: (1) B wants precisely the goods that A has to offer, and (2) B possesses precisely the goods that A wants. To grasp the essence of this problem, imagine the plight of a history teacher, say, in search of a dairyman, dry cleaner, or auto mechanic who is prepared to exchange his goods and services for history lessons. Equally awkward, imagine an auto worker in Detroit who gets paid in the form of Chevrolet Chevettes--or in tires, wheels, bodies, and other car parts--and then has to search out suitable trading partners (e.g., supermarkets, doctors, restaurants, etc.) willing to accept his Chevettes or car parts as payment for their goods and services. Or, how about the difficulty the Chevrolet company would have in inducing workers to accept wages in the form of cars or car parts in the first place.

This brings us to a second major difficulty with barter trade--the problem of divisibility of product. This problem of divisibility arises from the peculiar technical-physical properties possessed by a "unit" of product. For example, the divisibility of a unit of water (the gallon) is considerably greater than that of a hammer. A unit of salt is very variable (divisible), ranging from an ounce to a pound; in any quantity salt will still retain its specific usefulness. But the unit of an anvil or hammer is not divisible: it cannot be divided into a fraction of itself without destroying its specific usefulness. Similarly, a unit of silver or gold (e.g., ounce) may be more easily divisible than a unit of diamonds (karat). Thus it would be easier to pay someone in salt or gold than to pay him in hammers or anvils.

Problem of Payment

The combination of these two serious drawbacks of direct exchange generated a third handicap: What would producers use as a means of paying off their hired hands? To be sure, they could make payments in kind-- the farmer paying his hired hands in food, clothing and lodging, or the craftsman doing likewise for his apprentices. But what would the hired hand or apprentice, in turn, use to pay for the other things he might want to buy? Surely, if the hired help depended exclusively on the employer to provide all their consumption, this would restrict their mobility and the quantity and variety of goods they could consume. These restrictive working conditions would make employment unattractive to potential workers. In turn, employers would be limited in the quantities they could produce and market, and in the wealth they could invest in their farmlands or shops.

In other words, a barter economy based on a system of payments-in-kind would be feasible only if employers produced and marketed goods with the following properties: (a) employees are able to use these goods for their own direct consumption, and are therefore willing to accept them in lieu of any other form of payment; and (b) these goods are readily exchangeable or marketable for other goods which are available only in the market place and are valued by employees more than the payments they had received in kind.

Problems of Capital Accumulation

Payments-in-kind also must have made it diffi-cult to accumulate savings. Presumably workers could not save very much, if at all, since all of their income (in kind) came in the form of goods and services for current consumption. The producer-employer might have been in a better position to save by putting some of his current output into inventories, but only if these goods were not perishable. If the variety of goods produced and saved by the producer was too narrow to provide for all of his own needs, the producer himself would need to exchange some of his supplies for more desirable goods.

Finally, the producer would also have to specu-late whether the current exchange ratio or market price commanded by his product was more or less favorable than the future expected price. If the current market price seemed more favorable than tomorrow's expected price, he would be induced to exchange his product now rather than wait for a lower price tomorrow. In any case, all such speculation about possible future changes in prices-- which involves sophisticated guesswork about the future --is necessarily shrouded in uncertainty: no trader can know in advance exactly what price his goods will fetch at some future date. For instance, an egg producer may have enjoyed a market exchange ratio of one dozen eggs for one pound of sugar. Now, will this price remain the same tomorrow, or will market price change? That is, will it drop to a half pound of sugar or will it rise to two pounds of sugar?

Problems of Price Information

This brings us to still another difficulty under barter trade: How could the trader locate that one other trader who could offer him the best price (ex-change ratio) for his goods? This involved, in essence, a search for information--information in the form of exchange rates or prices. Very likely, the greater the quantity and variety of goods exchanged in a given locale, that is, the more developed the market, the less readily known was the desired price. But even if all market rates of exchange were readily available, barter terms of trade would create an overwhelming memory problem for the trader: for every additional product that was exchangeable in the market place, the number of exchange ratios (prices) would multiply at an ac-celerated rate.

For example, imagine a grain producer is seeking to exchange grain for oil and wool. His search for the highest price for his grain--or, conversely, the lowest price for oil and wool--would involve a relatively simple comparison of only three ratios: grain for oil, grain for wool, and oil for wool. This last price ratio, apparently irrelevant (since it does not directly involve grain), must also enter into the trader's calcu-lations if he is to be able to calculate the all-around best return for his grain. (For example, if the price

43

of wool was relatively favorable compared to oil, he
might be induced to buy more wool than he needs, in
order to end up getting his oil at a lower price, than
if he traded his grain directly for oil. Such three-
corner exchanges are called arbitrage.)

Problems of Economic Calculation

But, now, imagine our farmer wants to exchange
grain for six other commodities instead of only two.
Now there are seven products that are potentially
exchangeable with each other; however, the number of
exchange ratios that would have to enter into his
calculations would not be seven, but twenty-one! Again,
if he wants to trade for twelve other commodities, then
he would have to stuff his memory with seventy-eight
prices! (The mathematical formula for determining the
number of possible pairs of exchange ratios, given n
number of items, is n(n-1)/2. In the last example,
n would be 13.)

Truly, barter must have been an extremely
cumbersome and inefficient--if not totally frustrating--
undertaking. Lack of information on prices and
quantities of specific goods and on general conditions
of demand and supply, plus ignorance of specific
potential offers and bids by other traders, must have
greatly limited the efficiency and profitability of
exchange.

Thus, very fateful and directly related to the
problem of price information was the virtual
impossibility of conducting economic calculation in
order to determine which transactions would maximize net
gains or minimize net losses for the trader.

Direct vs. Indirect Exchange

At this point, it is useful to note an
apparently trivial fact, but one that is nevertheless
crucial to the analysis ahead. Obviously, barter
exchange was by nature a direct or one-step transaction.
The goods the trader desired for his own ultimate use
were acquired directly and simultaneously with the
exchange of his own goods; that is, it took but a single
transaction to acquire the ultimately desired goods.
For example, our grain trader, seeking both oil and
wool, traded directly by exchanging (a) grain for oil

and (b) grain for wool. Consider now an astounding turn of events: imagine that our grain trader decides not to wait until he finds his "coincident" oil trader and wool trader but seeks to make an interim exchange of his grain for another valuable commodity, say, salt.

Now, why would our grain farmer first trade for salt when what he really wants is oil and wool? Offhand, this roundabout or indirect approach seems to be an inefficient way of acquiring the ultimately desired oil and wool. Actually, this indirect method of exchange--which involved a two-step exchange (first, grain for salt, then salt for oil and wool)--represented a momentous stage in man's invention of money.

Money Enables Indirect Exchange

Reason suggests that our farmer saw fit to exchange indirectly for his oil and wool, by first acquiring and holding salt, because he was confident that salt would be acceptable as a means of payment to oil and wool producers just as it would be to producers of wood, leather, sugar, candles, and a host of other commodities, any of which he might have wanted to acquire. In other words, salt had become a generally acceptable commodity which people acquired not only for its usefulness as a consumers' good but also for its usefulness as a medium of exchange.

Thus it is reasonable to conclude that so long as traders were willing to accept salt as an intermediary product--not to be consumed but to be passed along to other traders in exchange for the goods they ultimately desired--the demand for salt acquired an additional dimension: a demand for it as an intermediary medium of exchange (that is, money) on top of the traditional demand for salt as a consumers' good.

Historically, as indicated above, a wide assortment of commodities have taken turns serving as the most exchangeable (marketable) commodity and, therefore, as the general MOE (money). Out of this motley collection it was gold and silver that eventually emerged as the most desirable money commodities.

The Qualities of Money

What specific qualities enabled these very

marketable commodities to be singled out for the extra role of general MOE? Above all, these commodities were relatively _scarce_ _goods_ in great demand--either for direct consumption (food, clothing, adornment, ornament, religious purposes), or as tools or other means of production. Beyond their scarcity value, however, the money commodities possessed other special qualities that enhanced their marketability. For one thing, they were generally more _durable_ than other commodities. Thus they could be held in stock and accumulated in the form of "cash balances," so to speak, until their owner preferred to exchange them--either to acquire other goods, say, or to profit from a more favorable exchange rate in the market.

These commodities were also physically _divisible_ into fractional units without losing their essential value. Salt, for instance, could be exchanged in ounces or pounds and still retain its physical usefulness. Divisibility provided these goods the flexibility required to conduct exchange transactions involving different quantities and different exchange ratios.

Furthermore, the money commodities were usually very _transportable_, even over long distances. This made them convenient, not only for transactions small and large, but also near and far.

Finally, the money commodity was _not easily counterfeited_. On the one hand, its quantity would be difficult to duplicate or replace except by increased production. On the other hand, it possessed _cognizability_: traders and merchants could readily determine whether it was the real thing or debased (diluted with baser materials, as in the case of metallic money) and whether it possessed the stated weight (as in the case of metal bars).

Metallic Money Dominant

Of all the money commodities, it was the metals which were best endowed with monetary characteristics and therefore emerged as the dominant money commodity-- first in the form of useful objects or simple bars, then later as coins. The metals most often used were iron, copper, bronze, gold, and silver--starting somewhere around 1000 B. C. Metallic _coins_ made from a natural alloy of gold and silver called Electrum can be traced back to Lydia in Asia Minor, in 700 B. C.

Metal coins were the first moneys to have their exchange value marked on their face. Hitherto, metallic money bore no mark or stamp for its exchange value, retaining its currency only by virtue of its shape or weight. Thus, recipients of money had to judge its value by sight or by weight, or by measuring its purity in an assaying process.

The Merchant as Coiner

Those who customarily handled a great deal of money, such as the merchants, were usually involved in a lot of weighing and assaying. Thus it was the merchant who created the first metal coins. By stamping his identifying mark as well as the face value, he sought to spare himself the chore of reassaying coins every time they passed through his hands. Wherever the merchant was trusted by others, his coins became acceptable at face value. Thus, historically, it was the merchant who invented and developed coinage--primarily to serve his own affairs and convenience, but incidentally for the benefit of the rest of the community.

This fact is of greatest moment. It means that, contrary to hearsay or tradition, it was not government that gave birth to money, but the market place, in response to the demand for a general MOE. As one writer has put it:

> Money does not depend on government; . . .[it] does not need legal sanction to perform its function . . . it is a natural outgrowth of the needs of the community. Nor did the government invent coinage; it was the child of private enterprise. . . . In money's younger days there was never any question of legal status. What was accepted as money depended entirely upon the desire of the community. Money was simply a commodity with certain characteristics that enhanced its general acceptability. Its value was determined in precisely the same way as that of any other commodity. [7]

---

[7]Haines, Money, Prices and Policy, pp. 32, 34.

Governments Take Over

Nevertheless, beginning already with the cities and temples of ancient Greece, a variety of governments and states have since managed to expropriate and monopolize the coinage of money. Although private coinage was, as a consequence, suppressed, it nevertheless managed to re-emerge periodically well into the 19th Century (e.g., during the California gold rush). By and large, however, government coinage during the past two thousand years has been characterized as a "dismal recital of broken faith." [8]

For instance, governments very early accused private minters of coins of tending to debase and counterfeit their own coins, and used this claim as an excuse to nationalize the coinage. Thus, suppression of coinage by the market was ostensibly for the purpose of providing a more "uniform" and "honest" system. Yet, once governments monopolized the coinage, they themselves, despite all their well-publicized pretensions, resorted to the very debasement which they had condemned in the market--and on a massive scale to boot, since money was now totally in the hands of government.

Government Debasement of Money

By a variety of well-known devices, governments tended to reduce the metallic content of coins below their nominal (face) value, and appropriated for themselves the value of the metal thus purloined. As Haines puts it, government debasement of coins became "the normal state of affairs" mainly because governments sought to spend more than their tax revenues. Compared to the nuisance of levying new taxes, it seemed preferable to reduce the silver content of coins, substitute cheaper materials, and thereby produce more coins from a given amount of silver. On which Haines properly comments: "How easy, how common, and what a fraud!"

This is not the place to belabor this perennial tendency of government to debase the money supply, including modern government fiat paper money and

---

[8]Haines, _Money, Prices and Policy_, p. 12.

commercial bank checkbook money.[9] Incidentally, the
ease with which governments can "debase" modern paper
money and demand (checking) deposits is explainable by
the fact that, on the one hand, debasement is technically much easier to accomplish than in the case of coins,
while on the other hand it is not so visible to the
public eye. Nevertheless, the effect of debasement in
modern money is the same as in coins: depreciation of
money's purchasing power and rising price levels.

Market Production of Money

        Thus far, we have merely outlined the reason for
the emergence of money on the free market as a replacement for barter trade. To explain why commodity-money
was not only desirable but practical, let us examine its
workings in greater detail. History reveals that the
money commodity originated and was exchanged in the same
way as any useful, scarce commodity in the market. In
the first instance, the money commodity originated and
was offered to the market much like any other commodity
useful for consumption (e.g., salt) or as a means of
production (e.g., fishhooks). In the case of gold or
silver, the original producer was the miner who invested
his resources in locating, producing and transporting
his valuable commodity to market. There it became
available for non-monetary as well as monetary uses.

        Whether or not it was worthwhile for anyone to
undertake the production of a money commodity (instead
of a non-money commodity) was based primarily on whether
(a) the production of a money commodity, or (b) the
production of other (non-money) commodities would make
it easier for the producer to realize a given level of
wealth or standard of living.

        Once the original producer of the money com-
modity traded away some of his supply in exchange for
other goods, it became possible for merchants or others
to acquire the commodity-money: they acquired it simply
by "purchasing" it--by exchanging their own commodities
or services for the gold or other money commodity.
They, in turn, could "sell" the newly acquired money for
other goods or services that they had originally desired

---

[9]Groseclose, in op. cit., devotes his entire book to this
central theme.

and for whose acquisition money had served as
intermediary.

Thus, production of useful goods and services
was the primary method of originating and acquiring
money. The non-productive methods of acquiring money
were through (a) borrowing, gift, and inheritance, or
(b) force, theft, debasement, and counterfeiting.

A Speculation

At this point it is noteworthy to speculate:
only the free market--not the designs or plans of kings
or other rulers--could have generated and crystallized
the commodity-money system. As we have already noted,
the characteristic qualities required by a commodity to
be crowned as "money" were scarcity, durability, divisibility, portability, and cognizability. Furthermore,
commodities varied greatly in their possession of these
requisites and, therefore, varied greatly in their
marketability and suitability for serving as MOE.

Clearly then, a more or less evolutionary process of trial and error must have transpired until such
time as one or a few commodities emerged as the most
marketable, thereby assuming the role of general MOE.
Thus, it was the accumulated wisdom gained by traders
from long experience in the market place, and not the
decision of rulers or governing bodies, that spawned
money proper.

Money as Cash Balances

Associated with the autonomous emergence of the
money-commodity as general MOE was the use of this money
as cash balances. First of all, acceptance of a general
MOE implied that while, on the one hand, all other commodities retained their usefulness "just being themselves," so to speak, the monetary commodity, on the
other hand, not only retained it original usefulness but
was now also being demanded for its monetary use as a
medium of exchange. That is, those commodities which
became useful as money (in addition to their non-
monetary usefulness) enjoyed an extra demand relative to
the demand for other commodities. Money thus became
that unique commodity which characteristically was no
longer desired mainly for itself--as a directly useful
consumers' or producers' good. Rather, it was desired

50

primarily as a general MOE--as a means of acquiring those _other_ goods which were directly useful for consumption or production. That is, money was desired primarily for its _exchangeability_, _marketability_, or _convertibility_ into other goods.

But this was only one aspect of the cash-balance role of money--the _marketability_ of the money commodity which made people willing to accept it as a general _means_ _of_ _payment_ in the first place. That is, people began to accept money because they were confident it could be passed along to others when they wanted to exchange it for other goods. Now we must explain why people were also willing to _hold_ this money for varying lengths of time as a "cash balance." Clearly, until people actually _spend_ their money, they must willy-nilly _hold_ it in the _form_ of a _cash_ _balance_--as a "temporary abode of purchasing power," so to speak. This is as true for commodity-money, such as silver and gold, as it is for modern money.

Money as Purchasing Power

Why are people willing to _hold_ money as a cash balance? The answer seems to be obvious: because they prefer not to spend all their money as soon as they get it. They may wish to postpone some expenditures to some more opportune time. But this is not the whole of it: the money commodity must also possess _purchasing_ _power_ (exchange value) in order to induce people to accept it in the first place. Possession of this purchasing power is the _sine_ _qua_ _non_ (necessary condition) for the use of money--not only as MOE, but also as cash balances.

Indeed, it is money's _purchasing_ _power_ that makes money so unique among all the world's goods: whereas all other goods are subjectively valued mainly for their physical usefulness in consumption or production--and not for their market (exchange) value-- the money commodity, in its role as "money," becomes valued primarily for its _exchange_ _value_ (purchasing power). Without this command of general purchasing power in the market, money would not appeal to people as an asset worthy of holding as a cash balance, regardless of its physical utility for consumption or production.

Thus, it is precisely the exchange value or _purchasing_ _power_ of money which induces people to hold it as a cash balance in waiting, so to speak, until such

time as they prefer to spend it.   The holding of money
as cash balances fulfills what is known as the store of
value function of money.

The Question of Stable Money Value

Can money really serve as a true store of
exchange value, maintaining constant or "stable"
purchasing power in terms of other commodities? Indeed,
can any commodity (even gold) serve as a fixed store of
value?   These questions cannot be fully discussed here.
It suffices to note that the purchasing power function
of money is derived solely from (made possible by) the
primary function of money as the general MOE; that is,
only because money serves as the general MOE can it also
serve as a store of value or wealth.

It should also be noted that money alone is not
qualified to serve as a convenient store of wealth.
Numerous commodities other than gold and silver have
also served as stores of value, the most familiar being
jewelry, diamonds, rare paintings and antiques. Indeed,
it would be fair to say that such non-monetary commodities often fared better as a store of value than
government-issued moneys subject to chronic debasement.
Why governments systematically alloyed and debased their
moneys is the subject of political and economic history
and, hence, beyond the scope of this book. (See the
references in footnote 5.)

Vital Role of Cash Balances

To go one step further, it should be stressed
that the use of money as a general MOE is inconceivable
without its ability to serve also as a cash balance. At
any given moment, the total money supply is necessarily
being held by people, in varying amounts, in the form of
cash balances. Even when some people are spending their
cash balances, this money is merely being transferred
from A's cash balance to B's.   For example, after the
buyer spends his money, it then becomes the seller's
turn to hold this money.   Indeed, the act of "spending"
may be defined as a "transfer of cash balances" from A
to B in exchange for other goods.   (Similarly, once the
saver lends his money, it becomes the debtor's turn to
hold it.) Thus it is that at any given moment the total
money supply is necessarily reposing in someone's cash
balances.

Were this not the case, the monetary system would simply collapse. Imagine, if you will, the extreme case in which everyone spends his money as soon as he gets it. Such an immediate and perpetual flow of spending would result in people never holding any cash balances. This getting rid of money by spending it would, in turn, cause prices to skyrocket and reduce money's purchasing power. This rapid depreciation of money would, in turn, induce sellers to reject money as a means of payment; instead, sellers would ask for payment in non-monetary goods and services--which means a reversion to barter!

The conclusion is inescapable: in order to maintain the monetary system of indirect exchange, it is essential that people hold money in the form of cash balances rather than spend it immediately. Historically, extreme cases of instantaneous spending of money have occurred only in exceptional periods of hyperinflation. More usually, however, people hold their money in cash hoards for various lengths of time. This is why, at any given moment, the entire money supply can be found dispersed throughout the population in the form of cash balances.

Cash Balances as Savings

Also noteworthy is the fact that the holding of cash balances can be viewed as an act of saving. The next chapter will explore the crucial role that saving plays in economic growth; here we merely note that savings, in the form of cash balances, are more liquid (cashable) than other financial assets. That is, whereas cash balances already consist of money and therefore do not need to be converted ("cashed") into money, the other types of savings must first be converted into money before they can be used for spending.

Furthermore, whereas the dollar value of a cash balance is always equivalent to the nominal or face value of the money comprising it--for example, one-hundred-dollar bills will always have a market value of $100--the same cannot be said of, say, a share of stock or a bond. In the latter case, the market value of the asset is subject to fluctuation--due to changes in demand and supply conditions in the financial markets--and will, therefore, tend to diverge from the face value stamped on the asset. Thus, susceptibility of face value to a drop in market value makes non-money types of paper assets less "liquid" than money.

In this connection we should note that a curious debate has emerged among modern economists on the basic question: "What, after all, is modern money"? How should "money" be defined? What forms of money should it include? The debate is curious because in the past there was no ambiguity of definition: money existed in its "full-bodied" commodity form, and its purchasing power was therefore intimately tied to its market value as a commodity. Thus, in their original commodity forms, cash balances obviously consisted of physical quantities of the given money commodity—say, ounces of gold and silver. In the modern world, too, cash balances consist of the money that people happen to use. Thus, today, the chief physical _forms_ of cash balances are (a) government-issued currency (i.e., coins and paper bills) and (b) bank-issued demand deposits, or check money, which together comprise the "money supply."

In modern times, however, most governments have severed all connection between money and its commodity heritage. In place of commodity-money, they have sub- stituted _token_ forms of money in which the face (nominal) value of the money far exceeds the exchange value of its commodity substance. Compare, for in- stance, the face value of a ten-dollar paper bill with the anemic value of its paper substance, or compare the 25¢ face value of a quarter with the fractional value of its "sandwich" contents.

How this drastic transformation of money took place—especially in the last few centuries—has been analyzed by the works in reference 5. Here it is enough to note that, in the radical change from commodity-money to (a) government-sponsored paper or token money and (b) government-chartered commercial-banking money, money has become "abstract." In this process of becoming more and more _abstract_ we can locate the root of the contemporary difficulty of defining the nature of modern money.

Money As Unit of Account

This brings us to another derivative use of money, also derived from its primary role as the general MOE; this is the _unit of account_ function. In this role, a _unit_ of money, such as a "dollar," is used as the element for expressing prices. That is, prices of

54

goods and services can be quoted in terms of the U.S. dollar, British pound, French franc, Italian lira, Japanese yen, or German mark. In this respect, too, money went through radical transformation which makes it difficult for a modern person, untutored in the history of money, to know the origin of this aspect of money.

For example, under commodity-money, when a particular commodity emerged as the general MOE, prices of all other commodities would be expressed or quoted in terms of the physical units of that commodity, mainly in units of weight. In the case of silver or gold money, for example, the unit of weight was the ounce, grain, or gram. Weight units of a given metallic money were convertible into each other at a fixed ratio--for example, an ounce was equivalent to a fixed number of grams--enabling the "size" of any particular money unit to vary with the size of the transaction.

This historically-based weight nature of the money unit is probably one of the most important, yet little appreciated, facts about money. Monetary units such as the British pound, the French livre, the German mark, the Italian lira, the shekel, the talent--even the "dollar"--all originated as names for definite units of weight of metallic money, usually silver, but often linked (or convertible) to unit weights of gold, varying in exchange ratio according to the market values of the metals. As Haines has put it:

> So closely related is the development of money to the development of weight standards that a number of currencies are named after their original weight. [10]

Modern Money Is Abstract

In contrast, today's monetary unit--for example, the dollar--has become essentially abstract, consisting merely of a piece of paper on which is printed a face value that has no connection with the market value of the paper, and no longer represents a weight of gold or silver. Nevertheless, this should not obscure the fact that the dollar as well as other major currencies were once related to monetary standards based on weight units of gold and silver.

---

[10]Haines, op. cit., p. 31.

Furthermore, as important as the unit-of-account function is for the quotation of prices, it too (like the store-of-value or cash-balance function) is essentially _derivative_--that is, derived from the primary function of money as the general MOE. It is important to stress this point, as will be explained in the following paragraphs. By way of review and emphasis then, it should be noted that traditional economic analysis of the functions of money lists the three functions described above: (1) medium of exchange, (2) store of value, and (3) unit of account. Not always, however, have economists agreed in this analysis. The present work regards the medium-of-exchange function as being money's _primary_ function. However, the other two _derivative_ functions are necessarily associated with the primary MOE function--the use of money as a store of value (cash balances) and as a unit of account. As important as the latter two must be, they are logically secondary to the MOE function, since they both presuppose the existence of money as the general MOE.

Primacy of MOE Role of Money

I stress the logical _priority of the MOE_ function because of the modern tendency to slight it or deny it. Indeed, some writers go so far as to place the unit-of-account function above that of the MOE function! The implication is that it matters not what money consists of so long as government, with its monopoly privilege, prescribes a given unit of account as the only one sanctioned by the state.

The "dollar" is a good example of how a money-unit was gradually transformed over the centuries from a weight-unit of silver to an abstract unit--a dollar sign printed on a piece of paper. Briefly, the word "dollar" is traceable to the 16th century silver coin issued privately by Count Schlick of Joachimsthal (Joachim's Valley) in Bohemia. This coin deservedly gained reknown for its fineness of content and uniformity of stamp; it was at first called a "Joachim thaler," then later simply "thaler," from which descended the word "dollar."

Today, the dollar is not convertible into anything else but another paper dollar--except, of course, if one spends it and exchanges it for other goods. Thus, one can no longer exchange a dollar for a given weight-unit of silver; in this sense the unit of money has become "abstract": It has become purely symbolic. The dollar, as a money unit, retains its acceptability and usefulness not because it represents the weight of a valuable commodity, but because it is the only game in town, so to speak: it is the only money permitted by law, hence called legal tender--and, being created by government decree, it is called fiat money. Today only government has the power to create such abstract, zero-cost dollar units and to outlaw the use of competitive forms of money, such as gold.

Conclusion

History demonstrates amply that a monetary system based on gold or silver would not require the legal sanction of government in order to perform its essential functions. True, it is widely believed that government alone has the responsibility and right to control the monetary system, and that the market cannot be trusted in this regard. Nevertheless, in the spontaneous evolution of commodity-money, the question of government monopoly and legal sanction of money was totally irrelevant. The substance and form of money were determined spontaneously in the market place: money emerged from those commodities that possessed the best combination of desirable characteristics and gave it the greatest acceptability and exchangeability. Furthermore, the exchange value of the money commodity was determined the same way as any other commodity, according to the law of supply and demand. The money commodity was unique only in that the demand for it contained an extra component: on top of the customary demand for the commodity for production and consumption, there was the extra demand for it as a general MOE.

Furthermore, monetary history discloses that the market not only invented coinage but also created appropriate forms of paper money--for example, warehouse receipts and bank notes--as a means of making the use of commodity-money more convenient. Just as coins were more convenient than metallic bars, so was paper more convenient than coins. But there was this crucial difference: Whereas metal bullion and coins were money proper, the new paper money was not so; rather, it was essentially a money substitute used for transferring ownership claims to money from buyer to seller and from debtor to creditor. [11]

Thus, in face of these historical perspectives and the modern government monopoly of the money supply—a monopoly that restricts the market's role in determining alternative forms of money—it seems reasonable to conclude as follows: modern forms of money tend to comprise a species of pseudo-money rather than money proper, such as silver or gold.

---

[11]Rothbard, What Has Government Done to Our Money?, is exceptional for his analysis of free-market money compared with government-controlled money.

CHAPTER IV

PRODUCTION, INCOME AND ECONOMIC GROWTH

Consumption is the act of satisfying a human want. As such, therefore, it is the most prevalent human action. Equally significant, however, is the fact that in the natural scheme of things consumption is the ultimate purpose of production. Human energies become "productive" to the extent that they are to be directed towards producing those things that are directly and indirectly useful to consumers. Only leisure and air are directly obtainable without any effort. Virtually everything else we want must be produced with the aid of scarce means; indeed, the latter become valuable precisely because they can serve productive purposes.

Elements of the Production Problem

What is the essence of production? Again, it is instructive to look at Robinson Crusoe in order to get the answer. A study of Crusoe also helps us better understand the complexities of the modern economy. The modern economy differs from Crusoe's not in its essential functions but only in (a) its great degree of specialization, division of labor, and interdependence; (b) its scientific and technological levels of production; (c) the quality and variety of goods it produces; and (d) its social-political institutions and organizations.

For Crusoe, a number of things are pretty obvious. Whatever he wants--other than leisure and fresh air--he must produce; he must expend time and labor effort to provide those goods which can still his hunger, quench his thirst, and protect his body. Furthermore, as an isolated man, it is necessary that he himself engage in production if he is to survive. Only in the context of a society--be it a family, tribe, or nation--does it become possible for an individual to consume without himself producing what he wants to consume.

For most purposes of production, however, Crusoe finds that his time and labor are not sufficient. He also needs two other things: producers' goods (i.e., capital goods) and technology. Producers' or capital goods refer to those means, other than his own time and labor, that he works up into such forms as (a) inventories of materials, food, clothing, and other forms of wealth useful in further production as well as for direct consumption; and (b) tools and implements useful in production, such as knives, axes, fish nets, and traps. On top of this he must also develop a technology (that is, "techniques of production" or "know-how")--a body of technical principles which guide him in coordinating and applying his resources to his production goals.

Crusoe Economy vs. Modern Economy

Thus, already in Crusoe's starkly simple, primitive economy, it is clear that man is impelled by his wants and by the "stinginess" of nature to devise tools and methods that will enable existence. In these respects, isolated man's predicament is essentially no different from that of people in the modern industrial economy. However, the modern production process involves a crucial difference: a characteristic specialization and division of labor.

As was noted in Chapter II, Robinson Crusoe is both producer and consumer. He therefore does not have to face the problem peculiar to the modern firm which produces for mass markets--of having to determine what and how much to produce for millions of other people. Crusoe the "producer" knows exactly what Crusoe the "consumer" wants. His only real problem is whether he possesses sufficient mental and physical resources to accomplish his production goals. In contrast, the modern firm faces the problem of uncertainty of market demand--what to produce (i.e., type of product, sizes, designs, quality), how much to produce (i.e., of each variety of product, at which season of the year, in which locality), and at what price. Uncertainty of market demand makes for uncertainty about the firm's profit-rate--the margin of difference between the firm's costs of production and the final selling price of its product.

Production as Utility-Creation

Finally, for both Crusoe and the modern firm, the results of production have no use-value unless the goods produced are capable of satisfying people's wants. Textbooks usually refer to this necessary quality of usefulness with the word utility, and not "use-value." In practice, the term "use-value" is less confusing than "utility." For instance, in Chapter V the word "utility" is part of the term "marginal utility" which connotes subjective value or a personally-felt degree of importance attached to a unit of a good (say, a loaf of bread). In that context, the term "utility" has a subjective connotation that contrasts with the objective physical connotation in the present context. However, since the term "utility" is more customary than the more appropriate "use-value," we will use it for convenience.

Types of Utility-Creation:
Form-, Place-, and Time-Utility

Probably the most familiar type of utility created by production is form-utility. Form-utility is created whenever natural or processed materials are "transformed," that is, are processed or converted from a less directly useful form into a more directly useful form. Examples of form-utility creation are easy to find: when grain is converted into flour; when trees are cut into timber to make lumber, pulp, and newsprint; when metallic ores are processed into iron and steel; when plants and animals are processed into oils, fats, meat, and leather--and when each of these materials is fabricated into a product used by manufacturer or household. Each case involves a process of conversion that yields form-utility.

Man has no alternative but to create form-utility: generally he does not find ready at hand the means that are directly useful to his purpose, neither as a consumer--even if he bakes his own bread or tailors his own clothes--nor as a producer.

Place-Utility

Another important group of productive activities centers around the creation of place-utility. This involves the transportation of goods and services from places where they are less preferred, therefore less valued, to places where they are more preferred and more valued. There would be no need to create place-utility if sources of supply were abundantly located at the right places--indeed, right at the foot of every

consumer and producer, immediately available at their
every beck and call. In the absence of such a paradise,
people must depend upon various transportation services
--rail, ship, road, and air--in order to save time and
effort.

Place-utility can be created by the movement of
people as well as goods--people who desire to be in more
preferred locations. For example, people may want to
visit friends and relatives, make business trips, and
migrate overseas in search of a new homeland. In
effect, transportation of things and people serves as a
way of "moving" geographic areas.

Time-Utility

Last, but not least, is the creation of time-
utility. Time utility can be provided in two ways. One
way is by means of loans. A loan enables a person to
obtain goods and services earlier rather than later, and
enables him to consume more than if he had to wait until
after he had worked and saved the needed money. Other
things being the same, people prefer to have their
satisfactions come sooner rather than later. (More on
this time-preference in Chapter IX.) Second, time-
utility is provided by storage and warehousing services.
In this case goods are stored until a later time when it
is more desirable to use them or sell them on the
market. Processing activities like freezing or preserving fruits and vegetables also create time-utility.
For example, production of frozen orange juice serves as
a storage of oranges; similarly, the preserving or
freezing of meats. In the above two ways, creation of
time-utility is valuable because it can make goods
available at a more desirable time in preference to a
less desirable time.

Utility Creation Enables
Increased Consumption

Curiously, time-utility can also be provided by
the same productive activities that yield form- and
place-utility. For instance, form-utility created by
the transformation of trees into a daily newspaper also
enables time-utility in communications; jet-plane
transportation provides time-utility as well as place-
utility. We can now see why all types of producers'
goods in essence provide time-utility. From the

simplest tool to the largest electric generator, from the simplest shelter to the largest warehouse, from the smallest shop to the largest assembly plant--all of these producers' goods not only increase the productive capacity of the economy but also increase consumption possibilities per unit of time.

Having said all this, utility is not enough. True, it is essential that goods possess utility in order for people to value them at all--but it is not a sufficient condition. Unless the utility possessed by goods has a subjective importance for people, people will not be willing to pay for them. Unless people want to use butter, for example, people will not buy it. Furthermore, it is the value that people attach to consumers' goods that becomes the source of value attached to the producers' goods (i.e., labor, capital, etc.) capable of producing those consumers' goods. Thus, the value of an auto factory is derived from the automobiles it can produce for sale on the market.

In other words, it is not production per se--the mere physical creation of utility--that is the source of value of consumers' goods. Rather, it is the consumers' subjective value attached to consumers' goods, and the prices they are willing to pay for them, which not only impart market value to consumers' goods but also entice firms to undertake production and, in turn, to hire labor and other factors of production. (More on this in Chapter IX.)

Technology, or Various Ways of Skinning the Cat

Implicit at almost every step in the creation of utility is the intangible role of technology and techno-logical progress. "Technology" may be defined simply as a body of technical knowledge or information on how to produce anything. The "anything" can be a physical product, a labor service, or a professional performance. Thus, there is a technology not only for making mouse-traps and automobiles but also for "producing" a carpenter, a chef, a barber, a doctor, an engineer, or a teacher.

Notice the use of the words "knowledge" and "information." This signifies that the essence of technology is an idea or concept, which may be expressed in a variety of ways--from a technical manual to a

63

cooking recipe. Technology is thus not to be confused with the physical form in which an idea may be embodied, such as a combustion engine or a rum cake. Thus, technology may be transmitted in a variety of ways--from word-of-mouth, schooling, and espionage--all the way to the final product which enables it to achieve practical utility.

Adam and Eve, being the first on earth, unfortunately had no technology to inherit. For us moderns, however, the vast accumulated body of technology inherited from the past is, for the most part, available free or at relatively low cost. Contrast this with Robinson Crusoe's plight in his lonely existence. Technologically, at least, he was more fortunate than Adam and Eve: he was able to bring with him--in mind or in manual--some rudimentary technological ideas on how to survive in primitive environs. If he had not already known how to fetch and prepare his food, clothing, and shelter, his days would have been numbered, indeed. Even if he had landed on the island totally empty-handed, so long as the natural environment was hospitable he would need only a few basic ideas on how to make an axe, a bow-and-arrow, a hut, and so on. He could then implement his ideas by working to produce the things required for survival. Otherwise, in dreadful ignorance, Crusoe would have to originate his own technology by trial-and-error, abandoning less efficient techniques for more efficient ones, and always perilously at the mercy of his own inadequate resources.

Technology Is Not Enough

These comments on the nature of technology are, strictly speaking, not of the essence of economics. Technology per se is primarily related to pure and applied science and engineering. Economics as such is not concerned with the creative mainsprings of specific technological ideas; rather, it is more concerned with how technology becomes physically embodied and implemented, and how its progress and diffusion are accomplished over the long run. Concerning these two aspects, economics can assert the following: the development and progress of technology necessarily involve economic processes of saving and investment, that is, capital accumulation. To these very crucial concepts we must now turn.

If our man Crusoe wants to produce a fish net in order to increase his fish catch and consumption, he will have to become a "capitalist." This may sound strange, since we usually associate capitalists with modern industrial economy, and not primitive economy. How can a primitive like Crusoe be a capitalist? Let us put ourselves in Crusoe's situation. Assuming we know how to make a net and nature provides all the required materials, we now face the primary <u>economic</u> task of <u>capital</u> accumulation.

The Role of Capital Accumulation

In order to build our fish net, what do we require besides technological know-how and some materials plucked from nature? One possibility would be <u>overtime</u> work to fetch and weave our materials. This <u>overtime</u> work involves a sacrifice of leisure--a precious consumer's good--a sacrifice made especially difficult by the hard day's work already put in. Another alternative is to <u>tighten our belts</u> by consuming fewer berries and other foods. This would enable us to allocate the time saved from fetching fewer berries, etc., to the making of the net. This, too, like the overtime loss of leisure, involves a sacrifice of current consumption.

There is a third possibility: we can work overtime or tighten our belts (or do a combination of both) in order to <u>store up</u> berries and other consumer items in sufficiently large quantities. This would enable us to devote all of our working time exclusively to net-making, without having to worry about our usual food-gathering chores. But this, too, calls for sacrifice of current consumption. And the same is true of the fourth alternative, which involves a combination of the other three.

Whichever course we resort to, there is no escaping the hard economic fact: production of the fish net requires an act of <u>sacrifice</u>--the forgoing of current consumption. The sacrifice of current consumption enables us to <u>save</u> some labor time which can then be devoted to (<u>invested</u> in) the fabrication of the net.

The Crux of Capital Accumulation

This economic necessity to <u>save</u> and <u>invest</u> confronts us whenever we have to build <u>anything</u>, be it a

65

shelter, a ladder, a wagon, or a weapon. Further, so long as we believe that any of these things would enable us to live better tomorrow, we will be willing to save and invest. On the other hand, if we did not wish to live better tomorrow, we could simply postpone or avoid the saving-investment decision, and settle back into our customary style of living.

This is the crux of capital accumulation and economic growth: higher consumption levels in the future rest essentially upon the sacrifice of some consumption; the saved resources are then invested in making the producers' goods (machines, etc.) that enable us to produce more consumers' goods. Only if we expect the improvement in future consumption to be worth more than the sacrifice of present consumption will we undertake saving and investment, that is, become "capitalist."

Capital Accumulation--Crusoe vs. the Modern Economy

Thus, the example of a primitive Crusoe enables us to understand the essence of capital accumulation: the sacrifice of present consumption (saving) and the allocation of saved resources to capital goods projects (investment) that enable increased future consumption. Indeed, there is no essential difference between Crusoe and the modern economy when it comes to the saving process. In both cases the source of saving is the sacrifice of present consumption.

For Crusoe, the sacrifice of consumption (saving) takes obvious forms: overtime work, tightening the belt, or storing up food. For us moderns, the sacrifice of consumption takes on institutionalized, more complex forms involving an elaborate system of financial institutions. Households can save by withholding from current income (from wages and salaries, rent, interest, and dividends) a portion that is "invested" in financial assets of all sorts (in check deposits, savings accounts, stocks and bonds, etc.). Firms can save by apportioning their undistributed profits and depreciation (i.e., "cash flow") from their current sales receipts, for the purpose of acquiring new plant and equipment and inventories. Cash flow funds are "saved" in the sense that the firm could just as well have "eaten them up," dispensing fatter salaries to executives and fatter dividends to stockholders and owners who could then spend these funds on consumption.

Similarities in Investment Processes

Nor is there any essential difference between Crusoe and the modern economy when it comes to the type of investments to which their savings can be allocated. First, both can invest in inventories of materials and other goods that will be useful for consumption-- directly useful, when consumers' goods are being stored, or indirectly useful, when the stored goods are raw or semi-processed materials. Second, both can invest in the making of tools and equipment (i.e., "durable pro- ducers' equipment") which, combined with labor, help man amplify his productive capacity far beyond anything that he could develop by the use of his labor alone. Third, both can invest by creating structures that are useful for dwelling and working space (i.e., "construction, residential and non-residential"). For each of these three investment purposes, the modern community no less than Crusoe must sacrifice (save) time and other resources, and reallocate them from the production of consumers' goods toward the production of producers' goods (invest).

Furthermore, even when it comes to the repair and replacement of their capital goods--when these goods become depleted, broken, worn out, or obsolete--both Crusoe and the modern economy face the same economic necessity to save and invest. In both cases the time, effort, and other resources required for the maintenance of capital goods against the ravages of time and productive use--commonly referred to as depreciation or "capital consumption"--can be supplied only by the sacrifice of current consumption.

Capital Accumulation and Living Standards

Finally, there is no essential difference between Crusoe and the modern economy in the significant increases in consumption that can be achieved through capital accumulation. Indeed, it is precisely this possibility of achieving great increases in consumption --or of forestalling threatened declines in consumption --that is the prime inducement for investment in capital goods. This investment can be done directly--as by a Crusoe, a peasant family, or a modern manufacturing firm.   Investment can also be done <u>indirectly</u>,   as when individuals   invest   in new stocks and bonds   issued   by firms,   and   thereby   provide the firms   with   funds   to acquire new plants and equipment.   In both   cases,   the basic inducement is the same: individual preference for both increased consumers' goods <u>and</u> increased leisure in the   future.   Only investment in capital goods has   enabled   the   combined   increase in consumers'   goods   <u>and</u> leisure   enjoyed by increasing numbers of people   during the   past   200   years of industrial   capitalism   in   the Western world.

Capital Accumulation and Technological Progress

Nor is this all.   Saving and investment are the <u>sine qua non</u> of <u>technological progress</u> itself.   Let   us see   why.   Technological "progress" simply reflects the <u>changes</u> in technology resulting from   the   introduction and diffusion of new technology.   Technological changes occur in two different dimensions: via (a) the creation of   new   types   of <u>producers' goods</u>,   such   as   new   and improved   machines   substituting for physical or   mental labor,   synthetics   substituting for natural   materials, assembly-line methods,   and computers; and (b) the creation   of new types of <u>consumers' goods</u>,   such   as   phonograph records,   radio,   movies,   television,   automobiles, jet air travel, and motels. In both of these dimensions, it   is   not   possible   to introduce the   new   technology-- whether   it be by the lone inventor or by the   corporate research   team--unless there is saving   and   investment, that is,   unless time,   effort,   and resources (otherwise available   for   current   consumption)   are   reallocated toward creation of the new technology.

Technology and Production Costs

Specifically,   producers   will   invest   in   new, improved   producers'   goods when they believe this   will reduce   the   <u>average</u> <u>cost</u> (<u>cost</u> <u>per</u> <u>unit</u>) of   output. Other things being equal,   a cut in the cost per unit of output represents <u>per se</u> an increase in <u>profit</u> rate per unit of output.   Furthermore,   a cut in production cost enables   a   reduction in the <u>price</u> per   unit   of   output (e.g.,   the price of each loaf of bread,   each car,   each television   set)   without squeezing the   profit   margin. Since   both   of these possibilities can give the   firm   a competitive   edge over rival firms that are not able   to

duplicate such cost savings, they constitute a strong
inducement for the firm to search for cost-cutting
technology.

Let us digress briefly to visualize the impact
of a new technique of production on the profit rate of
the firm. The profit rate will be analyzed in greater
detail in Chapter IX; here it suffices to note that the
profit rate represents the price spread or margin between the selling price and the per-unit cost of a
product (as shown by the "profit margin" in Figure 7).
"Outlays for factors of production" in Figure 7 include
wages and salaries, rent, depreciation, and expenses for
purchased services, materials, and supplies. The
"profit margin" in the first stage A represents the
profit rate which the firm earns currently. This profit
rate is not a money-expense or cost in the same sense as
wages or other outlays for factors of production.
Rather, it is a margin of earnings--the inducement
required by the firm to undertake a time-consuming and
risky production process whose payoff is only in the
future. The "profit margin" in stage B, however, is the
expected increase in profit expected from the new cost-
cutting technique.

Some Further Explanations

A further word of explanation about Figure 7 is
necessary. The decline in "outlays for factors" represents a percentage or relative change, not an absolute
one. It therefore does not signify a drop in the total
amount of money wages, etc., paid out. Also, the
numerical values shown are expressed only in terms of
unit (average) costs and prices; they imply nothing
about changes in the total volume (number of units)
produced, nor the total number of workers employed.

Also, note that the selling price of the product
is assumed to remain unchanged. In practice, reduction
of the unit cost and the associated increase in profit
rate would enable the firm to subsequently reduce the
price to consumers, to grant an increase in wage rates,
or a combination of both.

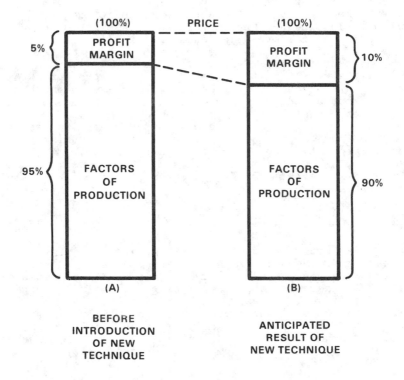

FIGURE 7:
EFFECT OF A NEW TECHNIQUE OF PRODUCTION ON
PROFIT-MARGIN PER UNIT OF OUTPUT.

Technology's Unique Function

Finally, the introduction of new technology has always had another important function: the accomplishment of things not otherwise possible. Examples include the innovation of optical devices, nylon, nuclear energy, computerized operations, space propulsion, as well as consumers' goods such as cars, television sets, and polaroid cameras. Here the inducement to apply new technology by firms is the potential new demand for the new product or technique and the potential new source of profits.

In both types of technological progress--that which enables reductions in unit costs and prices, as well as that which induces new demand for new products--the profit potential may be sufficiently large to induce firms to undertake major investment programs--to originate, develop, and implement the new ideas on a large-scale, commercial basis--despite the great uncertainty and risk usually attached to such new ventures.

"Innovation," the Culmination of Technology

The great economist, Joseph A. Schumpeter, gave a special name to the culminating phase of technological progress--the phase characterized by large-scale application of new ideas and inventions on a commercial, mass-market basis. He called it innovation. Innovation is not to be confused with (a) the exploration for and statement of new ideas, as exemplified by pure science or research, or (b) inventions and applied science, in which a new idea is physically embodied in a "model" or "pilot project," on a sample basis. We get innovation primarily through large-scale investment by firms in order to embody ideas or inventions in new and improved consumers' products on a scale sufficiently great to enable masses of people to raise their levels of consumption.

Thus, it is the lure of profits from innovation that motivates firms to invest large sums in product research and development as well as market research. DuPont, for example, many years ago spent more than $20 million to bring nylon to the pilot-plant stage. The several billions annually spent by large firms on product "R and D" prompted the economist, Sumner Slichter, to coin the phrase "industry of discovery" to describe corporate preoccupation with developing a back-log of potential new products. Firms search for new products to replace old ones when sales of the latter level off or decline, and thereby enable the firm to survive or grow over the long run.

Innovation Is No Guarantor of Profits

Innovation, with all its potential for profits, nevertheless does not in itself guarantee profits. In the market place there simply are no such guarantees. First, there is the unpredictability or uncertainty of market demand. Uncertainty of demand is caused by continuous change in consumers' tastes and preferences, in market prices, and the character of competition from rival firms at home and abroad. On top of this is the specific uncertainty due to the untested nature of the innovation itself: a new consumer product to which masses of consumers have not yet become accustomed, or a new production tool or method that has not yet been proved out under factory conditions.

In other words, as long as the market environment is haunted by constant flux in key dimensions—in the quantity demanded of product, in the prices at which the product sells, in the technological longevity of equipment, and in the character of competition—so long will profit expectations be subject to uncertainty and risk.

The Entrepreneurial Function

It is this pervasive, continuing uncertainty that prompted some writers to give the name entrepreneurship to the function performed by stockholding owners of firms. Admittedly, everyone else involved in production—employees as well as top management—is perforce in the same boat as the owners themselves with respect to market uncertainty; the firm's success or failure affects employees as much as it does the firm's owners. Nevertheless, it is the owners alone who specialize in the entrepreneurial function of contending with uncertainty and risk. It is their capital assets that are being laid on the line—that are willy-nilly subjected to increase or decrease, according to the uncertain twists of the market and competition.

So long as the firm faces uncertainty in the market, so long will it be driven to speculate about the future market demand and prices--and so long will it remain in doubt whether sales will bring profits or losses. Indeed, the peculiar characteristic of production in the market economy is the entrepreneurial function thrust upon the firm.

The Entrepreneur As Intermediary

There is another sense in which the firm is entrepreneur--a sense alluded to in Chapter II. There we described the transition from the direct-use mode of production to market-oriented production. As a consequence of the division of labor between households and firms, the firm emerged as an intermediary between (a) household members as consumers and (b) household members as owners of means of production (see Figure 4, part A, in Chapter II). How is entrepreneurship manifested in this intermediary role of the firm? In the following way: On the one hand, the firm finds itself facing a consumers' demand that is in constant flux and tinged with uncertainty. On the other hand, in order to earn a profit, the firm faces the task of obtaining resources (labor, etc.) at prices low enough to leave a profit margin between (a) the expected selling price to consumers, and (b) the unit cost of production.

Why do these tasks involve entrepreneurship? On the one hand, in spite of the uncertainty of consumers' demand, the firm must nevertheless decide upon a definite price at which it expects to eventually sell its product, in the hope that when the product finally reaches the market the planned price will prove satisfactory to both consumer and firm. On the other hand, there is no guarantee that the firm will be able to discover resources at prices low enough to keep unit costs low enough to assure that the planned price spread (profit margin) between selling price and average costs will actually materialize.

Derived Demand for Factors of Production

What makes the firm, as intermediary and entrepreneur, so crucial in the market economy? It is the fact that householders--as owners of labor power and

73

other resources--depend on the firm for employment and income (wages, salaries, etc.). It is the firm's demand for factors of production which determines employment opportunities for resource owners, and hence their incomes as well.

Yet, this demand for resources owned by house-holders, in turn, depends on the firm's estimate of market demand for consumers' goods. Thus it devolves on the firm, as intermediary between consumer and factor-owners, to convert its estimate of consumers' demand into a planned production program and a demand for factors of production. For this reason, the firm's demand for factors has been aptly described as a <u>derived demand</u>--derived from the expected consumers' demand for the firm's product (see Figure 4, part B). Thus, the greater the anticipated consumers' demand for its product, the greater the firm's demand for labor and other factors; and vice versa in the case of a reduced demand for its product.

Firms As Generators of Income

It should be evident by now that the primary source of income for households is simply firms invest-ing in the employment of workers, materials, and equip-ment for the purpose of production. This should be self-evident, but often it is not. Even among econo-mists, there is still a lingering notion that it is <u>consumers'</u> spending--not investment by firms--that is the source of people's income. Thus, it is claimed that consumers' spending is logically prior to investment by firms since consumers' dollars provide firms the where-withall to make income payments to wage-earners and others. As one writer has put it: " . . . [R]esource owners get their incomes from what consumers spend; but consumers' income doesn't come from what resource owners spend." [1]

But this merely begs the question. First of all, where do consumers get the money they spend in the first place? Clearly, consumers' purchasing power can originate only in the income earned by working for firms as wage-earning and salaried employees, or by otherwise

---

[1]John E. Maher, <u>What Is Economics?</u> (New York: John Wiley & Sons, 1969), p. 102.

participating in production as suppliers of services, materials, equipment, etc.

Second, how are we to understand the fact that when consumers enter the market with their purchasing power, the goods they want to buy are already on the store shelves waiting for them!? What does this imply? It means that the production of consumers' goods by firms had already occurred prior to the consumers' act of spending--and, as stated above, this flow of production had also generated an accompanying flow of income, the very same income that consumers only later spend in the market.

Where Do Consumers Get Their Money?

Thus we must ask: How is it possible for consumers' spending to be a source of income for workers who had already been paid by the firm for producing the goods only subsequently purchased by the consumer? Indeed, all the money in the world would avail the consumer naught if there were no goods produced in advance and waiting on the store shelves. (Indeed, an abundance of money in consumers' hands, in the absence of goods on the market, would simply drive prices sky-high in an inflationary binge.) To be sure, when consumers spend their money, they enable firms to stay in business and provide continued employment for wage-earners and others.

All of this recalls an amusing paradox once told by comic Nipsy Russell which, to the best of my recollection, ran as follows: "There's one thing that's really got me puzzled about the car I've just gotten," said Nipsy. "In Malaya there are people making the rubber for the auto tires; in England they have people weaving fabric for the car seats; in Ohio they're making the window glass; in Pittsburgh they're rolling the steel for the car frames and bodies; in Detroit they have thousands of people busy assembling all these parts into a car--but what I still can't figure out is how all these people all around the world can be making a living turning out a car that I can't even afford to pay for." For Nipsy, all of this constitutes a paradox. For us, however, it is a neat parable for the economic lesson drawn in these pages: people earn income by participating in production, which logically occurs prior to consumption and which economically is the primary source of purchasing power.

The Production-Income Regression

As a clincher, let us pursue this apparent chicken-or-the-egg problem by doing some chain-reasoning backwards in time and envision a past world devoid of the modern division of labor--a world based, instead, on the direct-use mode of production. As we saw in Chapter II, this pre-industrial world consisted strictly of households--peasant families, clans, tribes, and villages--which incorporated in their midst the production function as well as factor-ownership and consumption. In this former context, production as a matter of course is for the direct use of the households themselves, and not for sale in the market. To be sure, some product would occasionally be diverted from direct consumption toward exchange with other tribes or villages on a barter basis; these transactions, however, would be marginal or of secondary importance. In such a pre-industrial economy it was obvious that the only way people can acquire goods for their own consumption is by prior production. This brings us to the crux of the matter.

Production Is Prior to Consumption

The crux is this: The proposition that, in the modern economy, the firm is the primary generator of income is merely a roundabout way of saying that production is prior to consumption. Ironically, in the context of the complex, modern division of labor, this elementary fact may not be as readily discernible as in the simple, direct-use system of production. Nevertheless, in the modern economy, it is precisely because production is prior to income that it is also prior to consumption. In other words, the only difference between the pre-industrial direct-use system of production and the modern division of labor based on production for market sale is this: In the former case, producers acquire consumers' goods directly as a result of their own productive efforts for themselves, whereas in the latter case, producers such as wage-earners, etc., acquire goods only indirectly, via the money income earned and used as purchasing power in the market. Otherwise, in both cases, it should be clear that production is prior to consumption.

Furthermore, the thing that imparts effective purchasing power to the consumers' spending money is precisely the prior availability of consumers' goods on

76

store shelves in sufficient supply. Otherwise, as noted above, if the supply of goods is very low, an abundance of money in consumers' hands would merely cause prices to skyrocket in an inflationary spurt.

Production Requires Investment

Here's another way of looking at all of this. What would happen if the entire productive capital structure of firms would suddenly disappear and every consumer, therefore, had to return to Crusoehood to become his own producer? How much would consumers now be able to consume under these altered circumstances-- even if they were loaded to the gills with money? How long could they avoid the economic necessity to <u>save</u> and <u>invest</u> their own time and labor in order to <u>build</u> the rudiments of a productive capital structure, much the same as Crusoe? It doesn't take much thought to realize that money and consumption do not in themselves produce anything.

True, consumption remains the ultimate purpose of production, and it is therefore the ultimate goal of capital investment by producers--be they Crusoe or modern firms. Indeed, it is this ultimate purpose of consumption that furnishes the basic incentive to expend time, energy, and resources in production. Nevertheless, the fact remains that without prior <u>investment</u> in capital goods and other resources, there <u>would be</u> no capital structure capable of producing consumers' goods; neither would there be the <u>income</u> <u>streams</u> generated by firms in the modern economy.

In this connection it is important to stress that <u>investment</u> outlays by the firm include not only outlays for capital goods--such as machines, factories, inventories--but encompass <u>all</u> of the firm's expenditures on production, including wages and salaries, rent, advertising, trucking, and marketing. Without question, this makes <u>investment</u> <u>expenditures</u> by firms the <u>primary</u> type of spending in the modern economy, and <u>clearly</u> prior to consumers' spending. The fact that only a <u>few</u> undertake the entrepreneurial role of the firm, and <u>that</u> <u>most</u> people prefer not to do so--nor to revert to Crusoe-like self-subsistence as an alternative--leads to only one conclusion: Most people find it preferable to "leave the driving" (that is, production) to the firm, and to enjoy thereby the greater productivity that is

77

made possible by the modern industrial economy based on specialization and large-scale production.

The "Consumers' Sovereignty" Problem

None of the above denies the fact that household spending on consumers' goods does play a crucial role in the modern economy. It is the householder as consumer who plays the fateful role of ratifier or validator of the firm's sales goals and profit expectations. Indeed, in the modern division of labor the consumer necessarily plays this ultimately fateful role vis-a-vis the firm. The firm cannot escape the fact that only if it caters successfully to the consumer--by providing desirable products at acceptable prices--can it hope to be rewarded by the consumer, earn profits, and avoid losses. Only by satisfying the consumer can the firm succeed in recouping its costs and earn its expected profit margin. (This fateful role of the consumer, as the ultimate ratifier of the firm's sales and profit expectations, is also intimately related to the consumers' sovereignty problem which is discussed in detail in Chapter X.)

More precisely, one of the key problems facing the firm is determination of the price at which the consumer is willing to buy. The firm cannot escape the fact that the price of consumers' goods is ultimately determined by consumers--by their preference-scales and marginal-utility valuations (as will be shown in Chapters V, VI - VIII). It is this market price which signals to the firm whether and how much it will be able to produce. That is, only if the market price payable by consumers is expected to be sufficiently high--promising a margin of profit above the cost of factors of production--will firms be induced to invest in production.

"Working Back from Price"

Thus, it is very much to the point to describe the firm as having to work back from price. As already explained, only through validation by consumers--by their willingness to pay the price that firms expect, in order to recoup costs and earn a profit--can the firms survive and prosper. Contrary to what people usually think, it is not costs that determine the selling price set by the firm; rather, it is the prevailing or expected market price that determines the costs that the firm will find it profitable to incur.

More precisely, the firm "works back from price" in the following sense. It is primarily guided by its estimate of the market demand for its product, including the selling price at which it believes it can dispose of its output. Then it considers the profit margin it would like to earn on each unit of product (as shown in Figure 7). By deducting the profit margin from the expected selling price, the firm derives the limit to the factor outlays or costs that it can profitably incur in producing each unit of product. In this whole calculation process, entrepreneurial estimation of the profitable expected selling price is obviously of ultimate importance.

Discounting of Future Prices

First of all, only after the firm makes its most reasonable estimation of the future selling price, and discounts this price to allow for interest and risk, can it calculate the margin allowable for its factor outlays. Given this estimated limit or budget for factor costs, the firm must then calculate whether the prevailing market prices of factors of production (e.g., wages, rent) are low enough to permit the firm to obtain the required factors. (Chapter IX will discuss this relationship between selling price, profit margin, and factor costs in considerable detail.)

Second, and more basic, is the formidable task faced by the firm in determining the appropriate selling price in the first place. It is well known that selling prices are intimately related to consumers' demand in the market place: if the price is raised, less will be purchased; if the price is dropped, more will be purchased. So the relevant question becomes: Which price of all the possible prices that can be set by the firm will be the most profitable one to set? The market, of course, in no way reveals this precious information to the firm directly or unambiguously. Yet, in practice, the firm must face up to the task of discovering this price, albeit by a process of trial and error, aided possibly by market research.

Conclusion

The market, through the operation of demand and supply forces, is precisely the mechanism which can and does reveal to the firm, sooner or later, which <u>price</u> is the most profitable, and which <u>quantity</u> to produce at that price. The process by which the market-price system helps to guide the firm in making its price and quantity decisions is the subject of Chapters VI - VIII. First, Chapters VI and VII examine the <u>demand</u> side of the market, followed by an analysis of <u>how the</u> market, through the interplay of its demand and supply forces, determines the prevailing price (Chapter VIII). Since the market place, as the ultimate determinant of profits or losses, is the crucial environment for the firm, an analysis of the interplay between demand, supply, and price becomes the heart of our task. But before we tackle these topics, let us prepare some essential background (in Chapter V) on the nature of human wants, subjective valuation, and motivations underlying human action.

CHAPTER V

SCARCITY AND INDIVIDUAL CHOICE

Preceding chapters have been preoccupied with only one set of implications of scarcity--the need for man and society to engage in production for the provision of goods capable of satisfying wants. The relevant contexts were the direct-use and market modes of production, extending from Robinson Crusoe at one extreme to the complex social division of labor at the other extreme.

In this chapter a parallel analysis unfolds: the implications of scarcity for individual choice-making. In particular, the analysis explores in detail what it implies when we say that man's wants remain unlimited in the face of relative scarcity of means. This analysis will unravel a chain of propositions that, on the one hand, relate directly to the implications of scarcity while, on the other hand, they provide an array of new concepts required for the development of later chapters.

I. Wants, Preferences, and Marginal Utility

What more can economics say about the nature of wants, one of the two basic aspects of scarcity? (Recall Chapter II.) What is the significance of the role of wants, not only in economic analysis but in the study of human action in general? Can the economic analysis of human wants provide insights into human motivation in general? What are the implications of our basic proposition that human wants are "unlimited"? Answers to these and related questions in this chapter will involve a chain of implications and propositions of prime importance.

Implications of Unlimited Wants

Let us start with the basic proposition: Wants are unlimited. Or, as Alchian and Allen have put it: Every person seeks a "multitude of goods." Why is this so? For one thing, the concept of wants embraces every imaginable object, purpose or goal that man can strive

for--commercial or non-commercial, tangible or intangible, material or spiritual, aesthetic or vulgar.
Economics encompasses "non-economic" man as well as
"economic" man. Thus its analysis of wants must yield
propositions that are consistent with propositions made
about human action in general. That is, economics must
assume a common or unitary basis to human purpose and
motivation in every dimension of man's choice and
action.

Thus, in contrast to the textbook focus on economic man on the assumption that his desire for economic
gain or wealth sets him apart from non-economic man, or
whole man, here it is assumed that man's "economic" and
"non-economic" motivations are both prompted by the same
principle. Man seeks friendship and love for the same
basic reason that he strives for higher wages or greater
profits; he seeks prestige, status, or fame for the same
motive that he strives to accumulate wealth or fortune;
he seeks to help others--as preacher, physician or
healer--for the same reason that he develops new products for the market. Since there is no limit to the
variety of what man can aspire to, nor to the quantity
of things that would be desired by increasing numbers of
people, the conclusion is inescapable: man's wants must
be presumed to be "unlimited."

All Wants Are Competitive

This brings us to our first important implication: given the condition of scarcity, the existence of
unlimited wants makes all wants competitive with each
other. At any given moment, a person has a multitude of
wants; however, since he faces a scarcity of means, he
is not able to realize all his wants at any given moment. As a consequence, every human action necessarily
involves two aspects: (1) selection or choice of a
given course of action on the one hand, and (2) sacrifice, foregoing, or postponement of other, alternative
courses of action on the other. The first is referred
to as the act of choice or preference; the second is
referred to as the opportunity cost or sacrifice, which
is a necessary concomitant of every human action. In
this sense, every choice truly involves a "cost."

Thus, so long as man does not have the means to
satisfy all his wants at the same time, any given want
or goal must vie or "compete" with all other wants or

82

goals in order to catch a person's attention. Which brings us to an important additional dimension of scarcity not discussed in Chapter II. Even in a world of absolute abundance of physical means, such as the Garden of Eden, all wants would remain competitive. Why? For one thing, there is the scarcity of time: for human beings there are only twenty-four hours in a day, even in the Garden of Eden, and since every action takes time, there cannot be enough time to accomplish all of one's goals in a given time period. So, even with an abundance of other means at one's disposal, only some wants can be favored at any one time; other wants will have to stand aside for later attention.

On closer examination, however, it is not really the scarcity of time per se that is the reason why wants are competitive. The true basic reason is not the objective scarcity of means, including time, but man's own personal inadequacy or infirmity: man himself is simply not capable of satisfying more than a few wants simultaneously. Even if man somehow possessed endless physical means and was somehow able to live forever, he would still be frustrated by the fact that he is personally incapable of satisfying more than a handful of wants at a time. Given this subjective incapacity, man would always be faced with the task of deciding which goals to prefer and act upon, and which goals to sacrifice and forgo.

Substituting More for Less

Given the competitiveness of wants, economists have described human action as involving a process of substitution: in order to satisfy more of some wants or acquire more of some goods, man has to sacrifice other wants or other goods. That is, acquisition of more of A involves giving up some, or all, of B, C, D. . . . In this example, more of A is referred to as the "more-preferred package, while less of B, C, D . . . is referred to as the "less-preferred" package.

Following on this, human choice or action can be described as a process in which man exchanges less-preferred positions for more-preferred positions. Furthermore, the choice of A over B, C, D. . . signifies not only an act of "preference" but also an act of exchange, i.e., an exchange of the less-preferred B, C, D. . . for the more-preferred A. As one writer has put it, all action is an attempt to exchange a less satisfactory state of affairs for a more satisfactory one." [1]   Or, another way of putting the same thing: every human action is undertaken with the expectation or belief that it will place the person in a preferred state.

Subjective Values and the Preference-Scale

This brings us to the next important implication. If the multitude of wants must compete with each other for one's attention because they cannot be simultaneously fulfilled, then it implies that wants stand on some kind of ladder, referred to as the preference-scale or scale of subjective values. At any given moment, one's personal preference-scale ordinally ranks the degree of urgency or importance attached to each want, with some wants assigned to a higher rank and others to a lower rank of the subjective preference-scale. More precisely: since in every human action we opt to do a given thing in preference to other things, it is clear that we do not rank or value our wants equally--the importance or urgency we attach to individual wants is not of equal value. Those particular wants which we decide to act upon are thus revealed to have greater urgency or value for us than those which we reject or postpone at the time of action. At another occasion, of course, the tables may be turned: other wants, previously neglected or postponed, emerge to occupy our attention, while previously attended wants are shunted aside.

This implies that the personal preference-scale has another very important attribute: the subjective ranking of wants or goals according to their respective importance is not rigidly fixed and unchanging but is, indeed, ever changing. For example, as revealed by his daily behavior, man does not act as though food were always uppermost on his mind. Similarly, the act of attending a movie reveals that, in that case, the movie is more important than, say eating dinner at a restaurant. Indeed, throughout any given day we perform a host of tasks more important than eating food.

---

[1] Murray N. Rothbard, Man, Economy, and State, Vol. I (Princeton: D. Van Nostrand Co., 1962), p. 16.

The specific action we undertake at any given moment reveals the specific want we regard as highest ranked or the most important at the time. Since a person's preference-scale is subjective, personal, and therefore hidden from direct view, so to speak, it can be revealed to us only through specific actions and through patterns of action over time. Preference-scales have no objective existence; they become apparent only through people's actual behavior. To anyone who observes how people act out their daily lives, it is clear that a sort of musical-chairs game is being played by their numerous wants or goals, as each want or goal takes its turn occupying the highest-order rank.

Are There Such Things As "Needs"?

At this point, some readers may be unnerved by the implication that there is no fixed, absolute "hierarchy" of wants. This assertion conflicts with the customary belief that some wants are absolutely more important than others, and are therefore called needs or necessities. For instance, people regard food, clothing, and shelter as "needs" or "necessities," implying that since these items are required for life and well-being, the desire for them is therefore always more important than other wants. In contrast, of course, the term "wants," as used above, has a neutral, formal, or general connotation in that it does not imply that particular wants are always more important than others.

Indeed, as argued above, economics must assume that wants are a subjective dimension, and that the subjective value attached to each want is constantly changing, thereby preventing preference-scales from becoming a rigidly fixed "hierarchy" of wants whose topmost members constantly consist of "necessities" such as food, clothing, and shelter. Furthermore, for different individuals or in different cultures and living styles, a given goal such as food, clothing, or material possessions may be held in extremely different regard.

Are There Any "Absolute" Wants?

More to the point is the question: What does it really mean to say that a specific want can have absolute importance such that it is always regarded as a "need"? What is an "absolutely" important want? For example, life would readily be regarded as such an absolute want, and food, clothing and shelter also derive their great importance from their life-sustaining roles. Yet, we daily observe countless instances in which people behave as though life itself is not regarded as an "absolute necessity."

Examples abound all around us: young men enlist in the army to defend their country in war; young men accept military draft during a shooting war, and go to the fighting front instead of evading the draft; parents of drafted youth tacitly accept the possibility that their sons may not return alive from combat; political leaders of nation-states shout all manner of slogans to justify slaughter on the battlefield; men join the police force knowing full well they may become sitting ducks for wild cop-haters; people commit suicide; others practice euthanasia and promote "right to die" movements; people drive recklessly on the freeway; people continue to smoke tobacco despite the danger of cancer; and, finally, as the poet put it, "Greater love hath no man than to lay down his life for a friend."

Each of these instances is familiar testimony to the fact that motives and values other than life per se are often held in even greater esteem than life. These values include patriotism, "national interest," "saving the world for democracy," "public service," escape from an unbearable life (!), the heightening of immediate pleasure at the expense of long-term health, and the cherishing of friendship.

None of this, of course, denies the fact that most, if not all of us, clearly prize life above all else and behave accordingly. But the fact remains that it is not life per se that people value uppermost so much as the quality of life, however that "quality" may be interpreted: very often people seek an enhanced quality of life at the expense of known risk or hazard to their health or life per se.

Another View of "Needs" or "Necessities"

Thus, we are on firmer ground if we use the words "needs" or "necessities" in a less extreme sense, not to connote absolute wants--wants that we cannot live without, such as eating--but simply to connote wants that are very highly valued. But the same can be said for every want: every want is "very highly valued" or "very urgent" when we are in the act of satisfying it. A person values food more highly at the time of eating than when it is merely on the supermarket shelf; when we are not eating, other wants are being attended to, revealing that they are for the moment more important than eating.

Often the words "needs" and "necessities" are bandied about by politicians or social reformers who wish to endow their pet legislation or program with supreme value. What better way to get votes for one's pet project--be it a freeway, a military weapon, or hospital--than to call it a "need," implying that is has supreme urgency, without which "progress" is not possible or the "national interest" cannot be served? But here, too, as in the case of food and eating, the word "needs" merely reflects the subjective valuation of the politician or reformer: they use the term merely to induce the public to believe that their project is one that it "cannot do without."

To summarize: man has an endless variety of subjective wants. Because these wants are competitive with each other, only the more-valued ones are attended to at any given time, while the less-valued ones are put aside. This implies that the preference-scale on which man ranks his various wants--from the most urgent to the least urgent--is constantly subject to change, as each currently-satisfied want assumes the top-most rank, while the remaining wants fall to lower rank. The words "needs" and "necessities" do not connote the existence of absolutely superior wants, but merely highly valued wants. All of this brings us to the next big step in our analysis of wants.

Subjective Values Affected by Available Supply

So far, we have been looking at the purely subjective side of human wants. Thus we have regarded man as a sentient, feeling being who not only wants an endless variety of goods, but regards each want with a different sense of urgency or subjective value from moment to moment. Although the concept of wants involves an essentially subjective dimension, the subjective value attached to any given good depends not only on one's subjective preference-scale, but also on the available supply of means which are capable of satisfying the given want.

87

A quick example: In theory, the value attached to water, per se, would be extremely high because of its vital role as a means of life. In practice, however, the value we attach to a given quantity of water is significantly influenced also by the supply of water available; thus, the greater the number of gallons available, the lower the subjective value attached to any single gallon, and vice versa. Indeed, in general, the subjective value we attach to a unit of any desirable good or means (e.g., a gallon of water) is intimately and inversely related to the amount of goods or means available for satisfying the given want (i.e., drinking). (More on this in a moment.)

The Famous "Paradox of Values"

In the first half of the nineteenth century, this objective influence of supply on subjective values had been generally neglected by the classical economists (Adam Smith, et al), which prevented them from understanding the famous Paradox of Values. The paradox arises as follows: If you compare the respective prices of, say, water and diamonds in the market place, why is it that the price of a unit of water is but a fraction of the price of a diamond, even though water is ever so much more valuable for life than diamonds? Why, indeed, when life would be impossible without water, whereas we could get along without diamonds?

Implicit in the paradox is the traditional but misleading notion that the price of a good should be proportionate to some objective property of the good, such as its technical usefulness. For Adam Smith, propounder of the paradox, there was "nothing more useful" than water, whereas diamonds had "little or no" usefulness; therefore, he thought, the price of water should be very much higher than the price of diamonds. No wonder he was puzzled by the fact that market prices were exactly the reverse of what he expected.

Explaining the "Paradox"

Clearly, the fact that water is available in ever so much greater supply than diamonds does have a bearing on the "paradoxically" low price of a gallon of water compared with the high price of a karat of diamonds. Add to this the fact that, for drinking purposes, nature provides important substitutes, such as

milk and fruit and vegetable juices. Indeed, relatively
abundant supplies of water enable us to use water not
only for vital drinking and cooking, but also for less
vital car-washing,   swimming pools,   and decorative
fountains.

If supply conditions were exactly the opposite,
and water was as rare as diamonds, then surely its
market price would greatly exceed that of diamonds.
Imagine the predicament of an explorer in the desert who
has run out of water, having to bargain for some water
from a passing caravan of Bedouins. He would surely
offer them all the valuables he had (even diamonds) for
enough water to get him to his destination.

The Fallacy of All-or-Nothing

Furthermore, the paradox of values suffers from
the fallacious assumption that the choices daily facing
us are made on an all-or-nothing basis--that is, water
or diamonds,   food or movies,   clothing or books,
etc., rather than some amounts of each.   Of course,
if such were the case, no doubt we would always
choose food instead of movies, or clothing instead
of books.   Actually, the choices we typically make
are not of the all-or-nothing kind, but are more
along the lines of "some-of-this and some-of-that, or "a
bit-of-everything."

Thus, the subjective values we attach to the
goods we desire are not directed toward the whole class
or genre of the goods (e.g., food or liquids as a
whole), but rather toward single units of them (e.g.,
pounds, gallons).   Similarly, the prices we pay in the
market place are not for food as a whole, but merely for
single units of given foods (e.g., a loaf of bread).
Furthermore, we not only buy food in varying amounts,
but we also buy a host of other non-food items in
varying amounts, according to our individual preferences, on the one hand, and the prices of the respective
goods, on the other.

Summary

To conclude this section: We can now see more
clearly that, in practice, the entities we value most
directly are the goods or means (e.g., water) capable of
satisfying our wants (e.g., thirst), and not the wants

themselves which ultimately inspire the desire for goods
or means.   True, the personal or subjective want (e.g.,
thirst) is the fountainhead of the subjective value that
we attach to the goods or means (e.g., water) capable of
satisfying it.   But in practice,   only goods or   means
have the capacity of satisfying a want; therefore, it is
the goods,   rather than the ultimate want itself,   which
become the direct object of our subjective valuations.

        Nevertheless,   the value we attach to a good   or
means   (e.g.,   water)   indirectly reflects both (a)   the
subjective value attached to the uses or purposes served
by the good,   as ranked on our preference-scale, and (b)
the relative abundance or scarcity of the supply of   the
good   itself,   as well as the availability of close substitutes.   It is this latter aspect which now brings us
to the Law of Marginal Utility,   one of the most   fundamental principles in economics.

The Law of Marginal Utility

        The   classic   statement of the Law   of   Marginal
Utility   is   by Boehm-Bawerk in the form   of   a   parable
about   a   small farmer who had planted enough   seeds   to
harvest five sacks of grain.   Boehm used this parable to
illustrate the following principle: for any given good,
there   is an inverse (opposite) relationship between (a)
the   quantity (number of units) that we possess   of   the
given   good   and (b) the subjective value or   importance
attached   to   any single unit of that good   (called   the
"marginal utility"),   provided other things (subjective
preferences, personal income, etc.) remain the same.   In
other words,   the Law of Marginal Utility is a statement
about   the   inverse relationship between (a)   the   total
amount possessed of a given good,   on the one hand,   and
(b)   the   value attached to a single unit of   the   total
stock of that good.

        In a moment,   this principle will be illustrated
by means of Boehm's parable, but first we should add the
two   corollaries   that follow from the Law of   MU.   The
first   is the Law of Diminishing MU,   which runs as follows: The greater the quantity possessed of any   given
good, the lower is the subjective value attached to a
unit of the given good (the MU),   other things being the
same.   The   second is the Law of Increasing MU: The
smaller   the quantity possessed,   the higher the subjective   value   attached to a unit of the given   good   (the

MU), other things being the same. The best way to see this is through Boehm's parable.[2]

Parable of Five Sacks of Grain

In Boehm's parable of the farmer and his five sacks of grain, one form of wealth possessed by the farmer is grain, which he allocates as follows: food for himself, feed for his poultry, brandy-making, and food for his parrot. These uses are listed in order of descending importance on the farmer's preference-scale, with food in the prime position, followed by poultry, brandy, and parrot. This subjective ranking of the various uses of grain is revealed in the way the farmer allocates his grain when his crop is harvested.

For instance, if his harvest yielded only one or two sacks, the farmer would use the grain only for food. However, if his crop amounted to three sacks, he would allocate the third sack to feeding his poultry. Similarly, if he enjoyed a crop of four sacks, he could then also make some brandy. Best of all, if he harvested the expected five sacks, he could then indulge in feeding his pet parrot.

Thus, the value attached to a sack of grain reflected the value attached to the particular want being served by the grain. It follows then that the greater the size of the farmer's crop--and the more he can indulge his lower-ranked wants--the lower the value he attaches to a single sack of grain. Conversely, the smaller the size of his crop, the greater the value that he attaches to each remaining sack, since only the more important wants can then be satisfied. In other words, Boehm's farmer esteems each of his wants, not with an equal intensity, but with a variable intensity; for this reason, the subjective value he attaches to a single sack of grain is variable--not fixed or constant--varying according to the number of sacks harvested.

---

[2] Eugen von Boehm-Bawerk, Capital and Interest, Vol. II: Positive Theory of Capital (South Holland, Illinois: Libertarian Press, 1959), pp. 143-150.

The Significance of Boehm's Parable

Another way to understand Boehm's parable is as follows: imagine the farmer harvested a full crop of five sacks, but, on the way home from the fields, he lost one sack (which got torn, say, and its contents scattered on the road). Clearly, given the farmer's preference-scale, and given only four sacks instead of five, he will sacrifice the feeding of his parrot (the least-important of his several wants). Similarly, if he had lost two sacks instead of only one, we would expect him to abandon not only his parrot but also his brandy-making, which is his next lowest preference. In the extreme case, if he harvested a very meagre crop of only one sack, he would clearly allocate it to his highest-valued purpose--provision of food for himself.

Thus, in general, the smaller his crop and the smaller his wealth of grain, the greater the value he attaches to a sack of grain (i.e., the law of increasing MU). Alternatively, the larger the crop he harvests, the lower would be the value attached to a sack of grain (i.e., the law of diminishing MU), and the more he could indulge in his lower-ranked wants. Another way of putting this: he would be most sensitive to the loss of a single sack when his stock is only one or two sacks, whereas when his stock is larger (four or five sacks), the sense of loss of a single sack is "diminished."

Illustrations of the Law
of Marginal Utility

Thus, the law of MU helps us answer the very basic question: What is the subjective-value or degree of importance attached to a unit of anything? The general answer is simply: It depends on how much you have of the thing. To use a simple example: The value I attach to a cigarette depends on how many I have in my pack; if I have a freshly opened full pack, any one cigarette would have a lower value than if I had only a very few left.

The principle is illustrated in another common situation: the airplane passenger who has packed 60 pounds of luggage for his trip, only to discover that the airline limit (without charge) is 40 pounds. He has to discard 20 pounds of stuff--but which items will it be? According to the law of MU, each "pound" has a lower MU for the passenger when he has a 60-pound limit than if he has only a 40-pound limit; thus, whatever item he discards, we can presume it is of lower-ranked use, whereas the remaining 40 pounds comprise items of higher-ranked use.

One final example: Imagine the government imposes gasoline rationing, limiting purchases to only ten gallons a week. If, formerly, people were using gasoline an average of fifteen gallons a week, it is clear that, with five gallons less than before, drivers will have to cut back on their driving. But which trips will they sacrifice? According to the law of MU, whichever trips are sacrificed, they must be presumed to be trips of lower importance, while the allowed ten gallons will be used only for the more valued trips.

A couple of interesting historical notes on the origins of the law of MU come to mind. The principle has been traced back to Aristotle, the philosopher of ancient Greece. And the great poet Shakespeare certainly alluded to it, albeit unwittingly, when he penned these lines in Much Ado About Nothing:

> For it so falls out,
> That what we have we prize not to the worth,
> Whiles we enjoy it, but being lack'd and lost,
> Why, then we rack the value; then we find
> The virtue that possession would not show us,
> Whiles it was ours. [3]

"Marginal Utility" vs. "Total Utility"

Sometimes, upon first meeting the law of diminishing MU, the reader gets confused between what is here called "marginal utility" and another term, "total utility." We have used MU to stand for the subjective-value attached to a single unit of a stock of goods. On the other hand, TU stands for the "total usefulness" of the stock of goods, and depends on the physical/technical capacity of the goods to render services or satisfy wants. Compared with the subjective nature of MU, the concept of TU embraces the purely objective, physical dimension of technical usefulness embodied in given goods. In the case of Boehm's farmer, a larger stock of

---

[3] Quoted by Henry Hazlitt, in his The Foundations of Morality (Princeton: D. Van Nostrand Co., 1964), p. 323.

grain would, on the one hand, cause MU to diminish, but, on the other hand, would enable TU to increase.

To illustrate the difference between MU and TU: if Boehm's farmer harvested five sacks, he could satisfy all of his wants for grain and thereby enjoy a greater TU than if he had harvested only two or three sacks; nevertheless, the MU attached to any one sack would be less ("diminished"), as reflected by the fact that parrot-feeding is of a lower rank than food or poultry-raising. Yet this by no means contradicts the fact that, given the choice (and other things remaining the same), man would prefer more to less--a greater TU to a smaller TU; that is, he would prefer five sacks of grain to only one or two. On the other hand, Boehm's parable illustrates the principle that, whatever the quantity of his resources, man prefers to allocate them to higher-valued purposes rather than to lower-valued ones.

Conclusion

We have explored several major ramifications of the concept of wants under conditions of scarcity. In the process, we analyzed two key dimensions of subjective-value: (1) the existence of ordinal preference-scales, and (2) the law of marginal utility. Awareness of these two aspects make it possible to understand the degree of importance that we attach to anything. (Time-preference, which is a third dimension of influence on subjective valuation, is discussed at length in Chapter IX.)

To culminate our understanding of wants, two tasks remain: (1) an analysis of the general principle of motivation underlying all human action (in the remaining sections of this chapter), and (2) an analysis of the relationship of wants to their market form, the concept of demand (Chapters VI and VII).

II. The Maximizing Principle

We are now prepared to explore a fundamental proposition hereafter referred to as the maximizing principle. This principle follows logically from the preceding analysis of the nature of human wants, subjective valuation and preference-scale ranking, and constitutes the fundamental principle of motivation in human action. This principle acknowledges explicitly that human action comprises, yet bridges, the two time phases of all human action--the "beforehand" (ex-ante) phase on the one hand, and the "afterward" (ex-post) phase on the other. Exploration of these essentially different time dimensions, as well as their interconnections, will not only deepen our understanding of the nature of choice and decision-making, and human adjustment to the world around us, but will also be particularly relevant to later chapters.

The maximizing principle may be stated simply as follows: <u>Every</u> human action is undertaken with the <u>expectation</u> or belief that it will leave a person better off <u>than otherwise</u>. First, a few comments about the underlined words. "Every" literally means EVERY, and involves the annoying or distressful situations of daily life--Hamlet's "thousand slings and arrows of outrageous fortune"--as well as the more pleasant and enjoyable ones. <u>Expectation</u> indicates the <u>ex-ante</u>, beforehand, or anticipatory nature of human choice and action; choices and actions are always made in the present phase, whereas their actual final outcome or result comes only in the future phase. Expected future outcomes and results of human decisions are therefore more or less unknowable in the present; they can only constitute expectations, anticipations, or speculations.

Lastly, the phrase "than otherwise" refers to the fact that human choices and actions are made under unavoidable <u>limitations</u> or <u>constraints</u>. These limitations are imposed, on the one hand, by (a) one's personal resources, capabilities, etc., (e.g., budget, skills, energy, values, beliefs, knowledge) which are naturally relatively scarce, and by (b) one's environment (physical, legal) on the other hand. Together they serve to define the array of possible <u>alternatives</u> that confront the human actor and from which he has to choose the preferred alternative. To put it in more familiar terms: under given circumstances, we always do the best we can with what we have--and what Nature and the Law allow.

Categories of Human Situations

Every human action is prompted or induced by one of three possible categories of situation. The first category can be referred to as the <u>plus</u> or "net gain" situation, in which a person's goal is to become absolutely better off than he is, that is, to reach a

higher status or level of well-being in general, be it
by some tangible or intangible standard. This includes
such goals as a higher income level, professional
achievement and recognition, or the raising of a family.
Indeed, any kind of action whose purpose is to enable
the person to become "better than he was," so to speak--
for example, trying a new cooking recipe--would fall
into this "plus" category.

The second category is the type we face virtually several times a day, since it includes such things as
eating, drinking, sleep, sex, and clothing. Here the
person is typically acting to adjust to some discomfort,
uneasiness, or longing. The source of the "uneasiness"
may be either internal to his body or mind--as in the
case of hunger or depression--or external, as in the
case of a weather change. But the purpose of action is
merely to restore the customary level of well-being.
This case is referred to here as the equilibrium type of
situation, since the goal is merely to recapture a
customary plateau and not to reach a "plus" level.

The third and final category of situation may
also be encountered several times a day: the purely
unfavorable event--the disappointment, the frustration,
the "bad news" (again, Hamlet's "thousand slings and
arrows of outrageous fortune" that life is prone to).
These are purely minus or "net loss" situations which
leave us worse off than before, no matter what we do
about them. As a consequence, a person is merely trying
to "make the best of a bad situation,"--or is choosing
the "lesser of two evils." Examples include: business
firms that face losses and seek ways of minimizing them;
the youth who faces the military draft and wonders
whether military combat or draft evasion is the lesser
sacrifice; the taxpayer who, facing a higher tax bill,
has to decide on how to cut back on his consumer
expenditures.

Some Examples of Maximizing Behavior

Altogether, these three classes of situation
encompass every conceivable case. Yet in each and every
situation, whichever way a person decides to act, the
choice is presumed to be the one which he expects will
leave him feeling better off than otherwise.

For example, consider a plus situation as follows: a young accountant is offered a new job with

another firm at a $5,000 raise in pay. What are his alternatives? Plainly, only two. He can accept the new job, in which case it would indicate his belief that the change would move him up the professional ladder, and thus leave him "better off than otherwise." On the other hand, he could turn it down because, say, he believed the new working conditions would not be satisfactory, making the new job, despite the higher pay, appear worse overall than his present job. Nevertheless, he would still be maximizing if he decided to stay with his old job, since it implies a belief that this would leave him better off than otherwise.

At the other extreme--in the minus category-- imagine a 19-year old getting a military draft notice. What are his alternatives? Suppose he considers only the following three: he could comply and become a soldier, he could evade the draft and run off to Canada or Sweden, or he could apply for a C. O. status. None of these choices appeals to him because he believes each would leave him absolutely worse off than before. Yet, given his situation, he must select one of them. Which one will it be? The maximizing principle says that whichever choice he makes, it will be the one which he believes will be the "least of the evils," so to speak; that is, the one he hopes will leave him the "least worse off"--which logically will leave him better off than otherwise. As the balladeer, Tom Rush, once put it, "We're all making the best of a bad situation."

In the intermediate equilibrium category, consider the usual case of increasing hunger pangs which arouse one's appetite for the next meal. What are the alternatives? On the one hand, one could eat right away; on the other hand, one could postpone eating until it became more important to eat than to do anything else. Either way, a person will be maximizing since he has chosen to do that which he expects will make him feel "better off than otherwise."

Generalizing the Maximizing Principle

We are now in a position to see why it would not suffice to state the maximizing principle, as some have done, as follows: "A person always chooses that course of action which he believes will put him in a preferred position." The reason this statement would be unsatisfactory is that the word "preferred," by itself, is limited; it prevents the statement from being sufficiently general to qualify as a general "law" or "principle" of human action.

For example, in a "net loss" situation (e.g., military draft), no possible decision could lead a person into a "preferred" position in the sense that it leaves him better off <u>than</u> <u>formerly</u>. If a draftee decides to flee to Canada, for instance, this could be regarded as a "preferred" situation only compared to the <u>available</u> alternatives--not compared to his former <u>situation</u>. Thus, it is necessary to qualify the phrase "preferred position" as follows: "...a preferred position compared to the <u>available</u> alternatives." This is why our basic statement ends with the phrase <u>"than</u> <u>otherwise."</u>

Similarly, the earlier proposition that human action comprises exchanges of "<u>less-preferred</u> positions for <u>more-preferred</u> positions" can now be generalized by the addition of the qualifying phrase, "from among the available alternatives;" that is, <u>given</u> <u>the</u> <u>options</u> open to him, a person always chooses to act on the more-preferred goal and rejects the less-preferred ones. Thus, even if a person accepts military service under the draft, this choice is revealed as being the "more-preferred" one <u>compared</u> <u>to</u> <u>any</u> <u>of</u> <u>the</u> <u>alternatives</u>.

Possible Mismatch Between
Ex-Ante and Ex-Post

We must now make it clear that the maximization principle is relevant to the <u>ex-ante</u> phase of human action, not the <u>ex-post</u> phase. The <u>ex-post</u> could very likely reveal that a person's "best laid plans" did <u>not</u> turn out as intended. In the <u>ex-ante</u> there is no way <u>of</u> knowing in advance whether <u>one's</u> expectations will materialize. It is only in the <u>ex-post</u> that it becomes possible to discover whether <u>ex-ante</u> expectations, anticipations, hopes or gambles <u>will be</u> realized, or whether they are to be disappointed.

Ideally, of course, each of us prefers that his decisions enjoy a <u>certainty</u> of outcome--a kind of guarantee that <u>ex-ante</u> hopes would always be realized in the <u>ex-post</u>. In practice, however, this certainty of correspondence between <u>ex-ante</u> expectations and <u>ex-post</u> outcomes is clearly unrealistic. That is, the <u>ex-post</u> may very well bring disappointment and regret instead of

successful realization and satisfaction. Indeed, the
ex-post result may be such that, had we been able to
know it in advance, we would have made some other choice
instead of the choice actually made. Thus, we use the
term "regret" to indicate one's ex-post awareness that
he had not made the best ex-ante choice.

Imperfect Knowledge and
Ex-Post Regret

This brings us to the crucial question: What
prevents us from knowing, ex-ante, whether or not--or to
what degree--our maximizing choices will be disappointed, ex-post, and cause regret? To this we offer the
following general answer: The possible mismatch between
ex-ante expectations and ex-post outcomes is caused
basically by incomplete information or degrees of ignorance ("imperfect knowledge"), a condition that potentially characterizes all situations and decisions. Indeed, the natural human condition of imperfect knowledge
prevents the matching of the ex-ante plan and ex-post
achievement in a host of ways.

In the market place, for instance, we are all
familiar with the case of the regretful consumer who
discovers, only after his purchase, that he could have
bought the thing at a lower price elsewhere, or that he
could have acquired a better quality product for the
price he paid. In both types of regret, if the relevant
information about price and quality had been available
in advance--say, in the form of newspaper ads or TV
commercials--then a more careful reading of this information could have avoided the regretted choices.

Suppose, however, that the consumer did do his
homework and checked all the available ads. Even this
would not preclude the possibility that he missed some
attractive bargains simply because they were not adver-
tised at all. In this case, the consumer could only by
accident discover these bargains while shopping and,
regretfully, after he had already made his purchase at
the higher price.

Another familiar case is that of the firm which
typically has to decide how much to produce and at what
price. This decision requires some fore-knowledge of
consumers' demand (more on this in Chapters VI - VIII).
Yet, there is no way that anyone can know consumers'
demand with sufficient precision. The reason is that

consumers' tastes and preferences are constantly changing; so is their purchasing power. This creates a basic
uncertainty for any firm having to forecast demand.
True, a firm may engage in market research in order to
increase its knowledge of market demand, but it can
never really know it with certainty since there is
likely a remaining residue of unknown data. Thus, the
daily operations of firms provide a hotbed source of
possible regret in human decision-making.

Changes in Taste, Forgetfulness

Sometimes the source of regret can be attributed
to an ex-post change in one's taste or preference. For
example, there is the college student who first majors
in one subject--say, engineering--only to discover a
latent love for economics such that he is regretful of
his initial preference for engineering. Or take the
case of the young couple that decide to divorce after
several years of a marriage they now both regret. In
both cases there is a change of mind--be it due to
increased knowledge, or awareness of one's self, or of
the other person's self, or simply due to increased
personal maturity.

At times, regret may be caused by what appears
to be a change of taste but is actually a case of for-
getfulness. That is, a mere oversight may explain why a
person undertakes action A instead of B: if he had
remembered B, he would have acted on it rather than A;
having forgotten about B, he had reason to regret the
omission once he was again reminded of it.

Fraud, Self-Deception

Regret may also occur in interpersonal transactions due to fraud or deception committed by one of
the parties. For example, if someone paid $8,000 for
what the car dealer described as a "great car!" but
which actually turned out to be a "lemon," he is a
victim of a fraudulent transaction that he surely re-
grets: had he known better, he would not have purchased
the defective car. Similarly, if the car-buyer uses
counterfeit money to pay for the car, the dealer will
have reason to regret accepting the bogus money. In
neither case could the fraud or deception transpire if
the victim were informed to begin with of the deception
taking place.

In this connection, we should include the case where regret is attributable to the lack of information induced by self-deception. Here the relevant cause is not an objective lack of means for obtaining the required information, but rather a subjective tendency to rely on uninformed guesses--hunches, omens, or flips of the coin. Why would a person intentionally disdain reasonably obtained information in favor of a flight of fancy? It might be due to a belief that the necessary information is unknowable, and therefore a flip of the coin might be the easiest way to reach a decision. In other cases, however, where the necessary information might be ascertainable, the disdain of a search for this information in favor of deciding on the basis of un-examined data implies an act of self-deception.

Information is a Scarce Means

At this point it is relevant to stress that whether a particular bit of information is knowable or not, or whether a given transaction is economic or non-economic, the information required for reaching non-regretful decisions is, indeed, a scarce means: it cannot be acquired except by the expenditure of time, effort, or wealth. This is why, in the initial elucidation of the maximizing principle, information is included among the limitations or constraints affecting every decision. Furthermore, since every human decision is effective only to the extent that it is based on information that can avoid or minimize regret in the ex-post, since information is truly a scarce "means," and since economics is concerned with the implications of means-end relations, we can now realize that the analy-sis of information and regret provides still another link between so-called "economic" behavior and human action in general.

From Autistic to Bilateral Exchange

Before closing this section, it should be added that the maximizing principle, being applicable to all types of individual action, applies to interpersonal transactions as well. It is but a small step from arguing that (a) the individual always maximizes in the ex-ante by exchanging one state of affairs for another, to realizing that (b) if two people exchange with each other, whether personally or in the market place, each of them is seeking to maximize. In the former case, the maximizing is <u>autistic</u> or purely personal, involving only one person as the maximizer. In the latter case, maximizing is <u>bilateral</u>, involving two parties, both of whom seek to <u>maximize</u> through voluntary exchange with each other. It is this bilateral maximizing that is at the core of all interpersonal or social transactions, whether in the commerce or trade of the market place or in purely personal (non-economic) decisions.

We are all familiar with <u>market</u> exchange--for example, the type analyzed in Chapter III--in which two parties engage either in barter exchange (goods for goods or services) or in monetary exchange (money for goods or services). In all such transactions, exchange occurs because each trader believes he will be better off by exchanging than otherwise. But the same is also true for all so-called non-economic or social trans- actions between two people. Even though no money changes hands, the interpersonal transaction between two people is no less an <u>exchange</u> transaction than is the market transaction.

Whether the interpersonal relation involves mere conversation and pleasantries, recreation, friendship, sex, entertainment, or marriage, in every case there is a presumed voluntary mutual exchange of personal assets (tangible or intangible) in which each party expects to be made better off than otherwise. Indeed, every time two people, A and B, transact with each other, they are mutually "using each other" as a means of becoming better off than otherwise--that is, better off than being with persons C, D, E, etc., or better off than being alone. Thus it follows that <u>all</u> interpersonal transactions, whether "economic" or "non-economic," are in the nature of <u>exchange</u> transactions in which both parties exchange personal assets for mutual benefit in the effort to maximize.

III. Methodological Individualism

By now we should be aware that the analysis thus far has been primarily in terms of <u>individual</u> wants, goals, and motivation. Practically no reference has been made to corresponding dimensions of "society," "government," or other social or political entities. The omission is unavoidably due to the epistemological nature of the subject--the fact that it is impossible to talk about "society" or "government" in the same way as we can about individuals. That is, it is possible to analyze individual action in terms of a <u>unitary</u> human entity and motivation--a <u>single</u> mind, body, and personality capable of formulating goals and purposes that reflect and are consistent with the person's own nature and will. However, the same cannot be said of social entities--societies, nations, states--which by their very nature comprise numerous <u>separate</u> and <u>different</u> individuals possessed of separate and different minds and goals.

Individual is Prior to "Society"

The matter was succinctly put by Ludwig von Mises: "For the purpose of [human] science we must start from the action of the <u>individual</u> because this is the only thing of which we can have direct cognition. The idea of a <u>society</u> that could operate or manifest itself apart from the action of individuals is absurd. Everything social must in some way be recognizable in the action of the individual.... Every form of society is operative in the actions of individuals aiming at definite ends...." [4] (insertion and underlinings mine).

In a similar vein, Alchian and Allen assert: "The unit of analysis is the individual. The actions of groups, organizations, communities, nations, and societies can best be understood by focusing attention on the incentives and actions of members. When we speak of the goals and actions of the United States, we are really referring to the goals and actions of the <u>individuals</u> in the United States. A business, a union, or a family may be formed to further some common interest of the constituents, but group actions are still the results of decisions of individuals" [5] (underlinings in original).

Finally, take the following from the textbook by P. T. Heyne on the subject of political decisions concerning the choice of government projects: "...keep in mind that entities like <u>states</u> or <u>cities</u> never really want anything. Wants and goals are always attached ultimately to individuals. When someone says, 'The

---

[4]Ludwig von Mises, <u>Epistemological Problems of Economics</u> (Princeton: D. Van Nostrand Co., 1960), p. 43.

[5]Armen A. Alchian and William R. Allen, <u>University Economics</u> (3rd ed., Belmont, California: Wadsworth Publ. Co., 1972), p. 19.

people want...,' what does he mean? That all the people
want it? A majority?   Those who count?   It is usually
a good rule...to ask: Who wants...?"6 (underlinings   in
original).

In summary, the implications of methodological
individualism are clear: the only irreducible unit of
human action is the individual actor, even when he acts
as a member of a group. The "group" is merely an entity
that is itself reducible to the individual members who
comprise it. A group such as a committee or legislative
body cannot act as a "group" except in the purely technical or legal sense, as a unit empowered to reach a
group decision.   It is individuals who ultimately make
the decisions of groups; the group is merely a means
through which individuals act, albeit in a cooperative
fashion, to achieve goals ultimately serving its individual members.

Another way of seeing this: it is only the
individual who, acting through a group as one of its
members, is in the position of judging whether the
group's decision is a "maximizing" one for him.   Thus,
no group can claim that its decisions are representative
of the group's members; only the individual member can
determine the "representativeness" of the group's decision for him.

Some Cases in Point

A few more examples should clinch the point.
Suppose a "nation" goes to war. It is clearly illegitimate to claim that entry into war--say, on the basis of
Congressional decision--reflects the consent of every
individual citizen in the nation.   Similarly, it would
be illegitimate for a political leader to claim that a
given war is in the "national interest," since there
exists no such unitary, homogeneous entity: one person's "national interest" could mean going to war, while
for another person it could mean pacifism or isolation-
ism.   So long as individuals differ in their attitude
toward war--or any other specific issue, for that matter
--there is simply no way that a group can logically
claim to be "representative" of all its individual
members.

6Paul T. Heyne, The Economic Way of Thinking (Chicago:
Science Research Assocociates, 1973), p. 7.

104

In this connection, it should be noted that the principle of majority rule itself is vulnerable to criticism by methodological individualists. Groups typically decide by the principle of majority rule. The very concept itself concedes the existence of minority views and therefore implies that a majority decision cannot represent minority viewpoints. Therefore, no group or group leader can truthfully talk in the name of "all the people," be it in a democracy or a totalitarian state.

IV. The Primacy of Self-Interest

With the aid of the maximizing principle and methodological individualism, economics logically moves on to another basic proposition about human motivation: the primary purpose of human action is to serve the "self," or the self-interest of the individual; human action is therefore always fundamentally "selfish." As a corollary: human action that is apparently motivated by unselfish service to others (so-called "altruism" or "self-sacrifice")--that is, allegedly not egoism--is at the root also motivated by self-interest. That is, what appears to be unselfish or altruistic behavior is merely a particular manifestation of basically selfish behavior, albeit in the form of a gift or service to others.

Self-Interest vs. Altruism:
a Fallacious Dichotomy

It has been customary to regard self-interest and altruism as basically opposite or mutually exclusive principles of motivation. The implication is that an altruistic act on behalf of others (e.g., a gift of goods or services) could not possibly be motivated by self-interest. Conversely, it is customary to assume that a person acting "selfishly"--for example, by accumulating profits and wealth--could not thereby render service or benefit to others.

First of all, regarded purely as a practical matter, the alleged dichotomy of self-interest and altruism simply is non-existent. The successful doctor or surgeon, for example, whose practice necessarily involves ministering to others, is usually being handsomely rewarded for his services; his "altruistic" services do not preclude his desire to be well paid for them. Conversely, the person who undertakes a career as a doctor or surgeon in order to become wealthy simply could not succeed at this goal without "altruistic" ministering to his patients. It is similarly misleading to imply that farmers, auto mechanics, teachers, lawyers and others are incapable of rendering services to others simply because their remunerative work is motivated by self-interest.

What makes altruism at the root a <u>self-interes-ted</u> act is the fact that, while the altruistic act provides a benefit to its recipient, it is also a source of selfish satisfaction to its performer. Any "altru-istic" act that is a direct source of joy, contentment, or self-satisfaction to its performer is essentially a self-interested act. The principle of <u>pure</u> altruism cannot logically imply that, in practice, an altruistic act cannot be tinged with self-satisfaction--that its performer is necessarily deprived of any joy from "doing good" for others! This logical predicament was clearly visible to Mandeville, author of <u>Fable of the Bees</u> as early as 1705. More recently, Mark Twain elaborated on this theme in his sadly neglected essay, <u>What Is Man?</u> (1906).[7]

Self-Interest is Pervasive

For example, for Mark Twain the only impulse that moves a person in all his actions is the impulse to "content his own spirit;" man's prime need is to secure his own self-approval. ". . . Both the noblest impulses and the basest" emanate from but one source, as defined by Twain's own "law" of motivation: "From his cradle to his grave a man never does a single thing which has any FIRST AND FOREMOST object but one--to secure peace of mind, spiritual comfort, for HIMSELF." Thus, when a so-called "unselfish" man does a thing that is apparently only for another person's good, at his own expense, such an apparently "unselfish" act, as Twain put it, "must do <u>him</u> good, FIRST; otherwise he will not do it." What then becomes of "self-sacrifice"? It turns out to be merely another way of acting by which man can "content his own spirit." (Underlinings and emphasis by Twain.)

---

[7]Mark Twain, <u>What Is Man?</u>, Vol. 12: The Complete Works of Mark Twain (New York: Harper & Brothers, American Artists Edi-tion, no date), pp. 1-24.

Patriotism and Charity

For Mark Twain, examples of self-contenting "self-sacrifice" are not hard to find. Let us note two such cases. For instance, patriotism--"that noble passion, love of country;" as patriots, men will give up the peace of home and work and march into battle, danger, and death. Why? Why would anyone who was supposedly seeking "spiritual contentment" and "peace of mind" leave his pleasant home and his family in tears and march into battle?

For Twain, the solution to this paradox is straightforward: a man joins the army and goes into battle, even though he loves peace and dreads pain, because "there is something that he loves more than he loves peace--the approval of his neighbors and the public. And perhaps there is something which he dreads more than he dreads pain--the disapproval of his neighbors and the public." (Underlinings by Twain.)

Twain's second case involves the act of charity. On a stormy, snowy, bitter-cold midnight, a man is about to board the horse-drawn car to return home and avoid trudging home through the dreadful storm. At this very moment he is approached by a gray, ragged old woman ("a touching picture of misery") who extends her palm and begs for respite from hunger and disease. Without a moment's hesitation he reaches into his pocket, but finds only a single quarter--just enough for his car fare! Again, without hesitation, "he gives it to her and trudges home through the storm." How did he feel plodding his way home? Twain says he was in a "state of joy ...his heart sang ...unconscious of the storm." How come? Why such a state of joy and singing heart?

Why not, says Twain. Just look at the bargain that the man got for his twenty-five cents--and his stormy walk home! For one thing, he could not bear the pain of seeing the poor old woman suffer; "his conscience would torture him all the way home.... If he didn't relieve the old woman, he would not get any sleep." Thus, for a mere quarter-piece, he was able to (a) free himself from "a sharp pain in his heart," (b) escape the "tortures of a waiting conscience," and (c) buy himself a full night's sleep "...all for twenty-five cents!... profit on top of profit! ...first, to content his own spirit; secondly, to relieve her sufferings." (Underlinings by Twain.)

Self-Interest as a Formal,
General Concept

Essentially, Twain is telling us not to be misled by mere appearances if we want to understand the foundation of human action. Take the case of charity. To give away cash voluntarily is essentially no less selfish than to hoard it, since the pleasures derived therefrom can exceed the "self-sacrifice" involved; otherwise the cash would not be given away.

Take the case of danger. Facing danger is not purely self-sacrificial, nor is its avoidance the height of self-interest. As every car driver knows, driving on hazardous freeways is not a purely negative situation that one avoids under any and all circumstances. If one drives the freeway every day to work, it must be because the monetary and psychic rewards of the job more than offset the driving hazards.

Take the case of pain. "Pain" is not always the antithesis of "pleasure." For example, the experience of pain, whether physical or psychic, may often permit a more pleasurable outcome than the avoidance of pain. Thus, the pain of surgery can be more than offset by the pleasures of a repaired condition. In the case of "neurotic" persons, patterns of behavior that may strike the "normal" onlooker as self-defeating and painful--because they only lead to "failure"--are not necessarily painful to the neurotic: he may regard his neurotic patterns of behavior as being less painful than being forced to abandon them before he is willing to do so.

In other words, the concept of self-interest is here formulated as a general or formal axiom embracing and explaining all human action under the unitary principle of "maximization." Thus it can be asserted that all human action seeks to achieve net gain--benefits or satisfactions exceeding costs or sacrifices--or, at least, to achieve minimum loss or least-painful outcomes. As a general axiom, therefore, self-interest is no longer associated only with pure gain or profit; nor is altruism any longer to be regarded as pure self-sacrifice and the opposite of self-interest.

Altruism as a Source of Joy

The primacy of self-interest as the only underlying purpose of human action becomes even more evident when we realize that pure altruism is both impossible and absurd. Up to now, our argument has been: altruism is not in conflict with the principle of self-interest; indeed, the altruistic act is merely a peculiar form of essentially self-interested behavior. Now it is to be argued that pure altruism is simply an irrelevant concept to start with--logically untenable, impossible to implement, and therefore absurd.

Consider above all the following. If pure altruism is supposed to be the polar opposite of self-interest, it must imply an act of pure self-sacrifice that precludes any form of reward. That is, the pure altruist is precluded from receiving either payment in money or in kind, or even payment in the intangible form of joy or satisfaction. The latter would clearly constitute a benefit or gain no less self-serving than a monetary reward. The only way that the admitted joy received from giving or rendering service to others can be made consistent with pure self-sacrifice is to redefine such sacrifice as a kind of joyless joy, or, indeed, a form of pure pain! But this is patently absurd. On the other hand, if we deign to define altruism as an enjoyable act, per se, and not as joyless pure self-sacrifice, the ghost is up: altruism can no longer serve as a concept antithetical to and inconsistent with personal gain, satisfaction, and self-interest.

The Split: Altruists vs. Beneficiaries

To reinforce the argument, let us further grant the premise that altruistic self-sacrifice can be purely joyless, totally painful to its practitioners. It can then be argued that an "altruistic" society would necessarily generate a conflict of interest between the altruistic A's and the beneficiary B's. If the virtue of altruism lies precisely in the effective ministering to other peoples' wants, we must then conclude that the useful services provided by the A's' actually satisfy the B's' wants. If so, we end up with a society wherein the B's' self-interest is being served at the A's' expense; that is, A's altruistic behavior and self-denial merely enable B's selfish enjoyment of A's gratuities: one man's altruism is the vital source of another man's selfish joy.

Ironically, therefore, altruism by A's necessarily serves to foster self-interest in others (B's) rather than suppress it. But this means there can be no totally altruistic society! To get a society in which no one's self-interest is catered to, the B's, too, would have to be precluded from enjoying selfish contentment from the A's ministrations! Only thus could there be an altruistic society totally antithetical to self-interest. Once again, we reach absurdity--a society in which the gratuitous benefits provided by the A's must in no way give selfish joy to the beneficiary B's!

Some Additional Absurdities

Related to this absurdity is still another. Not only must the A's be purely self-sacrificing toward the B's--precluded from receiving payment from the B's--but the B's, too, must be precluded from rewarding the A's, even if they were willing to do so out of sheer gratitude! Note the paradox: despite their gratitude for the A's' goodness to them, the B's are by definition precluded from rewarding the A's in any way, for to do so would redound to the A's' benefit, thereby fostering the latter's self-interest!

A final note on the light side. The splitting of society into the A's and B's necessarily follows from the fact that for every pure altruist there must be a pure beneficiary, and vice versa. Since people logically cannot simultaneously be both pure altruist and pure beneficiary, society must be split up into two distinct camps, the A's versus the B's. This recalls the story in which Edgar Bergen, the ventriloquist, told his working dummy Charlie McCarthy: "Now, remember, Charlie, we're put on this earth to give help to others." To which Charlie queried: "Then what on earth are the others put here for?"

Moral Questions Raised by Altruism

The fact that the altruistic "society" is actually split into two societies--into the A's and the B's--raises some basic moral questions. What happens if some of the A's refuse to bestow further gratuities on the B's, giving as their reason the desire to take care of themselves first? Is it now immoral for these A's, in their own self-interest, to take care of themselves and leave the B's to be taken care of by themselves or

110

by other A's?   Do the B's have any right to force the
A's to sacrifice themselves in behalf of the B's?

        Furthermore,   would   selfishness   in the   A's   be
morally acceptable if they decided to share their wealth
with the B's only voluntarily, at their own discretion,
without compulsion?   How much of their wealth must the
A's   share with the B's before they cease to be   "selfish"?   What is the moral nature of an   altruism   that
requires force and compulsion rather   than   voluntary
choice for its implementation?   Why would it be moral to
serve others,   but   immoral to serve one's own   self?
Finally,   if the B's wished to pay the A's for benefits
received,   would they have the right to do   so?   Unfortunately,   these and related moral questions,   raised by
altruism and "redistribution," cannot be pursued in this
book.

Altruism Means Lower Living Standards

        There   are still other reasons why it is a   fal-
lacy   to   regard self-interest and altruism as   opposing
premises.   The fact remains that no person could survive
physically while acting purely altruistically.   If   a
person, as a pure altruist, works only for others, and
not   for   himself,   he himself can survive only   if   (a)
others,   in turn,   take care of him (tit-for-tat,   so to
speak) by providing him with food, clothing, etc., or if
(b)   he   steals from others whatever he needs.   But   in
both of these alternatives he is necessarily serving his
own self-interest (i.e.,   his selfish desire for   survival),   and   therefore   cannot be regarded as a pure   altruist.   Similarly,   if he does not resort to   alternatives (a) and (b), but begins to produce for himself the
things he wants, this too would be "selfish" behavior
and nullify his pure altruism.

        Furthermore,   alternative   (a) would result in a
reduced standard of living for the average person.   The
reason is that if, in addition to the A's taking care of
the B's, the B's are now to also take care of the A's,
we   end   up with a reversion to primitive barter   which,
despite   its altruistic veneer,   would signify a   woeful
regression from the advanced division of labor   achieved
since   the   Industrial Revolution of 1750-1850   (recall
Chapter III).   Gone would be the obvious benefits of the
monetary economy,   specialization,   and large-scale technology which have brought greater output per capita and
rising living standards.   Instead,   the barter   economy

111

would force people to live from hand to mouth under
conditions tantamount to poverty.

First Things Are Still First

Pure altruism also distorts the order of
reality: it overlooks the basic fact that what is
being sacrificed and given away consists primarily of
the "self" of the altruist. Therefore, in order for the
altruist to be able to give anything away, he must first
acquire some "self"--in the form of wisdom, skill, or
product; otherwise he would have little or nothing of
value to give away. And since, logically, preservation
of his own life is prior and requisite to his ability to
serve others, the conclusion is clear: self-interested
self-preservation is necessarily prior to altruism.

This can be readily seen in the case of Robinson
Crusoe, our mythical, isolated man. His every effort to
produce the means of his own survival is clearly in his
own self-interest; no one could logically smear this
selfishness with the taint of "immorality." How, then,
does Crusoe's situation change if he suddenly abandons
isolation and joins "society," to become one producer
among many producers?

Once Crusoe becomes part of the social economy,
it is possible for him to exchange his goods and services with other producers. He will trade with them so
long as this leaves him better off than otherwise, in
accordance with the maximizing principle. On the other
hand, if he finds no advantage in trading with others,
he will tend to revert to his former pattern of isolated, self-sufficient production.

Conclusion

Finally, it is appropriate to ask: Why should
pure altruism be regarded as superior in any way to
self-interest? To regard altruism as an absolutely
higher principle assumes either of the following: (a)
service to others is the only satisfying act, whereas
self-service is never satisfying; or (b) service to
others is always more satisfying than self-service.
Both of these assumptions are patently absurd; they are
totally contradicted by the behavior of real people.
Granted, people do not "live by bread alone," but
neither do they live by altruism alone. In practice,

people help each other gratuitously in many diverse
ways. More importantly, however, they primarily take
care of themselves first. Only in this way are they
able to become altruists at all. And, irony of ironies,
it is precisely because the so-called altruistic act is
at bottom a self-satisfying and, therefore, self-
interested act, that one is desirous of being
"altruistic" (without "compensation"?!) in the first
place.

CHAPTER VI

THE DEMAND SIDE OF THE MARKET

The market place is a social-economic context in which suppliers and demanders face each other in repeated instances of exchange--actual and potential. The rates at which they exchange their goods and services and money constitute the "prices" of the market. As we shall see in Chapter VIII, it is the free and spontaneous interplay of demand and supply forces which determines the prices that tend to prevail in the market. Having already discussed the basic aspects of production and supply in Chapter IV, and the ramifications of wants in Chapter V, we now examine the demand side of the market in all of its relevance to the firm.

Demand vs. Wants

Our first task is to clarify the distinction between natural wants (i.e., desires, wishes, needs, appetites, etc.) and the concept of demand, a distinction already noted in Chapter II and Figure 5. When we talk about "wants" in economics, we have in mind the natural fact that all human action is broadly motivated by one or another desire, wish, or purpose. Furthermore, as we have seen, a want can be satisfied only by the application of means--time, effort, or wealth--that is, some expenditure, sacrifice, or cost. In other words, in a world of scarcity, wants by themselves do not help us very much; means must be acquired and applied to achieving the satisfaction of wants.

Here is where the concept of demand comes in: it encompasses not only the fact that a person has wants or goals, but that he also has the means to satisfy them effectively. Thus, in a barter economy, demand is exercised by means of producing and exchanging one's own product for the products of other producers. By contrast, in the modern market economy, the means used for the purpose of exercising demand typically takes the form of money, which, as a means of payment, is exchanged for product. Besides money, other forms of wealth--such as financial assets--also serve as sources of purchasing power (albeit not as money proper), which must be converted into money before they can be accepted as a means of payment.

Demand vs. Needs, Consumption

Similarly, demand must be distinguished from the term needs, which we saw in Chapter V is a term used to emphasize a want to which one attaches a special degree of importance. "Needs," like wants in general, are also handicapped by the fact that, by themselves, they do not possess the means to be satisfied; and just like wants, needs can only impel people to acquire means to satisfy them. Thus there is no "need" that can be satisfied without some effort or cost.

Before we proceed, we should note another impor-tant distinction of terminology--the difference between "demand" and consumption. Demand, as has been shown, is related only to the act of acquiring goods; in contrast, "consumption" represents that act of actually satisfying the want for which the goods were acquired. More pre-cisely, demand is exercised by the use of means, through exchange or purchase transactions; however, the actual consumption of the goods thus acquired does not take place until the person actually uses them for the pur-pose of directly satisfying the given want or fulfilling the given goal.

More on Consumption

To be sure, a person's ability to consume rests principally on one's ability to exercise demand in the first place. Thus, demand is logically prior to con-sumption, and consumption is therefore predicated upon the exercise of demand. But this fact in itself does not imply anything as to when the final act of consump-tion will actually take place. For example, consumption may occur virtually simultaneously with the act of demand, as in the case of a frankfurter purchased at a hot-dog stand and eaten right there. Alternatively, consumption may occur only after a deferred period fol-lowing the acquisition of the goods, as in the case of frankfurters purchased and stored in the refrigerator, pending a subsequent picnic or other occasion.

Furthermore, in economics, consumption has a much broader or general meaning than the narrow,

116

materialistic meaning usually given to it by the layman.
For example, economics classifies as <u>consumers'</u> <u>goods</u>
such things as leisure, music, spiritual <u>worship</u> and
other intangible or non-material goods alongside such
material goods as food, clothing, or jewelry--and for
the same reason: any goods that have the capacity to
<u>directly</u> or <u>personally</u> satisfy a want or purpose, be it
material or non-material, must be classified as consumers' goods. Hence, the act of personally using a
consumers' good is regarded as "consumption."

Demand is Based on Production

As important as <u>means</u> are for the exercise of
demand, equally important is the fact that, whether the
economy is based on barter (direct) exchange or monetary
(indirect) exchange, means must be acquired typically by
<u>productive</u> effort. This productive activity yields
purchasing power to the producer-- whether in the form
of (a) <u>goods</u> produced in the case of Robinson Crusoe and
subsistence, direct-use economy, or (b) <u>money</u> <u>income</u>
earned in the modern monetary economy. It is this
productive effort which constitutes the basic sacrifice
or cost involved in the acquisition, directly or indirectly, of the means to satisfy one's wants. Since
means are required to exercise demand in the market, and
means must be acquired by productive effort, it follows
that demand must ultimately be based on productive effort. Thus, demand is more than mere wants or needs.

All of this brings us to a fundamental implication. The fact that, on the one hand, wants cannot be
satisfied without the use of means, plus the fact, on
the other hand, that the means are <u>scarce</u>, imply the
following: There is an inverse or opposite relationship
between the <u>quantity</u> or <u>extent</u> of wants to be satisfied
and the <u>sacrifice</u> or <u>cost</u> involved in achieving the
satisfaction of wants. That is to say, the greater the
sacrifice or the more it costs to satisfy a given want,
the less of that want will a person seek to satisfy;
conversely, the less it costs a person to satisfy the
want, the more of it will he be induced to satisfy.

Demand vs. "Quantity Demanded"

Here we have the essence of the economic prin-
ciple referred to as the <u>law</u> <u>of</u> <u>demand</u>. In order to see
how economics formulates <u>this</u> <u>law</u>, we must first intro-

117

duce and define the key, albeit simple, term quantity
demanded, which is not to be confused with the term
"demand." Indeed, the term "demand" itself remains to
be defined more precisely, since up to now we have used
it superficially.

For convenience, the term "quantity demanded"
will be expressed simply as "Qd." Qd stands for the
number of units of a good or commodity that a person
would purchase at any given price. This term acknowledges the fact that, in the market place, goods of
whatever class or grade are typically sold and purchased
in units of numbers (e.g., one, two, or more), weight
(e.g., ounces, pounds), or length (e.g., yard goods).
Furthermore, prices in the market place are typically
quoted in terms of such units; for example, the price of
hamburger meat would be quoted at $1.50 per pound.

Since the term Qd includes the word "demanded,"
it is evidently associated with the act of acquisition
(via purchase or exchange) and not with the act of
consumption. As a rule, therefore, Qd refers to the
rate of purchase--that is, the number of units that a
person would purchase at a given price--and not to the
rate of consumption. Thus, to paraphrase the implication stated at the end of the previous section,
economics asserts: there is an inverse or opposite
relationship between the price of a given good and the
Qd of that good. Specifically, the higher the price
asked for a unit of a given good, the smaller will be
the Qd; the lower the price, the greater will be the Qd.
This proposition brings us pretty much to the heart of
the law of demand.

Determinants of the Quantity Demanded

In order to fully appreciate the law of demand,
one more important bridge remains to be crossed. The
reason is that while the law of demand assumes that
price is the only determinant of the Qd of a product, in
reality this is not strictly true. As we shall now see,
there are several other determinants of Qd--other than
price, hereinafter referred to as non-price determinants, for convenience--that also exert important
influence on the Qd of a given product. So, let us
first examine each one of these non-price determinants,
and thereby gain a better perspective on the law of
demand.

118

What else does the Qd of a product depend on, other than the price of the product itself? We have already seen that the price of the product would be a "negative" or inverse influence on the Qd: a lower price would induce an increase in Qd, whereas a higher price would cause a decrease in Qd.... However, to be more precise, we should add an important proviso: provided that other (non-price) determinants of Qd are assumed to be passive and uninfluential. Why is this proviso necessary? Because these other, non-price determinants can influence Qd even when the price of the product has not been changed by the firm; that is, changes in one or more of the non-price elements could cause Qd to change even when the price of the product itself remains unchanged. The following examples help us to understand this.

Income and Population

The first non-price determinant of Qd that comes to mind is a fairly obvious one: the consumer's income or other purchasing power or wealth. Thus it would follow that, other things being equal, the greater a person's purchasing power, the greater would be his Qd of a given product. In other words, the rate at which we buy things depends on how "rich" we are. A person's purchasing power depends primarily on his income as well as on accumulated savings from past income; the latter may take the form of financial investments or assets (e.g., securities, deposits) that are readily convertible into money (i.e., are "liquid").

Another important determinant of Qd, also fairly obvious, is the size of the household unit, or of the total population. Other things being equal, we would expect that the greater the number of people in the household, or in the population as a whole, the greater would be the Qd of the given product, and vice versa.

Subjective Value: Tastes or Preferences

Another important determinant of Qd is something we discussed at length in Chapter V: subjective value, or the degree of importance attached to a unit of a given product. Thus, other things being equal, the greater the subjective value, the higher the price one would be willing to pay; conversely, the less important the product, the lower the price one would be willing to pay. If we recall, subjective value depends on two things: the character of taste, or the preference-scale ranking attached to the product; and the amount of stock of the given product already possessed by the consumer (the law of marginal utility). Thus, with reference to the preference-scale, the higher the rank of the product on a person's preference-scale, the higher the price one would be willing to pay; conversely, the lower the rank held by the product, the lower must the seller's price be in order to induce a purchase.

A few examples will suffice to illustrate this aspect of subjective value. Advertising by firms, one of the most familiar institutions in the market place, serves two important functions: the one is to inform consumers about the product--its price, quality, location of sellers, etc.; the other is to persuade consumers that they cannot live without the given product, hoping that the consumer will then place the given product on a higher rank of his preference-scale. Medical reports on the link between tobacco smoking and lung cancer have caused cigarettes to drop to a lower rank or disappear altogether from many people's preferences. Studies on the relationship between diet and health have played havoc with the position of eggs, butter, and processed foods in our preferences. Finally, changes in fashion play similar havoc with the position of older models or styles in cars and clothing, as well as living patterns in general.

The Law of Marginal Utility

Similar effects on subjective value can be exerted by variations in the amount of stock already possessed by the consumer of a given product. This is the aspect of subjective value where the law of marginal utility becomes relevant. If we recall, the law asserts the following: the smaller the stock, the higher is the marginal utility (MU) or subjective value attached to a unit of the product; conversely, the larger the stock on hand, the lower is the MU attached to each unit.

Now, applying this law to prices, we come up with the following: the smaller the quantity supplied by sellers and the higher the MU therefore attached by the consumer to each of the fewer units, the higher is the price that the consumer is willing to pay for any unit of the product; conversely, the greater the quantity supplied by sellers and the lower the MU therefore attached by the consumer to each unit of the available

120

supply, the lower must the price asked by the seller be in order to induce consumers to buy more units.

A clear example of the relevance of the law of MU was the gasoline shortage in late 1973. At the time of the oil embargo, in the fall of 1973, the supply of refined gasoline reaching the market had dropped significantly. When car drivers realized that considerably less gasoline would be available, it did not take long for them to adjust and begin to attach a higher MU to each gallon of gas obtained after much search and waiting in line at the gas pump. Simultaneously, they also adjusted upward the price they were willing to pay for each of the more precious gallons.

Complementary Products

Another important set of influences on the Qd of a given product involves the effect of changes in the price of other related products. Many products are "related" to each other in one of two possible ways--as complementary products or as substitute products. Complementary products typically go together; that is, they are usually jointly consumed. Good examples are bread and butter, beer and pretzels, cars and gasoline. As a consequence, a change in the price of one of the pair would be expected to exert an opposite effect on the Qd of the other. For example, a rise in the price of gasoline would be expected to cause a drop in car-driving--more precisely, a drop in the Qd of transportation mileage by automobile; conversely, a drop in the price of gasoline would be expected to induce an increase in car-driving--that is, an increase in the Qd of transportation by automobile.

Substitute vs. Complementary Products

Similar considerations apply to substitute products, that is, products that are regarded as "rivals" or "competitors" to each other with respect to a given use or purpose. Good examples are butter and margarine (for cooking); paper and cellophane (for wrapping); natural fibers like silk, cotton, and wool as against nylon, dacron, orlon, and other synthetic fibers (for clothing and textiles). Since these commodities are substitutable for each other in specific applications, it stands to reason that a rise in the price of the one (say, butter) relative to the price of the other (i.e.,

121

margarine) would induce a rise in the Qd for margarine, as people are induced to shift from butter to margarine. Conversely, a drop in the price of butter would be expected to induce a drop in the Qd for margarine, as people are induced to shift from margarine to butter.

In the case of complementary products, price changes in one of the pair are expected to induce opposite changes in the Qd of the other complementary product. Thus, a rise in the price of gasoline is expected to induce a drop in the Qd for transportation by car. On the other hand, in the case of substitute or rival products, price changes in the one are expected to induce Qd changes in its rival products in the same direction. Thus, a rise in the price of paper relative to its rivals (say, cellophane wrap) is expected to induce a rise in the Qd for cellophane. In general, therefore, changes in the price of one of the "related" products would be expected to induce Qd changes in the other of the related products.

Before proceeding, we should note that the preceding, non-price determinants of the Qd--such as income, subjective tastes or valuations, and size of households--were truly "non-price" in character. However, in the present case we were dealing with the possible effects of price changes in related products, so that, strictly speaking, the subject is not "non-price." For convenience, however, the effects of price changes in related products are treated as a "non-price" determinant.

Expectations of Future Price Change

A final, but nevertheless important set of determinants involves expectations about the future. This dimension of influence is made relevant by the fact that, so long as such determinants of Qd as price and income are subject to change, the future becomes uncertain. That is to say, tomorrow's price will not necessarily be the same as today's price, since it may be higher or lower than today's price; nor will tomorrow's personal income necessarily remain the same as today's. As a consequence, today's Qd will depend not only on today's price and income, but also on tomorrow's price and income.

For example, assume a situation in which prices have been falling, as during periods of price "deflation." A consumer therefore has grounds to expect that tomorrow's price (say, of clothing) may be still lower than today's price. Given such expectations it would be reasonable for the consumer to postpone his planned purchase of clothing until tomorrow, since he would prefer to buy at tomorrow's expected lower price rather than at today's relatively higher price. Conversely, assume that prices have been rising, as during periods of price "inflation." The consumer would therefore reasonably expect that tomorrow's price could be higher than today's price, and consequently decide to hasten his purchase and buy today rather than delay his purchase until tomorrow, since today's price appears relatively lower compared to tomorrow's expected higher price.

In sum, therefore, expectations of a change in tomorrow's price compared to today's price would reasonably influence the consumer's rate of purchase (Qd) today: an expected higher price would induce a hastening in the rate of purchase (i.e., an increase in the Qd today), whereas an expected lower price would induce a postponement of purchases (i.e., a decrease in today's Qd). So long as prices are not stable or constant, but are either rising or falling, it is clear that tomorrow's price will not be the same as today's. Therefore, at any given time, the consumer is faced with not one price but two prices: today's price and tomorrow's possible price. As a consequence, he is prompted to decide which of the two prices will be the relatively lower, and decide his Qd accordingly, that is, at the relatively lower price, according to the law of demand.

Expectations of Future Income Changes

Similar considerations apply to expectations of change in one's future income. For example, an expected increase in salary or wages due to an expected promotion would obviously herald an increase in future income; conversely, an expected reduction in working hours or loss of one's job, due to a slackening of business, would lead one to expect a drop in tomorrow's income. In either case, the expected change in tomorrow's income would induce a reasonable adjustment in today's rate of purchase (Qd).

For example, if a worker expects to receive a wage increase in the nearby future, it would not be unreasonable for him to spend that money now, in antici-

123

pation of his increased future income and on the assumption that "the money is as good as in the bank," so to speak. Similarly, if Congress announced a cut in tax rates effective within a few months, it would not be unreasonable for taxpayers to spend that money now. (Economists attribute the stepped-up rate of spending in the latter half of 1963 to the anticipated Kennedy tax-cut scheduled for 1964.) In both cases, the effect of the anticipated increase in future income is an inducement to increase the current rate of spending (Qd). The opposite would happen in the case of anticipated decreases in income. That is, wage-earners would be expected to reduce their current Qd if faced with lay-offs or curtailed working hours; taxpayers, too, would be expected to spend less today if faced with a tax increase tomorrow.

What About Changes in Supply?

Have we left anything out? Well, what about the supply of the product--that is, couldn't changes in supply conditions cause changes in Qd? For instance, couldn't increased supply cause an increase in Qd, and vice versa? Economics would answer as follows: changes in supply can affect Qd only indirectly, through the prior effects on the price of the product. Thus, other things being equal, an increase in supply would first have to cause a drop in price before it could induce a larger Qd; conversely, a decrease in supply would first have to cause a rise in price before it could induce a smaller Qd.

Restatement of the Law of Demand

Thus, we see that the quantity demanded (Qd) of a product in the present can be influenced not only by the price of the given product but also by a variety of non-price determinants. As a consequence, it would be reasonable to conclude that, even if the current price of a product remained unchanged, the current Qd could nevertheless be induced to change due to a change in one or more of the non-price determinants. In any event, the firm faces a difficult task in assessing which of the several non-price determinants is influencing the Qd for its product and to what degree. It is one of the primary functions of market research to study the importance of each of these determinants of market demand.

124

All of this enables us to state the law of demand with greater precision than before. First comes the general statement of the law of demand: there is an inverse, opposite, or negative relationship between the current price of a good and the quantity demanded (Qd) of this good, provided other things (i.e., the non-price determinants) remain the same. From this general principle are derived the two important corollaries: (1) other things remaining the same, at a sufficiently higher price the Qd will be expected to decrease; (2) other things remaining the same, at a sufficiently lower price the Qd will be expected to increase.

Before we proceed, it is important to note that the law of demand applies only to the case where the price of the given product is changed relatively to, or comparatively to, the prices of other products. Thus, a decrease in the price of product X can be regarded as a "lower" price only when compared to what happens to other product prices, especially substitute or similar products. Thus, a decrease in the price of product X can be regarded as a "lower" price only when compared to what happens to other product prices, especially substitute or similar products. If prices of other similar products are decreased in the same proportion as product X, then the drop in X's price is not a comparatively lower price. The price of X is truly "lower" only when it is decreased while other prices remain the same, or decrease less than X's price, or even increase. Conversely, X's price cannot be regarded as a "higher" price unless it is increased more than in proportion to the prices of other similar products, that is, only if other prices do not increase, or increase less than X's, or even drop.

The "Ceteris Paribus" Proviso

We can now see more clearly why the law of demand is based on the special assumption that "other things remain the same," and that the price of the given product is the only determinant of its Qd. The proviso "other things remaining the same" has become known in its latin form as the ceteris paribus clause (which literally means: other things being equal). In the real world, of course, it is more reasonable to assume that the non-price or "ceteris" determinants do not remain fixed or unchanged, and that any given change in Qd could be a result of a non-price change as well as of a price change by the firm. However, for the purpose of economic analysis, which seeks to intellectually _isolate_ the effect on Qd of the _price_ alone, it is logically necessary to abstract from the _non-price_ determinants and assume that they are, for the moment, passive or dormant.

In other words, the law of demand assumes that at any given moment it is reasonable to assert that the Qd of a given product X is influenced _only_ by the _price_ of X--that is, market exchange involves only P's and Q's, so to speak. This special assumption of _ceteris paribus_ is a kind of "mental experiment." It is the closest that economic analysis comes to duplicating a controlled laboratory experiment, as in the physical sciences, where it is possible to isolate and exclude all variables or determinants except one. In the human sciences, including economics, it is impossible to conduct such physically controlled experiments; the only intellectual recourse left, then, is the method of "partial analysis," which uses the logical device of the _ceteris paribus_ proviso.

Law of Demand Is Not "Automatic"

One additional explanation is needed. We have deliberately used the word "sufficiently" in the phrases "at a _sufficiently_ higher price" (corollary 1) and "at a _sufficiently_ lower price" (corollary 2). This is to exclude the case of very _small_ or _minute_ changes in price which, in practice, may not induce any significant change in Qd. Realistically, it would not be reasonable to expect that just _any_ size of price increase (or decrease) would _necessarily_ induce a decrease (or increase) in Qd; indeed, it is very possible that a very small or insignificant change in price would have practically no impact on Qd.

For example, it is possible that during the early stages of the gasoline shortage in the fall and winter of 1973-74, the relatively small initial increases in gasoline price did not in themselves cause any significant drop in Qd of gasoline. However, such unresponsive changes in Qd to the rise in prices would not constitute a contradiction of the law of demand, since, properly stated, the law pertains only to relatively _significant_ of "sufficiently" large changes in price. Thus, whereas a rise in gasoline price from, say, 40 cents to 50 cents a gallon might not in itself cause any significant drop in Qd, a "sufficiently" great increase from 40 cents to 80 cents, say, could be expected to cause a significant drop in Qd.

In other words, the law of demand does not assume that people react automatically or mechanically (i.e., immediately) in response to just any size of stimulus (e.g., a price increase). Indeed, it is rather usual for people not to react significantly to small or tiny stimuli, and it is only when stimuli are "sufficiently" large that they will react and adjust in reasonable ways.

Furthermore, even when the stimulus is substantial, people will respond only after they are able to discover the best way of adjusting to the stimulus--all of which will take some time. In the case of a price stimulus--for example, an increase in price--it will take some time at least before the consumer can adjust (a) by switching to a substitute product, or (b) by deciding to do with less of the given product, which involves a distinct change in taste or preference.

Graphic Presentation of Law of Demand

We are now at the point where the law of demand can be illustrated graphically. The graph shown in Figure 8 is based on the fact that the law of demand involves only "P's and Q's," that is, prices and quantity demanded; hence, only a two-dimensional graph is required. The vertical scale or "axis" on the left represents the various prices that could be charged per gallon of gasoline, rising up from lower to higher prices. The horizontal axis represents the quantities that would be demanded at various prices, showing increased quantities as you move from left to right.

Of course, Figure 8 is not based on actual market data, which could be obtained only by a market research survey. It is merely an illustration of what an economist might expect to find if he undertook a market survey by asking car drivers the simple question: "How many gallons of gasoline would you purchase at various prices, say, from 30 cents up to $1.20?" The resulting sample data represent aggregation of the data gleaned from the survey responses.

Each dot in the graph represents two bits of information: a given, potential price that could prevail in the market, and the corresponding number of

127

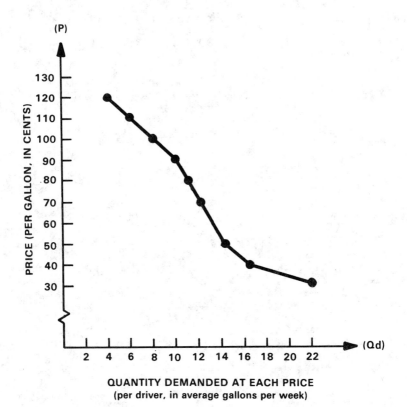

QUANTITY DEMANDED AT EACH PRICE
(per driver, in average gallons per week)

FIGURE 8:
DEMAND FOR GASOLINE BY
PASSENGER CAR DRIVERS.

gallons that would be demanded by each car driver. That is, each dot represents a given "P and Q," so to speak: a given price (P) and the corresponding quantity demanded (Qd). Thus, at $1.20 a gallon, very few gallons would be demanded, but, at successively lower prices, more and more gasoline would be purchased.

The Demand "Schedule"

Notice that the dots are linked to each other in sequence by straight lines, and form what is known as the demand curve. Ideally, the demand curve would be derived from data collected by a market survey, with the series of dots representing a discrete array of pairs of prices and Qd's. Indeed, the original statistical data obtained in such market surveys might very well assume the tabular form presented below in Table I. Notice therein the inverse relation between the prices and Qd's, with the P's going from high to low while the corresponding Qd's go from low to high. Together, this array of pairs of P's and Qd's, presented in tabular form, constitutes the demand schedule.

Table I

DEMAND FOR GASOLINE
BY PASSENGER-CAR DRIVERS
(in gallons)

Price (per gallon)	Weekly Quantity Demanded (per driver)
$1.20	4
1.10	6
1.00	8
.90	10
.80	11
.70	12
.60	13
.50	14
.40	16
.30	22

129

An "Instantaneous Snapshot"

Thus, Figure 8 is an illustration of the law of demand by means of the demand curve. Here the Qd's are shown to vary only in response to the different possible prices--on the ceteris paribus assumption, of course, that personal tastes, incomes, and other non-price determinants of Qd are dormant. In this sense, there-fore, the curve gives us, in effect, an instantaneous snapshot of how people "feel" about gasoline prices when expressed in terms of gallons demanded. It is this overall view of the various possible pairs of P's and Qd's which is designated as the total "demand" schedule, in contradistinction to the specific "quantity demanded" which is related to a given price.

Thus, even if we had no precise idea of the specific magnitudes that the market survey would reveal, the law of demand would lead us to expect that the demand curve would have this overall characteristic slope: downward from left to right. So, assuming the present price was 50 cents a gallon, a price increase to 60 cents a gallon would be expected to cause a drop in Qd to 13 gallons a week, whereas a price decrease to 40 cents would be expected to induce an increase in Qd to 16 gallons.

The "Elasticity" of Demand

In this connection it should be noted that, while all demand curves possess the characteristically general slope downward (from left to right), not every demand curve necessarily has the same degree of slope, technically referred to as elasticity of demand. The following Figure 9 illustrates three different sche-dules, each having a different degree of slope or elas-ticity. Curve D_1 on the left would be classified as "inelastic," curve D_2 in the middle displays "unitary" elasticity, while curve D_3 on the right would be re-garded as "elastic." Notice that the "curves" have been drawn, for convenience, as straight lines in order to emphasize the general degree of slope of the entire schedule. A more detailed analysis of demand elas-ticity, and the critical importance of the concept, will be the subject of the next chapter.

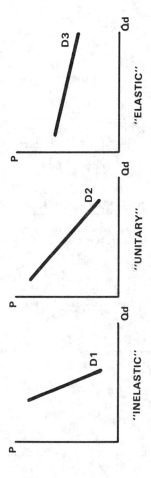

FIGURE 9:
DIFFERENT DEGREES OF ELASTICITY OF DEMAND

131

As a final note, it should be stressed that the demand schedule does not constitute an _actual_ rate of purchase, but merely an indication of people's _readiness_ to buy, based on their wants and modified by their economic ability, that is, their purchasing power. In other words, the use herein of the term _demand_, by itself, will connote not a sense of actuality but rather of potentiality.

"Shifts" of the Demand Schedule

We come now to an important question: What happens to the demand schedule when the basic _ceteris paribus_ assumption of the law of demand--that _non-price_ determinants are dormant or unchanging--is relaxed, and these determinants are allowed to change, as they do in the normal course of events? That is to say, what is the effect on demand of a _change_ in one or more of the non-price determinants? For example, what happens to the demand for product X when people's _incomes_ or _tastes and preferences_ change? Well, it all depends on whether these determinants increase or decrease.

For example, if there is a general _increase in income_ in the community--of wages, say--then we could expect that people would be able to purchase more units at _each_ possible price. This can be seen in Table II, where the quantity of gallons that would be purchased at each possible price (from $1.20 down to 30 cents) would be expected to increase in varying degree as shown for Period 2. Graphically, the resulting change in the state of demand is shown in part A of Figure 10. That is to say, the entire schedule or curve of D would be expected to _shift_ from position D_1 to D_2, from left to right, indicating that, at all possible prices, people would be willing and able to buy more. A similar graphic effect would be expected if, instead of an income increase, there occurred an increased taste or preference for a given product.

The same reasoning applies to the case of a _decrease_ in incomes in the community. Here we would expect that people, with reduced purchasing power, would be induced to buy less at _each_ possible price, and the demand schedule would correspondingly undergo a "shift" to left, as in part B of Figure 10.

132

Table II

AN INCREASE IN DEMAND FOR GASOLINE
BY PASSENGER-CAR DRIVERS

Price (per gallon)	Weekly Quantity Demanded (per driver)	
	Period 1	Period 2
$1.20	4	5
1.10	6	7
1.00	8	9
.90	10	11
.80	11	12
.70	12	13
.60	13	14
.50	14	15
.40	16	19
.30	22	27

Some Comments on Demand Shifts

It should be noted that in all such instances of change in non-price determinants--and in the corresponding shifts of demand curves--it is not possible to predict exactly the extent or degree of change; only the general direction of shift is predictable.

Finally, it should be stressed that a shift in the entire demand schedule cannot be caused by a price change--only by a non-price change. True, laymen customarily say such things as, "rising prices cause a drop in demand," or "falling prices cause an increase in demand." For economics, this language is not

133

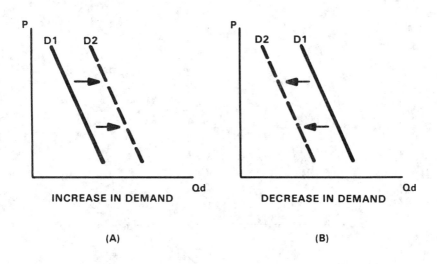

FIGURE 10:
"SHIFTS" IN THE DEMAND SCHEDULE.

sufficiently precise: in each statement the underlined word "demand" should be replaced by "quantity demanded" to make the statement correct.   Price changes can only cause specific changes in Qd along a given unchanged demand schedule ("a movement along the curve," so to speak);   on the other hand, only non-price changes can induce "shifts" of entire demand schedules.

The Role of Market Research

How would the firm become aware of such a shift in demand?   First of all, we must be sure that the change in Qd's was not caused by a change in price by the firm; that is, the selling prices of firms must be assumed to have remained unchanged, so that any change in Qd cannot be attributed to a price change but rather to a change in one of the non-price elements.   Thus, if a firm has not changed its price, and yet the Qd for its product has either increased or decreased, then it is certain that one or more of the non-price determinants were at work.

This raises the question: How can the firm discover which one or more of the non-price determinants of demand is at work, and to what extent?   In this connection, market research projects become very relevant.   The firm may have to undertake market research studies on each of the possible non-price determinants.   Such studies, even though very costly, may be worthwhile if the firm believes that knowledge of demand determinants would improve its ability to plan future production and marketing, and leave it better off than otherwise.

Explaining the Law of Demand

We have now reached a crucial point in the analysis. So far we have presented mainly a description of the law of demand, without really giving the rationale behind it, and without explaining why we would expect the demand curve to slope generally the way it does.   Although the law of demand makes a lot of common sense, it is nevertheless important to explain precisely why this is so.   Some writers have attempted to explain the "why" of the demand curve, and it is useful to briefly examine their efforts.

Substitution Effects

One explanation of the law of demand is based on the notion of the substitution effect, which assumes that all products have "substitutes," either in the form of rival brands or rival products, as in the case of butter vs. margarine. Thus, when the price of a given product X is decreased, potential buyers are supposed to be induced to switch their buying from other products to product X, and thereby cause an increase in the Qd of X. However, the trouble with this theory is that it does not necessarily follow.

This can be seen in the case of a price decrease. For one thing, there is no certainty that product X has any substitutes at all from which loyalty can be switched to it. Nor is it necessary that the savings resulting from the lower price of X will inevitably be used to buy more of X itself rather than more of some other unrelated product.

What about an increase in the price of product X? The substitution effect would be expected to work as follows: a higher price for X would induce purchasers of it to buy less of it, and thereby cause a decrease in Qd of X. Thus far, then, the "substitution" theory is still consistent with the law of demand. Beyond this, however, it falls down: substitution effects do not necessarily follow.

First of all, unless we know something about the price-elasticity of demand for X (to be discussed in Chapter VII), it is not even certain that a reduced Qd will yield any savings at all. Indeed, in the case where few or no substitutes are available, it is possible to get the curious result that the smaller Qd is associated with an increase in total expenditures on X (as would be expected in a product like gasoline, which people cannot easily cut back if they are heavily dependent on automotive transportation). Hence, if there are no savings to start with, there can be no increment of money, at least in the short run, with which to do any switching to substitutes.

To be sure, if substitutes are sufficiently available, the substitution effects could easily occur, as the higher price of X induces people to switch to the substitute brand or product and causes a decrease in the Qd of X. Furthermore, if product X is of the type that simply does not command any strong preference or

136

attachment among its customers, and people find they can easily do without it, (i.e., the demand for it is very "elastic"), then its Qd could be expected to decrease as a result of its higher price; however, in this case there need not ensue any substitution effects.

Income Effects

Thus, the substitution effect is not a sufficient explanation of the law of demand. Another explanation offered by some writers is based on the notion of the income effect, which correctly assumes that changes in the price of products affect the purchasing power of one's income. That is to say, a lower price for product X makes buyers of X "feel richer," whereas an increase in price makes them "feel poorer." However, this does not necessarily follow.

Let us first take the case of a decrease in the price of X. The fact that the lower price yields a kind of savings to buyers of X does not necessarily imply that this increment will be devoted to increased Qd of X itself. Indeed, it could just as well be devoted to some other unrelated products. But, for argument's sake, let us suppose the savings are used for buying more of X: unless we know something about the price-elasticity of demand for X (to be analyzed in Chapter VII), it is possible to come upon the curious result seen in Table I: for example, the drop in price from 40 cents to 30 cents could be associated with an increase in total expenditures--from $6.40 (40 cents x 16 gallons) to $6.60 (30 cents x 22 gallons)--that is, an increase in total spending of 20 cents that could be attributed as much to a strong subjective preference for additional travel as to any income effect per se.

How would the income effect occur in the opposite case of a price increase? The assumption is that, at the higher price, the decrease in Qd is induced by the feeling of being made "poorer" by the price raise. However, here too it is not entirely true that the reduced Qd is induced only by the impoverishment effect. Again, in Table I, we see a case where a price raise, say from 40 cents to 50 cents, would be associated with an increase in total expenditures--from $6.40 (40 cents x 16 gallons) to $7.00 (50 cents x 14 gallons). That is to say, even though the price raise caused a drop in Qd, the fact is that total spending increased by 60 cents, revealing not an income effect but rather a lingering strong preference for car

137

driving, such that drivers are willing to pay more money (in total) for fewer gallons of gasoline.

People Prefer Lower Prices

In summary, then, neither the substitution effect nor the income effect is sufficient to explain why the demand curve slopes the way it does. In this connection, it should be noted, there is a third type of explanation: the idea that the law of demand is merely a description of how demanders in general and consumers in particular "feel" about prices. Thus there follows this proposition: people prefer lower prices to higher prices. That is to say, in terms of the law of demand, this can be expressed as follows: preference for lower prices is reflected in the greater quantities demanded, whereas rejection of higher prices is reflected in the fewer units purchased. This proposition, that people prefer lower prices, turns out to be, in effect, a reverse way of expressing the law of demand: for any given quantity to be purchased, a person would prefer to buy it at a lower price rather than at a higher price; indeed, the lower the price, the better.

The Least-Cost Principle

Let us pursue this line a bit. The money price asked by the seller of a good in the market place represents a kind of cost or sacrifice that the demander must make in order to acquire the good. The element of sacrifice lies in the fact that the demander must give up leisure and go to work in order to earn the money with which to pay for the desired good. We can now restate the preceding proposition: for any given want or goal, the lower the cost or sacrifice involved, the better--other things being equal. Logically, this leads us to conclude that the least cost or sacrifice is the best.

Indeed, this leads us to yet another proposition: in order to achieve any given purpose or goal, man prefers the least-cost method, other things being equal. This would be thoroughly consistent with the maximizing principle (see Chapter V). As we recall, the maximizing principle asserted that man chooses to do that which he expects will leave him better off than otherwise. Since, in our present case, lower money prices, lower costs, or lesser sacrifices clearly leave man better off than otherwise, it is reasonable to assert that man would prefer not only the lesser cost (to the higher cost) but, indeed, the least cost.

When all is said and done, however, the fact remains that the least-cost principle is merely consistent with the law of demand (and the maximizing principle), but cannot serve as a sufficient explanation of why the demand schedule slopes downward from left to right. The reason is that it, too, can be criticized on the same ground as the income-effect explanation. The income effect operates on the premise that lower prices make us feel "richer;" the least-cost principle is relevant primarily to the case of a price decrease. In either case, the increased purchasing-power effect caused by a price reduction does not necessarily imply an increase in Qd of product X itself: the "income" increment could just as well be devoted to other, non-X products.

Again, The Law of Marginal Utility

This writer believes that the best all-around explanation of the law of demand is the law of marginal utility (Chapter V). The best way to see this is to raise the question: For whom does the law of demand have the greatest practical significance? Clearly, for the firm or the seller in general. As a first approximation, what the law of demand says to the seller is simply this: if you want to sell more (i.e., induce a greater Qd), you will have to reduce your price sufficiently; conversely, if you want to withhold supply from the market and offer fewer units for sale, then you can raise your price and this will reduce the Qd. But this still is begging the question; we have to invoke the law of MU, especially its corollaries.

First let us apply the law of MU to the case of a price reduction. Relevant here is the corollary on diminishing MU, which asserts that, other things being equal, an increased stock of a given good X is associated with a diminished subjective value attached to any one unit. How does this tie in with the law of demand? In this way: if the seller wants to sell more units of a given good X to people for whom each unit of this good is subject to a diminishing subjective value (i.e., because more units are available), then the seller must reduce his per-unit price sufficiently in order to induce people to buy more.

139

In other words, the buyer could not be expected to be willing to pay the same price for additional units of good X since, for him, acquisition of additional units is subject to the law of diminishing MU. Only a lower price per unit will induce him to buy more units. A very familiar example is the "economy-size" approach used in retail selling of detergents, coffee, and other consumers' goods: compared to the smaller-size package, the larger (economy) size package is priced so that each ounce or pound of the good costs less than in the smaller package.

Similar reasoning applies to the case of a price increase. Relevant here is the corollary on increasing MU, which asserts that, other things being equal, a decreased stock of a given good X is associated with an increased subjective value attached to each unit. This ties in with the law of demand as follows: if the seller makes fewer units available for sale to buyers, for whom each unit of this good would be subject to an increasing subjective value (i.e., because fewer units are available), then the seller could raise his price and expect to get it.

In other words, people would be willing to pay a higher price for each unit, albeit in fewer units than before, since each unit is now subject to the law of increasing MU. Here, too, the economy-size approach is relevant, although in reverse: compared to the larger-size package, each unit (e.g., ounce) of the smaller-size package is priced higher than in the larger package.

Are There Exceptions to Law of Demand?

One problem remains: people sometimes object that the law of demand does not apply as a general rule--indeed, they claim there are exceptions to the law of demand which destroy its general validity. We shall examine a few of these alleged "exceptions" and see why they fail to prove their case against the law of demand.

Before we proceed, however, we should remember that the law of demand is concerned only with the relation between prices and quantities demanded (Qd's). It follows therefore that each alleged exception to the law of demand--in order to prove its case--must be framed strictly in terms of this exclusive relationship between prices and Qd's, albeit in the opposite sense;

that is, an alleged exception must be able to show that (a) a lower price will induce a <u>decrease</u> in Qd, or (b) a higher price will induce an <u>increase in</u> Qd.

Selling More at Higher Prices

Let us first take up a familiar general case: The drug store which, after noticing that its bottles of aspirin did not sell very well at the discount price of 19 cents for 100 tablets, decided to <u>raise</u> the price to 49 cents! To its pleasant surprise, the aspirin sold much better at the <u>higher</u> price. This example is often given as an illustration of how a lower price induced people to buy <u>less</u> of the product, not more, thus contradicting the law of demand.

Is this really an exception to the law of demand? The first thing to notice is that: Was it <u>only</u> the lower price that had first induced a smaller Qd? Was it <u>only</u> the higher price that induced the increased Qd? It is well to recall that an exceedingly low price --such as the 19-cent price--may connote a product of lower <u>quality</u> as well, such that the lower price might induce a decrease rather than an increase in Qd! In the same vein, it is also well-known that a higher price for a given product often connotes to people a product of higher <u>quality</u> as well, such that the higher price could, not surprisingly, induce a greater desire to buy and an increase in Qd. Both of these cases appear to be clear contradictions of the law of demand.

Aspirins Fail the Test

To return to our aspirin case, it is relevant to ask again: Was it the lower 19-cent price <u>itself</u> that deterred purchases, or was it rather the fact that the low price also connoted inferior quality, therefore making the product not worth buying at all? Conversely, was it the higher 49-cent price <u>itself</u> that induced increased Qd, or was it rather the fact that the higher price connoted superior quality and therefore made the product more attractive?

To put this another way, in order to make the aspirin example a proper test case of the law of demand the following procedure would have to occur: at the same time that the seller raises his aspirin price from 19 cents to 49 cents he informs the customer that the

141

49-cent price is for the very same bottle that he could still buy at 19 cents--and then asks the customer: "Do you prefer to pay the 49-cent price or the 19-cent price for the identical commodity?" The outcome is predictable: For any given product, people would prefer to pay lower prices to higher prices, and the law of demand would still prevail.

In fact, of course, the drug store did not do this, and consumers were unaware that the aspirin quality was the same even at the higher price. Indeed, it was this ignorance of quality which explains why the Qd was greater at the higher price than at the lower price. Furthermore, the persistent tendency of sellers to resort to "sales" and "slashed prices," in order to sell out goods at a faster rate than at the former higher prices, is testimony to our contention that the law of demand remains intact.

Prestige Goods

Another alleged exception to the law of demand involves the class of products known as prestige goods. Familiar examples include mink coats and Rolls Royce cars, whose prices are characteristically very high. The allegation claims that it is the higher price of these goods that induces a greater Qd than otherwise. In rebuttal, however, it is not the higher price itself that induces the greater Qd, but rather the status or prestige attached to the higher quality of the product. That is, people are willing to pay a higher price for the added prestige or status.

Furthermore, the fact that a mink coat, for example, is of a higher quality than, say, a silver fox coat, means that it must be classified as a different type or grade of product, and therefore does not belong on the same demand curve as silver foxes or other lower-grade furs. That is, a separate demand schedule must be drawn for each different type or grade of product. Thus, the demand schedule for a given grade of mink coat would be expected to reveal the familiar downward slope, left to right, associated with the law of demand; in this case, people would certainly not pay a higher price if they knew they could get the very same coat at a lower price.

142

Price Expectations

A final set of alleged exceptions involves <u>price expectations</u>. Let us first take the case of expectations of <u>rising</u> prices, as during a period of price inflation. As we saw above, expectations of higher prices tomorrow would be expected to induce a greater Qd today. Hence, it is alleged that this is an example of how higher prices can induce a greater Qd, thereby contradicting the law of demand. Actually, this allegation involves a distortion: it is not tomorrow's higher prices that induce the greater Qd, but rather the realization that today's prices are <u>relatively lower</u> than tomorrow's expected higher prices; it is <u>this</u> realization that induces us to buy <u>more</u> today than usual. Hence, the law of demand remains intact.

The opposite case involves expectations of <u>falling</u> prices, as during a depression period marked by price deflation. As we saw above, expectations of lower prices tomorrow would be expected to induce a smaller Qd today. Again, the allegation claims that this contradicts the law of demand, since it shows that lower prices cause a drop in Qd and not an increase. This, too, is a distortion: it is not tomorrow's lower prices that reduce today's rate of purchase, but rather the realization that today's prices are <u>relatively higher</u> than tomorrow's lower prices. That is, at today's relatively higher prices it pays to postpone purchases until tomorrow, when prices will actually be lower. Once again, the law of demand comes through unscathed.

Conclusion

A careful review of the alleged exceptions to the law of demand reveals a common characteristic: each basically involves a <u>non-price</u> determinant of Qd. This includes the case of price expectations, which we have classified among the "non-price" determinants. Since the law of demand involves <u>only</u> the relation between <u>prices</u> and Qd, it cannot be contradicted by cases that hinge on <u>non-price</u> determinants.

CHAPTER VII

PRICE-ELASTICITY OF MARKET DEMAND

After all is said and done, the law of demand is not enough. The reason: demand schedules come in a variety of slopes or price-elasticity--which makes all the difference in the world for the firm. Hence this chapter.

In the preceding chapter we visually alluded to the concept of price-elasticity of demand (Figure 9) by showing how market demand schedules, even though they all slope downwards from left to right, will in practice vary in their degree of slope or elasticity. We also noted that, technically speaking, demand schedules fall into three categories: elastic, inelastic, and unitary. In the present chapter we will not only explain the meaning of these categorical terms but will also show their extreme practical importance for the firm, as well as the special factors--social, technical, and economic --that help determine the category into which a given demand schedule would be expected to fall.

I. The Anatomy of Demand-Elasticity

The concept of elasticity of demand reflects the fact that, while the quantities demanded (Qd) by buyers are affected by the price of the product--as under the law of demand--the degree of responsiveness of buyers to a change in the price may vary from product to product, from person to person, and from time to time. That is to say, while a lower (higher) price set by sellers will be expected to increase (decrease) the Qd by buyers, the sensitivity of response of buyers to the given change in price will vary in degree. These different degrees of sensitivity or elasticity in Qd, in response to a given change in price by the seller, necessarily make the elasticity concept of greatest practical importance to the seller.

The Law of Demand Is Not Enough

The best way to get into the concept of price-elasticity of demand--"elasticity," for short--is to

145

realize that it is directly related to a situation often faced by the firm: the firm seeks to increase its total dollar sales receipts (hereinafter noted simply as $\underline{TR}$ for total receipts) by means of a change in its selling price, that is, by cutting it or raising it.   Thus, in its quest for increased TR, the firm wants to determine the following: should it reduce its price, or increase it?

At first glance, this would seem a fairly simple decision: in order to increase TR, the firm should try to sell more units of its product.   To accomplish this, the firm should reduce its price, according to the law of demand (see Chapter VI).   So the decision seems obvious: cut the price.   Right?   No--wrong!   It does not follow that selling more units at a lower price will necessarily increase the TR as well.   True, the lower price will enable the firm to sell more units--according to the law of demand--but it does not necessarily follow that the quantity demanded (Qd) will increase sufficiently to offset the dollar loss due to the lower price received for each unit sold.   It all depends on the elasticity of demand.   Clearly, in such a pricing decision, the law of demand is not enough as far as the firm is concerned.   So, without further ado, let us pursue this matter of elasticity.

How To Increase Total Receipts

Imagine a firm that wants to increase its TR because, say, it is confronted by a union demand for wage increases.   Other things being equal, a wage increase would cause an increase in the firm's total dollar costs (hereafter referred to simply as TC).   Such an increase in TC, unaccompanied by a proportionate increase in TR, would in itself reduce the profit margin between TR and TC.   (Note: total profits = TR - TC.) Now, one of the things the firm could try to do to offset the profit squeeze is to increase its TR sufficiently to cover the increase in TC.

Of course, the firm could try two other things in order to offset the wage increase and restore its former profit margin.   Instead of increasing its TR, the firm could try to reduce its TC.   On the one hand, the firm could lay off some workers and reduce its total wage bill enough to keep the TC at its former level. Or, it could install more efficient methods of production; this, too, would enable the firm to reduce its TC

146

sufficiently to restore its former profit margin. In the present case, however, we assume that instead of reducing its TC, the firm seeks to increase its TR by selling a larger quantity of its product.

Quantity Demanded vs. Total Receipts

Now, according to the law of demand (Chapter VI), the firm would have to reduce its price in order to increase the quantity-demand (Qd) of its product. Since the law of demand is a matter of common knowledge, we would expect the firm to do the obvious and cut its price (P) in order to sell the larger quantity (Q) of its product. So far, so good--or so it would seem. But, as we have been intimating, the law of demand is not enough--not as long as the lower P fails to increase the Qd enough to offset the cut in price required to induce the increased Qd.

Let us illustrate graphically the problem of demand-elasticity now facing the firm. Figure 11 reveals a firm that has been selling 10,000 units at a price of $8 (see the dot O). If the firm now decides to reduce the price to $5 in order to sell more units, it has no way of forecasting precisely how much the Qd will increase. This much, however, it does know: it would like the Qd to increase enough to offset the drop in P of $3 per unit sold; that is, it would like the TR to increase despite the lower price received. Only after it has actually cut its price will the firm be able to determine whether its TR has increased, that is, whether the Qd is sufficiently "elastic" to offset the price cut.

Selling More But Enjoying It Less

If after the price cut from $8 to $5 the Qd increases from the current 10,000 units to 24,000 units (see dot E in Figure 11), it is visually apparent that the response in Qd was comparatively great. More important, simple calculation reveals that the TR increases from the previous total of $80,000 (derived from P = $8 multiplied by Qd = 10,000) to a total of $120,000 (derived from $5 times 24,000 units)--despite the cut in P of $3 per unit! That is to say, the Qd proved to be sufficiently responsive to the price cut, and therefore able to offset the drastic price cut. Whether or not the increase of $40,000 in TR is actually enough to

147

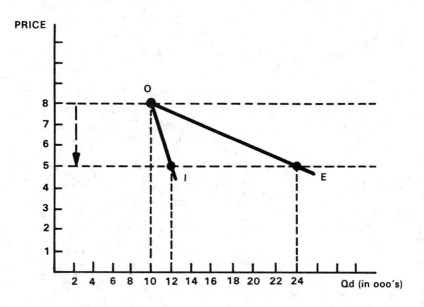

FIGURE 11:
ELASTICITY OF DEMAND IN THE CASE
OF A PRICE-CUT.

satisfy the firm's goal, the fact remains that such a sensitive response in Qd is technically referred to as elastic. Elastic responses are precisely what the doctor should order if ever the firm has to cut its price, for only in such cases would the TR be expected to increase despite the price cut.

Things could have worked out just the reverse! If the Qd, instead of increasing to 24,000 units, increased only slightly--to only 12,000 units, say--the TR would show a decrease from its previous $80,000 to $60,000! (This is the result of the lower P of $5 times the 12,000 units sold, shown by dot I in Figure 11). Clearly the increase in Qd here is relatively small compared to the sizable price cut--it does not increase sufficiently to offset the hefty price cut--so that on balance, the TR decreased from its former level. The relatively insensitive response in Qd, indicated by the demand segment OI, is technically referred to as an inelastic response. Inelastic responses are precisely what the firm does not want to encounter if it ever has to cut its price, for in all such cases the TR would decrease in spite of the increase in Qd. This amounts to selling more but enjoying it less, so to speak.

The Unknown Demand Schedule

At this point we should note some additional properties of the demand schedule that are practically important to the firm. First of all, only after the firm changes its selling price can it get some idea of the slope of demand for its product. More precisely, at best it could discover no more than the segment of the demand that lies in the range of prices around its current price (e.g., the segments OI and OE in Figure 11). Indeed, so long as the firm continues to sell a given quantity at a given (unchanged) price--e.g., 10,000 units at $8, in Figure 11--the only thing it really knows about the demand schedule is a single "dot"--the dot O in Figure 11, which represents the current selling P of $8 and the Qd of 10,000 units. Only by a trial-and-error process of changing its P can the firm discover the slope of the demand segment nearest to its previous position or "dot."

The second noteworthy thing is that the slopes of the demand segment in Figure 11 are basically different: the inelastic segment OI slopes more to the vertical, while the elastic OE segment slopes more to

149

the horizontal. And this is generally the case: whenever the demand schedule assumes a relatively vertical posture, it is technically identified as "inelastic," whereas the demand schedule that slopes toward the horizontal is identified as "elastic."

Elastic, Inelastic and Unitary

Omitted from Figure 11 is the oddball in-between case where the degree of elasticity is technically categorized as unitary--neither elastic nor inelastic. This is the extremely peculiar case where the TR remains the same as before--TR neither increases nor decreases--even though both the price and Qd have changed. In the case of a price cut, as shown in Figure 11, the unitary case would be represented by an increase in Qd to 16,000 units, which at $5 a piece yields a TR of $80,000, precisely the same amount as the original TR. Such a result can occur only in the very unlikely event that the Qd responds just enough to compensate for or offset the extent of the price change, as a consequence of which the TR remains virtually the same as before.

Third, it should be noted that the demand schedule (D), which consists of an array of possible "dots"--each of which represents a given P and the Qd at that price--for that very reason also consists of an array of potential TR's which can be calculated from the respective P's and Q's. In other words, the D schedule may also be interpreted as a TR schedule. As the firm moves from one selling price to another, it encounters not only a change in Qd but also a change in TR.

Elasticity of Demand and Uncertainty

This brings us to the fourth and probably most important aspect of the demand schedule--at least as far as the firm is concerned: the TR does not necessarily change in the same direction as does the Qd under the law of demand. That is to say, under the law of demand it is always true that a significant price decrease will cause Qd to increase, but it does not necessarily follow that TR will also increase. (Similarly, a significant price increase will cause Qd to decrease, but it will not necessarily cause TR to drop, too. More on this below.) It all depends on the slope, or degree of elasticity of demand. As we saw in Figure 11, in the case of a price cut, TR will actually decrease when the

150

D schedule is _inelastic_, even though the Qd is increased. Only when the D schedule is _elastic_ will a price cut increase TR as well as increase Qd.

The direct implication of this possible discrepancy between changes in Qd and changes in TR is the _uncertainty_ that it causes for the firm whenever it wants to change its price and increase its TR. Will a price _cut_, for example, increase its TR or decrease it? The same question, we will see, applies to a price _increase_. The firm cannot know for certain which of the two TR outcomes will occur unless it knows the degree of elasticity of demand--that is, unless it knows whether the D for its product is "elastic" or "inelastic" in response to a price change. How can the firm acquire such practical knowledge of the elasticity of D for its product? Before we answer this question, we must resume our graphic analysis of elasticity to include the case of a price _increase_.

A Note on Statistical Procedures

Before proceeding, we should note the technical problem posed by the fact that the raw sales data showing the TR change cannot be accepted at face value. The reason: in practice, some part of the TR change may be due not only to the given _price_ change (e.g., the price cut) but also to changes in _non-price_ determinants, such as tastes or income. As we saw in Chapter VI, the law of demand _abstracts_ from the impact of the various _non-price_ influences on Qd. In the present chapter, for the purpose of illustrating the elasticity concept, we are similarly abstracting from possible non-price influences on TR, in order to be able to focus only on the relation between _price_ changes and TR changes.

As a consequence of this technical problem, posed by the complex nature of the raw TR data, a variety of statistical procedures have been required to enable, at least approximately, the elimination of possible _non-price_ influences on TR and the calculation of an "adjusted" TR figure which is related purely to _price_. A similar statistical chore is required in order to compute the _coefficient_ of _elasticity_, which is the traditional method of explaining the concept of demand-elasticity (see Appendix to this chapter).

151

The Hazards of Price-Raising

Virtually everything we have said concerning the case of a price cut applies with equal force to the case of a price increase. Assume, now, that our firm has tried the price cut as a means of increasing its TR and discovered to its dismay that market demand was inelastic, so that its TR was now lower than before! The firm, being guided purely by the law of demand, might believe that its salvation lies only in a price cut--not a price increase--reasoning that only an increase in Qd could bring the desired increase in TR. Let us assume, however, that in sheer desperation it tries the price increase route to its goal.

In Figure 12, our firm has decided to raise its price from $8 to $10. Being ignorant of the degree of slope or elasticity of the demand schedule, it has no way of forecasting whether the extent of drop in Qd caused by the price increase will be dot E or dot I. As a starter, suppose the price-raise caused a drastic drop in Qd from the original 10,000 units (dot 0 in Figure 12) to a mere 4,000 units (dot E). Just by looking at the slope of the demand segment OE, it is apparent that the drop in Qd has been relatively drastic. It is clear that the price increase of $2 per unit was more than offset by the sharp decrease in Qd. It is no surprise, therefore, to find that TR, too, undergoes a drastic drop from the original $80,000 to only $40,000. The firm's worst fears have been confirmed: the price-raise did scare off too many customers.

Technically speaking, the demand segment OE revealed by the price increase in Figure 12 is regarded as elastic. Not only does Qd decrease in response to the price increase (and the law of demand), but more importantly, so does TR decrease, which is contrary to what the firm had desired. If ever the firm thinks that it must raise its price in order to increase its TR, it will learn at least one thing: to keep its fingers crossed lest demand turns out to be elastic.

Selling Less But Enjoying It More

In contrast to the dour outcome associated with Dot E in Figure 12, there is the totally opposite and happier possibility shown by dot I. Although here, too, Qd has dropped in response to the $2 price increase, it is apparent that the drop in Qd was relatively slight,

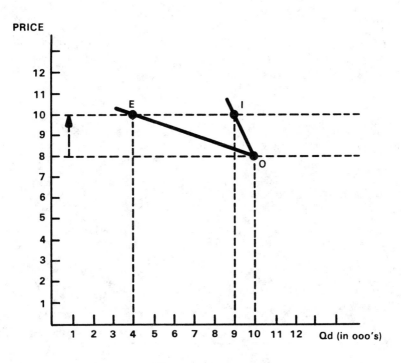

FIGURE 12:
ELASTICITY OF DEMAND IN THE
CASE OF A PRICE-INCREASE.

and not nearly as much as the dot E.   Indeed, when we
check out the result in TR terms, we see that TR has
increased from $80,000 to $90,000--despite the drop in
Qd!   Clearly, the drop in Qd proved to be sufficiently
small that it did not offset the $2 raise in price.

Whether or not the $10,000 increase in TR is, in
practice, enough to satisfy the firm, the fact remains
that, technically speaking, the demand segment OI is
regarded as inelastic.   Such "inelastic" responses are
exactly what the firm would like to experience if and
when it ever wants to raise its price, for only in such
cases could TR be expected to increase in spite of the
drop in Qd.   In other words, the firm may be selling
less but it is enjoying it more.

A Tableau of Our Results

Again omitted from our Figure 12 is the curious
in-between category of elasticity technically referred
to as unitary.   As noted above, a "unitary" degree of
elasticity is indicated only in those special instances
where the price change somehow does not affect total TR
even though the Qd changes; that is, TR remains virtually constant.   In Figure 12 this unitary response would
be indicated by a third dot placed right at the point
joining the new $10 price and the reduced Qd of 8,000
units, which together make for a TR totalling $80,000--
exactly the same as the original TR.   Since the unitary
response remains a relatively transitory case in practice, we will neglect it and devote our attention mainly
to the more practically significant elastic and inelastic cases.

It is now possible to summarize the results of
our analysis by the following tableau:

Type of Price Change	Change in Qd under the Law of Demand	Change in TR as Indicator of Degree of Elasticity of Demand
Price Cut	+	+ Elastic degree of elasticity - Inelastic degree of elasticity = Unitary degree of elasticity
Price Raise	-	- Elastic degree of elasticity + Inelastic degree of elasticity = Unitary degree of elasticity

Elastic vs. Inelastic:
Which Is Better?

Before we proceed, we should explain some of the entries in the tableau: the "plus" sign indicates an increase in the Qd or TR, the "minus" sign stands for a decrease, while the "equals" sign stands for no-change. Now, the first thing to note is that elastic cases emerge only where the TR changes in the same direction as the Qd--that is, when TR increases while Qd increases, or when TR decreases while Qd decreases. On the other hand, the inelastic cases occur only when TR changes in a direction opposite to that of the Qd--that is, when TR decreases while Qd increases, or when TR increases while Qd decreases.

The next thing to note is that an "elastic" or "inelastic" demand does not always have the same practical significance for the firm. Thus, as illustrated by Figure 13, if the firm is considering a reduction of price, it would clearly prefer an elastic to an inelastic demand segment, since only an elastic demand will bring with it the desired increase in TR despite the price cut. Conversely, when the firm is considering a price increase, it would clearly prefer an inelastic demand segment, for only in this case will the TR increase despite the drop in Qd. Put another way, an elastic demand would be "good news" to the firm only when considering a price cut, while an inelastic demand is "good news" only when a price increase is being considered.

The Practical Importance
of Demand-Elasticity

Once again, then, we see why knowledge of the law of demand is not enough as far as the firm is concerned. Of great practical importance is an awareness of the price-elasticity dimension of demand, especially as it operates through changes in TR. More precisely, only from its market experience can the firm learn, sooner or later, that elastic and inelastic demand segments will exert significantly different effects on TR when it undertakes a price change. Only through constant effort to adapt to changes in market demand, via adjustments in selling price and/or quantities supplied, can the firm learn anything about the elasticity of demand for its product.

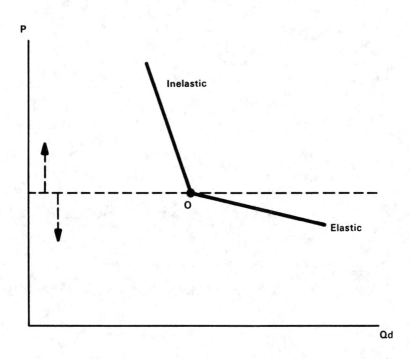

FIGURE 13:

DEGREES OF ELASTICITY PREFERRED BY THE FIRM.

By now, the preceding analysis must have raised at least two questions in the reader's mind: (1) What are the various social, technical, and economic forces that help determine whether market demand will be elastic or inelastic? (2) In what ways can the firm acquire knowledge of the elasticity of demand, which can guide it in forecasting the possible effects of a price change? It is these two practical questions to which we devote the next part of this chapter.

II. The Determinants of Elasticity

In the following analysis of the determinants of elasticity, we enumerate and analyze several basic dimensions through which the forces influencing the degree of elasticity of demand exert their effects. These determinants of elasticity ultimately boil down to but a few basic dimensions having to do with the product itself, the nature of the competitive environment, and the subjective conditions of the consumer. Our analysis will help us learn the nature of those conditions which tend to make demand elastic or inelastic, and which are therefore of direct practical relevance to the pricing policies of firms. As we will see, there is nothing in this common-sense analysis that the firm cannot, and does not, learn from its own trial-and-error experience in the market place.

(1) Availability of Close Substitutes

For virtually any given product X offered for exchange or sale in the market place, there can be found one or more close substitutes--other products that can serve the same purpose or provide the same utility (usefulness) as the given product X. One example already familiar to the reader involves butter and margarine (see Chapter VI). Substitutes need not be identical in physical properties. That is to say, the degree of substitutability or similarity of product is determined not only by the physical/technical properties of the interchangeable commodities, but also by the judgment of the consumer. Substitutability lies in the eyes of the beholder, so to speak.

If, for example, people use newspapers as well as wax paper for wrapping purposes, then this practice effectively makes them substitutes for each other with respect to the given purpose (wrapping), even though the two products are not physically identical. So long as the different products can be used to serve the same purpose, more or less, they are to that extent substitutable for each other--indeed, as far as the consumer is concerned, they may be viewed as rivals, in competition with each other.

Substitutes and Competition

Another equally important dimension of substitutability is the extent of competition provided by rival brands or firms producing the given product X. The larger the number of competing firms producing product X, the greater the degree of substitutability as far as the consumer is concerned. For example, if the consumer does not like Schlitz beer, for reasons of price or quality, he can find a half-dozen or more substitute beers produced by rival firms, all of whom offer a similar product that effectively serves as a close substitute for Schlitz.

We thus have not one but two dimensions of substitutability, both of consequence to the competition among products and firms. In effect, therefore, the availability of close substitutes is a reflection of the competitive environment facing the firm and its product. Hence, the greater the competition among both products and firms, the greater the availability of close substitutes--and vice versa. We now must ask: What is the effect of availability of substitutes on the degree of slope or elasticity of market demand? First, we will analyze the case of a price raise, and then the case of a price cut.

Substitutes and Elasticity

Assume, now, that a given firm has raised the price of its product, while other firms producing a similar product have not raised theirs, or have not raised theirs as much. It would be reasonable to assert: other things being equal, the greater the availability of substitutes, the more likely that the demand for the product will be elastic (see segment OE in Figure 14, part A); conversely, the smaller the availability of substitutes, the more likely that demand will prove to be inelastic (see segment OI in Figure 14, part A). The reasoning here is straightforward: the greater the competition, the better able are buyers to locate

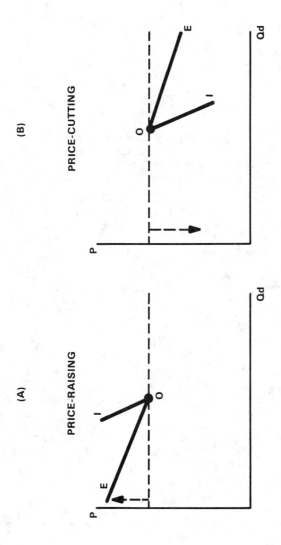

FIGURE 14:
PRICE-CHANGES AND PRICE-ELASTICITY OF DEMAND.

159

relatively cheaper substitutes and to shift their purchases to those alternatives. They would rather switch
than fight, to re-coin a phrase. Conversely, the smaller the extent of competition, the fewer the alternatives available to buyers.

What about the case of a price reduction? Here
it would be reasonable to assert the same propositions
as in the case of a price increase: other things being
equal, the greater the availability of substitutes, the
more likely that demand will be elastic (see segment OE
in Figure 14, part B), while conversely, the less the
availability of substitutes, the more likely that demand
will be inelastic (see segment OI in Figure 14, part B).
Here the reasoning would be as follows: if the ABC
Company cuts its price while all other firms fail to
follow suit, then the greater the extent of competition
from rival brands and products, and the greater the
number of customers that can be won over from competitors in favor of ABC's lower price. Conversely, the
smaller the extent of the competition, the fewer the
customers to be won away from competitors.

Notice that in both cases of price raising and
price cutting, the same conditions of substitutability
result in the same degree of elasticity. Thus, the
greater the availability of substitutes, the more likely
that demand will be elastic in both the case of a price
raise and a price cut. The same proposition applies to
the situation where substitutes are not very available.
As a consequence, the overall slope of market demand
would be expected to be elastic (E) when numerous
substitutes are available, and inelastic (I) when substitutes are not very available (see Figure 15).

Subway Fares and Oil Cartels

How does all this apply to the practical pricing
policies of firms? A couple of important examples will
suffice, although numerous others can be recounted.
Officials of New York City's subway system have been
periodically faced with the need to increase their total
subway receipts (TR), especially to finance increased
wage demands by union workers. Which way should they
go--reduce the subway fare or raise it?

History tells us that the subway authorities
have repeatedly resorted to an increase in the fare instead of a decrease. Why? Presumably, officials ruled

160

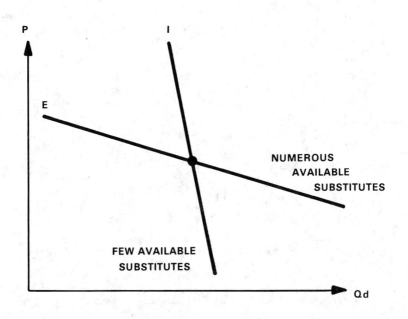

P

I

E

NUMEROUS
AVAILABLE
SUBSTITUTES

FEW AVAILABLE
SUBSTITUTES

Qd

FIGURE 15:
AVAILABILITY OF SUBSTITUTES AND ELASTICITY OF DEMAND.

out fare cuts on the belief that demand would be inelastic for a lower fare: they were probably skeptical that they could attract enough additional subway riders by the lower fare. So they turned instead to the fare increase, implying a belief that they had an inelastic demand for transportation. Clearly, the millions of workers going to jobs every day in Manhattan and other boroughs have little alternative to the subway. The comparative absence of any serious competition from alternative systems of transportation--taxis and owner-driven autos--would make for low substitutability and inelastic demand. Since the subway TR was increased as a consequence, the hunch about inelastic demand proved correct.

Another important example occurs in connection with the recent efforts of the oil cartel to increase total receipts (TR) by reducing supplies and charging higher prices. Intimately connected with this well-planned and orchestrated program were the gasoline "shortages" of the 1970's and the accompanying significant increases in gasoline prices. The oil producers must have been very confident that their Western customers were not only heavily dependent on oil, but also had few available substitutes, at least in the short run. Economic studies confirm their judgment: they show, for instance, that the demand for gasoline in the U.S.A. is very inelastic.

Before we proceed to the next determinant of elasticity, it is important to remember the proviso in our propositions: "other things being equal," i.e., ceteris paribus. This proviso reflects the fact that, in practice, there may be two or more determinants--not merely one--exerting their influence simultaneously on the demand for a given product. What makes this significant is the fact that the full array of determinants may not be exerting their influence all in the same direction, but rather in opposite directions. That is to say, one of the determinants may be imparting an inelastic thrust while another determinant may be imparting an elastic thrust. How does this affect our analysis of determinants? This will become clearer as we discuss other determinants.

(2) Relative Price of the Product

It is no secret that the various items we purchase in the market place have different price tags

162

attached to them, and that some of these prices are relatively low or insignificant--such as the prices of newspapers, bottles of coke, or cigarettes--while other prices are relatively steep or expensive, such as the prices of automobiles or refrigerators. Even though automobiles and other durables may be bought on an installment basis, involving lower monthly payments, the fact remains that such payments constitute relatively large-size items in one's budget. In any event, how would the relative dollar-size of the item affect the elasticity of demand?

The Case of a Price Increase

First, take the case of a price _increase_. For purposes of illustration, let us assume a price increase of 50 percent and compare the effects in the case of two differently priced products--say, a newspaper and an automobile. If the newspaper was selling for 20 cents, the new price would be 30 cents; if the car was selling for $6,000, the new price would be $9,000. Clearly, the impact on the elasticity of demand of the given 50-percent price increase would be vastly different in each case; the 10-cent price hike for the newspaper is virtually infinitesimal compared to the $3,000 boost on the car. As a consequence, a 10-cent boost would have virtually no deterrent effect on the rate of purchase compared to the deterrent effect of a $3,000 boost. Hence, it is reasonable to assert the following proposition: other things being equal, the smaller the relative price of the item, the more inelastic is the demand likely to be; conversely, the more expensive the item, the more elastic is demand likely to be--_ceteris paribus_.

This proposition can be confirmed by a variety of cases, but one important instance should suffice. A widespread practice among the governments of the world is the levying of _excise_ _taxes_, particularly on low-priced items, such as cigarettes, cosmetics, movies, and liquor. This "nickel-and-dime" method of public finance has been a successful revenue raiser mainly because the low-priced items involved show inelastic demand against price increases. This means that the price hike caused by the tax has relatively slight deterrent impact on the rate of purchase.

163

The Case of a Price Cut

What about the case of a price reduction? Here, too, it would be plausible to assert the same proposition as above, and for similar reasons. A price cut on a low-priced item will spare the buyer only small amounts, and hence constitutes a relatively weak inducement to buy more. On the other hand, a similar percentage cut on a high-priced item will mean a relatively huge saving to the purchaser, and therefore constitute a very great inducement to buy. Hence, an inelastic response in Qd would be associated with the low-priced item while an elastic response would be expected in the case of a high-priced item, ceteris paribus.

Finally, we should note that, since our propositions are the same for both cases of price raising and price cutting, the overall conclusion is that elastic (E) demand will emerge in the case of high-priced items, and inelastic (I) demand will emerge in the case of low-priced items (see the slopes E and I in Figure 15).

The Meaning of "Ceteris Paribus"

Before we proceed to a third determinant of elasticity, it is pertinent to recall our earlier comment on the "other things being equal" proviso. There we noted that, in practice, we are likely to find not one but possibly two or more determinants of elasticity at work, and in opposite directions. Now, with the automobile, at least in areas where people have few alternative means of transportation (such as Los Angeles), we have an excellent example of this case.

In the Los Angeles area, for instance, automobiles are not only expensive in price (like everywhere else in the country) and in upkeep (because of the great mileage travelled by each driver), but they remain virtually the only means of transportation. (About the only substitutability is in switching from "gas-guzzler" models to "economy" models.) This heavy dependence on the automobile not only makes for inelastic demand, but also accounts for families tending to own two or more cars--depending on the size of family, etc.,--which further adds to the purchase expense. Thus, we have determinants of opposite influence on elasticity: on the one hand, the lack of available substitutes causes inelasticity of demand, while on the other hand, the great expense of acquiring cars makes for elasticity of demand. This makes it more difficult for producing firms to predict the overall effects of an increase in the price of new cars as well as an increase in the price of gasoline.

(3) Subjective Preference Ranking

At least twice before--in Chapters V and VI--we have met the subjective preference-scale on which, at any given moment, we rank our wants and the means to satisfy them. The specific forces that shape and influence these subjective preference rankings--the importance we attach to things--are as numerous and varied as the human mind can imagine. They include such widely ranging factors as individual nutritional requirements, aesthetic tastes, and lifestyle--on to advertising, fashion, and professional/technical requirements.

Price Increases vs. Price Cuts

Before we examine some noteworthy aspects, let us first state the following propositions. If the firm is contemplating a price increase, it would be reasonable to assert: other things being equal, the higher the subjective preference-ranking for the particular product or want, the more likely that the demand will be inelastic in the face of a price raise. (In this connection, see Figure 14, part A, segment OI.) Conversely, the lower the subjective ranking for the item, the more likely that demand will be elastic in the face of the price raise. (See Figure 14, part A, segment OE.)

The reasoning here is straightforward. The more important the item is for the consumer, the less resistant will the consumer be to a price increase--ceteris paribus. The example of gasoline readily comes to mind. The inelastic demand attributed to gasoline in the face of price increases is as much due to the importance attached to the automobile as to the lack of available substitutes for automobile power. Conversely, the less important the item is for the consumer, the more likely that he will be deterred from buying at the higher price--other things remaining the same.

What about subjective preferences and price reduction? Here the propositions would run as follows: other things being equal, the stronger the subjective preference, the more will demand tend to be elastic,

165

while the weaker the subjective preference, the more likely that demand will be inelastic. (See Figure 14, part B, segments OE and OI, respectively.) And the reasoning here is also straightforward: the more important the item is to consumers, the more likely are they to take advantage of the price cut; the less important the item, the less likely are consumers to be induced to buy by the price cut.

Practical Implications

A further significant proposition follows from these considerations. On the assumption that firms prefer larger total receipts (TR) to smaller TR's, they will tend to produce goods of higher-valued preference, or cater to wants of higher rank, rather than produce goods or cater to wants of lower-valued rank.

In this connection, an examination of Figure 16 readily tells us why: higher-ranked goods or wants (see part A of Figure 16) are associated with demand segments whose degree of elasticity implies increased TR's if and when the firm wants to either increase its price (see segment OI) or cut its price (see segment OE); conversely, lower-ranked goods or wants (see part B of Figure 16) are associated with demand segments whose degree of elasticity implies decreased TR's when the firm raises its price (see segment OE) or cuts its price (see segment OI). To put it another way: if ever the firm is faced with the decision to change its price in order to increase its TR, it would clearly be better off producing goods of higher value than goods of lower value.

The Case of Agricultural Products

All of this has great relevance to government policy on agricultural products--their supply and pricing. Here it suffices to note that the demand for agricultural products and foodstuffs as a whole is over-all inelastic. This means that farmers face two alternatives. They could, on the one hand, increase their TR's by producing less and charging higher prices. On the other hand, they could increase production and reduce prices in order to increase the Qd; but in so doing their TR's would decrease due to the inelastic demand!

At least two interesting implications emerge from the agricultural case. One is the implication,

166

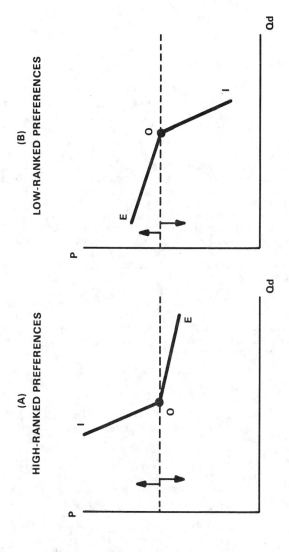

(A)
HIGH-RANKED PREFERENCES

(B)
LOW-RANKED PREFERENCES

FIGURE 16:
PREFERENCE-RANKING AND ELASTICITY OF DEMAND.

167

just noted, that farmers can be induced to increase their TR's by producing less and increasing prices. The other is an implication that applies to other goods that share a similar characteristic: while these goods possess great importance for people, they are nevertheless needed in only minimum quantities, such that the demand for them is inelastic both for a price raise and for a price cut.

Minimum Requirements

For example, in the case of foodstuffs, people generally desire certain minimum quantities for nutritional purposes (causing demand to be inelastic against a price hike). For this reason, they are not sufficiently attracted to opportunities to acquire more foodstuffs at lower prices, in preference to other goods (hence the inelastic demand to a price cut). Similar is the case of special technical instruments or equipment, such a slide-rules, pocket computers, or stethoscopes. For these items, people have only a limited professional or technical requirement--that is, they need but one unit, not more. Therefore, the firm would have to cut its price steeply in order to induce buyers to acquire a second unit or more. It may be noted, however, that at the greatly reduced price, additional customers can be picked up from two other groups of purchasers: people who have a relatively low-ranked preference for such items, and can be induced to buy only by a much-reduced price; and people in lower-income classes who can now afford to buy at the much lower price. This latter dimension of elasticity-determination will be examined in more detail in the next section.

(4) The Structure of Social Income

This dimension of demand-elasticity is relevant primarily to two cases. One involves a given product that has significant markets in each of the layers of the social income structure--from the higher-income strata, down through the middle-income, and into the lower-income strata--such that the problem facing the firm involves a judgment as to which price or price range will maximize its total receipts (TR).

Other things being equal, a relatively high price caters primarily to upper-income people, but because their number is comparatively small, the quantity

168

demanded by them will be relatively small (see the relevant inelastic segment of the demand schedule in Figure 17). On the other hand, a relatively low price caters primarily to lower-income groups, but since they exist in greater numbers, their Qd may be considerably large (see the elastic segment of demand in Figure 17). As a consequence, the firm must decide which of the two attractive segments of the market offers the comparatively greater TR, assuming the costs of producing the two different quantities does not significantly affect the pricing decision.

Closely related to this type of decision--which involves the question: Which level of price will maximize the firm's TR?--is another practical question: Which level of quality or grade of product will tap the most lucrative markets? Generally speaking, people associate higher prices with higher-quality products, and lower prices with lower-quality goods. Thus, assume an automobile producer who is able to turn out either a very expensive, high-quality, deluxe car (with a relatively inelastic demand) or a relatively inexpensive, lower-quality, mass-produced car (with a very elastic demand). The one car would cater to a select group of rich people or car enthusiasts; the other car would tap the untold riches of the mass market. If an entrepreneur were motivated primarily by the vision of a potential mass market, he would clearly undertake production of the inexpensive, mass-market car. Could this have been the paradigm for Henry Ford and his Model T car?

(5) Supplies On Hand in the Pantry

In pursuing this catalogue of elasticity determinants, we should also note a factor that must be presumed to be an important influence on elasticity, but its significance cannot be easily ascertained by the firm. It involves a wide variety of storeable commodities (from canned goods and linens to gasoline for the car), which are kept in consumers' refrigerators, freezers, pantries, closets, tanks, attics, or wherever. Typically, the quantity or stock in possession of the consumer can vary from zero or low to full or ample, so that the firm cannot gauge the state of consumer inventories of consumables with sufficient precision. Nevertheless, the law of marginal utility (Chapter V) enables us to assert the following propositions.

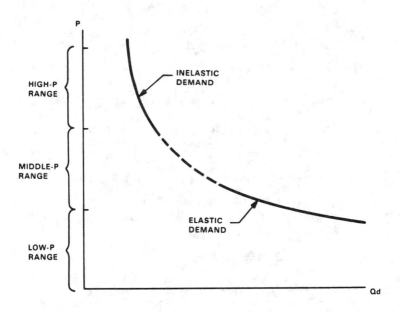

FIGURE 17:
SOCIAL INCOME-STRUCTURE AND
ELASTICITY OF DEMAND.

First, the case of a price increase. Other
things being equal, the greater the quantity of goods
already in consumers' stocks, the more likely that consumers' demand will be elastic in response to the price-
hike; conversely, the smaller the stocks on hand, the
more likely that consumers' demand will be inelastic
rather than elastic. The reasoning, based on the law of
marginal utility, would run as follows: with ample or
bulging stocks on hand (and the law of diminishing MU
therefore becoming relevant), consumers would be less
inclined than otherwise to pay a higher price; with
small or meager supplies on hand (and the law of increasing MU therefore becoming relevant), consumers
would be less deterred than otherwise from buying at the
higher price.

A parallel line of reasoning applies to a price
reduction. Other things being equal, the greater the
quantity in consumers' stocks, the more likely that
consumers' demand will be inelastic in response to the
price cut; conversely, the smaller the stocks on hand,
the more likely that demand will be elastic. Why? In
the case of ample stocks on hand, the law of diminishing
MU becomes relevant: the lower price is less of an
inducement to buy than otherwise. However, when stocks
are very low, and the law of increasing MU becomes
relevant, the consumer finds the lower price a greater
inducement to buy than otherwise.

Complexity of Determinants

As a concluding note to this analysis of elasticity determinants, it is necessary to stress again
that, in the real world, these determinants may exert
their influence in combinations of two or more simultaneously, but with mutually opposite impacts on Qd.
What we have done in this part of the chapter is a
"partial analysis"--a study of the effects of isolated
or particular forces at work, on the ceteris paribus
assumption that other influences are not simultaneously
at work. This enables us to explore theoretically the
full workings of any single factor. Then, equipped with
this knowledge of the workings of individual determinants, we should be better able to forecast the effects
on elasticity that may be exerted by the complex, real-
world conditions facing the firm in a given market.

In this connection it is important to recall
(from Chapter VI) that the firm knows little, if

anything, about the demand schedule for its product--
other than its current "dot," that is, its current
selling price (P) and the quantity demanded (Qd) at that
price. The only other thing the firm knows is that
there is a demand schedule out there in the market--
albeit unknown--and that if the firm raised (or lowered)
its price, the Qd would decrease (or increase).

Demand -- The Unknown

But surely this is not enough. The firm could
still not know in advance by how much the Qd would
decrease (or increase) when it raises (or lowers) its
price. Indeed, such information about the effect of a
price change cannot be known until the firm actually
institutes the price change. Even then, the firm would
discover the degree of elasticity pertaining to only one
segment of a potentially more complete demand schedule.
Logically, the only way the firm could discover the full
array of "dots" constituting the demand schedule would
be to conduct a kind of experiment: It could post a
series of price changes over a wide range in order to
uncover the full array of the respective P and Qd dots
that comprise the demand schedule--assuming, of course,
that the demand schedule does not shift throughout the
entire experiment!

In practice, however, firms cannot and do not
play such games. They do not change prices unless
provoked by special circumstances. For instance, they
have in the past raised prices mainly in response to
rising costs rather than to take advantage of increased
demand; from the public relations viewpoint, they prefer
not to be accused of "charging what the traffic will
bear." Conversely, they reduce prices mainly under the
pressure of increased competition or the need to dispose
of overpriced goods.

III. Some Important Questions

Can firms charge just any high price they want,
and still prosper? Do firms always charge the highest
price consistent with maximum profits? Do firms actually have complete knowledge of market demand so that they
know exactly which price will maximize their profits?
These and related questions can be answered, at least
partly, with the help of the demand-elasticity concept.
Let us see how.

The Firm as "Profiteer"

There is a widespread notion that, if left
alone, the firm would automatically charge the "highest
possible price" simply out of rapacious greed, and that
only fear of government reprisal (e.g., anti-trust
action by the Justice Department) keeps it from resorting to price "extortion" or "profiteering." Whether or
not it is true that fear of public reprisal keeps the
firm in check is strictly an empirical question, which
may or may not be open to investigation. As far as
economics is concerned, the market alone suffices to
keep prices of firms in check (as we will see especially
in the next chapter); it would be a waste of valuable
resources to set up a public agency merely to police
prices in the market place when, all along, the market
itself can serve this function.

It should be noted here, however, that no firm
in its right mind would blindly and steadily raise
prices regardless of the elasticity of demand for its
product. As we have amply seen, the only time it pays
the firm to raise its price is when market demand is
inelastic (not elastic!), for only inelastic demand will
yield an increase in total receipts (TR) and an increase
in total profits. (This assumes that cost-changes are
not a factor--that the smaller production rate due to
the drop in quantity demanded (Qd) does not affect total
costs in a way that affects the profit rate.) However,
if, following the price raise, demand proves to be
elastic, the result would be a drop in TR and (assuming
no cost-effects) a drop in profit rate, too, which
should suffice to check the price-raising! In other
words, the firm would go for a price raise only as long
as demand is inelastic; if demand turns out to be
elastic, the price-raising will stop.

Ex-Ante Ignorance

This brings us to a related question. Assume a
firm that, in quest of increased TR and believing market
demand to be inelastic, decides to raise its price.
And lo and behold, it discovers it guessed correctly--
its TR actually increases. This prompts the question:
How come the firm had up to now been asleep at the
wheel--selling at a lower price and TR--when all along
it could have been selling at a higher price and a
larger TR? Assuming costs of production were not a

173

factor, it looks like the firm had up to this point foregone higher profits. Why would it do so?

One possible answer is that the firm was more or less ignorant of the degree of elasticity of market demand when it had made its original ex-ante decision-- when it set the price at, say, $10 in the belief that this represented its most profitable price for the quantity produced. Had it known originally that a higher price of $12, say--and a smaller quantity of production --would have brought a higher TR, it would undoubtedly have opted for that combination of P and Q. But in view of its ignorance--its incomplete knowledge of the actual demand situation--it could not know in the ex-ante what it could know only in the ex-post, after trial-and-error. (See Chapter V on maximizing and the ex-ante/ex-post aspects of decision-making.) In other words, had the firm at the start possessed perfect knowledge of the market demand, it would have opened up with a $12 price--it would never have had to raise its price from $10 to $12, and consumers would not have any grounds to complain of "profiteering"!

"Social Pressures," Competition, and Income Changes

Another possible reason why a firm might only belatedly discover that its initial price had been set too low--in the sense that it was less profitable than the higher price it set later--is the widespread reluctance of firms to raise prices in the face of various "social pressures." One such pressure stems from the taboo, already mentioned, against "charging what the traffic will bear." In terms of elasticity this means: do not raise prices even though demand is inelastic and TR would increase! Another form of pressure stems from the fear of prosecution by the Justice Department under the anti-trust laws, on the grounds of "monopoly" or "market power."

A third possible reason is the firm's fear of competition from rival firms and rival products, such that a price raise might leave it out on the limb-- losing customers to rivals that had not raised their prices. In such cases it might occur to the firm that the best way to achieve higher profits is through collusion with its rivals. Such concerted action would involve a basic agreement among firms to restrict supply, rig prices, and bolster profits by means of pools,

mergers, or cartels. In other words, the firm may
overcome its fear of competition by, in effect, outlawing it in concert with its rivals. But history tells us
that such cartel-like arrangements have never worked
without the backing and legal sanction of government.

A Note on Cartels

In this connection, history also reveals that
cartels organized by commodity-producing nations--in
order to restrict supply and maintain the price of
copper, coffee, oil, etc.--have tended to underestimate
the degree of elastic response in consumers' demand as a
consequence of consumers' ability to find <u>substitutes</u> in
the long run. Indeed, all demand schedules possess some
degree of elasticity due to the availability, more or
less, of substitutes.

History reveals that in the long run there is no
such thing as a totally vertical (totally inelastic)
demand schedule. Man has not let himself be crucified
by a price hike. He has had the ingenuity to use
science and technology to find those substitutes that
enable him to reduce reliance on higher-priced resources. And this is probably the most productive as
well as the most effective way of bringing any cartel to
heel.

Rising Incomes and Price-Increases

Also worth mentioning is the following peculiar
situation. Imagine a case in which TR increases at the
same time that the firm raises its price--but not as a
result of inelastic demand. This is the case where
<u>market demand</u> had increased at the same time that the
firm had raised its price. In this case, the firm may
not have realized that demand had increased because
personal incomes of households had increased, thereby
causing a "shift to the right" in the demand schedule
(see Chapter VI). In this case the TR is increased not
because of inelastic demand but because, despite the
higher price, the increase in the demand schedule was
sufficiently large so that the Qd remains undiminished
or even increases!

Why Not Blame the Consumer?

The fact that the firm can raise its price and increase its TR raises another issue. There have always been people who regard price-raising by the firm as "reprehensible" or "gouging." Since it is usually inelastic demand that enables the firm to earn a larger TR when it raises its price, two further questions become very relevant: (1) Why blame the firm for inelastic demand, when only the consumers are ultimately responsible for that? (2) Does not the firm have the right to take advantage of a market situation which reveals an inelastic demand for a given product?

As to the first question, it should be noted that whereas consumers--not firms--should be blamed for creating the inelastic demand, these same consumers have it in their power to reverse the situation and create an elastic demand--simply by sitting on their hands and curtailing their spending! Therefore, if consumers think a firm's price and TR are "too high," and really want to bring them down, nothing stands in their way but their resolve to buy less.

A Question of Human Rights

As to the second question--concerning the firm's right to maximize its profit by increasing its TR--it suffices to note that it involves a moral issue. Virtually all attacks on the firm that concern their pricing and production policies--e.g., the firm's price is alternatively "too high" ("extortion"!), "too low" ("price warfare"!), or the firm is alternatively producing "too much" (beware of "growth" and "affluence!"), or "too little" ("monopolistic restriction"!)--these attacks are not only self-contradictory but also boil down to questions of fundamental human rights. Does a person have the right to ask any price he wishes for his goods and services? Does he have the right to produce as much or as little as he desires? These fundamental questions will turn up again in Chapter X, wherein we analyze the nature of a free-market economy.

Appendix

THE COEFFICIENT OF ELASTICITY

It is not usual to give the concept of demand-elasticity a whole chapter all to itself as we have just done. Nor is it usual to treat elasticity in "TR" terms, although textbooks are tending more and more to do so. More usual, because it is traditional, is to describe elasticity in "percentage" terms--that is, to compare the percentage change in quantity-demanded with the given percentage change in price. The purpose of this appendix is merely to alert the reader to the existence of this alternative concept, which he can pursue in greater detail in any introductory or inter-mediate textbook.

Theoretically, there is no basic conflict be-tween the TR approach and the percentage approach; they are two different ways of looking at the same thing. In the percentage approach, the criterion of elasticity is referred to as the "coefficient of elasticity," which is derived as follows:

$$\text{Coefficient Of Elasticity (COE)} = \frac{\text{Percentage Change in Qd}}{\text{Percentage Change in P}}$$

Thus, the COE turns out to be a number that reflects the numerical relation or ratio between the rate of change in P and the rate of change in Qd. The plus or minus signs that are involved mathematically can be conven-iently disregarded for the purpose of calculating the COE.

Let us take a simple example. Suppose a price cut of 15 percent results in a 20 percent increase in Qd. The resulting ratio is 20/15, equivalent to 1-1/3, or 1.333. Since any COE that is numerically greater than 1.0 is classified as elastic, the above case re-veals elastic demand. Another simple example: suppose a price raise of 20 percent results in Qd dropping only 10 percent. Calculation yields a ratio of 10/20, equiv-alent to 1/2 or .5. Since any COE that is numerically less than 1.0 is classified as inelastic, we have here a case of inelastic demand. Finally, the unitary case arises where the percent changes in Qd and P are exactly equal, yielding a COE of 1.0, the standard for unitary elasticity.

Notice that both the TR and percentage criteria
involve the same basic elements: P and Qd.   But the TR
figure , compared to the COE, has the advantage of not
requiring any further calculation once the raw TR data
have been statistically adjusted to eliminate the effect
of non-price influences on TR--a statistical procedure
that is also required in calculating the COE.   In contrast, the COE requires the further calculation of the
respective percentage changes in P and Qd, and then the
ratio of these percentage changes.

CHAPTER VIII

HOW THE MARKET DETERMINES PRICES

Prices, prices everywhere--indeed, prices are the most widespread aspect of the market place. And the market place is the preeminent theater of exchange transactions in our lives--the stage upon which we offer each other the services of our labor power, savings, or other wealth, in order to earn the income with which to buy the things we want. No wonder it is such a focal point of human action.

I. Free Markets vs. Interventionism

Market places are found in all modern economic systems--capitalist, socialist, or otherwise--in which a medium of exchange (money) is used as the means of payment for goods and services put on sale. But, although different economic systems share more or less the existence of market places, the specific way in which prices are established in the respective markets varies significantly. One of the ways in which price-formation processes differ involves the distinction between _free markets_ and _controlled_ markets.

Only Two Ways to Determine Prices

Indeed, throughout history only two principles have guided the formation of prices in the market place: the _free-market_ principle and the _interventionist_ principle of the "political means" (see Chapter I). Various facets of the free market will be examined in detail in Chapter X. For the present we concentrate on the market as a mechanism or process for determining prices, whereas in Chapter X we will examine it broadly, and fundamentally, in terms of its philosophical, institutional, and moral dimensions. A full-blown analysis of interventionism is beyond the scope of the present work.

For the present chapter it suffices to note that _free-market_ price formation is based on the principle of exchange of goods and services for money on a totally voluntary basis. That is to say, prices are agreed upon by mutual consent of the two exchanging parties, without

179

any forcible intervention by an outside third party, such as, for example, a government agency empowered to control prices and wages.

II. What Happens When Demand and Supply Meet?

We now tackle the key questions: How does the market determine prices? Toward what price will the market tend to move for any given product? That is to say, which of the several prices on the vertical scale of prices--relevant to the market demand schedule--will the market settle on?

Demand and Supply Determine Prices

Without getting into specifics here, this much can be said: the interplay of demand and supply forces is the crucial mechanism for answering each of these questions. Furthermore, despite the fact that the firm (i.e., its management) is responsible for personally setting the prices of its products, _ultimately_ it is _the market_ that determines prices, through the demand-and-supply mechanism.

Fortunately, it is possible to illustrate, by means of simple graphs, how the interplay of demand and supply manages to determine the market price. Chapters VI and VII have amply described the _demand_ side of the market. To understand the _supply_ side, our main preparation has been Chapter IV; with that chapter as background, we can now understand the supply schedule (S), as shown in Figure 18. There we see the so-called ex-post supply schedule (S), shown in two varieties (in panels A and B), both of which display the characteristic _vertical_ slope.

Meeting the Supply Schedule

First, we should explain the _ex-post_ aspect of this supply schedule. _Ex-post_ simply refers to the fact that once-planned production of a given good has already taken place, and a specified amount X has been offered for sale in the market (shown by X along the horizontal scale in Figure 18). _Ex-post_ represents a kind of _fait accompli_ situation; the firm's planned production program has finally been completed, and the finished product is now offered on the market in the amount X.

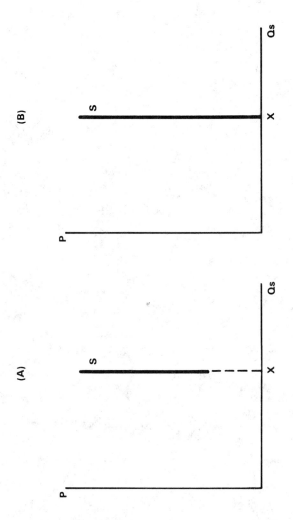

FIGURE 18:
THE EX-POST SUPPLY SCHEDULE.

181

Why is the supply schedule so characteristically vertical in the ex-post? Because the vertical line is the only way to illustrate the fact that the total quantity supplied (Qs) to the market is of a given fixed amount X. (See Appendix for analysis of ex-ante S.)

We should also explain the dashed portion below the lower end of the S schedule in panel A of Figure 18. This indicates the range of relatively low prices at which the firm would not want to sell any of its supply. In contrast, the upper (thickened) portion of the S schedule indicates the range of prices at which the firm would be willing to sell.

Minimum Reservation Prices

Now, what is the difference between the two S schedules in Figure 18? In panel A, the thick portion of the S schedule (as just explained) correlates with those prices on the vertical P scale at which the firm is willing to sell. Hence, the lower end of this thick line indicates the minimum reservation price acceptable to the firm, below which it will not sell. Thus, if market demand is disappointingly low, and buyers would be willing to buy only at the relatively low prices (shown by the dashed portion of S), the firm might decide to withhold the product from the market rather than to sell it at distress prices. In a sense, therefore, the dashed portion shows the prices at which the quantity X would not be offered for sale on the market.

In contrast is the S schedule in panel B, which does touch the horizontal Qs axis. This S illustrates the special but not unusual case where the firm has no minimum reservation price--its goods are placed on sale for whatever price the market will fetch. This includes selling out even at a zero price, which simply means giving the stuff away, with no price asked. Hence, the S schedule is drawn to touch the Qs axis, where P is zero. This means that regardless of the price buyers are willing to pay, firms enter the market prepared to dispose of their wares at any price they can fetch, from zero on up.

Perishables vs. Non-Perishables

A good example of this totally vertical S schedule, which touches the Qs axis, is the perishable

182

commodity (e.g., fish, tomatoes). These commodities may
be too costly to store, or not worth preserving, and
therefore must be disposed of at whatever price. In
such distress situations, the failure of the firm to
sell out its supply by the end of the planned sales
period puts it under pressure to slash its price sufficiently until it finally does sell out--even if it takes
a zero price to get rid of the unsold quantities. In
the worst case, where the goods become totally rotten,
the firm might even decide to pay a garbage collector to
cart the stuff away.

The more usual case involves non-perishable
goods--goods that can be stored for long periods of
time. Here the seller has an important option: not to
sell if the market is not willing to pay his minimum
reservation price. This is the case depicted in Panel A
of Figure 18. If prices offered are too low, the firm
can withdraw its supply and place it in storage. The
firm will select this option if it is confident that
demand will later pick up sufficiently--sufficiently,
that is, to raise prices enough to cover the temporary
storage costs. If this speculation fails--if market
demand remains weak and the prospect of higher prices
fades--the mounting storage costs could eventually induce the firm to sell out at whatever price the market
fetches.

Price-setting: Market vs. the Firm

In practice, of course, firms do not enter the
market totally ignorant of the prices the market will
fetch--without any preconception of the price demanders
are willing to pay. On the contrary, firms make appropriate efforts to determine that particular selling
price which would enable them to sell their given Qs at
the expected profit margin. (This was briefly discussed
in Chapter IV, and Chapter IX will deal at length with
the relationship between selling price, profits, and
costs.) But the point is this: Whatever price the firm
initially sets on its product, it must do so with its
fingers crossed, because only its eventual confrontation
with market demand will determine whether its best-laid
plans are successful or not--that is, whether it will be
able to sell out its Qs at the original asking P.

In this connection, we shall note that when the
S schedule in the graph pertains to the industry as a
whole--and therefore represents the market S schedule

183

instead of merely an individual firm's S--we must be careful how we interpret the lower end of the S schedule (for example, see the S schedule in Figure 19). As we saw above, the bottom tip of the S indicates the minimum reservation price at which the firm is willing to sell. But in the case of the industry or market S schedule, where several firms are involved--each with different costs, profit expectations, and selling prices--we cannot presume to have a single, uniform, minimum reservation price for every firm. These minimum prices will undoubtedly vary from firm to firm. Hence, the lower tip of the S merely indicates the minimum price of only those firms which, for reasons of cost and/or profit margin, are able to enter the market with the lowest minimum prices.

The Marriage of Demand and Supply

We are now prepared to bring both the demand (D) and supply (S) schedules together in the market place-- and examine the outcome, as shown in Figure 19. In the nature of the case, we assume that the firms competing in a given market are offering a similar product--as physically similar as is possible in the real world, and as similar as the eyes of the beholders (the consumers) make it.

The first thing to note about Figure 19 is the point E: This marks the intersection of D and S. This intersection point is technically referred to as the equilibrium point, but in simpler terms it represents the market-clearing price ($8 here) at which the total S (the quantity OX) could be sold. That is to say, the point E indicates the only price at which the quantity-demanded (Qd) would be just equal to the Qs--at which the given Qs of X could be sold out in entirety by the end of the planned sales period. This makes the equilibrium price a unique price--indeed, any other price would not have this fortunate market-clearing result, as we will see in a moment.

First, it should be realized that, since different firms are likely to open with somewhat different initial prices for the same product, the market-clearing price of $8 will not necessarily satisfy each firm to the same degree. Only those firms that opened up with an $8 price would discover they were able to sell out within the planned sales period they had set for themselves. On the other hand, those firms that had opened

184

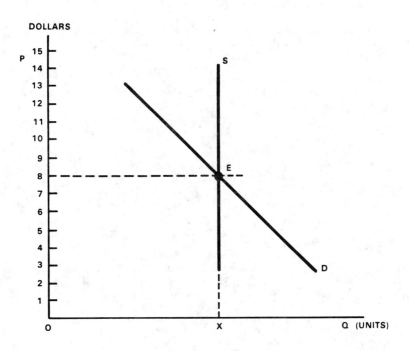

FIGURE 19:
DEMAND, SUPPLY, AND MARKET-PRICE

185

up with prices <u>higher</u> or <u>lower</u> than $8 would experience
a different result, technically referred to as "surplus"
and "shortage," respectively. Let us now see how and
why.

The Case of a Market Surplus

Assume that, instead of opening up at the happy
market-clearing price of $8, the firms had all opened at
a higher price, say $11, as shown in Figure 20. Clear-
ly, this $11 price is higher than the market-clearing $8
price. Now, under the law of demand the Qd at $11 will
be less than at $8--that is, Qd will drop from OX to OA,
as seen along the Q axis. But, since total market S
offered is the amount X, the firms now face what is
technically called a <u>surplus</u> or "excess supply": the Qs
is of the amount OX, while Qd is only OA. The size of
the surplus is indicated by the quantity AX, exactly the
horizontal distance by which Qs exceeds Qd at the price
of $11.

Let us make sure that we understand why the
surplus has occurred. The reason is that at $11 the
goods are <u>over-priced</u>, that is, what was a happy price
at $8--where Qd was <u>equal</u> to Qs--becomes too high at
$11. As a consequence of the too-high price, firms will
discover that by the end of the planned sales period--
during which they had expected to sell out the quantity
X--they are still stuck with an unsold quantity AX.
Indeed, well <u>before</u> the end of the sales period, firms
will begin to sense that something is going wrong--that
their goods are <u>not</u> selling as <u>fast</u> as they had planned.
This disappointing rate of sales causes the eventual
surplus.

The Case of a Market Shortage

So far we have seen two possible pricing out-
comes--one, the happy market-clearing price ($8 here),
the second, the too-high price ($11) which caused the
surplus. Now we come to a third possibility: the <u>too-
low</u> price which results in what is technically known as
the <u>shortage</u> or "excess demand." This is illustrated by
the $5 price in Figure 20. At this lower price, the Qd
will, of course, be greater than at $8 or $11, but since
the Qs being offered is still the same amount X, the
result is that Qd exceeds the Qs at the lower $5 price.
The size of the shortage is shown by the quantity XB,

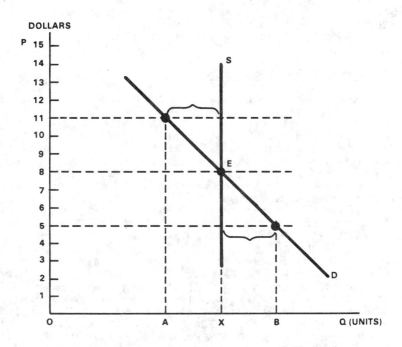

FIGURE 20:
SURPLUSES, SHORTAGES, AND SELLING PRICES.

187

exactly the horizontal distance by which the Qd exceeds the Qs at the price of $5.

Again, let us be clear why the shortage emerges. The reason is that, at $5, the goods are under-priced-- set below the market-clearing level. This is readily apparent when we compare this outcome with the market-clearing that occurs at the happy price of $8, and the surplus caused by the $11 price. Having set a too-low price, firms will discover that they will have sold out well before the end of the planned sales period. Indeed, they would very early have noticed that their goods were selling at a faster rate than anticipated, which could even make them confident of selling out their supply before the end of the planned sales period.

"Shortages" vs. "Scarcity"

At this point, we should digress to explain the important distinction between a "shortage" and "scarcity." In these days of politically-generated shortages in oil and other major commodities, it is important to avoid confusing these two terms. Scarcity, as we saw in Chapters I and II, is and always has been a natural condition of human existence--we live in a world which does not have enough resources to satisfy everyone's wants. As far as economics is concerned, scarcity can never be eliminated--it can only be alleviated. And the only way to alleviate scarcity is to increase production. It is quite otherwise with shortages.

When it comes to shortages, we are dealing with a purely man-made mess, which can be caused by either of the following actions: (1) by setting a too-low price for a given quantity supplied (as we saw in Figure 20, when a price of $5 was set for the quantity X supplied), or (2) by reducing the Qs on the market while keeping prices at former levels. We are already acquainted with the first case; the latter case is best illustrated by means of Figure 21, which is indeed applicable to OPEC's oil embargo or supply restriction.

How to Create a Shortage

Let us see how Figure 21 illustrates the OPEC policy of restricting oil supply and raising oil prices in order to increase their total receipts (TR) and profits. Assume that the pre-restriction situation is

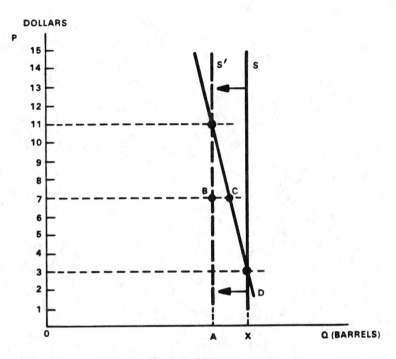

FIGURE 21:
SUPPLY RESTRICTION AND SHORTAGES.

depicted by the quantity-supplied (X) and the price ($3). Clearly the $3 price had been clearing the market of the quantity X. Now comes the restriction of oil supply, indicated by the shift of S to S' (i.e., from quantity X to quantity A). With this also comes the price increase. But then the question arises: How high can OPEC raise the P? Our diagram tells us that with the given D schedule and the new reduced S' schedule, P can go up to $11, at which there is a new intersection of D and S', indicating a new market-clearing P. Not only can P go up to $11, but TR, too, will apparently increase, because (here's the rub!) the D is inelastic.

Now, where does the shortage come in? The shortage occurs as soon as suppliers fail to raise P all the way to $11 at the same time that supply is reduced to S'. That is to say, if P stays at $3 or remains at any P below $11, a shortage will emerge! How? First let us see what would happen if the P is held down to $3. Clearly at the $3 price, the Qd will be at X, but since Qs had been reduced to quantity A, there will emerge an excess demand (i.e., shortage) amounting to AX. Now, what would happen if suppliers let P rise to, say, $7? At a $7 price, the Qd will drop to quantity C, but since Qs had been cut back to quantity B, there will still be a shortage amounting to the quantity BC, albeit a smaller one than AX. Only the $11 price would be sufficiently high to erase the shortage and clear the market.

To conclude this digression: Regardless of whether the shortage is initiated by (1) setting a too-low price for a given Qs, or by (2) reducing the Qs but keeping the price below the market-clearing level, the underlying cause of the shortage is, in effect, the same: the selling price is below the market-clearing level and therefore too low in the given demand and supply situation. It follows, therefore, that the shortage could be liquidated in jig time simply by raising the price to a new market-clearing level. Conversely, so long as the price is kept below the new market-clearing level, the shortage is sure to persist.

Surpluses and Shortages are Man-made

Now, to return to our main line. The reader may think it very curious, indeed, that one and the same quantity X supplied by firms could generate three different outcomes--either "shortage," "surplus," or "market-clearing"--simply by setting three different

prices. But this is precisely the point: for any given
quantity of goods offered on the market there is only
one market-clearing price--indeed, there never need be a
"surplus" or "shortage" so long as price is set at the
market-clearing level.

        To put it another way: In a world of universal
scarcity there is no such thing as an absolute surplus;
"surplus" can emerge only relative to a price being set
too high. Similarly, when it comes to shortages; scarcity is something that always exists, but shortages
arise only relative to a price being set too low.   To
repeat: For any given Qs on the market, a market-
clearing price is the only thing needed to avoid a
surplus or shortage.   Whereas "scarcity" is the natural
condition of human existence, "shortages" and "surpluses" are primarily man-made conditions.

The Planned Sales Period

        This brings us to an important question: Which
of the three possible outcomes--surplus, shortage, or
market clearing--would the firm prefer to experience?
Before we answer this, we should first recall something
about decision-making in the ex-ante.   In Chapter IV we
saw that the firm faces the prime task of determining
the selling price and the quantity of production that
will enable it to realize the desired profit rate--
a task made all the more difficult because of the uncertainty of consumers' demand and the competitive
environment. Hence, the firm is incapable of knowing in
advance exactly what the market-clearing price will be.
In addition to ex-ante ignorance, we should note a few
things about our concept, the "planned sales period,"
used several times in the preceding analysis.

        The planned sales period (PSP) is that period of
time by the end of which the firm expects to sell out
the quantity supplied to the market.   The PSP will vary
from product to product, firm to firm, and season to
season.   Since no firm has an exact pre-knowledge as to
precisely how long it will take to sell out its supply--
let alone whether it will be able to realize its price
and profit expectations--it can only make a best estimate as to the desired length of the sales period and
the rate of sales progress.   It can then compare the
actual rate of sales with the planned, desired rate, and
gauge its sales progress accordingly.

Indeed, given the firm's natural state of incomplete knowledge of market demand—that is, its ignorance of those market parameters affecting selling prices, quantity-demanded, and profit rates—the only alternative guide for measuring the rate of its sales progress is its PSP. The PSP at least enables it to judge whether or not sales are moving at the desired rate—that is, the rate that reflects the firm's best judgment, inadequate as it may be. From this experience—and this experience alone—the firm will be able to learn lessons as to what went right and what went wrong, and improve its ability to plan the next round of production and the next selling program. With this background we can now undertake the task of evaluating the surplus, shortage, and market-clearing outcomes.

Evaluating the Surplus Case

Let us first evaluate the surplus case. Remember: a surplus is the result of a too-high price, which reduces the Qd relative to the Qs. Indeed, even before the end of the PSP the firm will have noticed that its goods are not moving as fast as anticipated. Clearly, the surplus is a disappointing outcome in that the firm must slash its too-high price sufficiently—for example, to $8 in Figure 20—in order to sell out the unsold quantities under the given demand condition. This means that profits will be less than anticipated, and even losses may be incurred.

Furthermore, the firm will face a difficult decision as to how to adjust to the revealed market condition. Specifically, for the next time around, it must either cut its price—and hence its profit rate and/or cost of production—or produce less at the higher price. Either alternative may involve difficult adjustments for the firm, as we will see below.

Evaluating the Shortage Case

What about the shortage case? If you recall, this is the case where the Qd exceeds the Qs because the firm set a too-low price. As a consequence, the firm discovers that its goods sell at a faster rate than expected, so that its supply sells out even before the end of PSP. At first glance this seems to be a happy outcome, not marred by any disappointment. After all, the firm manages to sell out its total Qs at the planned price--and faster than it expected, to boot. What could be better? Upon close examination, however, we find reason for disappointment: the firm could have done even better. Let us see how.

If we assume firms prefer greater profits to smaller profits, it is clear from Figure 20 that, other things being equal, our firms could have sold out the same quantity X at a _higher_ price than $5--indeed, at any price up to $8 they would have been able to clear the market. The reason is that with the given state of demand, any price up to, but not including, $8 induces a Qd greater than the Qs at that price. That is, any price between $5 and $8 would have induced sales to run at a faster clip than expected, and supplies would have sold out before the end of the PSP. Since any price higher than $5 (up to $8) would have meant greater profits, the firms clearly missed a preferred opportunity by selling out at only $5.

The Lack of Advance Knowledge

It is clear that if the firms had _known_ _in_ _advance_ that their initial prices were too low, they _would_ surely have set _prices_ _higher_ than $5 in order to earn higher profits. Having failed to do so, they end up with profits being smaller than otherwise. And the firms have no one else to blame but themselves; they could have detected very early that their goods were selling at a faster rate than anticipated. Then and there they could have begun to increase their prices and watch carefully the extent to which the higher prices slowed down the rate of sales. If worse came to worse, they could always revert back to the $5 price they were happy to start with. Other things being equal, their failure to take advantage of market demand is surely a disappointing experience.

Another disappointment stems from the fact that the firms could have sold a _larger_ _quantity_ (OB) instead of the smaller quantity OX originally produced. That is to say, even if the firms had good reason not to raise their prices above $5--seeking public goodwill, say, or seeking to break into the market by means of this low price--it is clear they underestimated the _quantity_ demanded at the $5 price. This means their sales period ended with some unsatisfied customers--those who came to buy only after the bargain-priced supply had already been snatched up. If only the firms had known _in_ _advance_

that at the $5 price they could have sold quantity OB
instead of only OX, they would not be as disappointed as
they are now. And who knows if the disappointed customers will ever come back again to see if a new supply
is available?

Guessing the Right Price

        Compared to the surplus and shortage cases, the
market-clearing case clearly must be judged as the preferred outcome: it alone has no disappointment attached
to it. That is to say, things work out just as planned
whenever firms sell out their supply by the end of the
PSP. This is proof they have estimated the market-
demand situation perfectly--picking exactly the right
price for selling out the given quantity supplied. All
of this brings us to another key question: If market-
clearing is the preferred objective of the firm--because
it marks the perfect meshing of ex-post sales experience
with ex-ante pricing and production plans--what prevents
the firm from setting a market-clearing price every
time? What prevents the firm from realizing in the ex-
post its profit-maximizing plans of the ex-ante?   What
kind of knowledge would the firm require in order to be
able to avoid the less-preferred outcomes of surplus or
shortage?

Uncertainty and Market Information

        The answer to this question was, in essence,
already given in earlier chapters.   In the real world,
the perfect or complete information required by the firm
in order to realize its maximizing goals is simply not
available to it. Even trial-and-error experience, where-
by the firm learns the extent to which it has overpriced
or underpriced a particular product at a particular
time, does not provide information of a lasting quality.
Lessons learned from yesterday's sales experience do not
guarantee success for tomorrow's sales. The reason lies
in the uncertainty and unpredictability of changing
market demand: there are continuous shifts in demand
schedules (Chapter VI) as well as changes in price
elasticity of demand (Chapter VII).

        Only in a world in which market demand never
changes--in which tastes, incomes, and expectations are
constant, and demand schedules do not shift or change
their degree of elasticity--only in such a purely

imaginary world would today's demand be the same as yesterday's, and tomorrow's the same as today's. Only in such a make-believe world of no change could firms reasonably expect that tomorrow's P and Qd would be a mere repetition of today's. In such a world of repetition and certainty there would be no obstacles to acquiring perfect knowledge of the market demand--and trial-and-error search for the right price and quantity would become unnecessary! But a world of certainty is a pure figment of the imagination, useful only for the purpose of explaining why in the real world perfect knowledge is impossible.

Market as a Feedback Mechanism

It follows, therefore, that in the face of changing market demand, it is not logical to assume that firmis it logical to believe that any other group of people possesses such complete information, be they economists, consumer advisers, or politicians. The best that the firm can do is to arrive at approximate knowledge of the market--knowledge that reduces the areas and degrees of its ignorance. Approximate knowledge is the only kind of knowledge available to man--obtainable only from daily trial-and-error in the market--and trial-and-error experience is the only kind available.

Thus we can now see that the occurrence of surpluses and shortages is precisely the market's way of informing the firm that its plan has fallen short of the mark, and that it must henceforth make adjustments in price and/or quantities the next time around. In a moment, we will analyze these adjustments to market surpluses or shortages. Suffice it to emphasize here that the market is the only feedback instrument available for signalling to the firm that its price is not right, and that it had better change it.

Guessing the Right Quantity to Supply

This brings us to another crucial aspect. Not only does the market provide feedback signals to the firm when the selling price is not right, but it also sends up signals when the quantity supplied is not right --signals that likewise take the form of surpluses or shortages. Decisions by firms can result in surplus or shortage not only when they set prices too high or too low, but when they produce quantities that are too large or too small, relative to the selling price. This can be readily seen with the aid of Figure 22.

Now, in Figure 22, it is assumed that all firms are selling the same product at the same price of $8. On the other hand, it is assumed that different firms may produce different quantities. For instance, the market outcome is vastly different when firms produce excessive amounts--on the "surplus" scale OB, say-- compared to when they produce the relatively modest quantities on the "shortage" scale OA. There is also a third possibility--when firms produce on the scale of OX, which we will see is the market-clearing case. Let us examine each of these cases in detail.

When Firms Produce "Too Much"

First, why does the supply schedule Sb in Figure 22 represent a surplus case? Because the firms have produced a quantity (OB) that exceeds the quantity-demanded (OX) at the common $8 price--clearly they have overestimated the Qd at this price. As a consequence, they discover fairly early that their product is not selling as fast as expected, and at the end of their planned selling period they are stuck with a pile of unsold goods.

Had the firms been equipped with perfect know-ledge of the demand situation, this surplus could have been avoided in either of two ways. First, the firms could have offered the smaller quantity OX (Schedule Sx). The OX quantity would have cleared the market, since at the $8 price the Qd and Qs are exactly equal, as indicated by the intersection of demand (D) and supply (Sx). Alternatively, the firms could have avoided surpluses by selling the quantity OB at the lower price of $5, which, indeed, is a market-clearing price for the given quantity supplied: at this price the Qd (OB) is exactly equal to the Qs (OB). In the absence of perfect knowledge, however, the firms were ignorant of both the market-clearing price (given the Qs) and the market-clearing quantity supplied (given the P).

196

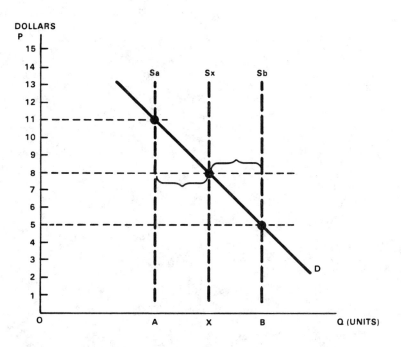

FIGURE 22:
SURPLUS, SHORTAGE, AND QUANTITIES SUPPLIED.

When Firms Produce "Too Little"

Next, why does the supply schedule Sa in Figure 22 represent a shortage case? Because while the firms are producing quantity OA, the Qd at the price of $8 exceeds the quantity being supplied by the amount AX. It is apparent that the firms undershot the mark: they underestimated the demand at the $8 price. And they could very early have spotted signs of the impending shortage : they could have noticed that the actual rate of sales was exceeding the expected rate of sales.

Had firms known in advance exactly where the market demand schedule was located, they could have resorted to more profitable alternatives. For one thing, they could have planned to produce the larger quantity OX (instead of OA), which would have cleared the market at the original $8 price. (This can be seen by the intersection of the Sx schedule and the D schedule at the $8 price.) On the other hand, the original output of OA (schedule Sa) could have been released at the higher price of $11 (instead of $8), and still clear the market, since at $11 the Qs would have been exactly matched by the Qd.

A Backward Glance

Before we proceed to examine how firms can adjust to the market's feedback signals--that is, to surpluses, shortages, or market clearings--we should briefly review the ground we have covered.

For any given quantity supplied by the firm, the problem becomes one of setting the right price--the price that will clear the market within the planned sales period (PSP). Otherwise, if it sets the P too high or too low, the result will be either a surplus or a shortage, respectively. Similarly, for any given price at which the firm wants to sell, the problem becomes one of gauging the right quantity to produce in order to clear the market. Otherwise, if it produces too much or too little, it will end up facing a surplus or shortage, respectively.

Also, for convenience, we will hereafter refer to a surplus or a shortage as a disequilibrium type of outcome. A "disequilibrium" simply means that, for the time being, the firm has failed to achieve its market-clearing or equilibrium objective within its PSP, and that it therefore faces a decision: What to do about disequilibrium?

III. How Firms Adjust to Market Conditions

By now it should be obvious that the firm's adjustments to market disequilibria can involve changes in its selling price (P) and/or quantity-supplied (Qs). Altogether, the firm can make three possible adjustments: (1) change its selling P, or (2) change its Qs, or (3) make a combination of changes in both P and Qs. Thus, in response to disequilibrium, the firm might institute a cut (or increase) in P, or a reduction (or increase) in Qs, or some combination of changes in both P and Qs.

Current Adjustments vs. the Next Time Around

Now, all of these adjustments can take place in either of two different time phases. One type of adjustment may be termed a current adjustment. As soon as the firm senses that its current sales are deviating from the planned path--that they are progressing at a faster or slower rate than planned--the firm can immediately change its P and/or Qs in order to improve sales or minimize disappointment before the end of the current PSP.

The second type of adjustment is not made currently but is delayed until the next time phase--the one following the current sales period--which we can term the next-time-around (NTA) adjustment. In this case the firm does not make any current adjustments: for one reason or another, the firm decides to do nothing now about the discrepancy between the actual rate of sales and the planned rate. Instead, it rides out the current period and reserves its P and Qs adjustments for the NTA.

Firms Cannot Rest on Their Laurels

None of this implies that an NTA adjustment in P and Qs is required only in response to a disequilibrium outcome. That is, it does not imply that a happy market-clearing experience will never induce the firm to make a subsequent NTA adjustment. In free competitive markets no firm can afford to rest on its laurels--even when it

199

enjoys a market-clearing experience. Market conditions are in constant flux, and changing demand is a constant source of uncertainty. Yesterday's success cannot guarantee tomorrow's success. Successful market-clearing is due more to good fortune--a happy coincidence of objective market conditions and entrepreneurial plans made by the firm--than to any precise foreknowledge of market conditions.

For example, if a firm succeeds in clearing the market as planned, should it merely repeat by producing the same Qs at the same P as before? Can it simply rely on market demand remaining the same as before? Or must the firm be alert to any possible shift in D, or change in elasticity of D? Clearly, in a dynamic changing market, the firm must be on constant alert. Thus it makes no difference whether the firm ends its PSP with a surplus, shortage, or market-clearing--it will always have to face the important entrepreneurial decision for the NTA: What should it decide for its next P and Qs?

Making Adjustments to a Surplus

We are now ready to examine the types of adjustments the firm can make in response to a surplus or shortage. In the case of a surplus, it makes no difference whether it was caused by (a) overpricing a given supply, or (b) overproducing at a given price--the analysis runs along similar lines. For the overpricing case, refer to Figure 20: there we see that the $11 price is too high for the given supply OX, hence the surplus of AX. For the overproduction case, see Figure 22: there it turns out that the $8 price is too high for the supply OB, hence the surplus of XB. In both instances, the basic cause of the surplus may be viewed as overpricing the given supply, or overproducing at the given price. Both instances turn out to be merely two sides of the same coin--an overpriced supply. With this understanding, let us focus on Figure 22 for convenience.

Now, what can the firm do in response to the surplus XB in Figure 22? If the firm spots the surplus in its incipient stages, during the current sales period --as soon as sales fail to progress at the expected rate--it can decide then and there to slash its current P from $8 in order to step up the rate of sales. However, so long as the reduced P remains above the market-clearing P of $5, some surplus would remain at the end of the PSP. In order to sell out the last unsold unit,

200

the P would eventually have to be cut to the $5 level. On the other hand, if the firm decides to avoid any P-cutting until the bitter end of the PSP, even then the same truth holds: P must at last be cut to $5 in order to clear out the remaining unsold units.

Next-Time-Around Adjustments

So much for current adjustments to the unfolding surplus. What about next-time-around adjustments? What lessons can the firm learn from its bitter experience and apply to its NTA production and pricing programs? One option is to produce the same quantity as before, which means a repetition of supply schedule Sb. However, this would call for a lower price of $5 as against the former opening P of $8.

This raises the relevant question: Can the firm manage to cut P to $5 without squeezing its profit margin? That is to say, can it also cut its costs as well as its P? This brings up a touchy practical problem: since wages are usually the major component of costs, can labor resistance to cuts in wage-rates prevent firms from cutting costs? If costs cannot be cut, will the firm be willing to accept a cut in profit margin?

Cutbacks in Production

A second option is for the firm to retain its former opening P of $8 but, instead, reduce its Qs to OX (schedule Sx), which, too, would be a market-clearing program. This would obviously call for a reduced rate of production and supply. Assuming that the reduced rate of production does not significantly affect the cost-per-unit of product, this cutback in output would not affect the margin of profit between selling P and cost-per-unit of product. Nevertheless, cutbacks in production could also mean layoffs and reduced employment, which may be as distasteful to workers as cuts in wage-rates.

The first two options give rise to a third option--a combination of both price and production adjustments in the appropriate direction--that is, a combination of price-cut and production cutback. More specifically, P could be cut to somewhere between $8 and $5, while Qs would be cut to somewhere between OX and OB (i.e., between schedules OX and OB). Technically speaking, any "dot" on the demand schedule in the segment located between the $5 and $8 P would yield a P and Qs combination capable of satisfying this adjustment.

Withholding Supply and Speculation

Since price-cutting can be bitter medicine, the firm may prefer a more palatable alternative: avoid any P-cuts but, instead, withdraw the unsold quantities from the market and withhold them until demand increases sufficiently to clear the market at the original price of $8. (Technically speaking, the expected increase in demand would be depicted in Figure 22 by a shift of D to the right, to the point where it intersects Sb at the $8 price.) However, withholding of supply from the market involves speculation; it is based on the expectation that the future holds a desirable market change in store. In the present case, the firm speculates that future demand will be sufficiently greater than today's; this would make it preferable to sell tomorrow at the desired $8 price rather than to sell out today at a lower price.

However, the withholding of supply for speculative purposes is not without cost. One speculative cost is the cost of warehousing the withheld quantities. Second, there is the uncertainty of how long the firm will have to wait until demand increases sufficiently. In the worst case, demand may not increase at all. In any event, the fact remains that withheld supplies constitute unsold products, and until demand increases sufficiently, the firm is haunted by a dilemma: to withhold or to sell out at slashed prices. Which will minimize its losses?

Which of these options should the firm resort to? Only the firm itself can decide which course is best. Economics as such is not capable of foretelling which course of action would be taken by any particular firm in a given circumstance. All it can say is that whatever adjustment the firm decides upon will be a maximizing decision, albeit in the given circumstances designed to minimize losses resulting from the surplus.

Making Adjustments to a Shortage

We now turn from the surplus case to the case of

202

shortages. How can the firm adjust to a shortage outcome? (The shortage is depicted in Figure 22 by the Sa
schedule and the $8 price, which together yield a
shortage amounting to AX.) In contrast to the surplus
case, the shortage generally poses fewer difficulties or
dilemmas for the firm. Other things being equal, a firm
would rather sell its product at a faster rate than at a
slower rate. Nevertheless, the firm does face a
tantalizing decision as soon as it notices that its
sales are moving at a faster rate than planned. It then
realizes that its goods will be sold out well before the
end of its PSP--and that there will remain unsatisfied
customers as long as the price is kept at $8 while Qs is
not increased. Clearly, the firm had underestimated
market demand, which turned out to be OX, whereas it had
produced only OA. What type of current adjustment
should it now make?

For one thing, firms could decide to immediately
raise their current price--indeed, according to Figure
22, they could raise P to $11 and still sell out their
total supply of Sa. But would they feel entirely at
ease raising the P in order to take advantage of market
demand being greater than anticipated? Would they feel
uneasy or hesitant about bucking widespread social
pressures and taboos against "charging what the traffic
would bear"?

On the other hand, if they decide not to raise
their P--in order to curry public goodwill, say--they
would be foregoing an opportunity to increase their
profits. Could they nevertheless compensate by stepping
up the rate of supply by dipping into inventories in
their warehouses? In this way they could release increased Qs to the market, reduce the number of unsatisfied customers, and increase their total profits. But
would this dipping into inventories be enough to quench
the unsatisfied demand?

Utilization of Existing Facilities

If firms do not raise prices, and inventories
are depleted before the shortage is eliminated, they may
still have an ace up their sleeves: more intensive
utilization of their existing productive facilities.

It is not at all unusual for plants to be operating at less than "full capacity." Indeed, by design,
most plants are built to scales larger than would be

203

required by the average rate of sales anticipated by the
firm. This oversizing of plant provides elbow room for
the firm--a margin of extra productive capacity--which
it can lean on if and when demand proves to be larger
than anticipated. The shortage case here calls forth
such an instance. If a shortage arises while firms are
operating at, say, only 75 or 80 percent of rated capacity, then they have a margin of capacity that can be
utilized to increase their Qs in the NTA.

     The problem here, however, involves a crucial
economic fact: if the plant is already at a high rate
of utilization (say, 85 percent or more), a further
increase in the rate of plant utilization would be
associated with an increased cost for each unit produced. The reasons for this increase in unit or average
cost (AC) are multifold.

     For one thing, the extra production load may
involve overtime labor at extra overtime rates of pay.
Also, there may be additional expenses due to breakdowns
in overworked equipment and the resultant bottlenecks.
Then, additional workers may have to be hired, but since
they are not likely to be as efficient as the regular
labor force, their labor will not be as productive and
their output will cost more per unit. All this adds to
the average cost of the product, with the consequence
that the firm has to ask for a higher price for its
product.

Price Inducement and Imports

     Even with a more intensive utilization of
existing productive capacity, the stepped-up rate of
output may not be enough to overcome the shortage. That
is to say, the industry supply schedule may not be able
to shift enough to the right, to where it coincides with
Sx in Figure 22. If so, as long as the Qd continues to
exceed the Qs and the shortage persists at the existing
selling price of $8, this price would be under pressure
to rise.

     As a matter of fact, this rise in P is precisely
what the doctor would order: it induces firms to step
up their rate of plant utilization since it compensates
for the increase in average cost of output. Otherwise,
the necessary margin of relief might have to come from
imports of goods from other countries. But the flow of
imports depends essentially on the ability of foreign

204

producers to sell at prices competitive with domestic producers, unimpeded by legal trade barriers such as tariffs and quotas.

The Next-Time Around Problem

Whatever the firms decide to do by way of cur-rent adjustment, they are still faced with a next-time-around adjustment. Here the problem facing the firm is no less ticklish than in the previous case. One option we have already seen: raise the price next time to $11 while producing the same amounts as before. Assuming that demand will stay the same, the total supply will still clear the market even at the higher P. After all, that's what the D schedule in Figure 22 says: at any price less than $11 the Qd will exceed the Qs. Hence, as long as P is not raised to $11, the firms will be fostering a shortage. Now, the main problem with rais-ing price is whether firms can either (a) suppress their collective fear of the public wrath against charging what the traffic will bear, or (b) make public opinion more hospitable to the idea that firms have a right to charge whatever price the public is evidently willing to pay.

Increasing Supply by Capital Investment

If firms prefer to leave the price as is, at $8, they can resort to another NTA adjustment: increase the Qs from schedule Sa to Sx. This would enable firms to eliminate the shortage by an expansion of supply. The increased number of units sold would result in increased total profits even though the profit rate per unit sold would remain the same as before: since the P remains unchanged at $8--and we are assuming the cost per unit of output is also unchanged despite the higher rate of production--the price spread between P and average costs remains the same as before. (Review Chapter IV on the "price spread.")

The main problem with increasing the Qs while holding P the same is that the expansion of output will involve capital investment of the type discussed in Chapter IV. As we saw there, expansion of output might require increased scale of plant operations, which, in turn, involves acquisition of additional machinery and space as well as hiring more labor. These expenditures, in turn, would require additional financing from

internal sources--such as profits and depreciation al-
lowances--and/or external funds from the money and
capital markets.

Once Again: Uncertainty and Risk

Underlying the investment decision, of course,
is the assumption that the firms know exactly by how
much their Qs should be increased.   But such an assumption is too glib.   It is one thing to play around with
diagrams like Figure 22, from which it is readily seen
that Qs should be increased from OA to OX, which would
still clear the market. But in the real world it is not
so easy to discover where the new market-clearing supply
schedule lies. Uncertainty of demand makes it virtually
impossible for firms to predict the location and slope
of D in the NTA period, and therefore creates considerable risk in the investment in enlarged productive capacity.   In any event, the fact remains that as long as
the Qs is not increased sufficiently, the shortage will
persist--which is, again, the market's way of informing
firms that sales opportunities still remain.

As we conclude this portion of the chapter, let
us pause once again to see how we can reach some simple
conclusions despite the possibly confusing details of
the complex analysis.   After all is said and done, the
following simple truth remains: however the firm
decides to adjust to uncertainty of market demand, this
adjustment always boils down to determining, as best it
can, that particular combination of P and Qs that will
clear the market. Still, so long as the market fitfully
turns up surpluses or shortages, the firm's adjustment
problems remain.   Indeed, even when it succeeds in
clearing the market as planned, such success is but a
fleeting fortunate outcome--the firm has no cause to
rest on its laurels in a world of seething uncertainty.

IV. The Law of Market Price

We are now at the point where we can assert the
key proposition of this chapter, the Law of Market
Price: in a free market unhampered by government price-
fixing or other market interventions, the selling prices
set by firms will tend to move toward the market-
clearing ("equilibrium") level, where the quantity supplied equals the quantity demanded at that price.

As a corollary to the law of market price we should add: any other price, higher or lower than the market-clearing price, would cause disequilibrium situations such as surpluses and shortages. Since these outcomes would be considered by firms as less than optimal compared with market-clearing prices, firms in the free, competitive market will be motivated to avoid or minimize them by appropriate price and quantity adjustments.

More on the Free Market

The free market will be discussed in detail in Chapters X and XI. Here it will suffice to note the following. In addition to the introductory remarks at the start of this chapter, the term "free market" includes the following two characteristics about firms. One is that firms are motivated primarily to make profits (and avoid losses), and to increase their total wealth in the interests of stockholders, while keeping non-monetary goals to a minimum. Thus, we exclude non-profit organizations from this context.

The second feature is this: firms have to make it strictly on their own--without paternalistic protection from government in the form of minimum prices, subsidies, bailouts, tariffs, or guaranteed markets. This implies that firms must earn their profits purely by their own ability to cater successfully to consumers, and that they will suffer losses for failure to meet consumers demands satisfactorily. As a consequence, firms will be strongly motivated to maximize profits and minimize losses.

"Supply Equals Demand"?

Next, let us be technically clear about the meaning of market-clearing price: it is the price at which "Qs equals Qd"--which is not the same as saying "supply equals demand." These are two totally different expressions. The latter expression is unquestionably the more popular, especially among people who are not sophisticated in economics. Yet, it is simply not correct to say, "S equals D" in the present context.

To be precise, "S equals D" literally is an absurdity. As stated, it implies that both S and D schedules are superimposed upon each other, which in turn means that at every price the Qs equals the Qd. This is an impossibility: ex-post supply schedules are vertical, whereas demand schedules slope downward from left to right; this permits only one point (i.e., the intersection point) at which the Qs equals Qd. That is, there is only one price at which there can be equality of Qs and Qd and market-clearing; at all other prices there is discrepancy between Qs and Qd, not equality. In contrast, the statement "S equals D" implies that, since Qs equals Qd at every price, there is market clearing at every price! Clearly an impossibility.

The Tendency to Market-Clearing

Also notable above is our statement that selling prices will tend toward the market-clearing level, and need not hit the mark every time the firm sets it price. Despite the firms' lack of perfect knowledge of D and S conditions, they are motivated to seek market-clearing outcomes and avoid disequilibrium outcomes.

For one thing, there is the economic incentive to maximize profits. As we have seen, surplus and shortage outcomes cause the firm less profit than otherwise under the given D and S conditions. Thus, in the case of a surplus, the firm will have to slash its P below the planned level, whereas in the case of a shortage the firm has missed an opportunity for greater profits by setting its P too low or producing less than the market was ready to absorb.

On the other side of this coin is the fact that, of the three possible market outcomes--market-clearing, surplus, or shortage--only market-clearing outcomes validate the firm's expectations and strengthen its confidence in its ability to judge market conditions. In contrast, surpluses and shortages are truly disappointments--sources of regret and diminished confidence.

What About Disequilibrium?

This brings us to the word optimal, which characterizes the market-clearing outcome. "Optimal" signifies that the firm's ex-post experience most nearly approximates its ex-ante expectations, and, hence, minimizes disappointment and regret. In effect, therefore, the law of market price says that, as long as firms are motivated to optimize the relation between ex-post

experience and ex-ante plans, selling prices will tend
to be market-clearing rather than disequilibrating.

Before we proceed, we should note that not all
disequlibrium outcomes can be blamed on the incomplete
knowledge of the firm and its planners. As we will see
in the next part, surpluses and shortages also occur as
a result of independent shifts in market demand and
supply--that is, demand shifts caused by changes in
tastes, income, population, or price expectations (see
Chapter VI), and supply shifts caused by the vagaries of
nature (e.g., bad crops caused by bad weather) or government policies (e.g., wheat price-fixing or oil supply
restriction). While such disequilibria are not the
direct result of decisions by the firm, they nevertheless exert significant impacts on profits and sales
opportunities, and the manner in which the firm responds
to them can determine its prosperity and growth.

Government Interventions and
Non-Profit Pricing

As we have indicated, because of uncertainty and
ignorance, firms will experience shortages and surpluses
about as often as market-clearing. In a free market,
such disequilibrium outcomes would tend to be short-
lived or temporary. However, if and when the surpluses
and shortages become persistent or long-lasting--a situation thoroughly inconsistent with free-market condi-
tions--the cause must be sought elsewhere: (1) in
government price-fixing or other interventions, and (2)
non-profit pricing policies. This is not the place for
a detailed analysis of government policies affecting the
free market; they will be briefly discussed in Chapter
X. "Non-profit" pricing by private organizations such
as colleges, theater companies, and civic groups will be
discussed here briefly.

Non-profit organizations include groups like the
Rose Festival Association--which, with its affiliated
colleges, produces the annual Rose Parade and Rose Bowl
game--as well as opera associations, and virtually all
fraternal and religious organizations. These organizations differ basically from profit-seeking corporations
in that they, for various reasons, do not seek to sell
their products or services at market-clearing prices--
prices that would maximize their profits and wealth.
Indeed, they characteristically underprice their goods
and services, causing inevitable shortages.

Why Blame the Ticket Scalper?

How can <u>non-profit</u> underpricing by a group like the Rose Bowl Association cause a shortage? Imagine, as in Figure 23, that there is a given supply of football tickets (S) for seats at mid-field, and that the demand for these tickets is great enough to clear the supply (OX) at an $8 price. Now, if the Rose Bowl people decide to sell these tickets at $5 instead, knowing full well they could easily sell out at a much higher price, they are clearly inviting a shortage--shown by the excess demand XB--with all of its familiar symptoms: excessively rapid rate of sales, long waiting lines of customers (queues), and black-market sales by ticket scalpers (since it is illegal to resell tickets at a price higher than paid for). By design, the Rose Bowl people had underpriced their product and, of their own account, brought on the shortage.

Indeed, the much maligned ticket scalper is merely rushing into a good thing when he sees it. The profits that he siphons off for himself could as easily have gone to the Rose Bowl group. Ironically, so-called "non-profit" pricing turns out to be an excellent source of profits for the speculators! Would our imaginary Rose Bowl people but realize that <u>they</u>--by their policy of underpricing--and not the ticket scalper, are responsible for inducing illegal speculation in tickets, they might question the wisdom of their "non-profit" pricing policies. It is proverbial in economics that whenever you spot illegal <u>ticket-scalping</u> or <u>black-market</u> activities, you can smell an underpriced product. It should also be noted that government rent controls and similar price-fixing policies, that characteristically <u>under-price</u> the product, are a prime cause of illegal <u>black</u> markets.

Ticket Scalpers on Broadway

One more example of non-profit underpricing suffices to reinforce our point. For a long time, tickets to Broadway shows had been priced according to arbitrary, traditional, or inflexible formulas rather than by flexible adjustment to demand and supply conditions. As a consequence, it was not unusual to see tickets for different shows selling at about the same price, even though some of the shows were smash hits while others were duds. In a truly free market, prices for the former shows should have been significantly

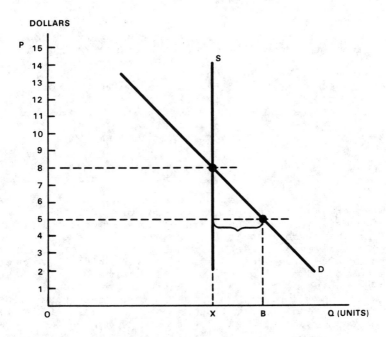

FIGURE 23:
NON-PROFIT UNDERPRICING.

211

higher than for the latter. In practice, however, even tickets to such classic Broadway smash hits as <u>South Pacific</u> and <u>My Fair Lady</u> were invariably underpriced.1

The results were inevitable. Induced shortages found ticket buyers scrambling for available tickets, while ticket scalpers, seeing a good thing in the under-priced tickets, moved in to make their profits. In some cases, dollar receipts of scalpers were about two to three times as great as box-office receipts! Indeed, even some of the managers and their box-office people were enticed by the situation and connived with scalpers for part of the latter's profits!

The bitter irony is that the theaters' hidebound adherence to underpricing, and their refusal to charge what the traffic would bear, constituted an open invita-tion to the ticket scalper to play his "evil" role. As a consequence, the profits that were diverted to ticket scalpers could have gone instead to the creative perfor-mers and professionals who made the hit show possible in the first place--the actors, musicians, authors, com-posers, lyricists, directors, and stage hands!

V. When Market Conditions Undergo Change

This final section of the chapter shows how demand-and-supply analysis helps us answer such impor-tant questions as: What kind of demand-and-supply con-ditions cause <u>changes</u> in prices? For instance, what D and S conditions enable or induce P to <u>rise</u>, or pressure P to <u>drop</u>? A related question is: If prices have been rising or declining for some time, what could have caused these <u>price</u> <u>trends</u>? Another group of questions focuses not directly on prices but on the underlying demand and supply conditions as <u>possible</u> cause of future price changes. For example, what will happen to prices and quantities if and when demand and/or supply increase or decrease?

---

[1]This section is based on Hobe Morrison, "Scalpers Gyp Legit Talent," <u>Variety</u>, Jan. 16, 1957, as reprinted in Paul A. Samuelson, Robert L. Bishop and John R. Coleman (eds.), <u>Readings in Economics</u> (3rd edition, New York: McGraw-Hill Book Co., 1958), pp. 184-188.

First, Some Diagrammatic Aspects

The analysis will be greatly facilitated by the use of diagrams showing how demand (D) and supply (S) schedules shift--that is, increase or decrease--and how these shifts cause prices to change. We have already seen in Chapter VI (Figure 10) how demand schedules can shift. Now, for the first time, we see (in Figure 24) how supply schedules can shift. Panel A shows a shift of S to the right (from S_1 to S_2), indicating an increase in S and Qs. Panel B shows the reverse happening, a decrease in S (from S_1 to S_2) and Qs.

We can now turn to the first set of questions raised above, specifically: Under which D and S conditions could prices rise? We are using the word "could" in the sense of "be able to." Thus, our question really is: Under which D and S conditions would P be able to increase? This kind of question is typical in the physical sciences, i.e., what conditions would be required in order to enable some particular event to transpire?

Enabling Prices to Rise

Imagine a market that has, up to now, been in a state of equilibrium, with supplies being cleared at the current $6 price (Figure 25). Now, along comes an increase in demand, while supply conditions remain the same as before. The increase in D in Figure 25 is shown by the rightward shift from D_1 to D_2, while the stationary supply schedule is shown by S at X. Why did demand increase? It could have been a general increase in wages and other incomes, or more intensive tastes, or some other non-price determinant of demand (see Chapter VI). For the sake of illustration, it makes no difference which it was.

Our diagram tells us immediately that the increase in D from D_1 to D_2 induces an increase in price (P) from $6 to $9. This is indicated by the new (higher) intersection point of the increased D_2 with the given S. At the $9 price the market would achieve a new market-clearing situation, in which the Qs once again equals the Qd, albeit it takes a higher price to accomplish it. Thus, higher prices will be associated with an increase in D, as long as S remains the same.

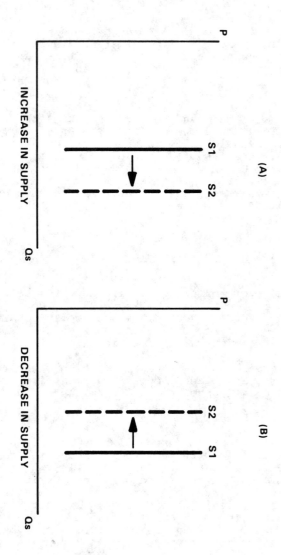

FIGURE 24:
SHIFTS IN SUPPLY SCHEDULES.

214

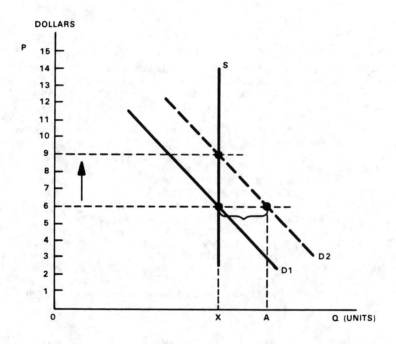

FIGURE 25:
INCREASE IN DEMAND WHILE SUPPLY
IS FIXED.

We are now able to start answering our first set of questions. For example, under which conditions would sellers be able to <u>increase</u> P? Figure 25 provides at least one answer: whenever D increases relative to S, P will be <u>able</u> to rise. Why? Because, with the increased demand, but <u>unchanged</u> supply condition, the ensuing shortage finds buyers are willing and able to buy the existing quantities X at any P between $6 and $9. That is, any P up to $9 still leaves the market unsatisfied: the Qd remains in excess of the Qs (i.e., a <u>shortage</u>). So long as there are demanders who, under the new schedule D_2, are willing and able to pay up to $9, sellers will obviously be able to ask and get the higher P.

A Decrease in Supply

Another situation in which a rise in prices would occur is presented in Figure 26. Here we see an increase in P that results from a <u>decrease in supply</u>--while demand conditions remain the same as before. The decrease in S is shown by the leftward shift in S from output X to A, while the D schedule remains fixed. Again, it is not necessary to know the specific cause of the drop in S--whether it is due to, say, work stoppages by labor unions, or the withholding of supply by producers (e.g., the OPEC oil embargo); it makes no difference for illustration purposes.

It is apparent from the diagram that the drop in supply from X to A induces an increase in P from $7 to $12. The higher P is indicated by the new (higher) intersection point of fixed D with the reduced Sa. Thus, a new market-clearing situation has been reached by means of the <u>increase in P</u> which reduces the Qd to equality with the reduced Qs (OA). Hence, a higher P would be associated with a reduction in S, so long as D remains unchanged.

Why are sellers able to raise P in the case of a reduced S? It is essentially the same <u>shortage</u> condition that arises in the case of increased D--except that now, with the reduced S but unchanged D, there are demanders who are still willing to buy the scarcer quantities (OA) at any P between $7 and $12. That is, any P below $12 would still leave Qd in <u>excess</u> of the Qs, hence shortage. As a consequence, sellers will clearly be able to ask and get higher prices--on up to $12--so long as the reduced S condition prevails and D is fixed in the previous position.

216

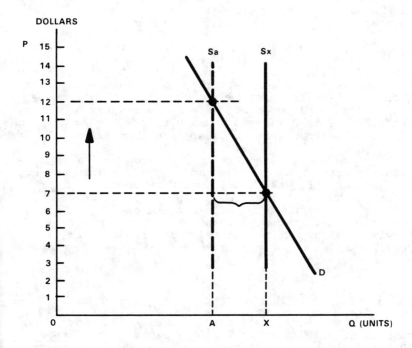

FIGURE 26:
DECREASE IN SUPPLY WHILE
DEMAND IS FIXED.

Edging Prices Downward

Let us now skip to the opposite side of the ledger and ask: Under which D and S conditions would prices be under pressure to decline? To answer this question, we go to Figure 27. Here we see that the decrease in P from $8 to $5 is spurred by a decrease in demand, while supply remains unchanged. The decrease in D is illustrated by the leftward shift from D_1 to D_2, while S remains fixed at output X. The cause of the drop in D might have been a decline in people's incomes or some other appropriate change in non-price determinants of demand, but it does not matter for our present purpose.

It is readily seen in Figure 27 that the decline in demand calls for a decrease in P from $8 to $5. The lower P, which corresponds to the new (lower) intersection point of fixed S with D_2, precisely enables the necessary market-clearing--the equality of Qd with Qs-- even though D has dropped while S remains fixed. Thus, the decrease in D is associated with a lower P, so long as the S that needs to be cleared remains fixed.

How do we explain the reduction in P associated with the drop in D? By the fact that if P were not cut, but kept at $8, the result would be an unsold surplus amounting to AX. That is, at the original $8 price, Qs exceeds the reduced Qd. Only the drop in P whittles away the initial surplus, and only when P has fallen to $5 will the surplus be entirely eliminated. If sellers really wish to clear the market of the given S, only the cut in P will do it.

An Increase in Supply

What else could cause prices to be under pressure to decline? Figure 28 tells us that an increase in supply would bring on a decrease in P. The increase in S is indicated by the rightward shift in S from quantity X to A, while the demand schedule (D) remains the same as before. The increase in S could have been caused by an expansion of productive capacity by existing firms, or by the entry of new firms.

Our diagram reveals, furthermore, that associated with the increase in S is a drop in P from $11 to $6. The lower P is indicated by the new (lower) intersection point between the fixed D and the increased Sa.

218

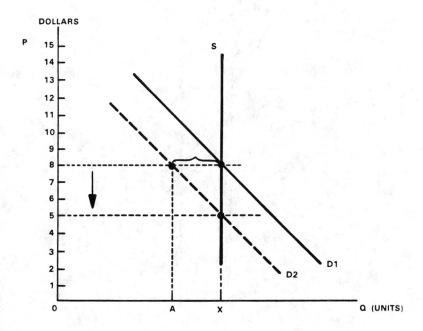

FIGURE 27:
DECREASE IN DEMAND WHILE SUPPLY IS FIXED.

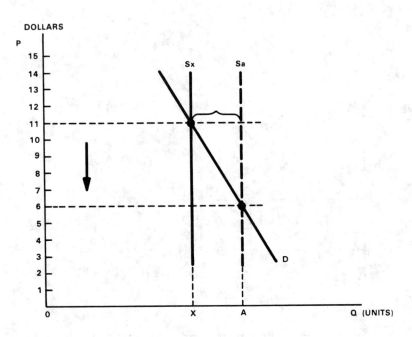

FIGURE 28:
INCREASE IN SUPPLY WHILE DEMAND IS FIXED.

It is the reduction in P which induces the Qd to increase enough to absorb the increased Qs (OA). Thus,
the reduced P is associated with the increase in S,
while demand remains the same.

By now it should be easy to explain the connection between the increase in S and the drop in P. It is
the same condition of surplus that occurs in the case of
reduced D. If P had been locked at the original $11 and
not allowed to fall, an unsold surplus (amounting to XA)
would have ensued. The $11 price would have left the
old Qd far short of the expanded Qs. Only the drop in P
induces the increase of Qd that absorbs the initial
surplus. Only when P eventually descends to $6 will Qd
be equal to the expanded Qs. Clearly, so long as suppliers wish to clear the market of the increased S, only
the reduction of P will enable them to do so.

A Brief Summary

By way of review, we can state in general that
changes in prices result from changes in demand or
supply--from shifts in the D or S schedules. Furthermore, the preceding analysis enabled us to kill two
birds with one stone. It not only showed how changes in
demand and supply conditions affect market prices, but
it also revealed a new source of disequilibrium. In
earlier parts of this chapter we saw how firms themselves could cause surpluses or shortages by overpricing
or underpricing, and by overproducing or underproducing.
Now we see that changes in the market--shifts in D or
S--can initiate surpluses or shortages.

Long-Run Decline in Prices

We are now prepared to see how demand-and-supply
analysis enables us to locate the basic forces behind
historical price trends. For instance, we know from the
history of the 19th century that the U.S. experienced a
general downward trend in prices through most of the
century. The only exceptions to the secular decline in
prices came during periods of war and economic boom.
Compared to the almost uninterrupted inflationary price
trend since World War II--in the U.S. as well as in
major Western countries--the 19th century deflationary
trend looms as a truly remarkable event. And yet it can
be readily explained by economics. How?

For clues to what could have caused the overall decline in prices, we can refer to our preceding analysis. One possible clue, diagrammed in Figure 27, is decreasing demand, which by itself could cause P to drop. But such a decrease in D cannot really serve as an explanation because D actually increased on a vast scale during the 19th century--and an increase in D itself would cause P to rise. However, since we also know that supply increased greatly during the 19th century, a more likely explanation is to be found in Figure 28: this shows prices crumbling under the pressure of expanding supply, a fact that obviously corresponds much more with 19th century experience than declining D. Indeed, the expansion of S was so great, especially after the Civil War, that it must have more than offset the effects of the long-run expansion of D. By itself, an increase in D would induce an increase in prices, but when it is accompanied by an even greater increase in S, the net effect is to cause a downward trend in P. This combination of forces is depicted in our new Figure 29.

Diagrammatic Aspects

First, notice the overall decline in prices over the long run, as indicated by the dashed line. Also notice the faster rate at which the S schedules increase compared with the increase in D schedules. For example, by the end of the second period, supply has reached the S_2 position, whereas demand has only increased to the D_2 position, so that D_2 intersects with S_2 only at a lower P. And so on. As a result of S generally running ahead of D, the successive intersection points between them come at lower and lower levels of market-clearing P. The reason is that, at previous prices, Qs exceeds Qd; hence, the faster-increasing S could be absorbed only at falling prices. Alternatively, the increased productive capacity and efficiency of the economy enable successive cuts in prices.

In Figure 29 we also have a diagrammatic novelty. For the first time, we show both demand and supply schedules shifting simultaneously. This is the more realistic case compared with the above cases in which only one schedule shifted while the other schedule stayed fixed. Indeed, this diagram illustrates a general proposition that follows from our preceding analysis: whenever the rate of expansion in S exceeds the rate of increase in D--based on increased productivity

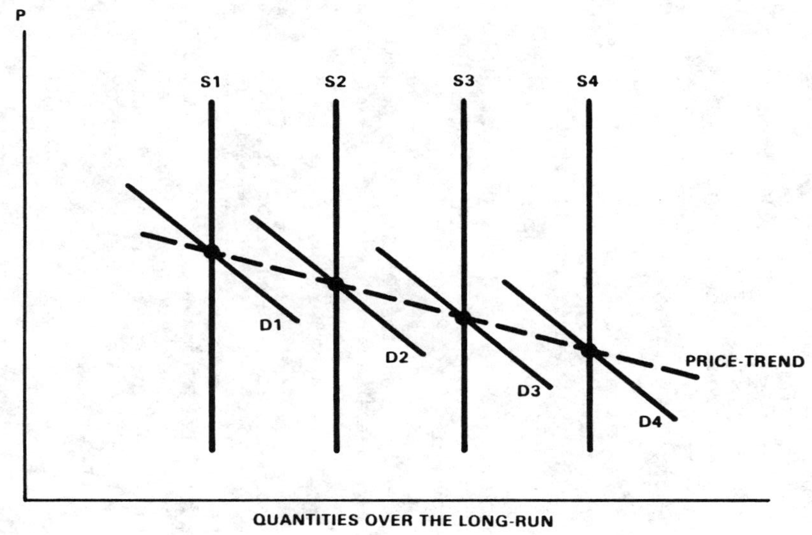

FIGURE 29:
LONG-RUN DECLINE IN PRICES.

and lower costs—prices will decline because of the pressure of excess S relative to D.

Long-Run Rise in Prices

Supply-and-demand analysis is also useful in explaining the long-run upward trend in prices, popularly referred to as inflation. For instance, ours has been called the "Age of Inflation," denoting the fact that prices have been rising more or less steadily in the U.S. and other major industrial countries since the 1930's. Indeed, inflation has become the predominant long-term problem of our times, which makes it an important subject for analysis. However, inflation would take us beyond the scope of the present work. Suffice it to say that, in spite of protestations to the contrary by many people who claim that modern inflation is something "new," and as yet without a solution—as though it were a mysterious visitation from a remote planet—the fact remains that the cause of inflation can be described simply in demand-and-supply terms. Let us now see how.

First, let us check out one possible explanation for rising prices in the U.S.—a reduction in the supply of goods. (This was diagrammed in Figure 26.) True, a continuous drop in S in the face of sustained D would, by itself, cause P to increase. But this possibility is disqualified as an explanation of modern inflation because, at least for the period since World War II, the U.S. enjoyed undoubted expansion of S (not contraction). And as we know, an increase in S by itself will cause P to drop. A more likely explanation is illustrated in Figure 25, which shows an increase of demand as the force that enabled P to increase. Indeed, demand in postwar U.S. must have increased on a scale sufficiently great as to offset the accompanying expansion of S. That is to say, D must have increased faster than S increased in order to enable or induce the overall rise in P. This combination of forces is depicted in the new Figure 30.

Diagrammatic Aspects

Again, notice first the overall rise in prices over the long run, as indicated by the dashed line. Also notice the faster rate at which the D schedules increase relative to the S schedule. Thus, by the end

P

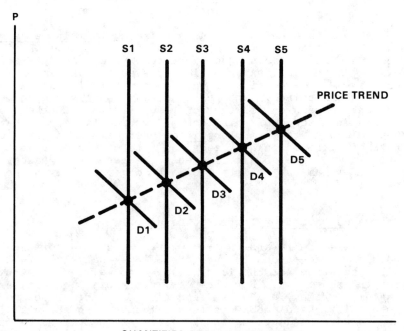

QUANTITIES OVER THE LONG-RUN

FIGURE 30:
LONG-RUN RISE IN PRICES.

225

of the second period demand has reached the D_2 position, whereas supply has increased only to the S_2 position. As a result, D_2 interacts with S_2 only at a higher P. By stringing out the succession of intersection points between a surging D situation and the lagging S, we discover that market-clearing P emerges at higher and higher levels. In this picture, Qd is generally exceeding Qs at previous P levels, so that sellers are able to ask (and get) higher prices.

How can the present inflation in the U.S. be analyzed in terms of Figure 30? Here, as in Figure 29, we show both D and S schedules shifting simultaneously in their historical directions and proportions. D is seen to be increasing at a faster rate than S--and exactly the same juxtaposition of events took place in postwar U.S. Details on why and how this inflationary process transpired, and the crucial role played by government expansion of the money supply would take us beyond the scope of this book. Suffice it to say that the following general proposition emerges: whenever the rate of increase in D exceeds the rate of increase in S, prices will be able to increase because the "excess demand" enables sellers to ask for and get higher prices.

Shortages Caused by Increased Demand

Before we end this chapter, we should note some possible exceptions to the preceding analysis. What will be true for the long run need not always be true for the short run. For example, it is possible that, at any given time, in a given situation, selling prices may not be increased when D increases faster than S. That is to say, sellers may decide for some peculiar reason not to take advantage of the excess demand situation and charge what the traffic will bear. This hesitancy of sellers to raise prices was noted in our chapter on elasticity of demand; we now can analyze it again in the present context.

Imagine the following scenario. It is the first full peace-time year of car production following the Korean War and the post-Korean recession of 1953-54. The auto industry had expanded output by the customary 10 percent. This proportion of increase in S was supposed to be sufficient to satisfy the expected average increase in demand of 10 percent, and would enable prices to remain stable. But the best-laid plans of the auto firms were upset by what actually took place. Whereas S was increased 10 percent, D increased some 30 percent as a result of wartime pent-up demand. Clearly, sales were running ahead of expectations. What effect did this excess demand have on selling prices at the retail level?

The first sign that D had increased relative to S was the acceleration in car sales at a rate faster than expected. It was apparent that producers had underestimated demand. There was little question that long before the end of the selling period the stock of cars on hand would have been sold out at the original selling prices, resulting in <u>shortages</u>. Plainly, dealers had a grand opportunity to immediately raise their prices, charge what the traffic would bear, and increase the profit margin per unit sold. What did they actually do?

Non-Price Rationing

Although selling tactics varied, dealers generally adhered to similar practices: they did not overtly increase their selling prices. How, then, did they ration the scarce cars among their scrambling customers? As follows: Those customers who did not want to wait in line for cars offered bribes to the dealers by paying above list-price, and dealers were disposed to accept. Thus, dealers did covertly what they feared to do openly: raise prices in line with the excess D and charge what the traffic would bear, bargaining with each customer.

In most cases, however, customers who did not want to pay the higher price in the form of a bribe paid it in another way: they waited in line on a first-come, first-served basis. Although queueing up on the dealer's waiting list does not incur a monetary cost, it does involve a psychic cost--the cost of waiting for something that one wants to enjoy sooner rather than later. (This time-preference will be discussed in Chapter IX.)

Now for the main question: Why didn't sellers, faced by an obvious excess-demand shortage, behave exactly as expected under the law of market price and raise their prices? One possible answer is: As noted on previous occasions, sellers may be fearful of the social taboo against charging what the traffic would bear. By not raising prices when it was economically feasible to do so, they were apparently currying the public's favor, foregoing short-term monetary gains in favor of long-run goodwill.

Connected with this possibility may have been the dealers' belief that the unexpected surge in D was abnormal, purely temporary--that next season's sales would return to normal--so why bother to raise prices and alienate customers for a purely short-term gain? Thus, it is not unusual for firms to forego short-term profit opportunities in favor of possibly greater profit opportunities in the long run.

Price Controls and Precautionary Pricing

We have seen that social taboos against sellers charging what the traffic would bear may exert a deterrent effect on price increases during periods of increasing demand. Social forces can also work in the opposite direction: they may induce firms to increase prices sooner than otherwise. In the early 1970's, government wage and price controls induced firms to abandon their policy of not raising prices until their costs had increased.

In the past there were fewer social taboos against firms raising prices in response to rising costs. This is why firms had, for a long time, avoided raising prices during periods of increasing demand until such time as their costs began to increase. In this way they could blame rising costs (not rising demand) for their price increases. Today it is a different story. Government wage-price controls--real or threatened--have introduced a new source of uncertainty--a stop/go tendency of first imposing controls, then relaxing and terminating them. During the 1970's this induced firms to resort to precautionary price increases.

Reliance on precautionary price-raising can be explained by the excess-demand environment created by inflationary policies of government. These inflationary policies have consisted of vastly expanded Federal spending, on the one hand, and deficit financing by the Treasury and the Federal Reserve monetary authorities, on the other hand. As a result, total purchasing power in the economy had exploded at a faster rate than the

supply of consumers' goods. This inflationary environment is very hospitable to the raising of prices by
firms--indeed, it is the prime factor that enables
prices to rise in the first place.

When selling prices are eventually raised, and
continue to rise as long as excess-demand conditions
permit, government threatens to move in with wage-price
controls. Since these controls freeze selling prices
for an indefinite period, firms realize that it may be
profitable to rush to raise their prices and beat the
anticipated price freeze before it is too late. Thus,
we have the bitter irony of government inflationary
policies, on the one hand, and the expected wage-price
controls, on the other hand, working in tandem to induce
firms to raise prices sooner than otherwise.

Conclusion

It is market demand that ultimately determines
prices. True, in practice it is the firm that establishes the selling prices and determines how much to
supply the market. But in the final analysis, this is
about all the firm can do; in all cases it ultimately
has to reckon with the market. It is market demand that
ultimately ratifies or vetoes the firm's price and quantity decisions. Will the firm set P too high or too
low? Will its Qs be too high or too low? Or will there
be market-clearing? Only the market can tell.

Appendix

WILL THE REAL SUPPLY STAND UP?

The point of this Appendix is simply this: the
reader should be alerted to the fact that the treatment
of the supply concept in this chapter is radically
different from the usual treatment in other books.
Thus, the reader should know that in contrast to this
chapter, which treats supply as an ex-post concept, the

229

standard text treats supply mainly as an ex-ante concept. [2] The distinction between ex-ante and ex-post was used in Chapter V to analyze the nature of decision-making and to state the maximizing principle. However, it also applies directly to the present analysis of the firm's supply decisions concerning how much to produce and at what price to sell. Let us see how.

We have already seen that, in the case of supply, the ex-post concept is relevant only to the actual provision by the firm of goods for sale in the market. For this reason, ex-post supply is graphically depicted as a vertical line or curve, indicating that a given total quantity is being offered by firms at varied prices. It is, indeed, the only way to properly depict the actual supply situation in any given market, for any given type of product. Furthermore, for the purpose of graphically depicting the market, with its array of demand and supply sides, only the ex-post supply curve should be used to intersect the demand curve, as in Figure 20 above.

In stark contrast, the typical textbook depicts the market as an intersection of the familiar demand curve with an upward-sloping ex-ante supply curve (as shown in the following Figure B). The ex-ante supply curve looks essentially different (see the following Figure A) from the vertical ex-post supply curve for the simple reason that it is relevant only to the pre-production phase, when the firm is still contemplating or planning its production program, in preparing to decide: How many units should be produced? What price should be set?

In the ex-ante phase of its decision-making, the firm has not yet produced anything—it has not even launched any production and it surely has not yet put a single unit of its product for sale on the market. Thus, in the ex-ante state, there exists no such thing as a "supply" of any sort; at this point, "supply" is nothing more than a gleam in the firm's eye; the firm is merely preparing to produce varying quantities, depending on which of various possible prices it thinks is likely to prevail.

---

[2]A noteworthy exception is the treatment by Armen A. Alchian and William R. Allen in University Economics (3rd ed., Belmont, Calif.: Wadsworth Publishing Co., 1972), Chapter 6.

FIGURE A:

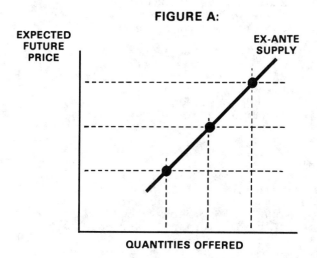

EXPECTED
FUTURE
PRICE

EX-ANTE
SUPPLY

QUANTITIES OFFERED

FIGURE B:

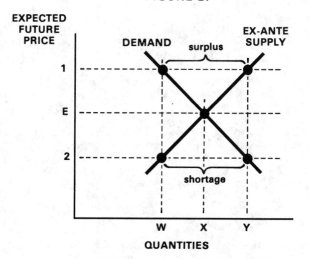

EXPECTED
FUTURE
PRICE

DEMAND   surplus   EX-ANTE
SUPPLY

1

E

2

shortage

W   X   Y

QUANTITIES

EX-ANTE SUPPLY AND MARKET PRICE.

The mind set of the firm in the ex-ante planning stage is illustrated in Figure A. As a first approximation, it says: If firms expect prices to be higher tomorrow, they will be willing and able to produce more and, vice versa, if they expect prices to be lower, they will produce less.

The reasoning behind this upward-sloping ex-ante S involves considerations of costs and profit margins. With respect to costs, we will see in Chapter XI that higher rates of production (i.e., at higher rates of productive capacity) involve higher unit costs, whereas at somewhat lower rates of output unit costs are less. Thus, expectations of higher prices are supposed to induce firms to produce more, either because profit margins will be higher or, at least, the higher costs will be covered by the expected higher prices. Conversely, expectation of falling prices puts a damper on the firm's plans: lower prices threaten expected profit margins, which can be preserved only by falling back to lower rates of production and lower unit costs.

So far, so good. We return now to the main point of this Appendix. My argument is not with the idea of the ex-ante S curve itself: it is a useful snapshot of how firms feel about producing varying quantities at various expected prices. Rather, what I find disturbing is the textbook tradition of using the ex-ante S curve for the purpose of describing the market process (as in Figure B), a procedure that contrasts sharply with use of the vertical ex-post S curve in this chapter (see Figure 20 above).

True, both of these figures are similar in being diagrams of demand-and-supply concepts; both have intersections of D and and S to indicate the market-clearing (equilibrium) price which the market will tend to reach; and, in both cases, surpluses will occur when prices are set too high, while shortages will emerge when prices are set too low. But there the similarities end. Whereas the vertical ex-post S curve of Figure 20 is a realistic, appropriate depiction of actual market supply, the ex-ante S curve is a pure phantom, having no real existence except in the ex-ante minds of those planning future quantities to be produced by the firm.

To be sure, textbooks find it useful to rely on diagrams like Figure B for the purpose of outlining the potential causes of surpluses and shortages, for which modest purpose such figures may be suitable. Thus,

Figure B is able to show that surpluses would arise if ex-ante plans set prices and supply in excess of demand (at level 1) and that shortages would emerge if prices and supply are set too low (at level 2). In contrast, the vertical ex-post supply curve is not only more realistic and correct, but, no less significant, it also enables a more complete analysis, as already shown in this chapter.

It is in this latter respect that the ex-ante S curve suffers a serious and embarrassing lapse, specifically in attempting to analyze the case of a surplus. First, let us assume that firms set their prices too high (at level 1) and produce quantities Y; but at that high price the quantity demanded falls back to only quantity W, creating a surplus of WY. Then the argument goes, firms begin to slash prices to get rid of surpluses, and they also cut back on production until, at price E (equilibrium level) they produce only quantity X, and thereby are able to clear the market. However, what is usually overlooked by texts is the following curious lapse in analysis.

What is overlooked is the fact that, in order to dispose of the surplus WY, the firms must slash prices from level 1 all the way down to level 2 in order to clear the market of the quantity Y they had produced at the expected price (level 1). Thus, the market-clearing price in this case is at level 2, not level E as Figure B would have us believe! That is, price-level E could serve as a market-clearing price only if the firms had initially produced only quantity X to sell at price E; since they, instead, produced the larger quantity Y to sell at price-level 1, there is simply no way they can clear the market of the total quantity except by slashing prices all the way down to level 2.

In fact, if they had cut prices only down to level E, there would still remain some surplus--the amount XY! Clearly, there is no market-clearing here--not until prices are slashed to level 2. In this price-slashing binge firms would be gliding right past price E, precisely because it would not clear the market. Thus, in this first go-around there is no way the firms can discover the market-clearing price E--something which they would be able to discover in Figure 20 above, with its ex-post curve. To repeat, use of the ex-ante supply curve prevents realistic analysis of the market as a feedback mechanism and of the price adjustments firms must make to achieve market equilibrium.

233

CHAPTER IX

PROFITS--AND OTHER INCOMES

This chapter is mostly about profits. Wages and other incomes are briefly touched upon, but the spotlight is on profits. The importance of profits should be clear: the firm which earns profits is also the prime generator of other incomes, including wages and salaries, as we saw in Chapter IV. In that chapter we also saw how profits can be increased by improved technology and cost reduction. In Chapter VIII we saw how changing market conditions affect selling prices and profits. In the upcoming Chapter X we will see how profits serve as the central motivating force of free-market firms. In the present chapter, our primary purpose is to explain the nature of profit itself--why the firm necessarily seeks profits and why profits are a justified return.

Controversy over profits--their justification and morality--has raged since the ancient and medieval taboos against the taking of interest on loans ("usury"). People did not understand why the money-lender should get back more than he lends. In modern times, Marxists and other socialists have maintained that profits are the result of "exploitation" of workers by capitalist owners of the means of production. For Marxists, profits belong to the workers in the first place, and are taken from workers only through capitalistic "monopoly" ownership of the means of production. Hence, for Marxists, profits are no more a deserved or earned income than is interest. In the following pages we will see why the taboos and attacks on profits are wide of the mark.

I. Introductory

First of all, production takes time. This fact is obvious, and may even seem trivial, but for economics the element of time is crucial. Why? Before we answer this question, we should briefly describe why production is not an instantaneous process but takes time to unfold and materialize.

Phases of the Production Process

As we have already seen, the entire production process involved at least three time phases. First comes the ex-ante phase during which the firm is engaged in estimating, speculating, planning, and investing activities--all centered around its decision as to what to produce, how much, and at what price. This is followed by the actual physical production phase. During this period, means of production are combined according to appropriate techniques that bring the product through stages of maturation until it is made ready for market. Finally comes the ex-post phase during which the product is supplied to the market, and the firm is able to see whether the sale of its product proceeds as planned.

Thus the entire production process embraces more than a physical-technical coordination of production resources in some appropriate technical combination. It includes also the ex-ante planning period and the ex-post or after-the-dust-has-settled period of reckoning. Even if physical production were somehow magically instantaneous, it still takes time to plan it (especially prices and quantities) and to assess results in the aftermath of market sales.

Moneylender vs. Entrepreneur

Overall, then, the production process involves not only the acquisition and use of means but also a prolonged waiting period until the product is completed, marketed, and hopefully sold. Seen from another viewpoint, when the firm undertakes production, it is making current outlays on factors of production in anticipation of future sales or payoff. To paraphrase a once popular commercial, the firm typically pays out now in order to fly later. In a general sense, therefore, the firm is essentially in the same position as the moneylender: both make a current outlay of money in exchange for a future payoff.

True, there is a technical difference between moneylending and entrepreneurial production by the firm. The moneylender makes his current outlay of money to the borrower in one lump sum, whereas the firm makes its current outlays mostly in the form of a series of regular payments to workers (wages), landlords (rent), power companies, and other resource owners from whom it purchases or hires the necessary means of production.

But this is merely a superficial technical or institutional difference, and does not alter the essential similarity between moneylending and production: both processes are inter-temporal in that they span a period of time from the present into the future. Furthermore, they are similar because the future payoff is characteristically expected to be greater than total current outlays. In the one case this increment is called interest; in the other it is profit.

To be sure, profits earned by firms consist of more than the equivalent of interest. As we will see, total profits earned by the firm include not only (a) a pure interest component but also (b) an entrepreneurial component due to uncertainty and risk, and (c) a purchasing-power component to compensate for changes in the value of money associated with changing price levels. Each of these components plays a vital role in determining the size of the firm's price spread (profit margin) between the expected selling price and the unit costs incurred in production. Let us first examine the interest-rate component.

II. Time-Preference and Pure Interest

The first question we must ask is: What exactly is the connection between the interest rate earned in moneylending and the profit rate earned by the firm? The answer given by economics is straightforward: The common basis for both the interest rate and the profit rate is man's natural time-preference. But what is "time preference"? Briefly, and somewhat crudely, it means that man prefers the present time to the future, other things being equal.

Meaning of Time-Preference

To be more precise, the time-preference axiom refers to the deeply-rooted and widely observed fact that, other things being equal, people prefer to enjoy any given satisfaction or good in the present rather than to enjoy the same good in the future. To put it another way: For any given goal set by a person, he would prefer to realize it sooner rather than later. The less the waiting time, the better. As one writer has put it, a bird in the hand is worth more than a bird in the bush. It makes no difference whether the goal is material or spiritual, tangible or intangible--man

237

prefers to achieve his goals in the shortest possible time, _ceteris paribus_. Conversely, the more distant the future achievement of any given goal, the less valuable does the goal become. Man attaches a "disutility" to _waiting_: postponement of consumption involves sacrifice.

It is important to stress the sameness of the object of satisfaction whose present availability is preferred to its future availability. Unless it is the same satisfaction that is being time-compared, it would be possible to raise the following objection: In wintertime, why would anyone prefer ice delivered then to ice delivered in the following summer when the weather is very hot? The fallacy here is the assumption that summer ice is literally the same good or satisfaction as winter ice. To be sure, ice is ice when regarded purely in terms of its physical-material properties. But the fact that cooling ice-in-summer provides significantly greater, and hence different, satisfactions than ice-in-winter compels us to regard the two ices as different goods rather than the same good.

Life Is Not Forever

Why is time-preference so deeply rooted in the nature of man? Some writers explain it in terms of an obvious physiological fact: Man does not live forever. Alas, man is mortal! The life he enjoys must someday be ended. Nothing is more certain in life than death--unless it be taxes, to paraphrase Dorothy Parker.

Furthermore, although death may be as certain as taxes, uncertain is the duration of the life-span of any given person. The mortality tables have it all clearly laid out--the variability of individual life-spans. This only compounds the time-scarcity problem for the individual. How much time does one have left? How much time does one need to accomplish his goals? Is there time enough? If not, which time priorities are to be assigned to one's goals? Can one tailor any given goal in order to fit the cloth of time available? Can one afford to postpone any given goal?

Time a Scarce Resource

As Böhm-Bawerk once put it: "[We] humans live out our lives in a temporal world ... our Today, with

238

its needs and cares, comes before our Tomorrow, and ...
our Day-After-Tomorrow may perhaps not be assured as at
all." There it is. Finite but indeterminate lifetime
makes it even more uncertain that we can satisfy all our
wants, regardless of other means available. So long as
tomorrow is "not assured," any satisfaction postponed
today may never be realized.[1]

In this connection we can also invoke the maximizing principle (Chapter V) according to which man
always acts in the expectation that his action will
leave him better off than otherwise. This implies that,
other things being equal, man will want to accomplish
more rather than less within his given lifetime. Given
man's mortality, it becomes clear that time is the
scarcest of means at man's disposal. No matter how any
given person manages his own time-scarcity, the fact
remains that the only way to assure fulfillment of a
given goal is to realize it sooner rather than later,
ceteris paribus. Postponement of a goal only courts the
likelihood it will never be fulfilled.

Time-Preference Axiomatic

Best of all, however, the validity of the time-
preference theorem does not need to rest on psychology
or physiology as above (e.g., the temporal limitations
of human life, impatience, the disutility of waiting).
As L. von Mises has put it, time preference is simply a
"categorical requisite" of human action:

[E]ach individual in each of his actions is
forced to choose between satisfaction in
various periods of time.... The very act of
gratifying a desire implies that gratifica-
tion at the present instant is preferred to
that at a later instant. He who consumes a
nonperishable good instead of postponing
consumption for an indefinite later moment
thereby reveals a higher valuation of present
satisfaction as compared with later satisfaction.... If he were not to prefer satisfaction in a nearer period of the future to that
in a remoter period, he would never consume

---

[1]Eugen von Boehm-Bawerk, Capital and Interest (South Holland,
Ill.: Libertarian Press, 1959), Vol. I, p. 266.

and so satisfy wants.... The knowledge provided by this insight ... refers to every
kind of want-satisfaction, not only to the
satisfaction of the vital necessities of mere
survival.[2]

Present Goods vs. Future Goods

At this juncture, we should introduce the important distinction between "present goods" and "future
goods." This distinction is based on the fact that any
given good can be made available for consumption either
in the "present" or the "future." Present goods, then,
are simply goods which are presently available for
present consumption. This category embraces all consumers' goods that are ready at hand for direct or
immediate consumption, including leisure and money.
Money, to be sure, is not directly consumable itself,
but since it is readily exchangeable for consumers'
goods, it is a present good par excellence. For
example, the money lent by the moneylender or paid out
currently to workers and other resource-owners by the
firm is classified as a present good.

In contrast to present goods are future goods.
As the term suggests, these embrace all goods that only
in the future can be regarded as present goods. Thus,
this category includes future product--goods that will
be completed only at a future date. It also includes
goods-in-progress that are expected to emerge as consumers' goods at some future date, as well as capital
goods that enable production of consumers' goods for
consumption only in the future. They also include any
claim on present goods in the future, such as money to
be repaid by borrowers to moneylenders; hence, the
promissory note (IOU) given by the borrower at the time
of the loan is a future good. Similarly classified as
future goods are securities such as stocks and bonds,
which constitute claims to future income.

Inter-temporal Exchanges

We can now readily describe the activities of
both the money-lender and the firm in terms of present

---

[2]Ludwig von Mises, Human Action (New Haven: Yale University
Press, 1949), pp. 480-485.

goods and future goods: both are essentially engaged in exchanges of present goods for future goods. The money-lender typically exchanges a lump sum of money (present goods) for the borrower's promissory note or IOU (future goods). Since the IOU promises repayment to the lender at a future date, it constitutes a future claim against the borrower. All loan transactions therefore are in essence an exchange of present goods (creditor's money) for a future good (the debtor's IOU).

Productive activities by the firm can be similarly described as involving essentially inter-temporal exchanges of present goods for future goods. The firm's current outlays of money on wages, rent, materials, and utilities can be classified as present goods. These current outlays are made in exchange for an ownership claim or title to the future product turned out with the help of workers, landlord, suppliers, and utility companies. Thus, all employment transactions between firm and worker involve an exchange in which the firm makes a series of present payments to the workers in exchange for rightful title to the product. Furthermore, the firm's outlays of money for factors of production also constitute an investment made in the present in expectation of profits at a future date (Chapter IV).

Premium vs. Discount

We can now restate the time-preference theorem in terms of present goods versus future goods. Man attaches a greater subjective value to present goods presently available to him than to the same goods available only in the future. For example, a person would rather hold a $100 bill now than hold it, say, five years from now, other things being the same--that is, disregarding the possible risk of not getting it back later from a borrower, and disregarding possible changes in the value of money due to a changing price level. Conversely, man attaches a lower subjective value to future goods, available only in the future, compared to the same goods available in the present. Thus, a money-lender who is promised a $100 bill in future repayment by a borrower (future goods) will now lend the borrower less than $100 (present goods) in exchange for the IOU of $100.

In effect, we have just described the difference between "premium" and "discount." Even though these two terms are actually two sides of the same coin, there is

241

a difference. Premium reflects the higher subjective value we attach to present goods that are presently available rather than in the future--the greater value attached to the convenience of earlier availability as compared to deferred availability. In the market place, present goods always command a premium or higher price over future goods.

In contrast, discount reflects the lower ("discounted") subjective value that we attach to future goods because they suffer from deferred availability--they are characteristically available only after a period of waiting. That is to say, discounting reflects the sacrifice involved in postponing present consumption and in waiting for its future availability. Hence, the market attaches a lower price to future goods compared to present goods that are presently available.

A Loan Transaction

For example, assume A possesses a given stock of wealth, say, ten barrels of sugar. Along comes B and asks to borrow the 10 barrels for one year. To this A replies: Okay, but I request repayment of 11 barrels. B agrees, and it's a deal--a deal that reflects a premium of one barrel of sugar, or 10 percent attached by A to the one-year loan. This case is one possibility. An alternative scenario could run as follows: B offers to repay A 10 barrels of sugar one year from now in return for 10 barrels borrowed today. But A protests, and suggests instead that he lend B only 9.1 barrels in exchange for the deferred repayment of 10 barrels. If B agrees, it's a deal--in effect, the same kind of deal as above, except that it reflects the other side of the coin, the discount: 10 barrels available a year from now is today worth only 9.1 barrels to A, revealing a present discount rate of 0.9 barrels, or about 10 percent of the 9.1 barrels lent.

Thus, premium and discount turn out to be merely two sides of the same coin. These two different ways of expressing valuations always refer to the same goods or object. They differ only with respect to which end of the time-span of goods availability one happens to focus on--on whether the goods availability is present or future. The premium emphasizes the greater value attached to presently available goods, whereas the discount emphasizes the lower value attached to the same goods available only at a later date.

Firm Discounts the Future

Just as we can describe loan transactions in terms of "premium" and "discount," so can we describe production and selling by the firm as involving a premium or a discount. As we saw in Chapter IV, the firm "works back from price" whenever it plans its current production. That is to say, it peers into the future to estimate its future market demand--its expected selling price and the quantities to be produced at that price. It then determines the profit rate it would like to earn on each unit to be sold (the unit profit rate). The residual obtained by subtracting the unit profit margin from the unit selling price represents the self-imposed limit on how much the firm can profitably spend currently on factors of production for each unit of output. Now, where does the premium or discount element enter into these calculations?

Let us assume a firm that is making product X and expects to sell it at some future date--say, a year from now, for $100. At this price it expects to sell its entire future output of X, which is currently in the works. Thus, there is a time-spread between current factor outlays and future selling of its product. The firm will have to wait until some future date before it can sell its output and reap the harvest of its current outlays on production. For the firm, therefore, the future selling price of $100 constitutes a future good. Like any future good, which is naturally handicapped by its deferred availability, this potential future $100 for each unit sold will have a lower present value compared to the same $100 were they presently available. That is to say, the future $100 is translated into a present discounted value.

The rate at which the future $100 is discounted is, of course, a subjective matter, depending on the subjective valuations of the firm's executives. For instance, if the firm is willing to expend only $90 now on factors of production on each unit produced, in exchange for the future $100, the $10 difference represents the rate of discount. Conversely, the future $100 price represents a $10 premium attached to the current total outlay of $90.

Pure Interest Rate

This brings us to a crucial point. Implicit in the concepts of "premium" and "discount" is the pure interest rate, which is actually the subjective time-preference rate. Hence, the "pure" interest rate should not be confused with the actual market or "loan" rate of interest, of which the pure rate is but one component. The other two components of the market rate allow for (a) uncertainty and risk factors attached to the loan, and for (b) changes in the purchasing power of the dollar. (More on this in Section III.) Thus, the actual rate of interest paid on loans in the market comprises all three components: subjective time-preference, uncertainty and risk, and changes in the value of money. In our present discussion we will focus on the time-preference or "pure" rate of interest, unless otherwise specified.

In our sugar-loan illustration, the premium rate of 10 percent actually represents a pure interest rate; so does the discount rate. Both of these rates also reflect Mr. A's subjective time-preference rate at the time of the loan. For example, if A had felt otherwise, and either (a) had asked a premium of 1.5 barrels for the 10 loaned, or (b) offered only 8.7 barrels in return for repayment of 10 barrels, both of these cases would have reflected a 15 percent rate of time preference: in the first case this rate is reflected in the 1.5 barrel premium, and in the second case the rate is reflected by the discount of 1.3 barrels. In both events the time-preference rate is the same 15 percent, which is also A's interest rate.

We can now also see why the pure interest or time-preference rate can be described as the inter-temporal exchange rate between (a) present goods presently available and (b) future goods available only at a later date. In our sugar illustration the 10 percent premium rate of interest was derived from the ratio of 11/10, while the 10 percent discount rate of interest was obtained from the ratio 10/9.1.

The "Price of Money"

The reader should not be misled by the customary notion that interest rates are related only to money loans. We have just seen, in our sugar illustration, that a loan transaction between creditor and debtor can

244

take the form of non-money goods. Indeed, history tells us that as far back as the Babylonian King Hammurabi, more than 2,000 years B.C., people were making loans in non-money commodities. The only difference between a sugar loan and a money loan is that the former is transacted in barrel units of sugar, whereas the latter involves units of money (e.g., dollars).

For this reason it is also misleading to define the interest rate merely as the price of money, rather than in the basic universal terms of time-preference. First of all, interest-bearing loans can be made in non-money goods as well as money units, as we have just noted. True, in the modern economy, interest is usually paid in the form of money, but this does not make interest a purely monetary phenomenon. Indeed, at heart, interest is a reflection of universal time-preference.

For another thing, the word "price" is literally misused. A money "price" represents the full number of money-units asked by the seller in exchange for a unit of his goods. In contrast, an interest payment is only a fractional payment, only a part of the total sum of money-units being exchanged. For example, an interest payment of $10 on a loan of $100 is only part of the total value of the transaction.

Furthermore, the present "price" of $100 is simply another batch of 100 dollar-bills--no more, no less. That is to say, anyone who wants to "buy" some money can go to the bank and buy, say a $100 bill by paying with a check or 100 dollar-bills, the "price" of money here being simply $1 for $1.

Additionally, and more precisely, the "price" of any good--say, X, be it money or a non-money good--is equal to the amount of other goods that this good X can be exchanged for in the market. For example, if the market price of X is $5, it means that one unit of X is exchangeable for five dollar-units. (The "exchange rate" is 1:5.) On the other hand, from the point of view of one dollar bill, the "price" of that dollar is how much it can be exchanged for in terms of X (which is one-fifth of X). For this reason, the "price" of a dollar is not the interest rate but rather how much the dollar can be exchanged for in terms of the full array of alternative goods. Technically speaking, it is approximately the inverse or reciprocal of the general "price level" of all non-money goods. Thus, the higher

245

the price level, the lower the "price of money," and vice versa.

Saving and Investing

Finally, and most fundamentally, the "price of money" concept mistakenly implies that the natural phenomenon of the interest rate arises only in <u>loan</u> transactions between parties A and B. This misconception gives rise to the expression that interest is "the price of a <u>loan</u>," which implies that a loan necessarily involves two <u>separate</u> parties, the lender and the borrower. However, a person can "lend to himself" as well as to others. For example, individual savers or groups of savers can "borrow" <u>their</u> <u>own</u> accumulated savings and invest these savings, without resorting to loans from other parties. Indeed, the classical concept of the "capitalist-entrepreneur," who was a central figure in spearheading the Industrial Revolution, was based on this notion of the saver and capital accumulator investing <u>his</u> <u>own</u> wealth without recourse to borrowing from others.

In all such cases, where people indicate a relatively lower time-preference by saving and investing in productive ventures--whether their own or others'--the presumption is that the saver-investor believes his investment in production will yield him a <u>future</u> <u>consumption</u> that will be <u>greater</u> than otherwise. This does not mean that savers-investors value the future absolutely over the present, but merely that they prefer a future consumption that would be greater than otherwise. In working to make for themselves a "better future" than otherwise, they in effect hasten the realization of their future.

Interest-Rate Tables

We have now seen that inter-temporal exchange transactions can involve money and non-money goods, and can also involve an investment of one's own accumulated savings rather than a loan transaction. We should also note that loans can be made for consumption purposes (consumer loans) as well as for production purposes (commercial loans). In any case, the various possible <u>rates</u> of exchange between present goods and future goods --that is, the various <u>rates</u> of subjective time preference as well as premium and discount--can be numerically

246

expressed in the form of <u>interest tables</u>, such as Tables
III and IV, which are condensed versions.

        For example, Table III can illustrate the terms
of a <u>premium</u>-type loan transaction. Imagine a current
loan of $1,000 to be repaid in 5 years at 15 percent
interest per annum. Table III tells us that the premium
rate attached to each dollar borrowed is 2.01 (see the
first column for the year 5, then across to the 15
percent column). We then multiply 2.01 by $1,000 and
get $2,010. This is the total to be repaid by the
borrower: it consists of $1,000 principal plus $1,010
premium interest.

TABLE III

Compound Interest on One Dollar

End of Year	3%	5%	10%	15%	20%
1	1.03	1.05	1.10	1.15	1.20
2	1.06	1.10	1.21	1.32	1.44
3	1.09	1.16	1.33	1.52	1.73
4	1.13	1.22	1.46	1.74	2.07
5	1.16	1.28	1.61	2.01	2.49
10	1.34	1.63	2.59	4.05	6.19
15	1.56	2.08	4.17	8.13	15.4
20	1.81	2.65	6.72	16.1	38.3
30	2.43	4.32	17.4	66.2	237
40	3.26	7.04	45.3	267	1470
50	4.38	11.5	117	1080	9100

        In contrast, we can use Table IV to illustrate
the terms of a <u>discount</u> interest loan. Imagine a borrower who offers to repay the lender $1,000 at 15 per-
cent interest, at the end of 5 years. Table IV tells us
that the rate at which the future $1,000 should be
discounted by the lender is .497 (see the first column
for year 5, and then across to the 15 percent column).
We then multiply .497 by $1,000 and get $497. Hence, in
a 15 percent loan, $497 is the present discounted value
of $1,000 to be repaid 5 years from now; that is, the

247

lender who wants to receive $1,000 in a 5-year, 15-percent loan should lend out no more than $497.

TABLE IV

Present Discounted Value of a Future Dollar

End of Year	3%	5%	10%	15%	20%
1	.971	.952	.909	.870	.833
2	.943	.907	.826	.756	.694
3	.915	.864	.751	.658	.578
4	.889	.823	.683	.572	.482
5	.863	.784	.620	.497	.402
10	.744	.614	.385	.247	.162
15	.642	.481	.239	.122	.0649
20	.554	.377	.148	.0611	.0261
30	.412	.231	.0573	.0151	.0042
40	.307	.142	.0221	.0037	.0007
50	.228	.087	.0085	.0009	.0001

Some Propositions

        While we have these two interest tables at hand, we should examine them for several important propositions implied in their numerical structure. The first implied proposition should be familiar by now: the greater is the time-preference rate, the greater is the numerical rate of interest, or the lower is the present discounted value. This can be seen by scanning each year-line from left to right. In Table III, for example, the numbers increase in value to reflect the higher time-preference or interest rates. Similarly, Table IV tells us, as we scan from left to right, that lower and lower present discounted values apply to the increasing rates of time-preference or interest.

        We now come to a second proposition implied in these interest tables: the longer the time-span involved in the inter-temporal transaction, the greater is the premium rate of interst, or the lower is the present discounted value. This can be seen by scanning each

248

percent column from the top down. In Table III, for example, the numbers increase in value, reflecting the greater premium attached to transactions of longer duration. In Table IV they drop in value, reflecting the increased rates of discount applied to such transactions.

A third proposition implied in our tables runs as follows: the time-preference or interest rate is always positive, never zero or negative. In other words, inter-temporal exchanges will always be transacted at a premium or discount rate of interest. For instance, A will never lend B 100 units of X now for only 100 units or less to be repaid at a later date, other things being equal. This assumes A's time-preference rate is the only determining factor in the terms of exchange, excluding personal considerations such a friendship or blood relationship with B.

Time-Preference: Relative vs. Absolute

In this connection it is important to note that positive time-preference is relative, not absolute. An absolute time preference means that a person provides only for present consumption or acquires only present goods, and never saves any current income for future consumption (those "rainy days") nor acquires any future goods (such as IOU's or securities).

Such absolute time-preference is conceivable only under two unlikely conditions. One would be a catastrophe-ridden world, where everything was going to "come to an end" at any moment, and there would truly be "no tomorrow." With catastrophe hanging overhead like a Damocles' sword, no one could be blamed for living it up today, with nary a care for the morrow. The other condition would be a non-scarcity world of absolute abundance, like the Garden of Eden. Here everyone could truly be a pure consumer (a pure non-saver), never having to worry about saving something for future consumption.

At the opposite extreme is the case of absolutely no time preference. This means that people have no desire to live "in the present"--to do any consuming now--but prefer to save everything for the future. At this extreme rate of abstinence, the human species clearly could not survive; it would simply perish!--which makes this condition totally unrealistic. Furthermore, if people literally never consume anything,

249

including the things they might buy with their savings, there is obviously no point in doing any saving in the first place.

However, there are people who have relatively low time-preference rates and, therefore, tend to be savers as well as consumers. That is to say, even while they consume significant portions of their current income, they also set aside significant amounts for future consumption by saving for those rainy days, retirement, or other future goals. Savers characteristically have longer time horizons than non-savers: for them the future stretches over a greater span of years than for non-savers; the latter care more about "living it up" today, care less about future consumption. Yet, even among savers, the rate of saving will vary according to one's age, circumstances, and preferences.

Time-Preference: High and Low

Clearly, then, real-world rates of time-preference must lie mostly between the one extreme of absolute time preference and the other extreme of absolutely no time preference. Real people are characterized by relative rates of time-preference, ranging from relatively "high" to relatively "low" time-preference rates, and varying from individual to individual and from age to age. That is to say, even though people prefer to consume now rather than later--other things being the same--they do save some of their income and allocate it toward future consumption. By saving varying proportions of their income, they divert varying amounts of current consumption toward future consumption.

People with relatively high time preference tend to use most or practically all of their income for present consumption, and save very little, if anything. Indeed, some people may consume more than their current income ("live beyond one's means," so to speak) either by living off their accumulated savings, or by borrowing the savings of others whose time-preference rate is lower and who, therefore, save more.

On the other hand, people with relatively low time preference tend to postpone present consumption at a greater rate than people with high time preference. They are the people who defer much consumption by saving significant parts of their current income. These are the savings that are usually channelled into investment

250

--via the financial system (e.g., the stock and bond markets)--in the growth of productive capacity of firms. Firms depend on these savings to supplement their own internal saving or cash flow, and invest them in new capital goods (see Chapter IV).

Because investment by firms in capital goods tends to increase productivity and reduce unit costs of production, thereby increasing profits, savers are reasonably induced to share in these profits by investing in firms. Thus, people are always tending to balance their time-preference and the disutility of postponed consumption against the advantages of investing in the higher productivity of expanded capital structure. Hence, it is the saver-investor, possessed of relatively lower time preference, who provides the capital for ever more elaborate ("longer") processes of production which, in turn, increase the productivity and standard of living of the community. In other words, the saver-investor provides the present goods that enable the firm to produce future goods, in return for which he acquires a claim to a share of the profits.

Calculation of Profits and Costs

We can now see how Table IV, on present discounted values, can help illustrate the profit calculations of the firm. Since the firm is a discounter of future values--seeking to keep its present costs below its expected future selling price--Table IV becomes the relevant table. On the one hand, this table deals with present discount factors, while on the other hand, the firm must necessarily attach a discounted value to its current factor outlays--a value calculated on the basis of its expected future selling price.

Assume, for example, that the firm is producing a computer to sell at $100,000 a unit, each of which takes two years to produce. The firm wants to earn a 15 percent profit as its pure interest rate. Working back from its future price of $100,000, the firm knows it must limit its unit costs to something less than $100,000. The question now is: What is this cost-ceiling that will allow the firm to earn 15 percent pure interest over two years on each unit produced?

If we were, instead, involved in a loan transaction, the calculation would be fairly simple. A two-year loan at 15 percent, repayable in the sum of

251

$100,000, would call for a present cash outlay by the lender of only $75,600 (obtained by multiplying the discount factor .756 by $100,000). That is to say, $75,600 represents the present discounted value of $100,000 repayable at the end of two years. The firm, too, like the moneylender, makes a present discounted payment in exchange for a greater payoff in the future. But there the resemblance ends. For practical reasons, the firm does not make its present discounted outlay to workers and other owners of production-factors in one lump sum as does the moneylender. In practice, the firm breaks its total outlays down into a series of regular weekly or monthly income payments, which enable wage-earners, rent receivers and materials suppliers to make their own current expenditures for consumption and production purposes.

Discounting Current Factor Outlays

Thus, the difference between making a series of current payments to factor-owners, stretching over two years, as compared to a mere lump-sum loan of cash, introduces an insignificant complication in the calculation of present discounted values of current cash outlays. Whereas the lender makes only one lump-sum outlay at the start of the two-year period, and then waits a full two years for repayment of every dollar of principal, it is otherwise with the firm.

The firm does not have to wait a full two years for a payoff on each of its currently paid-out dollars to factor-owners. Indeed, the first month's outlays wait 23 months for their payoff; the second month's outlays wait 22 months for their payoff; the third month's outlays wait 21 months; and so on, until the final monthly outlay waits no longer.

Over the two-year period as a whole, therefore, each of the firm's current monthly outlays to factor-owners involves not one present discount factor (e.g., 0.756) but rather a series of them, each numerically lower than the preceding one. Theoretically this implies that each month's outlays would have to be determined by use of lower and lower discount factors, and therefore payments to workers and others would be larger each successive month. In practice, however, it is more convenient for both the firms and factor-owners to have the payments made in uniform, unchanged amounts. How can this practical institutional complication be handled?

252

Making Regular Payments

Since the firm will be making twenty-four identical monthly outlays, the firm can calculate an approximate present discount factor by using the twelfth or
mid-point month as its guide. In Table IV we see that
the discount factor for the end of the twelfth month, at
15 percent interest, is 0.870. This implies that the
average of all monthly discount factors is 0.870, and
that the sum of the different present discounted values
will total about $87,000 over the two-year period. That
is to say, the firm must limit its current outlays to
$87,000 per unit produced, yielding a profit margin of
$13,000 for each unit sold at $100,000.

In practice, of course, there is no assurance
that the firm will be able to hire or purchase factors
of production at market prices (wage rates, rents, etc.)
that will be low enough--that is, low enough to keep
unit costs from exceeding the $87,000 limit which the
firm will be willing to spend for each unit produced.
The firm's inducement to employ labor and other resources depends crucially on the current market price of
the resources. Thus, if one or more of the resources
needed is overpriced, the firm may have to cancel the
venture altogether--unless it finds a way to economize
on some inputs, or decides to accept a reduced profit
margin.

Relevant Costs of Production

This brings us to a vital consideration: Which
costs should the firm include in its calculation of the
cost of production? First of all, costs can be calculated either as a marginal cost (MC) or as a per unit or
average cost (AC). The MC is simply the total cost that
will be involved in producing a given quantity or batch
of products. The AC is simply the total cost (or MC)
divided by the number of units to be produced, yielding
a per-unit cost. Now, to return to our question: Which
types of costs should be included in the calculation of
MC or AC?

It helps to realize, at the start, that not all
expenditures by the firm are to be regarded as relevant
costs--costs that will necessarily be incurred by the
forthcoming production. For example, as we will see
below, not every dollar expended for plant and equipment
is a relevant cost. Furthermore, relevant costs must be

broken down into (a) explicit costs, and (b) implicit costs. Leading examples of each category are as follows:

Typical explicit costs include:

　　Wages and salaries,
　　Rent,
　　Interest,
　　Materials,
　　Power,
　　Repairs and maintenance.

In contrast, implicit costs include such items as:

　　Depreciation of plant and equipment,
　　Implicit wages and salaries of owner,
　　Implicit rent on owners land and factory facilities.

　　　　What is the real difference between explicit and implicit costs? Explicit costs, usually referred to as "out of pocket" expenditures, always involve an outlay of money for goods and services purchased or hired for the given production program. They can be measured strictly on the basis of the purchase price of the given factor. Also, these factors are usually "short-lived" and therefore "expire" in the process of production: the factor is either technically transformed (e.g., materials) or is "embodied" in the product (e.g., labor, power). They are readily measurable or calculable. Implicit costs, in contrast, usually involve one or another complication when it comes to their calculation.

Implicit Earnings

　　　　For instance, in cases where the owner of the firm provides professional services (managerial, legal, etc.) so that the firm does not have to hire these services on the market, resources are being used even though no specific money expenditures are involved. Thus costs of production are incurred which are equivalent to the wages and salaries that the owner could have earned by selling his services to other firms. These foregone earnings constitute an opportunity cost whose value is imputed from the market value of the owner's services to his own firm.

254

Similar reasoning applies to the use of land and factory facilities that are owned by the firm but which are used in production instead of being rented to the market. Here the <u>rent</u> that could have been earned by selling these resources directly to the market are definitely an opportunity cost. Therefore their use in production by the firm involves a cost of production whose value is imputed from the rent that could have been earned on the market.

Depreciation and Interest

Why is <u>depreciation</u> of plant and equipment placed under implicit costs rather than explicit costs? Does not the acquisition of equipment, for instance, involve an outlay of money and, therefore, should be treated as an explicit cost? Well, equipment usage is complicated by the fact that it is durable or "long-lived," and therefore does not get used up ("consumed") in a single act of production. This has two important implications. First, the value of the equipment used up in a single act of production is usually only a fraction of the total purchase price. Second, at any given moment, equipment commands a <u>resale value</u>--either as productive equipment that still is useful, or as mere scrap. How does this help us calculate the economic cost of using equipment in production?

From the above it should be clear that the cost of equipment used in production--and the same goes for the physical plant--is measured not by its original purchase price but only by the portion of it that is actually used in the current production program. This portion is measured by the difference between the equipment's <u>current</u> resale value (at the start of the current production period) and its <u>prospective</u> resale value (at the termination of the production period). This difference in resale values is called <u>depreciation</u>, and reflects the economic cost of the wear-and-tear of the equipment used in production.

A final note about <u>interest</u> costs listed among explicit costs above. On loans received by the firm, only the interest portion of the obligation--not the principal--is included as an explicit cost. Inclusion of the principal would involve double-counting, since the proceeds of loans typically become embodied in explicit expenditure items such as wages and salaries, materials, etc.

·Specifically, the funds could have been invested in stocks and bonds, and could have earned dividends and interest for their owners. When owners of the firm invest in production instead of stocks and bonds, they are foregoing an opportunity to earn income elsewhere. The interest and dividends they could have earned on the financial markets they now want to exceed by investing in production instead--for earnings that are expected in the form of profits.

Profits as Opportunity Costs

We have now completed the first, and main, leg in our journey to uncover the nature of the profit margin. It is time, also, to briefly survey our results. Our first goal has been to link the basic component of the profit margin to the pure interest (time-preference) rate. Both moneylender and firm are engaged in the inter-temporal exchange of present goods for future goods. Since the present value of future goods is typically discounted, both moneylender and firm naturally attach a discount to their future payoffs. Here lies the reason for both the interest on money loans and the profit margin earned by firms.

We can now also see why the profit margin reflects an opportunity cost--the equivalent of what the firm could have earned elsewhere, by investing in financial assets instead of in production. Owners of the firm always have the option of investing their savings in the purchase of securities that yield interest or dividends and capital gains. By investing, instead, in production, they expect to earn at least the equivalent of what they could earn in the foregone investment opportunities. In effect, the owners of firms are merely lending their capital funds to themselves instead of to others. Furthermore, it makes no difference if the firm, in addition to investing its owners' savings, also borrows the savings of others via the financial markets: in both cases it will want to earn at least the equivalent of alternative earning possibilities.

III. Uncertainty and Inflation

We said at the start that the profit margin consists not only of a time-preference or pure interest component, but also of "entrepreneurial" and "purchasing power" components. The entrepreneurial component is included because of the hazards and risks faced by the firm due to the uncertainty of selling successfully in the market. The purchasing-power component is included because of changes in the value of money that are related to changes in the money supply and general price level.

Uncertainty and Changing PPM

If we were living in an imaginary world devoid of any uncertainty and risk, and in which the purchasing power of money ("PPM" hereafter) was perfectly stable, the profit margin could then consist only of pure interest. In the real world, however, there are no riskless markets or stable PPM.

Instead, there is constant uncertainty of market demand and selling conditions, and the PPM is subject to depreciation due to government monetary inflation and rising price levels. Both market uncertainty and changes in PPM affect ex-ante planning and ex-post sales experience in unpredictable ways and, therefore, compel the firm to provide against adverse effects by appropriate provision for both entrepreneurial and PPM components in the planned profit margin.

Impact of Uncertain Demand

How does market uncertainty influence the firm's ex-ante planning of its profit margin? In our preceding illustration we had the firm earning a $13,000 profit on each unit sold at $100,000, representing a 15 percent return on a two-year production project. But this assumed certainty of sales--that the firm would actually sell every unit produced (say, 200 units) at the expected selling price of $100,000. Such certainty of sales is possible only in the unreal world of static, unchanging market conditions in which the firm has complete knowledge of market demand and exactly how many units to produce.

However, unchanging market conditions do not exist in the real world, where demand and supply are in constant dynamic flux and market-clearing prices become unpredictable. In a world of market uncertainty and unpredictability, ex-post realized sales may or may not turn out as planned in the ex-ante. How does this uncertainty prospect affect ex-ante profit planning?

Impact of Reduced Sales

Suppose, for instance, that the firm wants to hedge against the possibility that it will not sell all of its 200 units, in which case it would have to slash its price in order to sell out the remaining unsold units. Such a prospect would, of course, also reduce the expected profit rate of $13,000 per unit. In order to minimize the effects of these adverse prospects on profits, the firm can, say, add a five percent margin for uncertainty and thereby enlarge its ex-ante planned profit rate from 15 to 20 percent. In principle, this increase in profit rate can be sought in two ways: (a) by lowering the ceiling on its unit costs from $87,000 to $83,000 (discount factor 0.833 multiplied by $100,000), or (b) by raising its expected selling price to about $103,700. Or it could plan a combination of (a) and (b). Its final choice will, of course, depend on whether it can effectively reduce its unit costs or whether, in its judgment, the market demand is inelastic against a price increase. In any case, the greater the uncertainty and risk attached to a given project, the larger will be the entrepreneurial component of the ex-ante profit margin.

If market demand is seriously disappointing, quantities sold will be less than expected, selling prices will have to be slashed, and profits will be less than expected. The drop in profits may either be slight or so great as to wipe out the profit margin or even prevent the firm from recouping some of its factor outlays.

Impact of Excess Demand

Of course, the market could throw a pleasant surprise by having demand exceed the firm's expectations. For example, assume demand increases at the same time that product is being released to the market, resulting in an excess demand for the product. As we saw in Chapter VIII, the firm might be able to spot this incipient shortage fairly early in the selling period, and decide to raise its price to take advantage of the unanticipated bulge in demand for its product. If so, its ex-post profit margin would surely exceed its ex-ante planned margin due to the emergence of entrepreneurial profit.

Thus, we see that the entrepreneurial profit
component enters into the picture only after the firm
makes due allowance for pure interest or time-preference. It can emerge both in the ex-ante planning phase
and in the ex-post selling phase. In view of inevitable
and pervasive market uncertainty, the entrepreneurial
component must be regarded as a categorical element of
the firm's profit margin. But whereas the pure-interest
component is always positive, the entrepreneurial component can be either positive or negative.

Impact of Inflation

Finally, the firm's profit margin must make due
allowance for prospective changes in the purchasing
power of money (PPM), especially in periods of rising or
falling prices. Since we are living in an "age of
inflation" marked by rising prices and shrinking PPM, it
is reasonable for the firm to anticipate a decline in
PPM by the time its product is selling on the market.
Rising prices and declining PPM, in turn, mean that the
dollar buys less and less as time goes by. Failure to
allow for this inflation effect in the profit margin
will, other things being equal, yield profits whose real
purchasing power is less than planned.

In order to minimize the inflation impact on the
purchasing power of its ex-post profits, the firm will
include an inflation component in its ex-ante profit
margin. The size of this PPM component will vary, of
course, with the anticipated rate of inflation: the
higher the rate of price inflation anticipated, the
larger will be the inflation component, and the larger
will be the ex-ante profit margin. So long as inflation
is anticipated, the firm will hedge against it by in-
flating its profit margin.

But this can be a hazardous game. There is no
guarantee that the anticipated market demand will increase sufficiently to absorb the inflated profit
margin. As we saw in Chapter VIII, increases in selling
prices can be realized only when market demand is increasing faster than market supply. If for any reason
such buoyant demand is checked, or even slowed down, the
roof can cave in; market demand will resist the inflated
selling prices and the firm will fail to realize anticipated sales.

259

Market Rates of Interest

At this point we should note that market rates of interest charged in the <u>loan market</u> will tend to reflect entrepreneurial risk and PPM considerations as well as pure interest rates. Thus, market rates of interest will tend to increase not only when subjective time - preference increases, but also when investments become riskier and when price-inflation intensifies. For this reason the loan-market rate of interest will tend to reflect gross profit margins in the economy.

IV. The Tail That Wags the Dog

In a sense, the preceding is merely prelude. In the present section we draw a variety of <u>implications</u> of both economic and general significance that follow from the preceding sections. Human action in the "economic" spheres of production and exchange is merely a particular expression of principles of human action in general. We have already argued this with respect to the maximizing principle and self-interest. We now argue similarly with respect to the implications of the preceding discussion of time - preference and profit planning.

Futurity of Human Action

A moment's reflection should make us realize how extensively man's goals and actions--be they centered on consumption or production--apply to the <u>future</u>, near or remote. We have seen again and again that the firm's production decisions are always made in the present with an eye to the future. But this principle applies as well to virtually the entire realm of human decisions, not only to economic affairs. Other things being equal, the only difference among goals is how far each one reaches into the future. Many goals pertain to the very near future, while others are posted in the remote future. By contrast to the future, <u>the present</u> permits man time to do but two things: (a) make <u>choices</u> of future goals, and (b) <u>apply means</u> for the accomplishment of those goals.

Economics as such cannot tell us anything about the making of <u>ex-ante</u> choices, except that they are individual or <u>subjective</u> and that, except where man has full knowledge of the data related to his decisions, choices cannot be made with certainty of outcome in a world universally subject to changing conditions and uncertainty. Thus, economists as such are no more qualified than anyone else to advise people on what decisions to make in their personal or business affairs. However, with respect to the application of means for the achieving of goals or ends, economics is qualified to assert certain principles of universal relevance.

Imputation Process: Ends and Means

The first significant implication is the existence of an imputation process, a general process by which value is ascribed from one source to another. More precisely, the imputation process describes how means or resources acquire value from the value attached to the product they help produce or the goals they help realize. As a general principle, people value the means at their disposal strictly according to the value they attach to the given end which the means can achieve.

In the case of the firm, the discounted present value attached to current outlays on factors of production is an example of an "imputed" value--a value derived from a prime source, the expected future selling price of the product to be produced by labor and other factors. For example, the value of a bricklayer's labor (e.g., his hourly wage rate) is imputed from the value of the building he helps build. Similarly, the value of machinery in a factory depends on the value of the steel or automobiles it helps produce. As a general principle, the greater the value attached to a future product or other goal, the greater the value that can be imputed to the means employed in achieving the given end.

Capital Value

This helps us understand the technical concept of capital value. "Capital values" are involved whenever you hear questions like these: What is the value of a given piece of land? What is the value of a given building that consists of office-space or residential apartments? What is the value of a given piece of machinery? In each case, the general answer is the same: The value of these capital goods depends on the value of the product or service they can help produce. Thus, land that is sitting on major oil deposits will be valued more than land suitable only for cattle-grazing. Machinery that is useful for producing automobiles will

261

be valued more than machinery useful only for making motorcycles. In the case of buildings, let us imagine the following case.

Assume an office building has been put up for sale. What price can its owner expect to get for it? What price should the potential buyer be willing to pay for it? In both cases, Table V can help. Basically, we need to know the following: (a) the physical durability of the building, specifically the years of "life" left in it; (b) the estimated total rent (income) expected from occupants of the building during the remaining lifetime of the building; and (c) the rate of profit the buyer seeks to earn on the funds invested in the building. For illustrative purposes let us assume that (a) is 20 years, (b) is $40 million, and (c) is 10 percent. (Let us also assume there are no risk and PPM elements involved in the deal.) Given this basic information, the following Table V helps us derive the capital value of the building, which then can serve as the price to be negotiated between seller and buyer.

TABLE V

Present Discounted Value of a One-Dollar Annuity

End of Year	3%	5%	10%	15%	20%
1	0.97	0.95	0.91	0.87	0.83
2	1.91	1.86	1.73	1.63	1.53
3	2.83	2.72	2.48	2.28	2.11
4	3.72	3.55	3.16	2.86	2.59
5	4.58	4.33	3.79	3.35	2.99
10	8.53	7.72	6.14	5.02	4.19
15	11.9	10.4	7.60	5.87	4.68
20	14.9	12.5	8.51	6.23	4.87
30	19.6	15.4	9.43	6.57	4.98
40	23.1	17.2	9.78	6.64	5.00
50	25.7	18.3	9.91	6.66	5.00

An Illustration

In consulting Table V, we locate the desired information by scanning across the 20-year line until we spot the factor 8.51 in the 10 percent column. This factor is a present discounted value, compounded annually. It tells us that it is worth paying $8.51 today for an annuity that promises to pay one dollar annually for the next 20 years, that is, a total income of $20, stretched out evenly over 20 years (i.e., $1 each year, hence called "annuity").

How do we apply this tabular information to our problem? Since the estimated expected total income is $40 million, and assuming this income will be evenly distributed over the 20-year period, we therefore have an investment that promises to yield $2 million a year (equivalent to 2 million one-dollar annuities). By multiplying the factor of 8.51 and 2 million, we arrive at a capital value of $17,020,000. This means that an investment today of $17,020,000 (a) would yield a 10 percent return when taken in the form of $2 million a year over 20 years, totalling $40 million, and (b) $17,020,000 is the top price the buyer should offer for the building. Of course, less should be offered if there is any risk attached to the investment.

A Definition

We can now define capital value without too much difficulty: it is the present discounted value imputed to a stock of productive assets or factors that is expected to yield its owner a stream of earnings over a given future period. The concept applies to any durable good whose future earnings can be estimated. It also applies to securities, such as stock, which represent shares of ownership in the capital assets of a firm, and, hence, are a claim to a share of its earnings (i.e., profits) in the form of dividends.

Capital Losses, Capital Gains

What would happen to capital values if estimates of future earnings of the asset increased or decreased? This question is very relevant in a dynamic real world of perpetual flux in prices and earnings. This brings us to the twin concepts of "capital gains" and "capital losses." Suppose that, in the case of our 20-year

263

building, while negotiations for sale/purchase are underway, the earnings prospects suddenly drop because of the construction of new competitive buildings in the same neighborhood? Say, instead of the expected $40 million, prospective income is revised downward to only $32 million.

Given the same desired 10 percent rate of return, we now apply the 8.51 factor to 1.6 million (i.e., $32 million divided by 20 years) and come up with a capital value that has, to no one's surprise, dropped to $13,616,000. This drop in capital value from $17,020,000 to $13,616,000 constitutes a capital loss for the owner of the building. He would now have to shave the price of his building in order to induce someone to buy it.

Just as a drop in prospective earnings results in a lower capital value or capital loss, so does a rise in prospective earnings mean a capital gain. Thus, if there is an increased demand for office space that appears long-lasting, and earnings prospects increase to $50 million, say, this would bring a rise in capital value to $21,275,000 and enable the owner to ask for a higher price on the market.

Share Prices and Wealth Effects

The stock market is notorious for its daily fluctuations in the earnings prospects of traded shares of common stock. For this reason, the daily quotations of share prices undergo echoing changes. When the earnings prospects of Company X spurt upward--due to a very promising new product, say--you can expect an immediate upward surge in the market price of its shares. And vice versa, if this company's earnings face a downturn, you can expect a dip in its share price. Once again, prospective future values determine current values.

Furthermore, capital losses and gains also signify corresponding changes in one's wealth status. Even when one is not actually buying or selling productive assets or securities, it is possible to undergo a change in wealth status; so long as one owns such assets, he is vulnerable to fluctuations in their capital value.

To go one step further, an increase in the capital value and wealth of any firm represents, in effect, an increase in its profit rate as well. And vice versa, an increase in its profit rate brings with it an increase in capital value and wealth. The three change in related fashion. In any case, such are the hazards of the market: constant change in prospective earnings, and related changes in capital values and wealth, place a premium on being able to read the uncertain future.

Imputation and MR vs. MC

Although our illustrations of the imputation process have come mostly from economics and business, imputation processes apply in a general way to all human action. In making choices and in applying means toward achieving given ends, future value always determines present value; that is, the value attached to one's goal, purpose, or object of future enjoyment determines the present (albeit discounted) value of the means that can be applied toward achieving the given end.

In our present context, a corollary implication runs as follows: man will apply means toward the satis-faction of a goal only when the value attached to the goal exceeds or at least equals the value attached to the means of achieving that goal, depending on how distant in time is the goal. Colloquially put, man will put out effort so long as the eventual payoff seems worthwhile, or the benefit exceeds the cost. Or, con-versely, man acts because the goal is sufficiently worthwhile to warrant the cost.

In the language of economics, man will act on a goal only when its marginal revenue (MR)--that is, the total amount of gain or benefit expected from the goal-- promises to exceed or at least equal the marginal cost (MC)--that is, the total costs involved in achieving that goal. Since MC represents current outlays, it is calculated as a present discounted value. Therefore, the more distant the goal, the more must MR exceed MC. Also, in the case of the firm, since MR and MC consist of "batches" or "lumps" of dollars, these dollar totals must be divided by the number of units produced in order to yield a unit profit margin comparable to the concept of unit profits hitherto used.

Derived Demand for Factors

Another fairly obvious implication is that the firm's demand for factors of production (labor, etc.) is a derived demand--derived from the anticipated demand for its product. As we saw in Chapter II (Figure 4), the firm is essentially a go-between between people as demanders of products (consumers) and people as owners of resources (workers, etc.). In this intermediary role the firm relies on its estimate of future market demand as a guide to its current demand for labor and other resources.

In the case of consumers' goods, the demand for factors is derived from the anticipated consumers' demand; in the case of producers' or capital goods, the demand for factors is derived from other firms' demand for capital goods. In both cases, the firm will not hire or buy services, supplies, or equipment before it has estimated the market demand for its product. These estimates of market demand can be optimistic, pessimistic, or merely moderate, but in all cases the firm can be either right or wrong, due to market uncertainty.

The significance of this is that anticipated market demand emerges as the ultimate determinant not only of the quantity and selling price of the firm's product but also of the quantity of resources the firm uses and the factor prices (wage rates, rent, etc.) it pays to resource owners. The quantity of resources used, multiplied by the prices paid to resource owners, constitutes the total cost of production as well as the income earned by resource owners. The total cost divided by the number of units produced yields the unit or average cost (AC). It is this AC which represents the present discounted value that the firm derives when it "works back from price," to determine the profitable limit to costs.

"Cost-of-Production" Theory of Price

A still further significant implication of the imputation principle is that it undermines the cost-of-production theory of price. This popular concept was given authority by classical economists of the early 19th century, and was converted into the "labor theory of value" by Marxists for partisan purposes. In response to the traditional question in economics, "What determines price?", this theory has alleged that it is the

266

cost of production that determines selling price. In effect, it is a "cost-plus" theory of pricing.

With a bit of simplification, the cost theory runs as follows: First, the firm calculates its cost of production per unit of output; it then adds on a profit margin, and voila!, it arrives at the market selling price. In the Marxist version, all costs boil down to but one: labor effort expended by workers. Labor alone creates the "value" of products that is the basis of their "exchange-value" in the market place. Thus market price is supposed to reflect the number of man-hours of labor embodied in the product.

Marxist vs. Non-Marxist Versions

Marxist proponents of the labor-value theory of price claim that the firm's profits represent "exploitation" because their source is the "value" created by workers. On the other hand, non-Marxist proponents of the cost-theory of price allege that firms in the market economy can earn profits at will. For them, profits are merely an addendum to the costs of production, and their size is determined entirely at the discretion of the firm.

More precisely, firms are alleged to have the power to "administer" prices--to raise prices whenever they wish to increase profit margins. This power to "administer" prices is also the core of the "cost-push" theory of price inflation, which holds that firms cause inflation merely by raising prices. The fallacy of the "administered price" concept will be discussed in Chapter XI. Here it suffices to assert that, in the real world, firms in no way possess the magical power to increase profit margins at will merely by raising prices.

Market Determines Prices

The general cost-of-production theory of price runs smack against the theory of price presented in this book. As we have maintained all along, it is the market, with its forces of demand and supply--and not the firm--that is the ultimate determinant of selling prices. In Chapters X and XI we will see even more forcefully that it is not of ultimate importance that in practice it is firms who post selling prices. No firm can regard its posted price as the underline(ultimate) selling price--the price at which the demander actually decides to buy. The final selling price is entirely up to the state of market demand and supply. And, after all, it is this _final_ market price that really matters; the _initial_ price posted by the firm in the ex-ante phase is, by the nature of the case, no more than a tentative price, subject to final validation by the marketplace. In no way can the firm be consoled by its ability to post a price that straightaway must face the market test.

"Working Back from Price"

Furthermore, we have seen in the present chapter that far from costs determining prices--as is commonly assumed--it is just the reverse: market price determines costs! Before the firm can profitably decide how much to spend on labor, materials, rent and other costs, it must estimate the price at which it can sell its product. Only after the firm has made its best estimate of the future price can it then profitably work back from price--that is, subtract its unit profit margin from the price and determine the limit to its current outlays or AC.

This is not the place to get bogged down in the doctrinal history of the controversy over the cost-of-production theory of price and the Marxist labor theory of value. It suffices to note that the cost theory was massively challenged by economists of the late 19th century such as W. Jevons, C. Menger, and E. von Böhm-Bawerk. By 1913, P. H. Wicksteed could confidently assert the victory of the "marginalist" revolution against the cost-of-production theory as follows: "[T]he idea that cost of production already incurred determines exchange value [i.e., price] turns out to be a reversal of the true relation. It is the anticipated value in exchange [i.e., expected selling price] that determines what cost of production the producer will be willing to encounter...." (underlining and brackets mine). [3]

---

[3]Philip H. Wicksteed, "The Scope and Method of Political Economy in the Light of the 'Marginal' Theory of Distribution" (1913), reprinted in R. L. Smyth (ed.), Essays In Economic Method (New York: McGraw-Hill Book Co., 1963), p. 249.

Labor's Claim to Product

Let us discuss some further drawbacks of the Marxist "labor" theory of price. After this will come a critique of the more general "cost" theory of price.

First of all, in the modern division of labor there is no way that workers can legitimately claim the full market value of the product. The reason is simple: labor is <u>not</u> <u>the</u> <u>only</u> resource used in production. Alongside workers are landlords, moneylenders, materials suppliers, and equipment owners, among others. As it is, workers account for the bulk (more than 70 percent) of the national income; the remaining 30 percent goes to several other groups. Unincorporated business--e.g., self-employed professionals, farmers--gets about 10 percent, while earners of profits, rent, and interest account for the other 20 percent.

There is an even more important reason that labor cannot lay claim to the full product. On the basis of what we said in Section II, in the case of our computer firm, it is clear that the final product--the 200 computers--belongs to the firm and not the workers. This is based on the nature of the exchange embodied in the employment contract: the workers agree to offer 40 hours, say, of labor in exchange for $5 per hour wages. That is to say, their <u>only</u> claim on the firm is $5 for each hour worked. Therefore, since the <u>product</u> is owned by the firm, the full proceeds from their sale on the market, including the profits, belong to the firm and not the workers. Hence, there can be no "exploitation" in the sense of taking from the workers what belongs to the workers.

True Source of Profits

Furthermore, the true <u>source</u> <u>of</u> <u>the</u> <u>profits</u> themselves is the market demand for computers; more precisely, the expenditures made by final customers. It is physically impossible for the firm to earn profits from any other source except the <u>customers</u> <u>in</u> <u>the</u> <u>market</u> who like the computer enough to buy it. In no way can workers be the source of profits when it is entirely up to <u>the</u> <u>market</u> to yield them. That is, the product must sell out in the market place before the firm can earn profits <u>as</u> <u>expected</u>.

Imagine, for example, what would happen to profits if planned sales of the computer <u>fail</u> <u>to</u> <u>materialize</u>. Indeed, let us assume the worst of all possible outcomes: not one unit is sold--the firm loses out in competition with a rival's cheaper, superior model. In this extreme case, we get an interesting result: workers and other resource-owners have <u>already</u> gotten their $87,000 income (in wages, rent, etc.) from the firm's previous outlays for each unit produced--but the firm, alas, gets no profits at all!

It should be evident, therefore, that it is <u>not</u> the workers' labor that is the source of profits <u>but</u> the market demand. Indeed, since the market determines whether there are profits, and how much, it is the market that also determines whether there is "exploitation" in the Marxist sense!

For example, assume that our computer firm sold all 200 units at $13,000 profit for each unit after resource-owners had earned their $87,000 (with workers getting $60,000, say) for each unit produced. The emergence of profits makes this a case of "exploitation" in the Marxist sense. But if, on the other hand, none of the computers was sold, yielding zero profits to the firm, we would have to conclude that the <u>same</u> $60,000 received by workers for each unit produced was <u>not</u> an "exploitation" wage after all! We thus arrive at the curious conclusion that the deciding factor as to whether there is "exploitation" is the market! That is to say, it is the customers who, every time they like a product and buy it, thereby validate the firm's profit expectations and thereby cause the workers to be "exploited"!

"Labor" Unit a Fiction

This brings us to the critical point: There is <u>no such thing</u> as a standard unit of "labor value" in the <u>first place</u>. There is no such entity that is supposedly produced by the worker. There are only <u>man-hours</u> of labor expended on the product, the wage-rate for which--in a market economy--depends ultimately on the market demand for the product. The best way to see why the "labor value" unit is a fiction is to visualize the following case.

Imagine a self-employed worker who has no "boss" to "exploit" him, but who makes his living by producing and selling leather shoes for barter-exchange with others in the market. He works some 60 hours a week, say, and produces 10 pairs per week. Thus, each pair of shoes takes six hours of labor. On the market, he seeks to sell the shoes in exchange for sugar, candles, oils, and other consumers' goods.

Theoretically, in order to give his labor a uniform market value over time, our shoe craftsman should seek in exchange the same amount of other goods for each pair of shoes. That is to say, he should seek the same "price" for each hour of labor expended on his shoes. For example, he expects that one pair will always fetch ten pounds of sugar, or one gallon of oil, or three dozen candles, and so on. But in practice, this expectation is rarely fulfilled. Sometimes he gets more sugar, oil, or candles for a pair of shoes, sometimes less. In effect, the "purchasing" power of his shoes--that is, of hours of his labor--is not stable but fluctuates from day to day.

Labor's Fluctuating Value

What is it that causes this fluctuation in the "value" of our shoemaker's hour of labor? How is it possible for the product of an hour of labor to fluctuate in its exchange-rate with an hour's product of another worker?

Let us first rule out changes in the quality of product; we assume the quality is uniform over time. Given this uniformity of quality in product, the shoemaker reasonably expects the same, constant exchange rate between his pair of shoes and other goods. Let us also rule out changes in the shoemaker's subjective valuation of his shoes, which might induce him to sell them at higher or lower exchange-rates because of a higher or lower subjective value attached to his shoes compared with other goods.

We will also rule out any changes in productivity or "efficiency"--in the number of shoes produced per man-hour. We assume productivity is constant: one pair produced every six hours. For example, if his productivity somehow increases--say, to one pair every five hours--his total weekly output also increases and he can offer more pairs for each unit of other goods "purchased" in the market. Thus, his increased supply would compel him to reduce the "price" of his shoes.

271

Conversely, if his productivity declines, and he produces only one pair every ten hours, each hour of his
labor now exchanges for less of other goods.   It is as
though he had raised the "price" of his shoes relative
to that of other goods. All this we assume away.

Role of Market Demand and Supply

There remains only one possible answer as to why
his hour of labor fluctuates in exchange-rate with other
goods: fluctuations in market conditions of demand and
supply. And we do not mean changing conditions in the
shoe market alone, but in all other goods markets as
well. As we saw in the preceding chapter, shifting
demand and supply conditions bring on changes in price.
It makes no difference whether it is a barter economy or
a money economy: shifting D and S conditions will cause
changes in exchange-values or "price relationships"
between one good and another.

For example, in a monetary economy, the changes
in "price" occur in the changed exchange-rates between
units of   money and units of other goods--for example,
the exchange-rate or price of beer can go from one can
for 20 cents to one can for 30 cents. Similarly, in the
barter economy, the exchange-rate or price commanded by
a pair of shoes can go from one pair for one gallon of
oil to one pair for a half-gallon of oil.

Thus, the market emerges as the primary cause of
changes in the exchange-value of an hour of labor and,
hence, is the ultimate determinant of the market value
of a labor hour. And, as far as the market is concerned, it makes no difference whether the worker is
"his own boss" or works for a firm; it is the market
that determines the "price" commanded by any given product and, indirectly, determines the value attached to
labor (or any other factor input) as well as the size of
the profit rate.

Workers' Control of Firms

Otherwise, in the free-market economy--which
will be further analyzed in detail in the next chapter--
workers are totally free to abandon their role of
alleged "wage-slaves" and themselves undertake the
entrepreneurial role of the firm. This they can do by
organizing their own firm under so-called workers'

control; they can pool their savings, or borrow the
savings of others through the financial institutions,
and invest these savings in their own firm. But even
so, they would themselves then have to make current
outlays for wages and other factor payments, and to wait
until their product is completed and sold before they
could recoup their expenditures and earn profits for
themselves.

Since, in fact, workers do not generally rush to
buy out existing firms or establish new ones
themselves--in order to specialize as entrepreneurs
themselves--we can conclude that they prefer the existing division of labor between themselves as "workers"
and others as "firms." Whereas the firm must wait for
its returns (profits), the worker gets his payoff now,
without waiting. He prefers to take his money and run,
as the saying goes. Thus, those who have relatively
high time preference will tend to be attracted to the
role of the "worker," whereas those with relatively low
time preference will tend to be the savers and
"capitalists" who invest their own wealth in production.
That is, the latter look upon their investment in firms
as the means of achieving a future consumption that is
greater than if they had not saved and invested.

Costs Are "Prices"

Now, as for the general cost theory of price, it
too is heir to all the objections levelled against the
Marxist labor-theory of value. In addition, it is embar-
rassed by an economic truth: costs are themselves
"prices." A wage-rate for labor is a price; so is rent
a price; materials costs, too, resolve themselves into
prices. And in every case these factor prices are
determined by the same market forces of demand and
supply that determine consumers' goods prices. Thus, it
is circular reasoning to argue that factor costs explain
market price when these costs are themselves determined
by the very same market forces they are supposed to
explain in the first place!

Market Determines Wage-Rates

The dependence of factor prices and costs on
market demand and supply can be exemplified by the wage-
rate--the price paid for labor. In Figure 31 we see how
the hourly wage-rate would be determined by market
D and S.

273

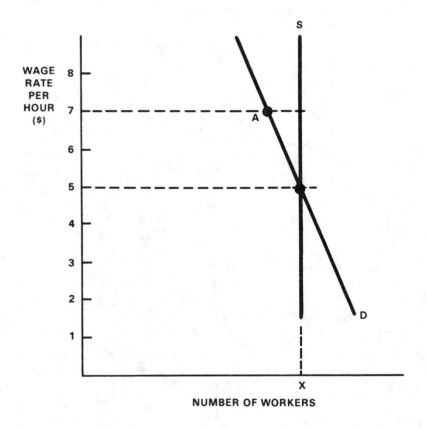

FIGURE 31:
MARKET DETERMINATION OF WAGE-RATE.

274

To simplify the exposition, let us assume a 40-hour work week. The demand schedule relates to the firms; it reflects their demand for workers--the number of jobs they would offer at various wage-rates. It possesses the characteristic slope downward from left to right, which means that, other things being equal, more workers would be employed only at lower wage-rates, and fewer workers would be employed at higher rates of pay.

On the other hand, the supply schedule relates to the workers: its verticality indicates that, at the given moment, there is a fixed number of workers who are seeking to work a 40-hour work week. But each worker has his own minimum "reservation price"--the minimum wage-rate below which he will not accept work. Thus, the hourly wage-rates acceptable to workers run from as low as $1.50 on up.

Cause of "Unemployment"

How does the market determine the wage-rate in a given field? Figure 31 says that any worker seeking a job can find one if he limits his wage demand to $5 an hour or less. The $5 rate would exactly clear the market: at this wage, the number of workers seeking jobs (X) is just equal to the number of jobs being offered (X). But at any higher wage-rate, say $7, workers would be inviting some unemployment: while the number of workers seeking jobs remains X, the number of workers being sought by firms has dropped to A, causing unemployment for AX workers. Clearly, at $7 the workers would be overpricing themselves, and as we saw in Chapter VIII, overpricing leads to unsold surplus which, in the case of workers, means "unemployment." Unemployment is the market's way of penalizing the overpricing of labor--the way it limits wage demands made by workers.

At first glance, it is the demander--the individual firm--which decides the highest wage-rate it is willing to pay, a limit it establishes as a result of "working back" from the expected selling price of its product. All firms together, therefore, comprise the market demand for labor. But, since firms are merely intermediaries between consumers and resource-owners, they come to realize sooner or later that it is the consumer who ultimately determines the limit to the wage-rate payable to workers.

Factor Costs Are Opportunity Costs

The cost-theory of price is mired in circular reasoning for another reason. The "costs" of producing a given good X are essentially <u>opportunity costs</u>: they reflect foregone opportunities, i.e., the other things that the given resources could produce if they were not used in producing X. Where technology permits, resources are generally useful in the production of a <u>variety</u> of goods. Labor, indeed, is the most <u>nonspecific</u> resource of all, since it can be applied in producing an infinite variety of goods and services. In lesser degrees, the same is true for land, materials, and many types of equipment. They are all more or less capable of serving <u>diverse</u> production purposes. For this reason, their utilization in producing any <u>given</u> good necessarily involves an opportunity cost. Indeed, the "opportunity cost" concept is made relevant precisely because of the diverse or non-specific uses to which resources can be applied.

Furthermore, the opportunity cost itself is measurable in terms of the earnings which the firm--or the resource-owners themselves--could have earned from using their resources in alternative uses. The market enables us to place a <u>market value</u> ("price") on the alternative goods and services that could have been rendered with the given resources. Hence, for the firm, the "costs" of producing X merely reflect the potential profits from foregone opportunities to produce and sell other things. For the resource-owner, the "cost" of offering his resource to the producer of X reflects the <u>earnings</u> he could have received in some alternative production program.

To be more precise, the firm will employ resources for producing X only when it expects to earn <u>more</u> this way than using the resources to produce Y, Z, etc. Similarly, the resource-owner will offer his goods or services to the firm producing X only when he can receive <u>more</u> from this firm than he can receive from producers of Y, Z, etc. Thus, a producer of motorcycles will stick to producing them rather than motorized bicycles so long as--other things being equal--earnings from the former exceed potential earnings from the latter. Similarly, a design engineer will stick to his job at General Motors rather than switch to Ford so long as--other things being equal--his salary at GM exceeds the salary offered by Ford.

276

What Determines Opportunity Costs?

Although the concept of "opportunity cost" is valid as far as it goes, it nevertheless prompts us to ask: Doesn't this concept itself beg the question? Indeed, there are several additional questions that beg for answers.

First, what determines the value of the given resources in their alternative, foregone uses? For example, if the value of resources used in making motorcycles is related to their value in making motorized bikes, it is proper to ask: What, then, determines their value in making motor bikes? This raises a second question: Why is the producer of X induced to use the given resources in making X rather than in making Y, Z, etc. Also, a third question: What induces General Motors to pay its design engineer a higher salary than he can get at Ford?

To the first question, the answer could very well be as follows: The present discounted value of resources used in making motor bikes is, as we have seen above, determined by the market price that demanders are willing to pay. Essentially the same answer pertains to the second question: The market demand and price for product X are presumably more attractive than in the case of product Y, Z, etc. An additional answer could be this: The firm is more efficient--is able to achieve lower unit costs--in making X than in making other products. This increased efficiency enables it to earn a higher profit margin. Both of these answers are also relevant to the third question: Either the greater demand and price for GM automobiles enables GM to pay its design engineer a higher salary than can Ford, or GM's greater efficiency and profit margin enable it to do so.

Conclusion

What could have been a relatively narrow discussion of profits has turned into an economic Odyssey through the world of time and time - preference, pure interest, risk, and inflation--to say nothing of imputation processes, capital values, opportunity costs and the labor theory of value. From the simple concept of "production takes time" we went a long way to show that present values mirror future values. But this is

277

in the nature of things. It is the "tail" of the future
that wags the "dog" of today; tomorrow's expected benefits induce or warrant the incurring of today's costs.
The "future" and "today," it turns out, are linked
inextricably in terms of benefit and cost.

CHAPTER X

THE CONSUMERS' SOVEREIGNTY PROBLEM

Consumers' sovereignty may be the central political-economic issue facing people in modern society. The question of consumers' sovereignty is not merely an empirical one--a question of whether the consumer is actually "king" in the market place, or to what extent the consumer exercizes any "sovereignty." The more important question is the normative one: Should the consumer be "sovereign" in the market? In this chapter we will understand why the consumer should be "sovereign," and how this "sovereignty" could be made optimal. We will then see why consumers' sovereignty is not only crucial in a free society but may also be one of the central issues facing all of modern society.

The "Matching" Problem

Two basic facts lie at the root of modern economic systems. One fact is essentially natural and economic: the primary purpose of production is consumption. Man engages in production primarily or ultimately only for the purpose of producing the consumers' goods he wants, including the capital goods with which to produce the consumers' goods. As Adam Smith put it in The Wealth of Nations, "Consumption is the sole and end purpose of all production...."[1]

Alongside this, however, is a great socio-logical-historical fact: man has become predominantly dependent on specialization and the social division of labor (hereafter termed DOL, for short) characterized by its elaborate system of exchange transactions among specialists of all types (recall the analysis above in Chapters II-IV).

Since man's primary purpose in production is the creation of desired consumers' goods, the logical arrangement would be one in which people, as producers, are producing or helping to produce things that they

---

[1] Adam Smith, The Wealth of Nations (New York: Modern Library, 1937), p. 625.

themselves want to consume. That is to say, it would seem reasonable that there should be a correspondence or matching between people's demands and the quantity, variety, and quality of goods that get produced. Wherein, then, lies the modern problem? It lies in the fact that people are, by and large, no longer engaged in producing directly for themselves; instead, they depend on others to organize the sphere of production and sell goods to them. As a consequence, there arises the matching problem.

Households vs. Firms

The modern social DOL, as we saw in Chapter IV, characteristically created a functional separation with respect to production. The functional separation emerged historically when households relinquished to firms the special task of organizing production so that firms became the "producers" while household members specialized both as owners of resources (labor, land, etc.) and as "consumers." The advantages were unquestionable: Firms have been better able than households to take advantage of the immense economies accruing to large-scale productive methods, and these gains were then shared with households in the form of tremendous output at lower costs and prices.

However, the overwhelming consequence of the separation of production from households under the DOL is the matching problem, whose outlines are drawn in Figure 32. (This is a duplicate of Figure 2 in Chapter II.) Formerly households combined all three economic functions within a single social unit--that is, the functions of owning the means to produce, production, and consumption. Now, in the DOL, we find production concentrated, by and large, within the framework of firms who have become the "producers," while the other two functions, naturally, still reside with the households. Since households by definition include everyone in society, they naturally include all the owners of resources and consumers. This gives rise to a problem of the first magnitude: How can households influence firms to produce what households want as consumers--in the quantities, variety, and quality they want?

Interdependent Relationships

Once again, what are the primary relations

280

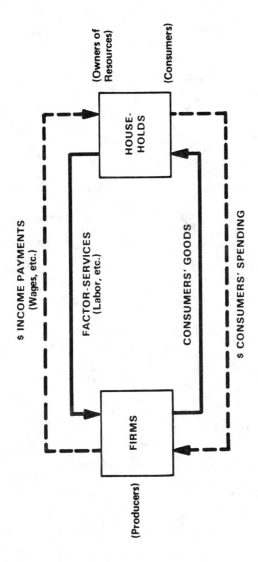

FIGURE 32:
RELATIONS BETWEEN HOUSEHOLDS AND FIRMS.

between households and firms, as shown in Figure 32? For one thing, firms are necessarily dependent on house- holds for the supply of labor, loanable funds, and other resources. Without these resources, firms simply cannot produce the consumers' goods they want to sell to house- holds. This brings us to a second dependent relation- ship: the firms' dependence on consumers' demand as the market for their consumers' goods output. These two lines of dependence are shown by the two inner lines in Figure 32. Vitally related to these two inner lines are the two outer (dashed) lines, which represent monetary counterparts--the upper dashed line being the wages, interest and other income payments made to resources owners, while the lower dashed line is the consumers' payments for goods purchased from firms.

On the other hand, in what ways are households dependent on firms? Clearly, since households no longer serve as the locus of production, they now must look to the firms to produce for them the things they once produced themselves. Thus, there emerges in the DOL a mutual interdependence between households and firms. But beneath it all smolders the basic matching problem: How can households influence firms in producing the things that households want but which they no longer produce for themselves?

Optimizing the Match

There is another way of viewing the matching problem: How can society minimize the likelihood of mismatch between what consumers want and what firms actually produce? In the modern DOL, the likelihood of such mismatch is ever-present. Let us briefly review the argument.

As abundantly described in earlier chapters, firms naturally cannot possess perfect knowledge of market demand in a world of constant change. They have to chart their way in the market with varying degrees of ignorance and uncertainty. Thus there can be no guaran- tee that what firms produce at any given time matches exactly what consumers want. Thus it would seem to be desirable to create social arrangements that would be able to minimize the likelihood of mismatch--or, con- versely, to optimize the correspondence between what consumers want and what firms actually produce. What would these optimal social arrangements look like? This is the central question which this chapter addresses.

282

When Mismatch Is Rare

It is ironic that the matching problem simply could not exist in Crusoe-like self-subsistence with its small-scale peasant families, clans, or tribes. True, such economies were characterized by primitive technology, low productivity, and low living standards, with their poverty, disease, and misery. But as to modern problems of "mismatch" between households and firms-- between what people want and what actually gets produced? None of those! In the world of self-subsistence, what the people wanted they produced for themselves. The variety of goods produced may have been narrow and quantity meager, but at least there was a direct correspondence between goods produced and goods desired. How could it be otherwise when product was for direct use of producers themselves and not for sale in the market place.

Nor does the matching problem pertain when goods are made to custom-order. Whether it is a suit of clothing, a house, an automobile, or an industrial product--components, equipment, or buildings--the customer's specifications and instructions to the producer minimize the likelihood of mismatch between what is ordered and what is actually produced. Even though the producer here is not the same person as the consumer, customized production can, by mutual agreement, achieve minimal or zero mismatch.

Similarly, in the area of services provided by doctors, lawyers, mechanics, and other professionals and artisans, the direct arrangements between consumer and producer enable a minimizing of mismatch. Finally, do-it-yourself activities by the householder who does his own repairs, maintenance, building, or other productive activities for his own direct use, permit a like degree of correspondence.

High Price of Self-Subsistence

Nevertheless, Crusoe and other self-subsistence or direct-use modes of economy come at a very high cost --isolated existence, primitive science and technology, low levels of production, and impoverished living standards. Man working with only primitive tools faces nature almost alone with bare hands. The existence he ekes out is meager in quantity and variety. So, while he suffers no correspondence problem, he suffers the

283

threat of infertile soil and poor crops. And his technological backwardness narrows his scope of adjustment
to alternative varieties of product and methods of
production.

Yet, in contrast, the modern social division of
labor (DOL)--with its ever-expanding exchange and
production, application of science and technology, and
use of money--inherently posits the matching problem.
Therefore, to the extent that people become involved in
the modern DOL, to that extent will the matching problem
affect their interpersonal transactions, and to that extent does the crucial question become: How can people,
as consumers, exert optimal influence over firms to
produce the things they want?   How can firms be made
most responsive to consumers' preferences?

The State and Planners' Preferences

In this connection it is important to note that
under socialism--especially in highly centralized models
like the U.S.S.R.--the matching problem becomes irrelevant as far as the ruling party is concerned, even
though such systems rely more or less on extensive
division of labor. In the rulers' eyes, the state must
maintain a total monopoly of production, including
ownership of all physical resources used in production,
and power to control all incomes and prices. In contrast, householders, shorn of property rights in the
means of production, are not permitted access to own
such means in order to produce for themselves what the
state's enterprises fail to provide. As far as the
state is concerned, the only recourse left to the consumer is simply not to buy--to do without.

True, the consumer living under socialism can
exercise more or less freedom of choice in his market
purchases--freedom to choose from among the existing
array of goods produced for him by the state. But
that's all. His "freedom" is limited in the most confined sense: He has no alternative but to buy or not to
buy what the state proffers.

In this connection it should be noted that even
in so-called free-market countries such as the United
States, there are areas in which the matching problem
also becomes irrelevant. For example, to the extent
that the government intervenes into the economy to provide so-called public goods, such statist production

necessarily competes for scarce resources and diverts them from the free-market sector that is consumer oriented. Since consumers are taxed and thereby <u>forced</u> to pay for public goods--goods that are by definition not subject to the free-market test of <u>voluntary</u> purchase--they are denied effective influence over what gets produced.

Optimizing Consumers' Influence

Thus far we have mainly described the nature of the <u>matching problem</u> and why it is peculiar to the modern DOL. We have also indicated why it is a crucially important problem: because of the natural primacy of consumption as the purpose of production. Thus, to the extent that people are concerned about the primacy of consumption and in optimizing their influence over producers as to what ultimately gets produced, to that extent it becomes relevant to find an answer to the central intellectual problem imbedded in the matching problem: Under <u>which conditions</u> would it be possible to <u>optimize</u> the influence of consumers over what <u>ultimately</u> gets produced by the firms? That is, what social-political conditions--philosophy and ideals, on the one hand, and institutions and practices, on the other--would enable consumers to exert optimal influence over the assortment of goods ultimately produced? Alternatively, what conditions are required to make firms most responsive to consumers' wishes?

Information and Motivation

Given the nature of the problem, some basic methodological considerations are in order. For one thing, required is some efficient mechanism for the transmission of <u>information</u> to firms about consumers' preferences--as to what consumers want and as to whether their wants are being satisfied. Required is a vehicle that will reveal consumers' preferences to the firms, so that the latter are guided as to what to produce, how much, and at what price. In other words, there must be an efficient method for "getting the message" from consumers to firms. Let us call this the <u>information requirement</u>.[2]

---

[2] A major work on the vital interdependence of the market-price system, information generation, and freedom, is by Thomas Sowell, <u>Knowledge and Decisions</u> (New York: Basic Books, Inc., 1980).

The second basic consideration involves incentives--the motivation of firms to produce according to revealed consumers' preferences. Specifically required is an incentive system that, on the one hand, provides rewards to firms that cater successfully to consumers' wishes and, on the other hand, penalizes them for failure to do so. The rewards must be sufficiently great in the long run to induce the firm to persevere despite short-term fumblings and setbacks. Initial difficulties are sure to confront the firm in its entrepreneurial ventures in the seas of competition and uncertain demand. The rewards must be large enough to justify the firms' plans to survive and prosper.

On the other hand, punishment for failure to cater successfully to consumers must be severe enough to deter firms from ever believing that they could get away with putting out less than their best effort at all times. No matter how successful in the past, firms must be deterred from resting on their laurels; they must be kept on their toes. Good reputations must be deserved, not guaranteed. We will call this system of rewards and penalties the incentive requirement.

The Meaning of "Optimum"

Before proceeding, the meaning of "optimum" consumers' influence should be explained. Above all, "optimum" calls for the listing of as many conditions as necessary to satisfy the requirements for optimal consumers' influence.

Second, "optimum" does not mean that firms must produce exactly what people want. Not even in the best of real worlds would such optimality be possible in the social DOL. We can only define an "optimum" for the realm of the possible. Real-world firms cannot escape making decisions under conditions of uncertain demand. Thus we must allow for the likelihood that there will be some mismatch between what consumers want and what firms actually produce.

Nor does "optimum" mean maximum quantity of output. The matching problem is not about quantities of goods produced. Rather, it is concerned with the problems faced by firms seeking to produce what consumers want under conditions of the modern division of labor.

Consumers' Dollar Ballots

The first step in our journey to discover the optimal conditions for consumers' influence over firms is realization of the key role played by the so-called consumers' dollar ballot--the dollar votes cast by consumers every time they buy something in the market. (It is represented by the bottom dashed line in Figure 32.)

At first glance, it might seem reasonable to be skeptical about the ultimate significance of the consumers' dollar ballots. After all, consumers typically spend their money on goods that have already been produced by the firm. Typically, consumers come into the market only to find that producers have already anticipated their desires by proffering products for the consumers' inspection and purchase. That is, firms do not wait for direct orders by consumers to tell them what to produce, how much, and at what price. They go ahead and produce in advance what they in their entrepreneurial judgment think people will want to buy. As we saw in Chapter IV, it is a system of "production first... buying later," so to speak. So, how can consumers' dollar ballots make for consumers' sovereignty after the fact, so to speak?

The fact remains that firms, precisely because they "produce first," are in a sense sticking their collective necks out for inspection by consumers, the latter being placed in the role of a final judge who has the power to accept or turn down what the firms proffer --to ratify and validate, or to veto and condemn. If consumers like what firms offer them, they will buy; otherwise they will not buy. In the modern DOL it cannot be otherwise. No matter whether it is capitalism or socialism, this is the predominant economic-socio-logical fact. To paraphrase Alchian and Allen, firms typically "proffer" goods, but it is the consumer who decides which goods to "prefer." [3] That is to say, consumers, after all, do have the final say. It remains for the consumer to decide whether the output of firms passes muster.

---

[3] Armen A. Alchian and William R. Allen, Exchange and Production (Belmont, Ca.: Wadsworth Publishing Co., 1969), pp. 142, 143.

Dimensions of Competition

On what basis do consumers vote aye or nay on the goods proffered in the market? Primarily on the basis of price, quality, and variety. For any given quality of product, consumers prefer to buy at the lowest price. For any given price line, consumers prefer to obtain the highest quality. Finally, consumers look with favor upon firms that anticipate consumers' tastes by producing an increasing variety of goods. In this way, price, quality, and variety are not only the main yardsticks by which consumers measure the popularity of firms, but they are also the main dimensions of competition among firms. That is, the ability of firms to survive and grow depends vitally on their competing successfully in terms of lower prices, better quality, and differentiation of product.

Economic Democracy and
Proportional Representation

Thus, consumers' voting with dollar ballots converts the market place, in effect, into a kind of economic democracy. Consumers' ballots are the means by which consumers indicate whether they like the job being done by firms and whether firms are catering successfully to their preferences. It is presumed that so long as consumers buy a firm's product, to that extent they show satisfaction with the firm's efforts. Conversely, when they do not buy its product, they are indicating dissatisfaction.

Thus, consumers' dollar ballots serve as the information mechanism through which consumers' preferences are transmitted to firms. It follows that output by firms will increase where consumers' dollars flow, and will decrease where consumers' spending dries up. In this way the array of goods and services produced for the market will constitute a kind of "proportional representation" of consumers' preferences.

In its working as an "economic democracy," the market is not to be judged by the subjective standards of any one arbiter, be they aesthetic, philosophical, or religious. The issue is not whether the market produces too much or too little of "culture," "material" goods, or rock music. So long as people buy what they think satisfies them, to that extent firms are producing what the people want.

288

Profit-and-Loss System

Furthermore, consumers' dollar ballots play a second vital role: They directly determine the profits and losses of firms! When consumers buy, firms will earn profits, and when they sit on their hands, firms will suffer losses. More precisely, only when people buy at the price and in the quantities initially set by firms will firms earn the expected profit rate. Otherwise, profit rates will be squeezed, or even losses may be incurred--that is, firms may fail to cover their average cost-per-unit of product. In this way consumers' dollar votes directly determine the economic fate of firms.

Seen from the individual firm's point of view, consumer dollar ballots determine whether the firm reaps profits or losses. However, from the point of view of the market system as a whole, the casting of consumer ballots creates a profit-and-loss system. While some firms succeed in reaping the expected profits, others suffer disappointing earnings or losses. Although all firms seek profits, not all succeed. As long as it is possible for any given firm to suffer losses, there is no guarantee of profits.

"Consumers' Sovereignty"

This brings us to the crux. To the extent that the very survival and growth of the firm depend vitally on its ability to earn profits and avoid losses, to that extent does the consumers' dollar ballot determine the very fate of the firm. Indeed, to the extent that the only way for the firm to survive is by earning profits, to that extent does the consumer achieve "sovereignty" in the market place.

"Sovereignty" is really not the best word for what is meant here; the dictionary defines it as rule or dominion over others, whereas what is meant here is optimal influence by means of the consumers' dollar ballots over what firms produce. Nevertheless, sovereignty is the term customarily used in economics, and we will hereafter use it, for convenience, to stand for the consumers' ability to determine ultimately what firms produce. Thus, our original task can be restated as a search for those conditions that will optimize consumers' sovereignty in the market.

Production for Use... for Profit

At this point it is appropriate to lay at rest an old cliche that the free market is inferior to the socialist economy because the former is merely a system of production for profit whereas socialism is production for use. The implication is that firms in the free market, being primarily motivated by profits, try to make profits by any means possible, by hook or crook, and the consumer be damned. In contrast, socialist firms are allegedly motivated primarily by the desire to produce useful commodities, with profits being a secondary or non-existent consideration. Yet it doesn't take much to realize that the cliche "production for profit" versus "production for use" involves a fallacious dichotomy, to wit.

There is no doubt the free market is production for profit, but it does not necessarily follow that it cannot, in the same breath, be a system of production for use. Indeed, history has amply shown that only by producing goods that consumers think are useful can firms earn profits and stay in business. Clearly, it would be inconceivable that firms could survive by producing shoddy goods or anything less than useful commodities. Furthermore, history reveals that only paternalistic protection by the state--in the form of tariffs, subsidies and bailouts--has enabled firms to survive even though consumers themselves had already rejected the firms for failing to compete successfully for their dollars.

Profits Under Socialism

In this connection we should note that profits exist under socialism, too--both in theory and in practice--although they are called something else. Marx's vision of socialism distinctly called for a profit margin to be earned by state enterprises. In the U.S.S.R., Soviet economists even boast that socialist profits are native to socialism and not an imitation of capitalism. Nevertheless, a profit margin by any other name is still a profit margin--a price spread between selling price and cost per unit of product. Socialists have variously called it a "common fund," "turnover tax," or "enterprise tax," terms which vainly disguise the fact that each constitutes a price spread or profit margin.

290

There is a key difference--not in the name given to profits but in the way the profits originate. In free competitive markets, profits are earned from the voluntary purchases of consumers. Under socialism, however, profits derive primarily from the monopoly position of the state. The Soviet state, for example, is the only producer--without any competition. It uses the price spread as a tax margin: prices of products are set on a cost-plus basis and are adjusted up or down, depending on the state's revenue requirements. Given the monopoly position of the state as producer, the pricing system used is, in effect, a tax mechanism.

Socialist Monopoly Profits

Another key difference between socialism and the free market is the way profits are used--that is, the extent to which profits are used for producing consumers' goods. Firms in the free market are virtually compelled to reinvest their profits in the same useful way that they were earned in the first place, by catering successfully to consumers. Socialist firms, however, are under no such compulsion. To start with, socialist profits are practically guaranteed: All firms are monopoly agents of the state, facing virtually no competition. Their selling prices, as we have noted, are a form of tax. Profits, therefore, are not a measure of performance but of extortion; consumers have no alternative but to buy from a monopoly source.

In contrast, the free market, as we will amply see, is by definition predicated on unrestricted competition--on optimum access to alternative sources of consumers' goods. Compared to the free market, socialism or any other system of controlled production by the state constitutes a drastic constriction of production opportunities; thus under socialism, firms are inherently incapable of optimizing consumers' sovereignty.

The Meaning of "Free Competition"

This brings us to the next requirement for optimal consumers' sovereignty. We have already discussed the need to make the earning of profits the only means by which the firm can survive. Now it is necessary to add another stringent condition: the fostering of maximum competition among firms. Availability of competition is one of the crucial differences between the free-market economy and socialism. The free market is "free" primarily in the sense of freedom to compete: "free competition" means precisely the liberty for anyone to enter into production. Let there be no artificial barrier or restriction on competition. Let all comers be free to compete--all for the purpose of optimizing consumers' sovereignty.

Thus, if for any reason consumers become dissatisfied with the products of firms, the market must always be open for the entry of another firm that thinks it can do better. And if anyone thinks he can do a better job than the existing firms, but merely remains on the sidelines--ranting, raving or complaining about the disappointing performance of those firms--such mocking behavior in no way serves the consumer. Talk is cheap. To really serve the consumer, mere bystanders would have to roll up their sleeves and get into the competition to prove that they can truly do a better job than existing firms. Indeed, the condition of free competition constitutes the only true test of optimal catering to consumers. Any artificial restriction of competition or barrier to entry results in a less-than-optimal degree of competition.

Government Monopoly Grants

Restrictions on entry into production can take a variety of forms. Historically, the predominant source of obstruction to entry has been government regulation: The state possesses the monopoly power to determine who shall and who shall not produce by its requirement of charters and licenses and similar controls. In some fields government itself runs the enterprise, as is the case with first-class mail. In other fields--for example, so-called public utilities such as water, electricity, and gas--government assigns only one firm to provide the given service, thereby granting a monopoly privilege to the selected firm.

If we use the word monopoly in its correct literal sense, it simply means: one single seller--the only seller. Traditionally, governments alone have been able to grant monopoly privileges in trade and production. In creating public utilities, the rationale is that water, electricity, and gas are "natural" monopolies due to the peculiar economic nature of their product. In fields where production is on a smaller scale

292

(such a taxicabs, barbershops, beauty parlors, plumbing, medicine, law, teaching... you name it!) government usually requires a special permit, license, or certificate in order to practice the given service.

Whether or not the doctrine of "natural monopoly" has any validity, the fact remains that it--or any other form of state-granted monopoly--is essentially a <u>restriction</u> of competition. By granting a legal privilege to one firm to be the <u>only</u> producer in its field, the government is blocking entry to any other firm, thereby protecting the monopoly firm against any competition. The legal muscle of the state prevents every potential competitor from getting a chance to outperform the monopolist and take his business away by driving rates (prices) down or by giving better service. In this respect, government protects the privileged monopolist from having to perform for the consumer in terms of price and quality. Far from being "natural," the state-granted monopoly privilege is an unnatural, arbitrary restriction of the natural freedom to produce.

Monopolies in the Free Market?

In a true free market, by contrast, a monopoly position could emerge--and properly so--only by the firm outstripping its rivals in behalf of the consumer. Under <u>open,</u> <u>unrestricted</u> competition, no firm--whether it produces electricity or milk or drives taxicabs-- could expect to become a monopoly except by excellent performance in terms of price and quality, by outperforming other firms in open competition for the consumers' dollars.

Nor could this hard-earned monopoly ever be considered a <u>privilege</u> guaranteeing the firm protection against any potential competition. The free-market monopolist would daily have to prove himself the best against all comers; as "King of the Hill," he could wear his crown only so long as he outperformed everyone else. And so long as the market remained open to one and all, his crown could not rest easily upon his head. There would never be respite from the threat of new competition. Without the state to protect him against potential rivals, his only shield against invasion of his market by competitors would be his low price and high quality.

Natural Obstacles to Entry

It follows then that in a free, open market the only obstacles to competition would be the truly natural ones that exist in any society at any time: scarcity of productive resources and the limited size of market demand.

For instance, not everyone can himself own all the necessary resources (of land, labor, capital) required to enter production. Nor does "free" competition mean costless entry--not requiring resources or sacrifice. Any new competitor would have to purchase, hire, or borrow resources from others for which he will have to pay a price, wage, or interest rate. Furthermore, individual differences in managerial and entrepreneurial skill will enable some potential competitors to be more successful than others.

Can Investors Be Attracted?

In this connection it is important to note the crucial financial role played by the money and capital markets--the former consisting primarily of commercial banks, and the latter consisting of financial intermediaries, such as the stock and bond markets, savings banks, and managers of trust and pension funds. It is through this vast, complex array of financial institutions that the owners of savings and other liquid wealth ultimately determine the availability and cost of their investment funds and, hence, the firm's access to resources and production. However, the essential criterion for investors, in deciding whether or not to invest in a given firm, is the ability of the borrowing firm to succeed in market competition. Investors' estimates of a firm's competitive ability are, in the nature of the case, necessarily subjective, resting on intangibles such as the quality of the firm's personnel, the morale and efficiency of its labor force, and the potential size of market demand.

Demand Cannot Be Guaranteed

On the demand side, as indicated, the obstacle to entry will be uncertainty about the size of market demand. Such uncertainty will usually be a problem in the case of a new product to which the market has yet to become accustomed. This does not necessarily mean that

the market is foreclosed forever. Indeed, experience
tells us that there is no way to foretell whether or not
a new product will click upon introduction to the
market. This is precisely what entrepreneurship is all
about: the undertaking of projects in the face of
uncertain market demand.

To be sure, market research and related investi-
gations of market demand can help reduce the degree of
uncertainty as to whether a new product will succeed.
Otherwise, the only ultimate test as to whether the
market is ready to welcome a new product and shower the
firm with profits is for the firm to take the plunge
into the cold waters and see for itself. There is truly
no other way to find out if the demand is there or not,
at least initially. If the demand is not there at the
start, it may develop eventually if and when the product
finally catches on. But this requires persistence and
perseverance to wait it out--yet even then success cannot be guaranteed.

Competing Against Incumbents

Another reason to doubt the adequacy of market
demand for the newcomer may be the apparently entrenched
position of the firms already established in the market,
each of which has already won for itself a seemingly
impregnable share of the market which no upstart entrant
dare think of capturing. But such incumbency of firms
is, in the nature of things, a fact of life. The newcomer in the market must nearly always expect to compete
against incumbents no less than does a presidential
aspirant who has to decide whether or not to throw his
hat into the ring.

Even if a new product were involved--one not
produced by any existing firm--it would still not
guarantee clear sailing. Its producer would still have
to face an incumbency problem, one that takes a special
form. Say the new product is a "smidget," which its
promoters regard as a sure-fire bet to catch on. Nevertheless the fact remains that, initially at least,
consumers' purchases of the new smidgets could only be
made by their buying less of other things. (Think of
television's first days.)

Let us briefly expand on this. In practice,
competition exists not only between different brands of
a given product but also between different products

295

themselves. Since all consumer wants are "competitive"
with each other, it follows that all products are also
in competition with each other--and no less than all the
brands that compete with each other.   In other words, a
dollar spent on smidgets means, other things being
equal, a dollar less spent on something else.   Even if
there were only one firm producing all products, there
would still be this product competition, and the monopolist would not necessarily have a guaranteed market for
his new product.

Competition of All Against All

          Up to now we have described free competition
mostly in terms of the absence of legal or other artificial restrictions on entry into production.   New we must
meet the other face of free competition--the variety of
sources of competition from which new firms and new
products can be expected to flow.   Indeed, once we
remove all barriers to competition, sources from whence
will come the new competitors are unlimited.

          To start with, existing firms in industry A
could decide to invade industry B, and vice versa.   It
would be competition of all against all, regardless of
the industry with which a particular firm is normally
identified.   For instance, a firm in industry A could
decide to invade industry B.   That is to say, it may
decide to produce, in addition to its old product A, a
new product B.   Furthermore, it may be a fairly big
firm,   well-heeled and capable of giving firms in
industry B a run for their money.   No longer could the
successful fat cats in B rest on their laurels, even
after they have attained major shares of the market from
the smaller firms in B.   The reason is that well-
established producers in industry A, as well as in C, D,
and so on, stand as a constant threat to enter B and
compete in it.   And the same threats constantly face A,
too, and C, and D, and so on!

          This possibility of inter-industry competition
opens up vistas of a vastly expanded arena of competition. Not only would firms in the same industry compete
with each other, but so would firms in different
industries compete with firms in other industries.
Thus, competition would be pervasive--product against
product, firm against firm.   It is therefore reasonable
to expect the emergence of conglomerates--firms that

296

would be grandly diversified, so much so that some would
be hard to classify in terms of the particular "industry" to which they belonged.

In Numbers There Is Strength

        Thus it is appropriate to question the tradi-
tional notion that "bigness is bad"--that "giant" firms
are "bad" because they are so big and efficient that
small firms are too weak to compete against them. Such
popular notions turn out to be fallacious; real-world
experience is not so neatly stacked in favor of the big
firm.

        For one thing, there are those giant firms in
the other industries (mentioned above) who often constitute the truly fearsome rivals of any big firm. For
another, let us not underestimate the power of even the
small firm. After all, smaller firms may be able to
produce a given product as cheaply and capably as the
large firm. Examples abound: toasters, radios, and a
variety of other appliances. True, in any given market
location, it would seem that a giant General Electric,
for example, could easily muster all of its resources to
drown out any one small competitor. But in practice it
cannot actually do so, for GE faces not one but numerous
small competitors in any given locale, as well as in
many other locales throughout the country. Taken together, all these many small competitors add up, in
effect, to a pretty big-size firm.

Consumer's Last Resort

        Last but not least, truly free competition would
enable consumers themselves to take up the cudgels and
compete in the market place. That is, if existing firms
dared to disdain the consumers' dollar ballot, and per-
sistently failed to respond to consumers' preferences,
then the consumer would have the ultimate recourse: the
freedom to undertake himself the production of what he
wants. In the free market, the consumer himself--a
"sovereign" in search of a crown--would also have freedom of access to the sphere of production. Since we are
all consumers--each and every one of us--this means
that, in the nature of things, each of us should be free
to enter into production, unobstructed and unhampered by
anyone.

Herein lies one of the truly vital differences between the free-market economy and socialism. Under socialism, because of its state monopoly of the means of production, the individual is prohibited from access to such property and hence to the sphere of production. In the free market, however, he is free to set up an individual proprietorship or a partnership, or form a corporation of stockholders or cooperative owners--it makes little difference which, at this point. The organization of production can take whatever form is deemed appropriate by the owner or owners of the firm.

It is therefore not surprising to learn that, almost from the very inception of the Industrial Revolution, ordinary people from all walks of life--given the environment of a relatively free market--were able to abandon their roles as workers, tinkerers, professionals, or peddlers and undertake the role of entrepreneurs. Their individual "success stories" abound in the pages of economic and business history of the Western world. [4]

These success stories are testimony to the readiness and ability of the "vital few" to venture forth with ideas for a new or improved product. Not satisfied with merely standing on the sidelines, they themselves seized the opportunity to undertake what others were not undertaking. It is this constant flow of new products which prompts the rest of us to remark, when we see them offered in the market for the first time: "Gee, why didn't I think of that?"

Foreign Competition

As if all of this were not enough, free competition must also invite competition from still another source--from producers in foreign countries. So far we have considered only domestic sources of competition, but if we are talking about optimizing the conditions of consumers' sovereignty, we must look to the world as a whole as our oyster, as far as sources of consumers' goods is concerned.

---

[4] See John Chamberlain, The Enterprising Americans (New York: Harper Colophon Books, 1963).

One has only to point to recent economic history, particularly to the invasion of U.S. markets by foreign producers of automobiles, cameras, optical products, electronic appliances, textiles and a host of other commodities to see how important this foreign source of competition can be. So, on top of inter-industry competition and competition from consumers entering production, we now must add the crusher: the foreign producer. Truly, there would be no rest for the weary in the world of free competition.

Free Trade vs. Nationalism

This brings us, therefore, to the related requirement, free trade--freedom of exchange. This freedom is accepted as a matter of course at home, in the domestic economy, but unfortunately it is not consistently extended to trade and exchange between people of different nation-states. Indeed, all sorts of restrictions on trade and exchange--in the form of tariffs, quotas on imports, bounties for exports--have become traditional. To the extent that trade between nations is restricted, to that extent is free competition itself restricted, and the consumer remains less than sovereign.

It should be noted that, historically, the restriction of trade between nations had its roots in the nationalistic policies of Europe's mercantilist states from the 16th century onward. This is not the place to examine the pro's and con's of nationalism--as a phase in the history of people, on the one hand, and as an obstacle to truly free contact and exchange between people of different backgrounds, on the other. Suffice it to note that a policy of protecting domestic firms from foreign competition by means of tariffs, quotas, and non-quantitative barriers in general--apart from its denial of free competition and consumers' sovereignty--is, from the consumers' viewpoint, illogical: it is no more logical to protect the Chrysler Company from competition by Toyota or Honda than it is to protect it from competition at home by General Motors and Ford.

Role of Government

It should be clear by now why the consumer stands to gain most by a condition of free competition and free trade. Only open, competitive markets would cause firms to fear and tremble before every consumer, wondering whether the consumer will cast his dollar ballots for their product or for their rival's? So far, so good. But, as already indicated, the greatest force for obstructing free entry, free trade and competition is government—the political power of the nation-state. This brings us to the next leg of our analytical journey towards optimum consumers' sovereignty: What should be the proper role of government in the free market? What can government do to help optimize conditions for consumers' sovereignty?

There is no need here to present a detailed analysis of government interventions in the market. Suffice to note that government possesses the power to fix price minimums (favoring producers) and price ceilings (favoring customers), and to prohibit exchange and production in varying degrees (e.g., allocations and rationing, labor laws, monopoly grants, tariffs, minimum wages). Here the discussion will be limited to a few main points.[5]

Removing Government Impediments

First of all, what is it that government should not do? As the preceding analysis implies, government should not place obstacles in the path of producers. This means an end to all restrictions on entry, such as licenses, charters, or monopoly grants. In the free market, it is not logical to force a practitioner to obtain a certificate or license in order to qualify as a producer. Let the practitioner decide for himself whether he needs a certificate. Let his concrete achievements—his successes and good reputation—suffice to speak for him, be he certified or not. And let consumers decide for themselves with which practitioners they prefer to deal. If some consumers, for instance, prefer their doctors, lawyers, teachers, and dentists to

---

[5]An excellent introductory analysis of the adverse, long-run effects of government interventions is by Henry Hazlitt, Economics In One Lesson (New York: Arlington House, Inc., 1979).

possess certificates of qualification--licenses, degrees, etc.--they are, of course, free to hire only
those who have such certification, and shun those who do
not.

No More Government Props

Nor should government come to the aid and rescue
of ailing firms by providing subsidies or other financial nostrums. If firms get into trouble in the competitive market, it is due primarily to their inability
to do as well as rivals in catering to the consumer. If
consumers' ballots have already spoken fatefully, "Exit
from the stage," no one else should thereupon tear this
verdict asunder. After all, there are firms that do
make profits because they are successfully catering to
consumers--and these firms should be cheered on; on the
other hand, firms who can only suffer losses should be
booed and hissed off the stage. From the consumers'
viewpoint there should be cheers for the profit-maker
but boos for the loss-makers.

As far as consumers are concerned, it is rubbing
salt in their wounds for the government to take their
tax money in order to subsidize non-competitive firms.
Instead, government should defer to the consumer and let
him decide which firms shall survive and which shall go
under. For only when the firm is not protected by
government against its failures--failure to cater to
consumers and failure to match its rivals' successes--
does the consumer have a chance to be sovereign in the
market. Conversely, any propping-up of firms by the
state only weakens the effectiveness of the consumers'
dollar ballot: it prevents the consumer from effectively rewarding firms in accordance with their responsiveness to his wishes, and penalizing them for negligence
or indifference towards him.

Meaning of Laissez-faire

Such a hands-off pro-competition policy by
government was known from its inception in 18th century
France as laissez-faire. Literally it means: let the
people make or do; but figuratively it means: let the
people, pursuing their own peaceful, productive ways,
determine their own lives. "Laissez-faire!" was the
great cry of the 18th century French economists, the
Physiocrats, who sought a radical dismantling of the

301

overregulated mercantilist economy of France in order to
move it towards free production and free trade. Leave
the market alone, unhampered by government regulations,
and the people will flourish--that was the battle cry.
Today, however, laissez-faire is in general disrepute--a
much maligned and distorted concept, with a connotation
totally opposite to its original meaning.

Adam Smith, who knew the Physiocrats well, car-
ried the message to England. He, too, egged his generation to nail the lid on the coffin of Mercantilism in
Britain. For Smith, Mercantilism was, among other
things, a system of state protection of the special
interests of producers against the consumer. He wrote:

> ... [I]n the mercantile [read: mercantilist]
> system the interest of the consumer is almost
> constantly sacrificed to that of the producer;
> and it seems to consider production and not
> consumption as the ultimate end and object of
> all industry and commerce....[6]

Adam Smith registered specific complaints against
government "restraints" upon imports of foreign goods
that were competitive with domestic output, and
"bounties" (subsidies) to exporters of goods not able to
compete on world markets. For him, both of these
policies favored the domestic producer at the expense of
the consumer.

Laissez-faire vs.
Privilege and Protection

Thus it was that laissez-faire, far from being
a policy of favoring the firm and sheltering it from
consumers and competitors, originated as the great cry
for free trade and competition--for the smashing of
mercantilistic protectionism and monopoly privilege
based on state charters, franchises, and licenses.

To be sure, one would not expect the entrenched
propertied and business interests of the 18th century to
rally behind the new banner of laissez-faire and free
competition. For them laissez-faire represented a most
unwelcome threat: the need to compete in the open
market in order to acquire and preserve new wealth.

---

[6]Smith, The Wealth of Nations, p. 625.

Whenever possible, threatened interests balked and attempted to restore the system of paternalism and protection; in time they managed to chip away at the foundations of increased competition and freer trade laid in the Industrial Revolution in England and the American republic.

Property Rights and Production

Having just outlined the negative side of the coin--what government should not do for the market--let us outline the positive side: What positive government actions would promote optimal consumers' sovereignty? Proponents of classical laissez-faire, consistent with their concept of non-interference in production and exchange, envisioned a system of limited government. That is to say, government should limit itself to a "nightwatchman's" role of protector of individual property rights, since property rights--especially the right to own means of production--were naturally basic to production and exchange. Thus, property rights became a fundamental tenet of classical liberalism-- "liberalism" meaning liberty or freedom from state interference and coercion.

For Adam Smith, it was sufficient to rely on the individual's natural desire to seek gain or profit. Since individuals participating in the market economy could gain only be rendering useful products or services for exchange on the market, it followed that such gain-motivated actions would necessarily result in benefits to society. For Smith, as well as for other liberal theoreticians, this was the truly seminal insight into the wondrous working of the market. Smith attributed the miracle of gain-motivated social productivity to the "invisible hand," a term whose metaphysical connotation unfortunately overshadowed the basic wisdom of his insight.[7] What remained, then, for government to do? For Smith, it was a relatively few things: national defense, police, some public works (roads, for instance). In today's world, that's not very much when compared with the leviathan proportions of modern governments.

---

[7]On the "invisible hand," see pages 34-35 above.

Consumer Under Socialism

With the institution of property rights, especially in the means of production, we come to the last of the conditions required to optimize consumers' sovereignty. The property-rights requirement is one of the central features differentiating the free market from socialism or any government-controlled system. Socialism, by definition, is the abolition of property rights in the means of production. By extension, it also means the end of the free market: its price mechanism, its productivity, its rising living standards and expectations. What does all this imply for consumers' sovereignty under socialism as compared to the free market?

Imagine, if you will, that you are living in the Soviet Union instead of the U.S.A. Each day you face the typical chores of the Soviet consumer: your daily rounds of shopping leave you thoroughly frustrated and dissatisfied because the selection of consumers' goods in the state-owned stores is a far cry from the virtual cornucopias back in the States.

What was it specifically that left you dissatisfied? Was the price of goods too high? Was the quality inferior relative to the price asked, or unacceptable at any price? Was the variety of goods—in size, style, and design—too narrow? Or was the variety unbalanced (e.g., plenty of radio sets but not enough TV sets, cars, cameras, phonograph records, tape recorders, typewriters, or do-it-yourself supplies)? Was it the absence of competition among firms—that the state was the only producer? What on earth can you do about it all?

First of all you can simply refuse to buy—learn to do without. Even in the totally monopolized economy of the Soviet Union every consumer has this option. You try shopping at another store—but only to find the same story there: the array of goods is practically a carbon copy of those in the first store. So you look for a third store, but there may be none—or simply not enough stores as far as your tastes are concerned.

Planners vs. Consumers

When you came home you decide to dash off a letter to the state-owned newspaper, venting your frustrations roughly as follows: You have learned that the

Soviet Constitution proclaims that "all power... belongs to the working people...." If so, it appears that the state is much too indifferent toward people as consumers; that the planners don't seem to be doing enough toward "raising the material and cultural standards" of the people as promised in Article 11 of the Soviet Constitution (1958 edition).[8] You would much prefer to see some competition introduced in the market. To you, competition among firms makes perfect sense: consumers have everything to gain when firms are compelled to compete for the consumers' rubles!

Then, having gotten this letter off your chest, you sit back and wait for some editorial response. You wonder, first, if they will dare publish your letter in the first place: Why should the state newspaper--the only paper in town-- give your complaint the widest possible publicity? If your letter does get published, millions of other sympathetic consumers might read it and join you in a chorus of protest. Hopefully the state planners will get the message--especially if there ensue consumer boycotts and disappointing sales figures, and Party leaders will want heads to roll.

So the planners decide to make some concessions to consumers. They introduce a few new lines of clothing, negotiate a contract for a foreign automobile factory, add a few other product lines--only to find their efforts are in vain: consumers remain frustrated, want still more changes instituted, and write still more complaining letters--occasionally also asking why state resources are allocated for moon shots, space satellites, and imperial ventures in the Third World instead of consumers' goods. And so on and so forth.

Property Rights a Necessary Condition

At some point you go into deep reverie of the way it was back in the U.S.A.--why it was so different there compared to here. In the U.S., individual property rights are recognized and implemented in great measure: almost anyone with sufficient capital--his own or borrowed--can go into business. You realize this is why private property, especially in means of production,

---

[8]Quotations from the Soviet Constitution in this section are based on Robert LeFevre, Constitutional Government Today in Soviet Russia (Larkspur, Colo.: Rampart College, 1962).

is the crucial difference: in the U.S., individual ownership of property provides the freedom to jump into production and fill any perceived gap in the market.

In the U.S.S.R., however, individuals are denied the right to own means of production. Here is the way the Soviet Constitution (Article 4) puts it: "The economic foundation of the U.S.S.R. is the socialist system of economy and the socialist ownership of the instruments and means of production, firmly established as a result of the liquidation of the capitalist system of economy, the abolition of private ownership of the instruments and means of production..." (underlining mine).

Socialism Inherently Restrictive

It may be reasonably asked: Why is it legal for Soviet citizens to own consumers' goods, which they can buy with their rubles, but it is not legal for them to own means of production—such as materials, machines, factories, work shops—to produce consumers' goods for themselves, things like sweaters, cosmetics, stockings, cameras, and endless other things they can find a happy use for?

More specifically: Why is it legal for the Soviet state to be the monopolistic employer of labor services, but it is illegal for Soviet citizens to compete with the state by becoming employers in turn, entering into voluntary agreement with others as employees, and conceivably offering higher wage-rates than the state? To put it bluntly: Why is it illegal for Soviet citizens to undertake productive activities that increase the standard of living?

If a Soviet citizen can make a better mousetrap than the state, what reason could the state have for preventing him from competing with it? By outlawing private property in the means of production, is not the Soviet state simply stifling opportunities to increase production and consumption? Is it not sheer arrogance for the Party and planners to believe they alone know what and how much the people should consume? By what test can the state prove that it is "raising the material and cultural standards" of the people?

306

When Is a Socialist a Capitalist?

These questions are crucial: they penetrate to the essential anti-humanism of socialist prohibition of private ownership of the means of production. Before we explore this anti-humanism, we must first note a characteristic fallacy in socialist thinking. Article 4 of the Soviet Constitution correctly states that the U.S.S.R. has abolished private ownership of means of production; but it also claims the U.S.S.R. has abolished "capitalist" methods of production--which is grossly misleading.

First of all, we saw in Chapter IV that what makes production "capitalistic" is investment and use of capital goods and roundabout (indirect) methods of production, in cooperation with labor. Thus, there is no necessary connection between a "capitalist" method of production, on the one hand, and private ownership in the means of production, on the other.

It is true that capitalist methods of production have historically been most widely applied by systems based on private ownership, such as Britain and the U.S. The consequences are well known: greatly increased levels of consumption for tens of millions of people. But the economic fact remains that there is nothing in the economic concept of capital goods per se that implies private property.

Free Market vs. Mere "Capitalism"

Thus we can see the fallacy stated in the Soviet Constitution: its confusion of the terms "capitalist" and "private ownership." To be sure, no one can deny the U.S.S.R. has legally outlawed private ownership in means of production, but certainly has not outlawed the use of capital goods--indeed, quite the contrary! Soviet emphasis on the use of machines and other capital goods in production--especially since the first five-year plan in 1928--makes the Soviet economy as capitalist as any so-called "capitalist" economy. For some reason, Soviet leaders as well as socialists around the world perpetuate a fallacy attributable to Karl Marx, the notion that there is an inherent relation between capital goods and the concept of property rights as the foundation of the free market.

307

Ironically, the Soviet Constitution, while deny-
ing people the right to own means of production, does
not hesitate to offer them "freedom of religious worship," the "right to vote," "freedom of speech ...of
the press ...of assembly ...of street processions and
demonstrations." This raises a question: Why pronounce
such "human rights"--so familiar in the Western world--
but omit the human right to own resources for productive
purposes? We will return to this issue below.

The Question of "Human Rights"

This brings us to the truly basic question: In
the U.S.S.R., are not the "freedom of religious worship," the "right to vote," "freedom of speech ... press
...assembly ...street processions and demonstrations"
--all proclaimed by the Soviet Constitution--no more
than mere words?   How can Soviet citizens really implement these human rights in any practical sense?   The
issue is not whether the Soviet state is able to implement these rights according to its own lights--according
to its own interpretation of the meaning of "human
rights." Rather the issue is whether the Soviet individual is able to implement these rights according to his
own wishes.   A few examples suffice to illustrate the
point.

For instance, take the frustrated Soviet consumer. Suppose the state newspaper refuses to publicize
his consumer complaints. What other recourse does he
have?   What if he wanted to start up his own newspaper,
or a consumer's newsletter, in order to bring his
opposition message to fellow consumers?   How on earth
could he implement his "freedom of the press" when the
state owns all the required means of production--the
newsprint, the printing presses, the printer's ink, the
factory space, the delivery trucks, the mail service--
and when the state also prohibits the hiring of wage
labor?   Is this real freedom of the press?   As A. J.
Liebling once put it: "A free press exists only when
you own a press."

Freedom of Speech, Assembly, and Religion

If freedom of the press under socialism is a
mere hoax--a promise without substance--how about "freedom of speech and assembly" and "freedom of street
processions and demonstrations"?   What if activist consumers decide to take their cause into the streets--to

308

shout their protest from every street corner, to parade
with banners down the main boulevards, and to picket
with signs in front of the appropriate ministries?
Could they even get to first base?

Assume that protesting consumers actually march,
speak out and picket--only to have the police storm them
and break up their protest? Consumers might then set up
a cry: Are not the streets the "people's property"?
The police reply that the protesters are "disturbing the
peace" and "obstructing traffic." How can this apparent
conflict between the people and the state police be
resolved? Who really owns the streets when the chips
are down? So long as the state, and not the people, is
the de facto owner of the "socialized" streets and
sidewalks, then it is clear that human rights in the
U.S.S.R. are at the mercy of the state's minions.

Finally, what about "freedom of religious
worship" in the U.S.S.R.? True, disgruntled consumers
do not ordinarily resort to prayer in church as the
solution to their shopping difficulties. But for people
who are regular church-goers--what about them? What
does their right to worship really amount to? Do they
have the right to land on which to build their shrine?
Can they hire labor to build it? Are firms free to
produce church organs, velvets and raiments? Are
printers free to produce prayer books? In other words,
in what effective sense does a citizen possess true
freedom of worship? The land belongs to the state, as
do all the other means of production, and wage labor is
prohibited. In a word, only the state has the political
power to build the church and to control worship.

"Human Rights" Are Property Rights

It should be obvious by now that human rights
such as freedom of press, speech, assembly, and religion
ultimately depend on property rights. (By "property" is
meant ownership.) Property rights in the means of production are crucial for all human rights. In practice,
man must have the right to own the means with which to
implement human rights. If a person does not have means
of his own, then he must at least be free to hire them
or borrow them from owners of means. Without property
rights, human rights become de facto mere will-o'-the-
wisps.

309

We can now also see why the familiar cliche that "human rights" are superior to "property rights," is actually a fallacious dichotomy. We have just seen that there is no effective way to implement human rights without property rights in the means of production. Indeed, not only is the implementation of human rights dependent on property rights, but property rights are prior to "human rights."

To go one step further: "Human rights" are derivative from property rights in the same sense as are products--the fruits of one's labor: they both come to fruition only by use of one's own means. Far from there being a conflict between "human rights" and "property rights," the former are naturally based on the latter, and flourish only to the extent that the latter flourish. As one writer has put it: "...property rights are indissolubly also human rights."9 It follows that a proper defense of "human rights" necessarily implies the defense of property rights.

Right of Self-Sovereignty

This basic truth is obvious in the case of Robinson Crusoe, isolated man. For Crusoe, his "human right" to life implies the right to keep the fruit of his labor--this alone sustains him. It follows that, if Crusoe has a natural right to own the fruits of his labor, he must possess the natural right to own and use the means of producing these fruits, including his own labor power. In turn, Crusoe's right to own his labor power implies that he has the natural right to own his person and being. That is to say, he is by nature a self-owner. It is this natural property right in his own being--this natural right of self-sovereignty--which generates Crusoe's right to the material goods that he produces.

What happens to Crusoe's property rights--in himself, his means, and his product--if and when he comes into social contact with other people in society? Is it proper that these rights be in any way compromised or denied by "society"? For instance, imagine that one day Crusoe meets Friday. Friday, not wanting to work

---

9Murray N. Rothbard, Power and Market (2nd ed., Kansas City: Sheed, Andrews and McMeel, Inc., 1977), pp. 238-240.

for his own sustenance, decides to set upon Crusoe and
exploit him. Using his superior physical strength, he
initially seizes Crusoe's product and accumulated
wealth, and then forces Crusoe to give him a portion of
his product on a regular basis. To Crusoe it is obvious
that Friday is exploiting him--forcibly enslaving him--
invading his natural right of self-sovereignty. Now, it
is clear that if Friday is not justified in exploiting
Crusoe, then neither is "society" justified in similarly
exploiting all the productive Crusoes. All of this
raises moral issues beyond the scope of this book.

Socialism versus Property Rights

What does this excursion into the nature of
property rights imply for socialism in general? By
maintaining state monopoly ownership of the means of
production, socialism must be viewed as a fundamentally
exploitative system. Far from being "humanist," as some
socialists claim, socialism is ultimately anti-humanist
precisely because it denies individual property rights
in the means of production and, in consequence, denies
the basis of human rights in general.

Thus an important truth emerges. The free
market economy is not only the proper economic framework
for optimizing production and consumers' sovereignty; it
is also the optimal social-political framework for the
exercise of human rights in general. Just as interference with the right to own means of production, enter
into production, and exchange goods is, willy-nilly, a
restriction of consumers' sovereignty, so is the denial
of property rights a denial of human rights. We are all
consumers, to be sure, but--more important--we are all
human beings. The free market not only optimizes opportunities for consumers' sovereignty but may also be the
road toward optimal human rights.

Conclusion

The fact that we are all consumers has, in
itself, a fundamental implication: the market-price
system must be, above all, a system for consumers'
sovereignty--for the benefit primarily of people as
consumers and not for the protection of business profits
or political privileges. So-called capitalism or free
enterprise is virtuous primarily by reference to its
service to people as consumers. As one observer has put

311

it: "...[B]usiness is not the element which benefits from [capitalism]. Businesses, in fact, are punished-- or at least disciplined--by the free enterprise system. Only consumers benefit. ...And we should not ask businessmen to assure market competition. If ever we're to keep what economic freedom we still have, or roll back the smothering blanket of controls, we'll have to ... do it as consumers, not as businessmen."[10]

Appendix

THE GALBRAITH EFFECT

This chapter primarily addresses two basic questions: <u>Why</u> should the consumer be "sovereign" in the market place? <u>How</u> can this sovereignty be implemented in optimal fashion? With very few exceptions, these fundamental questions have been curiously neglected or treated all too briefly or casually by economists. As noted in the first paragraph of this chapter, the alternative tendency has been to discuss consumers' sovereignty primarily as an <u>empirical</u> issue involving such questions as: Is the consumer actually the boss in the market place? If so, to what extent? Does the consumer exert any direct or meaningful influence over what firms produce?

In this latter vein the main contribution has been made by John Kenneth Galbraith, who has concluded that there is no effective consumers' sovereignty in the market place.[11] It is this point of view on which this Appendix is focused.

According to Galbraith, the general reason for the absence of consumers' sovereignty is that the modern firm has a kind of unfair advantage over the consumer.

---

[10] James E. Foy, letter to editor, <u>Reason</u> (October 1977), p. 9.

[11] John Kenneth Galbraith, <u>The Affluent Society</u> (College Edition, Boston: Houghton Mifflin Co., 1958, 1960), Chapter XI.

In the modern social division of labor it is necessarily
the case that production by the firm comes first, and
then only subsequently comes the consumer to buy the
goods thus profferred to him by the firm. That is,
since the firm does not take direct orders from the
consumer but, instead, takes the initiative to proffer
the menu of goods supplied to the consumer, the consumer
apparently has no choice but to buy what the firm places
in front of him in the shops and markets.

In this way, continues Galbraith, the consumer's
wants necessarily become "dependent" on what the firm
produces--that is, the consumer's wants are directly
influenced by the firm's offerings. Because of this
dependence effect, as Galbraith dubs it, the consumer
can in no way exercize any sovereignty over the firm.
He puts it this way: "...[P]roduction creates the wants
it seeks to satisfy....[T]he process by which wants are
satisfied is also the process by which wants are
created....[T]hus, wants are dependent on production.
...The producer [has] the function both of making the
goods and of making the desires for them." (Brackets
mine.)

Before I elaborate on this, by now classical,
Galbraithian formulation and analyze its flaws, we
should first note a basic agreement: the sociological
fact that, in the modern division of labor between
households and firms, production by firms necessarily
comes first and consumers' buying comes only afterward
(see Chapters II, IV, and IX.) But then note the significantly different implications drawn. For the
present author, this basic sociological fact, given the
natural priority of consumption as the purpose of
production, constitutes the essence of a weighty universal problem, the "consumers' sovereignty problem," which
preoccupies this chapter.

For Galbraith, however, it constitutes the basis
of a determinist argument, to wit: Consumers' wants are
necessarily "dependent" on (shaped by) what the firms
produce; hence, consumers are in no way able to exercize
any sovereignty over firms. Thus, for Galbraith, the
fact that the firms produce consumers' goods in advance
so that they typically appear on store-shelves in
advance of consumers' purchases, necessarily pre-
determines consumers' tastes and preferences, denies
them the possibility of making "spontaneous" or
"independent" choices, and therefore precludes any consumers' sovereignty.

313

For this author, however, this argument involves a determinist fallacy--the idea that firms can prefix the consumer's tastes and preferences, and thereby virtually compel him to buy their products. Such determinism overlooks two things. On the one hand, consumers are always free to decide whether to buy or not, or from whom to buy, and whether to change their tastes and preferences in the face of ever-changing offerings in the market place.[12] On the other hand, successful sales to consumers can only superficially be said to originate exclusively in the supply side--in the firm's initiative. On a deeper level, such sales reflect a successful appeal to pre-existing dispositions of consumers to accept the firm's offerings.

In support of his main argument, Galbraith relies on a bisection of wants into two familiar categories. On the one hand he postulates "urgent" wants--wants that are "original" with man himself, that would be experienced "spontaneously" if the individual were left to himself, that are "independently" determined or established (that is, independent of advertising influence or the inducement to "emulate" what others are consuming). (Some have called these the "basic" or "innate" wants.) Curiously, Galbraith does not seriously catalogue or exemplify these "urgent" wants, except to incidentally refer to "hunger" and "physical want." ("A man who is hungry need never be told of his need for food.") One can reasonably assume that Galbraith would feel at home with the concepts of "absolute wants" and fixed "hierarchy" of wants discussed in Chapter V.

In contrast to these "urgent" or innate wants, Galbraith poses the category of "created" or "contrived" wants which emanate exclusively from the dependence effect described above. Created wants are typically imposed on consumers by the production process itself, in which firms, by producing first, are able to "create" consumers' wants. For Galbraith, the created wants are generated in two ways. One is by the innocent "passive"

---

[12] People as consumers are surely no less free to choose in the market place than in the voting booth on election day. Indeed, it can be easily argued that the individual's "sovereignty" as consumer exceeds his sovereignty as citizen-voter at the ballot box. At least, in the market place a person is not forced to buy what he does not want, whereas on the day after elections he can find himself stuck with things he did not want to "buy"--that is, with candidates and propositions against which he voted.

314

process of "emulation." ("One man's consumption becomes his neighbor's wish," familiarly known as Keeping Up with the Joneses.) The second is the more active and "more direct" way to create wants: by "advertising" and "salesmanship."

For Galbraith, advertising and salesmanship are associated primarily with the emergence of the higher or "affluent" standards of living achieved in the industrial age. Furthermore, the "central function" of advertising and salesmanship is precisely to "create desires--to bring into being wants that previously did not exist." Indeed, for Galbraith, such want creation is "the most obtrusive of all economic phenomena" in the modern economy. It becomes easier to "synthesize" and "catalyze" people's wants when they have already achieved loftier levels of consumption and are therefore "so far removed from physical want that they do not already know what they want. In this state alone men are open to persuasion." (Underlines mine.)

Noteworthy is Galbraith's reference to "already known" wants, presumably his innate wants--"independent-ly determined" by life's "physical" requirements (such as food, clothing, shelter). (Recall his bon mot: "A man who is hungry need never be told of his need for food.") For Galbraith, any wants introduced beyond this basic level of urgency would merely "fill a void" in which alone people become "open to persuasion." (As he puts it: "production only fills a void that it has itself created.") Such persuasion, of course, becomes more effective the more the "value system" esteems keeping up with the Joneses and the more firms resort to advertising and salesmanship. That is, were it not for emulation and advertising, the "created" wants would simply not exist, since there is no natural "urgency" or "spontaneous need" to satisfy them.

Now to return to the original point. Galbraith's bisection of wants, while superficially appealing, turns out to be inadequate and confusing. First of all, Galbraith's innate wants are unjustifiably narrowly circumscribed, confined to wants usually dis-paraged as materialistic--wants that cry for the crea-ture comforts satisfied by food, clothing and shelter. (Recall his relevant references to "hunger" and "phy-sical want.") However, in the broader perspective of the full stature and strength of man--giving man and human nature its proper due--Galbraith is clearly short-changing us!

For instance, immediately coming to mind are Abraham Maslow's five categories of basic wants: (a) physiological wants, to which Galbraith's innate wants are limited; (b) desire for safety and security; (c) desire for affection and belongingness; (d) desire for self-esteem; and (e) striving for self-realization or self-fulfillment. This is more like it! Here is a range of wants that encompasses much more of human nature. But even Maslow's list is incomplete--for the panoply of man's wants most assuredly must include human preoccupations, propensities, and passions in such expressive dimensions as literature, music and the other arts (so-called "culture"); philosophy, religion and science; and--not the least--technology and technological progress.

Not only is Galbraith's concept of basic wants unreasonably confined, his analysis is avoidably obfuscating: he seems unaware of the implication of the fact that the satisfaction of wants requires means. Thus, whereas the several categories of human wants-- even in the broadest sense--may be regarded as finite or determinate, the variety of means or devices by which we may satisfy our wants must, in the full view of human historical achievement, be regarded as potentially unlimited. It is precisely in the area of means, instruments, implements and devices that man has been the most "creative" and "contriving" (innovative) of all creatures.[13]

If, therefore, Galbraith is complaining of the "created" and the "contrived," it surely cannot be in the area of wants; since their number and type are finite and determinate by nature, there is no more room for man to "create" or "contrive" new wants. Instead, it is in the realm of means that man, in all of his reason and ingenuity, is the constant creator, contriver and innovator. Unwittingly, Galbraith is actually lashing out against this most precious of man's proclivities! In view of man's time-honored, ceaseless creativity and innovation, Galbraith's case for a cessation of the "created" and the "contrived" would

---

[13]Friedrich A. Hayek argues, in effect, that virtually the whole of "civilization" and the spread of "culture" among the world's peoples are attributable to innovation and emulation in the means of producing goods and services. See his "The Non Sequitur of the 'Dependence Effect'," Southern Economic Journal (April 1961), pp. 346-348.

appear to be not only tilting at windmills but also reactionary to boot.

An illustration of this point should be instructive. While the basic drive to assuage hunger--which leads us to the act of eating--is a constant, the same cannot be said of the class of means called food, capable of satisfying hunger. The virtually endless variety of foods that clutter human diets and menus is necessarily created or contrived, mainly as a consequence of on-going social and cultural interaction and emulation. For example, take the lobster: To many people its appearance is so disgusting or outrageous as to deter them from eating it--at least until they first see it prepared and enjoyed as a food by others. Yet, for many others, it has been a traditionally natural food of unquestioned credentials. In Galbraithian terms, does the lobster represent a "basic" means or a "contrived" means?!

Or take the staple food, meat. So natural a component of the American hamburger would be treated as an unwelcome, unnecessary food for many people of India. How about insects? Such a natural component of the diet of Venezuelan tribes would be abhorred as an unseemly food by most Americans. Then again, it took some 200 years between 1550 and 1750 to overcome resistance in Europe and North America to one of the most nourishing and easily cultivated vegetables--the potato! What is illustrative here of the relation between eating (a constant want) and the variety of foods (man's contrived means) can be multiplied by illustrations from virtually every other dimension of human wants.

In this connection, we should recall the significant symbiotic relation discussed in Chapter IX that exists between wants, or goals, purposes and ends, and means--a relation that involves the imputation of values. Specifically, the value a person attaches to any given purpose or want is naturally imparted or transmitted ("imputed") to the means that are capable of satisfying the purpose or want. Thus any given want that is regarded as worthwhile by a person necessarily makes the means capable of satisfying that want equally worthwhile. Conversely, means, no matter how contrived or varied, are no less important than the wants they can satisfy.

317

It follows, then, that if we have no grounds for putting down or denigrating another person's <u>wants</u> or desires, we have no basis for denigrating the value attached to the <u>means</u> that can satisfy those wants or desires. That is, there is no putting down of a means without implying a putting down of the want itself. Thus it is that when Galbraith puts down means by labelling them as "created" or "contrived," he is willy-nilly also putting down the wants satisfied by these means. Given his fixation on "physical" wants, he would seem to be condemning us to egalitarian asceticism.

CHAPTER XI

COMPETITION: "PERFECT" VS. REAL

It is traditional to believe that competition is a good thing. The U.S. government, under the anti-trust laws, is empowered to achieve pro-competition and anti-monopoly goals. But what have the administrators used as their theoretical, intellectual guide for achieving increased competition? It has not been the neglected classical liberal concept of laissez-faire competition outlined in Chapter X. Instead, they have leaned primarily on the economists' perfect competition model for guidance on how to reduce "monopoly power" and increase "competition." In this chapter we will examine the perfect competition model featured in every economics textbook, and offer alternative perspectives for a desirable competition.

I. The "Perfect Competition" Model

The most popular textbook model for market competition is so-called "perfect competition." As we will soon see, however, perfect competition is neither "perfect" nor "competitive." Furthermore, taken literally, it is a most unrealistic model--impossible to implement in the real world. Even if perfect competition were possible, it would not necessarily be desirable. Yet, here we are, about to devote the major part of this chapter to perfect competition. Are we giving it more importance than it deserves? Let us see why this subject does deserve special treatment.

Standard for Government Policy

For one thing, perfect competition (hereinafter referred to simply as PC) is important simply because it is the main economic-theoretical standard by which real-world competition is measured, and by which government regulation of business is guided. Since the business sector is a dominant element in our economy, government policy designed to regulate business practices and promote competition, especially as it relates to prices and production, should be of prime interest to all.

319

Furthermore, a serious critical analysis of the PC model has been relatively neglected in introductory texts. The PC model is widely used as a standard for desirable competition, yet, as will become abundantly clear, it is based on unrealistic assumptions--assumptions that are unnatural and undesirable. If the PC model proves to be an unsuitable model, it should not be a guide for public policy.

What Does "Competition" Mean?

If competition is the desired goal, and more competition is supposed to be better than less competition, it behooves us to understand precisely what is meant by "competition." How is it to be defined? How can we tell when there is competition or when it is absent? In what ways is competition supposed to be beneficial? And for whom? This chapter will confine itself to answering some of the preceding questions and to furnishing perspectives for understanding the PC model. It will also try to show why the free-market model outlined in Chapter X is a more commendable and practical model than perfect competition.[1]

Competition as Rivalry

Right off, it should be noted that economists themselves are not agreed on how to define "competition." Some economists use a common-sense definition that is akin to what the layman means when he uses the term, and what the dictionary describes as "rivalry: the effort of two or more parties to secure the business of a third party by the offer of the most favorable terms." In this popular concept the key sense is rivalry--competition as a dynamic process engaging firms in "rivalrous" behavior with respect to each other, in an ongoing contest for the consumer's dollar.

More precisely, the dimensions of rivalrous competition are basically: price, quality, and variety. Consumers tend to favor the firm which, other things being equal, sells at a lower price than its rivals, offers a better quality product than its rivals, and

---

[1]A noteworthy analysis of the problem of defining competition is by P. J. McNulty, "Economic Theory and the Meanings of Competition," Quarterly Journal of Economics (November, 1968).

offers a greater variety from which to select (e.g., styles, designs, colors, materials, sizes). Hence, competitive firms will be constantly striving to curry the consumer's favor by (a) distinguishing or "differentiating" their products in one way or another, or by (b) imitating and catching up with rivals who have differentiated their product to profitable advantage or have been able to cut costs and price.

The "Market Structure" Approach

In contrast to this dynamic, rivalrous model of competition stands the comparatively static textbook model of PC competition. The PC model is an example of the market-structure approach to competition, to which economists have become so dedicated.

Market-structure competition is regarded as "static," not dynamic, because its competition is determined by its looks or physical attributes, and not by its dynamic action and interaction in a rivalrous environment. It reminds one of the Geraldine line by Flip Wilson: "What you see is what you get." Thus, if you observe a type A market structure, you can expect to get a type A competition; if you see a type B market structure, you should expect a type B competition; and so on. As we will see, one type of market structure--perfect competition--is preferred to all the others. To appreciate this we must first analyze the various market structures.

First, what is a "market structure"? A market structure is described in terms of four dimensions: (1) the type of product or service produced by firms in the industry, (2) the number and size of firms, (3) the conditions of entry and exit, into and out of the industry, and (4) the degree of information or ignorance prevailing among firms and consumers. Let us examine each of these dimensions in detail.

Dimensions of Market Structure

(1) Product. Products are classified either as "homogeneous" or as "differentiated." Homogeneous means that the product produced by each firm in the industry is identical, bearing no brand name, trademark or other mark of distinction. Similarly, firms that render customer services along with their products--such as

guarantees, complaints, repairs, returns, or financing--
are likewise identical with respect to these services.
As a consequence, consumers have no way of distinguishing the product or service of any one firm from that of
other firms.

In contrast to the class of homogeneous products
are the differentiated products. This is a much more
realistic classification: here the products of firms in
a given industry can be distinguished from each other in
some respect--by brand name, trademark, design, style,
advertising, customer services, or location. Indeed,
such differentiation of product is one of the mainstays
of competition in the real world.

It is important to stress that, in practice,
even if products of a given class are, for all practical
or technical purposes, virtually similar--as in the case
of shoes, clothing, canned goods, appliances--so long as
the consumer perceives these similar products to be
somehow differentiated, this suffices to make them "differentiated." It is the eyes of the beholder, the
consumer, which ultimately determine whether there is
differentiation--"whether real or fancied," as one
writer put it.

(2) Firms, number and size. At one extreme of
this dimension is the case of "monopoly," which literally means a single seller. At the other extreme is the
case of infinitely numerous firms. In between these two
market structures are two others, one consisting of a
"few" firms, and the other consisting of "many" firms.

(3) Conditions of entry and exit. A major condition of entry-exit depends on the presence of artificial or legal barriers, such as licenses, permits,
patents, and copyrights. These devices tend to restrict
entry by new producers and sellers because they are
special privileges that impede access to the market.

Another aspect of entry-exit pertains to the
degree of mobility of resources, especially labor and
capital goods. "Mobility" here refers to the ease with
which the resource or resource-owner can be induced to
move into or out of the market in response to changes in
prices or profit margins. Mobility, in turn, is influenced by one's geographical location and the ease
with which one can acquire new skills or apply new
technology.

322

With respect to <u>exit</u> conditions, pertinent are such questions as: Is the firm at liberty to close down its plant and dismiss workers if and when its losses are too heavy? Or are there legal hurdles or regulations that prevent or impede such moves?

One way of classifying market structures according to entry-exit conditions is to distinguish between "open" markets and "closed" markets. <u>Open markets</u> include market structures that have no legal or other "artificial" barriers imposed by government. In effect, an open-market structure corresponds to the condition of "free competition" described in Chapter X: the liberty or freedom of anyone to enter production. In contrast is the <u>closed market</u>, characterized by all kinds of legal blocks to entry, ranging from outright monopoly privileges granted by the state to public-utility firms and taxi companies (e.g., Yellow Cab) to license requirements for barbers and beauticians.

(4) <u>Information or knowledge</u>. Does everyone participating in the market know all the prices of concern to him? For instance, do <u>consumers</u> know where they can buy at the lowest price? Do <u>firms</u> know the selling prices of all their rivals? Do <u>workers</u> know where they can get the highest wage-rate for their labor? Do <u>resource-owners</u> in general know where they can get the best prices, rents, or interest rates for their resources (e.g., materials, rental space, loanable funds)?

All of the preceding questions pertain to <u>current</u> market prices or rates; but what about <u>future</u> prices or rates--how well informed are people about them? At one extreme, as we will soon see, there is a market structure--perfect competition--which postulates "perfect" knowledge or information (i.e., "omniscience"): all participants in the market know everything they need to know in order to make non-regretful decisions, to assure that <u>ex-ante</u> decisions are always realized in the <u>ex-post</u>. The other market structures, being more realistic, postulate degrees of ignorance on the part of firms, consumers, and resource-owners.

The Four Market Structures

Having noted that the market-structure approach to competition is akin to a "what you see is what you get" way of describing the market, exactly what is meant

323

by this? Textbooks usually list four types of market structure, as follows:

1. Perfect Competition
2. Monopoly
3. Oligopoly
4. Monopolistic Competition

Which of these structures assures the best type of competiton? According to the market-structure approach, it is perfect competition (PC). Why? Why is PC esteemed above all? Before the answer is given, we must first describe each market structure in terms of the four dimensions outlined above. Only then can we draw connections between market structure and the character of competition expected therefrom.

The "Perfect Competition" Model

(1) Perfect Competition. First, the kind of product produced by firms in PC is characteristically homogeneous. Products are identical by definition-- there is not an iota of differentiation between one firm's product and another's. There are no brand names or trademarks. The consumer has absolutely no way to tell which firm produced which product. For example, all TV sets would be turned out exactly alike by every producer, and each set would be a perfect substitute for every other set. In this way consumers would choose a product strictly on the basis of price--i.e., at the lowest price available--and would be indifferent as to which firm produced it.

What about the number and size of individual firms in PC? By definition, the number of firms in PC is virtually infinite--great enough to make each firm extremely small relative to the size of the industry, and its output insignificant compared to the total output of all other firms. Generally speaking, for any given amount produced by an industry as a whole, the more numerous the firms, the smaller is each firm; and vice versa, the fewer the firms, the larger is each firm. In PC, therefore, since the number of firms is virtually infinite, each firm must clearly be very tiny. Indeed, the individual firm in PC is so tiny that it is totally powerless to affect the market supply or price.

For example, if any one firm closed down, its missing supply would hardly cause a dent in the total

324

supply of the industry and, hence, could not cause a rise in market P. Remember, in Chapter VIII we saw that a drop in the industry S schedule would cause a rise in P, assuming demand remained the same. Well, in the PC model, the industry S schedule would hardly drop at all if one firm closed down, since the firm is too small to affect S and P. The same reasoning applies to the entry of a new firm: practically no increase in S and drop in P would occur. Indeed, the PC firm is so small that the word "atomistic" has been used to describe it--a firm as small as an atom!

The crucial importance of atomism in the PC firm cannot be exaggerated. By any reasonable interpretation of the literature, one must conclude that the conditions required to fulfill the PC model logically imply a virtually infinite number of firms which, in turn, implies a puny, atomistic firm.

How about entry and exit conditions in the PC model? By definition, PC calls for freedom of entry and exit--no legal or other artificial barriers--and for perfect mobility of resources or resource-owners. With respect to free entry or open markets, the PC model shares a feature in common with free-market competition as described in Chapter X. In the latter context, in the quest for consumers' sovereignty, open markets and free competition were eminently reasonable and desirable.

However, the second requirement--perfect mobility of factors--is really asking too much. Even if we assume no legal constraints on the mobility of people and capital goods, there are significant natural constraints that might dissuade people from being perfectly mobile, such as geographic loyalty, great distance to a new job, and lack of incentives and personal skills.

The fourth and last structural requirement of the PC model is no less extreme than the first two: every participant in the market--firm, consumer, and resource-owner--has perfect knowledge or complete information. First of all, everyone has perfect knowledge with respect to prices. Everyone knows all the future-- as well as current--prices. Each firm knows exactly what every other firm's selling price is, and therefore knows whether it is overpricing or underpricing its own product. Each consumer knows whether the seller is charging him more or less than rival sellers. Each worker knows whether his employer is underpaying him compared with other employers.

Perfect knowledge of current prices implies furthermore that firms are also instantaneously aware of any changes in demand and supply conditions. Somehow the market operates like a magical computer: it not only computes and reports instantaneously--to one and all--every nuance in D, S, and price, but it also senses these nuances to start with. As for future prices, firms possess not only the prescience to know future D and S conditions but also its underlying determinants.

Finally, the assumption of perfect knowledge extends also to the sphere of technology and technological progress. We saw in Chapter IV that innovation of (a) a new product or (b) a new technique of production can give the firm two competitive advantages, respectively: in the first case, it enables the innovator to win customers away from the old products of other firms; in the second, it enables the innovator to cut costs and prices below those of his rivals. In PC, however, with its generalized perfect knowledge, any firms that lag behind the front-running innovator need not worry for long: possession of perfect knowledge enables them to be instantaneously apprised of any rival's innovation and, because of perfect resource mobility, are instantaneously able to marshal the resources necessary to duplicate the innovator's feat and recoup their lost share of the market. Implied, then, in the assumption of perfect knowledge and resource mobility, is instantaneous adjustment by firms to any changes in the market--adjustments made without any time lag. What any one firm accomplishes technologically can be duplicated by all the others--and immediately! "Anything you can do, I can do," so to speak.

Given these structural features the first question usually asked is: Are there any examples of the PC model in the real world? Strictly speaking, there are none. Almost without exception, economists admit that the PC model is "palpably unrealistic," as one writer has put it. In fact, "unrealistic" is putting it mildly: the PC model is outright "impossible," as another writer put it. If PC is an impossibility, why would economists offer it as the standard for real-world firms? We will return to this question later in the chapter.

Textbooks do suggest some real-world approximations to the PC model. Agricultural markets are believed to present some analogies to PC, due to the large number of farms, the relatively small size of firms, the

relatively homogeneous products, and their commodity
exchanges. But we should not stretch the analogies too
far. For example, homogeneity of product may be more
apparent than real. Thus, fruit and vegetable farmers
do not all produce merely homogeneous products, undifferentiated from their rivals' products by fertilizers,
soil, and growing conditions. Finally, the growing
importance of large-scale corporate agriculture ("agri-
business") is significantly reducing the role of the
small, family-size farm.

More important, major segments of farming are
really "closed" markets rather than "open" ones, owing
to various government regulations which prevent open,
unrestricted competition. Examples include wheat, oats,
cotton, tobacco, oranges, milk, and lemons. That may
leave cattle-growing, beef and other foods, and truck
farming as possible vestiges of open markets. Some
economists include housing, both residential and owner-
occupied, and restaurants as approximations of PC. In
any case, there are no pure examples of PC in the real
world.

The Case of "Monopoly"

(2) Monopoly. This is the extreme opposite of
perfect competition. Literally, the word "monopoly"
means only one seller and therefore should be applied
only to market structures in which there is only one
firm in production. Obviously, the monopolist has no
rivals.

But the term "monopoly" is not without
ambiguity. Some writers claim that the meaning of the
term depends on whether it is given a narrow or broad
definition. If "product" is defined narrowly enough,
then every producer or seller can be regarded a monopolist, since he is naturally the only seller of his
product. Bobby Fischer, the chess grandmaster, was once
a monopolist because he was the only practitioner of his
brand of chess--even though there were many other grand-
masters on the scene. On the other hand, if the product
is defined broadly enough, then no one producer can be
regarded a monopolist. For example, the Du Pont
company, although once the only producer of cellophane,
could not really be considered a monopolist when broadly
classified as a producer of "wrapping or packaging
materials," since these include such competitors as
brown paper, waxed paper, aluminum foil, and newspapers.

327

Instead of using the word "monopoly" alone, some economists modify it by using also the words "closed" or "open," thus giving us two types of monopoly, i.e., closed monopoly and open monopoly. These useful terms help us understand that monopoly can arise in one of two ways. One route to monopoly is by a government-granted privilege that forcibly excludes any other firms. This has been the historical, traditional meaning of monopoly since the 16th century. A few examples will suffice: the wine and playing-card monopolies granted to Crown favorites by Elizabeth I; the charters granted to the East India trading companies; charters granted to railroads and airlines; licenses granted to radio and TV broadcasters; the monopolies granted to the telephone, gas, electric, and water "public utilities"; and patents granted to inventors. Such legal monopolies are referred to as closed monopolies, meaning the market is closed by the government to potential competitors.

The other road to monopoly is in sharp contrast: it is monopoly achieved by means of successful competition in the open market--by selling at the lowest price for the given quality, or by offering the best quality at a given price. As a consequence, rival firms fall by the wayside because they are incapable of matching the superior price-quality performance of the emerging monopolist.

So long as potential rivals cannot outperform the successful monopolist in competition for the consumers' dollars, so long will the monopolist reign. But such monopolies remain open monopolies because they do not depend on the power of the state, or the organized violence of a Mafia, which can forcibly exclude potential rivals from entry. The only "power" to exclude rivals is the economic power of the monopolist's ability to keep his costs and prices low enough to dissuade potential rivals from trying to invade his market.[2]

Nevertheless, an open monopoly cannot be a permanent one. As a consequence of its "openness," the mere absence of current rivals does not preclude the emergence of future rivals. If the monopolist decides

---

[2]Important contributions to the understanding of open monopolies are by W. S. Leeman, "The Limitations of Local Price-Cutting as a Barrier to Entry," Journal of Political Economy (August, 1956) and J. S. McGee, "Predatory Price Cutting," Journal of Law and Economics (October, 1958).

to exploit the market by abandoning his low cost and price policy and switching to a higher price and profit-margin, he is only looking for trouble: potential rivals attracted by the increased profits of the monopolist will be induced to invade his market. If the monopolist ever tires of the struggle to maintain his low-cost and low-price policy to keep rivals at bay, he might try seeking protection through a government-granted monopoly. If successful, the open monopoly would then be converted into a closed one.

Sometimes the word "monopoly" is imprecisely applied to the case where, like barbershops, there is more than one firm producing the given service under a license granted by the state. Nevertheless, since there is a monopoly feature involved--the fact that the granting authority, the state, is the only source legally empowered to grant the privilege of entry--the word "monopoly" is not entirely out of place. It is as though the state were acting as the only supplier of barber services, and is merely opening up new branches every time it chooses to grant a barber a permit to operate. In effect, barbers become mere agents of a monopoly firm, the state. The same reasoning applies to every field in which the state requires that firms obtain a permit or license to operate.

What about the size of the monopoly firm? Obviously, it is very large since only one firm is supplying the entire market, and the demand schedule facing the monopolist is identical with the market de-mand schedule. As for the monopolist's product, it is regarded as being differentiated since no one else is producing it, making it unique in that sense.

What about entry conditions? In the case of closed monopoly, entry is obviously precluded by the force of state-granted privilege. In the case of open monopoly, however, entry is as open as in "perfect competition" or free-market competition; there are no legal or other artificial barriers to keep existing or potential firms from joining in the fray. The only impediment to entry is the monopolist's ability to out-perform other firms in terms of price and quality.

The Case of "Oligopoly"

(3) Oligopoly. Between the two extremes of perfect competition and monopoly lie the two remaining

329

market structures, "oligopoly" and "monopolistic competition." These two structures encompass the bulk of firms in the real world.

"Oligopoly" literally means _few_ _sellers_. Because of this fewness, each firm is relatively large or "giant"-size. Steel and automobiles are good examples of oligopoly industries. The degree of oligopoly is usually measured by the percentage of industry output accounted for by the four largest firms--a percentage that could run from 50 percent on up.

It is important to note that although oligopolies dominate the output of their industry, they do not necessarily account for all 100 percent of it. Oligopoly industries may contain fringes of smaller firms which together account for as much as 30 percent or more of the industry's output.

The _product_ turned out under oligopoly conditions is generally regarded as differentiated. For one thing, the product of individual firms typically carries a brand name or trademark that distinguishes it from rival firms' products. In the case of automobiles and other consumers' goods, the product itself is also differentiated by design, style, and color. Differentiation may also occur in industrial products, such as special-grade steels made for special purposes and, hence, not easily duplicated by rivals. Even where the industrial product is fairly standard or similar, as in cement and steel, the attached brand name or trade-mark makes for differentiation.

What about conditions of _entry_ under oligopoly? Although, in theory, oligopoly industries are open markets, in practice they may become closed by one or another type of government intervention or protection (e.g., environmental regulations). Some writers, however, believe that the mere existence of oligopoly causes a "barrier" to entry. They point to the large size and "concentration" of output in the hands of a few firms, and to large advertising budgets and established reputations which allegedly make it difficult for new firms to get a foothold in the industry.

What makes oligopoly of particular interest? When people talk heatedly about "big business" or the "giant corporations," it is usually oligopoly they have in mind. Because of their large size, they account for major shares of manufacturing output, and therefore are

330

allegedly in a position to raise prices and increase profit-margins, causing "administered" price inflation. (This question of "administered" prices will be pursued below.)

"Monopolistic Competition"

(4) <u>Monopolistic Competition</u>. This is the last of the market structures which, together with oligopoly, encompasses the bulk of output in the economy. Offhand, the term sounds contradictory due to the combination of "monopolistic" and "competition." Actually, "monopolistic" here signifies that the industry is characterized by product differentiation, brand names, and trademarks, while "competition" refers to the presence of numerous firms and the absence of comparative giants. Furthermore, the product differentiation is often effectively slight, not enough to prevent the different brands from being regarded as close substitutes for each other. Leading examples include the manufacture of textiles, clothing, cigarettes, beer, chewing gum, bread, soap, TV sets, magazines, and aspirin.

"Monopolistic Competition" can, therefore, be briefly characterized as follows: the product is differentiated, albeit relatively slightly so that the different brands can be effectively regarded as close substitutes. Firms are many in number, and few, if any, are "giant"-size. Entry conditions are typically open.

Which Market Structure Is Best?

We are now ready to tackle the question: Which market structure is the <u>most desirable</u> model for competition, and why? As noted above, the market structure theory regards competition with a "what you see is what you get" approach: different market structures presumably yield different kinds of competition. Of the four market structures described above, it is <u>perfect competition</u> (PC) that is regarded by virtually all standard texts as the "optimal," most desirable form of competition.

The other three structures suffer by comparison with the PC ideal, and, hence, are lumped together under the classification of <u>imperfect competition</u>. And the reason given is very simple: under PC the firm is presumed to produce more Q (quantity) and sell at a

331

lower P (price) than any firm under imperfect competition (hereafter referred to as IC). Conversely, each firm under IC is presumed to produce less and sell at a higher price than any firm under PC.

Clearly, the basic criteria for preferring PC over IC are selling price and quantity produced. In themselves, these are eminently reasonable criteria. Other things being equal, consumers would surely prefer to buy at a lower price than at a higher price, and to get a larger quantity for their dollar than a smaller quantity. Since the PC firm, compared with IC firms, is purported to produce more at a lower price per unit, it wins the contest hands down. Compared with the standout performance of PC, the IC structures of monopoly, oligopoly, and monopolistic competition all yield "impure," inferior results. The simple graph in Figure 33 illustrates these comparative performances.

How Come PC Is Best?

Figure 33 shows that for any given capacity of production, the PC firm outperforms the IC firm in terms of quantity produced and selling price. The PC dot indicates that the PC firm produces at a higher rate of capacity than does the IC firm, and sells at a lower price, to boot. Right off, however, the reader may be prompted to ask: How is this possible? How can a tiny PC firm operate at a greater Qs and lower P than, say, a giant oligopolist (subsumed under the IC dot) who operates with economies of large scale?

For example, how can a puny "atomistic" PC firm produce more automobiles than a General Motors, and sell its car at a lower price than the mass-produced GM car? Something is out of whack here. Surely any GM plant can outperform--in terms of quantity, costs, and price--any tiny backyard, atomistic car maker. How do textbooks arrive at a conclusion so manifestly in conflict with experience? The textbooks do explain how they reach their curious conclusion, but what they generally omit telling us is that their exposition incorporates a fallacy. The nature of this fallacy, however, cannot be fully understood without additional technical analysis, to which we now proceed.

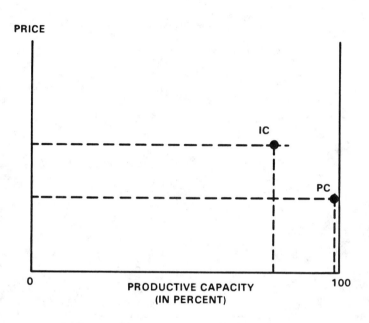

FIGURE 33:
COMPARISON OF PERFECT COMPETITION AND IMPERFECT COMPETITION

333

II. The Horizontal Demand Schedule

The technical textbook analysis which ends up concluding that the PC model is superior to any of the IC models runs along two related paths. One path explores the fact that the <u>demand</u> <u>schedule</u> facing the PC firm becomes <u>horizontal,</u> whereas the IC firm retains the familiar downward sloping D schedule. Along this path we will uncover several implications of the horizontal D curve compared with the sloping D curve. This analysis will involve elements covered in Chapters VII and VIII.

The second path is concerned with the question: Assuming both PC and IC firms seek to <u>maximize</u> <u>profits,</u> and given their respective horizontal and sloping D curves, which particular combination of P and Q will enable each firm to maximize its profits? That is to say, of all the possible dots (i.e., P and Qd) along their respective demand schedules, which one should the PC and IC firms select as the profit-maximizing one, such that any other P and Q would be less than profit-maximizing? To prepare for this particular analysis, some new technical concepts, such as "marginal cost" and "marginal revenue," must be introduced.

From Inelastic to Elastic

How do we start to understand the <u>horizontal</u> <u>demand</u> curve of the PC firm? How does the D curve lose its downward slope from left to right and acquire a horizontal slope? Figure 34 helps us reach an answer. Imagine, first, a real-world firm with the <u>inelastic</u> D schedule. The dot indicates the firm's initial position with respect to P and Q. If it raised it price, it would lose some unit sales, but because of its inelastic D its TR would increase. Other things being equal, the increased TR would leave it better off. Let us now take the next step in the analysis.

Imagine that just before our firm could take advantage of its inelastic D by raising its price, the industry is invaded by a host of new competitors from home and abroad. One consequence of this massive influx of competition and increased supply is a downward pressure on market price, as we saw in Chapter VIII. But more important for our purpose is the effect of the increased competition on the <u>slope</u> of our firm's D curve. As we saw in Chapter VII, an increase in the number of firms producing similar products will tend to

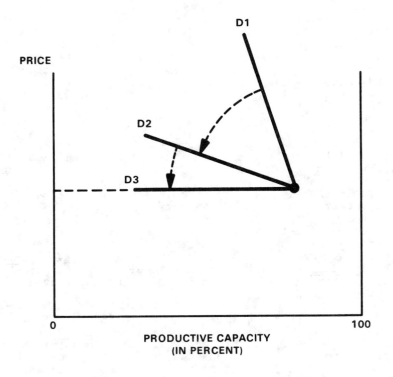

PRICE

D1

D2

D3

0   100

PRODUCTIVE CAPACITY
(IN PERCENT)

FIGURE 34:
ORIGIN OF HORIZONTAL DEMAND SCHEDULE.

335

make D more _elastic_, that is, D will slope more to the horizontal, as shown by D_2 in our diagram. And what a difference this makes! Let us see why.

Infinite Supply of Close Substitutes

Compare the new demand D_2 with the former D_1. First of all, D_2 clearly looks _elastic_, which means that if our firm now dared to raise its P it would lose proportionally more unit sales than under D_1, and its TR would decrease! Not only is this bad news for the firm, but it also reflects the effect of the increased availability of close substitutes caused by the huge influx of new firms producing a similar product. As we saw in Chapter VII, the greater the availability of close substitutes, the more elastic will D be. Now, let us go one step further in our analysis.

Imagine now _the ultimate_--that the influx of new firms into the industry continues indefinitely. Here is where we must stretch our imagination a bit: the continuous influx of new firms producing a similar product will infinitely increase the availability of close substitutes. The ultimate theoretical and graphical consequence is shown by the perfectly _horizontal_ D_3. Freedom of entry and the infinite availability of close substitutes have achieved their ultimate effect by causing _perfect elasticity_ of D--that is, _perfect horizontality_ in the demand schedule. We now have the explanation of the horizontal D. But our travels are not yet ended.

At this point we should note that our firm and its industry have reached the general condition characteristic of _perfect competition_: all firms are producing a similar, highly substitutable product (homogeneity); the number of firms has become "infinitely" great and, therefore, the size of each firm (relative to the total size of the industry) has become "infinitely" tiny (atomism); and freedom of entry has made possible the endless influx of competition. This awareness that we have reached essentially PC conditions will help us as we proceed.

No One Dares Raise His Price

We must now ask: What would happen to our firm if, faced with D_3, it would again try to raise its

336

price? How many unit sales would it lose? The perfectly flat D_3 tells us. The firm would lose all of its
remaining customers! Not even one unit could be sold at
the above-market price! All of this can be explained:
if our firm dares to raise its P, while other firms do
not, no consumer would want to buy from it when he could
get the same thing from its rivals at the unraised
price. Given the virtually infinite number of competitors, the consumer finds it extremely convenient to buy
from competitors whose unraised prices still prevail.
If we simply remember the assumption of perfect
knowledge, the consumer automatically knows where
alternative suppliers and unraised prices are available.

    In this connection it helps to emphasize that
real-world firms typically face the familiar downward
sloping D schedule, which looks like D_1 or D_2 in Figure
34. This means that if any firm dares to raise its
selling P above its rival's price, it would lose some
but not all of its customers. The important thing to
note is why the firm would not lose all of its
customers: customers cannot find perfect substitutes
for the firm's product. Consequently, some of them
continue to patronize the firm. The reason for this
continued loyalty might be one of the following:
customers still perceive the product as being sufficiently differentiated from rival firms' products; or
there are too many rival firms which makes it too costly
to search for and locate a lower-priced source.

    There is a more technical way of putting this:
the horizontal D follows necessarily from the PC market
structure. Product homogeneity assures perfect substitutability among products of separate firms. Unlimited
competition means that each firm is necessarily a teeny
atomistic entity, accounting for only an itsy-bitsy
fraction of the industry output. Indeed, each PC firm
is so small that it can readily sell all of its output
(i.e., 100 percent of its productive capacity) at the
current market price. Since consumers possess perfect
knowledge, and all products are homogeneous, firms do
not need to advertise or otherwise promote their
product.

Meet the "Price-Taker"

    In effect, all these special PC conditions cause
the PC firm to end up as a totally passive, submissive
agent--a mere price-taker, as some writers put it--

337

obediently accepting the market price as its own selling price. Our new Figure 35 helps us see this connection between the PC firm as price-taker and the horizontality of its demand schedule, as it perceives it. In panel A, the market dishes up a market-clearing price based on the momentary D and S conditions. Then, somehow, by some magical mystery device, the market automatically transmits information about this price to every firm, as shown by the arrow pointing to panel B. Panel B shows the firm "taking" the market price, adopting it as its own selling price, at which price it can then sell as much as it wants to produce.

In other words, the horizontal D schedule facing each price-taker is merely saying to the firm: the market says there is only one price at which you can sell your current product, and this is it; there is no sense in trying to sell at any other price. For instance, if you set your price above the market price, you will lose all sales to your rivals. On the other hand, there is no point selling below the market price since the market says you can sell all you want at the (higher) market price. Thus, the horizontal D schedule is essentially a price line in the same way that the familiar downward-sloping demand schedule constitutes a "price line": all demand schedules, regardless of degree of slope, indicate the price at which a given quantity can be sold to demanders.

A Possible Confusion

In this connection, let us anticipate a question concerning the apparent conflict between the traditional downward-sloping market demand schedule and the perfectly horizontal demand schedule facing the individual firm under PC. Actually, there is no real conflict: the horizontal D is an abstraction related to an unreal PC model, and hence is an impossibility, whereas the downward-sloping market D is a real-world concept. Market demand schedules will always have the familiar downward slope (remember Chapter VI). As for the demand schedule facing the individual firm in the real world, it too will possess varying degrees of downward slope so long as its product is differentiated and the number of rival firms is more or less limited (see Chapter VII on elasticity of demand). In contrast, the horizontal D schedule is merely the logical outcome of extreme conditions postulated by the PC model: absence of product differentiation and unlimited number of rival firms.

338

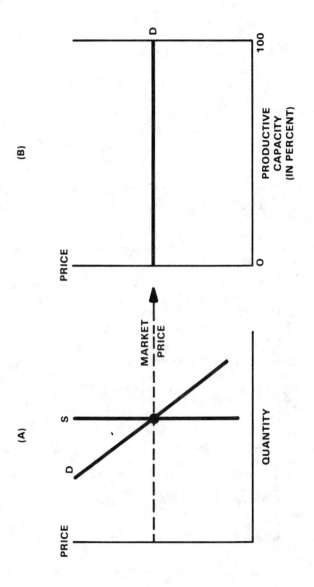

FIGURE 35:
PRICE-TAKER'S HORIZONTAL DEMAND SCHEDULE.

339

III.   Profit Maximization: MC vs. MR

We have reached the half-way point on our trek to discover the secret of Figure 33: why the perfect competition (PC) firm is alleged to produce more and sell at a lower price than the imperfect competition (IC) firm. On the first leg of our journey we explored the nature and implications of the horizontal demand schedule. We now explore the method by which firms are supposed to maximize profits, that is, the "marginal cost" versus "marginal revenue" method. In order to understand this rather technical approach to profit-maximization, we must first explain the concepts of marginal costs (MC) and marginal revenue (MR).

Costs, Fixed and Variable

The concept of marginal costs (MC) is simply derived from the concept of total costs (TC). As the term indicates, TC includes all current and capital expenses incurred by the firm in production. Generally speaking, the higher the rate of production--that is, the higher the rate of productive capacity utilized--the larger is TC.

Textbooks distinguish two main components of TC: "fixed costs" (FC) and "variable costs" (VC). Again, the terms indicate their respective meanings. Those costs which are classified as fixed costs are so called because, by their nature, they remain fixed or unchanged in total dollars regardless of the firm's rate of out-put. The other costs, which are classified as variable costs, are so called for the opposite reason--they do not remain the same but, rather, vary in amount accord-ing to the different rates of output. These general characteristics of the TC, FC, and VC schedules are shown in Figure 36, panel A.

Leading examples of FC--which textbooks also call "overhead" or "sunk" costs--are rent, depreciation, property taxes, and salaries of overhead personnel (e.g., executives, department chiefs). Leading examples of VC are wages of direct labor, materials, water, and electricity.

We can now see in Figure 36 why TC rises as the rate of output increases: it is due to the VC com-ponent, since FC remains constant. The reasons for this characteristic behavior of VC are several: the increase

340

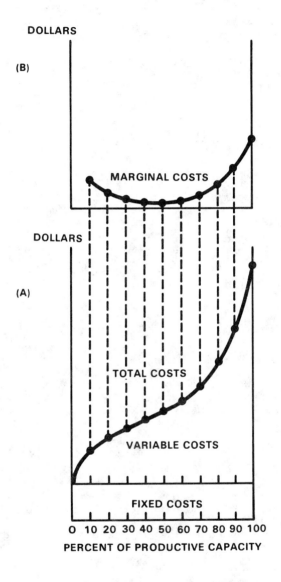

FIGURE 36:
TOTAL COSTS AND MARGINAL COSTS.

341

in output generally requires more inputs of labor, materials, and power. However, at the highest rates of output (say, 85-100 percent of capacity) premium rates of pay for overtime labor may be incurred; overtime operations are regarded as less efficient than day-shift operations; any additional workers hired may be less efficient than the regular labor force, thereby causing an increase in unit costs of output; and continuous high rates of plant utilization often cause equipment break-downs and expenses for repair.

Classification of Costs

How does one determine whether a given pro-duction outlay should be classified as "fixed" or "variable"? Theoretically, it is very simple: it depends on whether the dollar outlays for the given expense item are affected by, and vary with, the rate of output. If they vary whenever the rate of output varies, it is a variable cost. Otherwise, if they stay the same in dollar amount, regardless of the rate of output, it is a fixed cost. In practice, however, the accounting for such expense allocation may be more complicated than in principle.

The reader should be alerted to the fact that Figure 36 depicts a typically short-run situation. The "short-run" is defined as that time period during which the productive capacity of the firm is presumed to be fixed, unchanged. In our analysis, whenever we refer to "productive capacity," we are assuming a given, short-run situation during which plant, equipment, and other overhead items remain the same; the only things that vary in the short run are the variable expense items, such as labor and materials.

From TC to MC

It is from TC that we derive the marginal costs (MC) in a straightforward way. First, MC is defined as the increment of increase (or decrease) in TC when production is increased (or decreased) by one unit of output. For instance, if an increase in output of one unit increases TC from $1,200 to $1,300, then the MC is $100, the increment of increase in TC.

Although Figure 36 is drawn in terms of rates of output (e.g., increments of 10% each of productive

342

capacity), and not in terms of single <u>units</u> of output (e.g., one ton of coal), the principle of derivation remains the same, as shown in panel B. By extracting the increments of change in TC from panel A and connecting their heights in panel B, we are able to derive a characteristic <u>MC</u> <u>curve</u>. Indeed, the MC schedule turns out to be a reflection of the incremental changes in VC as well as TC. The reason for this, as we saw above, is that the marginal changes in VC account for the marginal changes in TC to start with.

From TR to MR

Derivation of the <u>marginal</u> <u>revenue</u> (MR) schedule of the firm is less complicated. Indeed, all we need to start is a demand schedule: an array of prices (P) and the quantity demanded (Qd) at each respective P. This D schedule enables us to derive <u>total</u> <u>revenue</u> (TR); and it is this TR from which marginal revenue is derived in the same <u>incremental</u> way as MC is derived from TC.

The following Table VI (A) illustrates the simple arithmetic involved. When P is reduced, Qd increases and, in this case, so does TR. MR, in this case, is the <u>extra</u> revenue from selling an additional unit. Thus, as TR increases from $1,000 to $1,089, MR amounts to $89, and so on. Indeed, MR can be defined simply as the <u>increment</u> of change in TR when one more-- or one less--unit is sold.

"Spoiling the Market"

Notice the following characteristics of the TR and MR schedules derived from the D schedule in Table VI (A). First, for all downward-sloping schedules, so long as the TR schedule increases when P is reduced (i.e., D is elastic), it increases at a <u>diminishing</u> rate--by diminished increments--as seen in the MR column: MR decreases even though TR increases.

The diminishing rate of growth in the TR, and hence the MR, is itself a consequence of the "spoiling-of-the-market" effect that naturally occurs when firms <u>reduce</u> their P in order to increase the number of units sold. Since the lower P is applied to <u>all</u> units offered for sale, the firm necessarily takes a beating, so to speak. For example, in order to sell 11 units instead of 10, the firm must reduce its P for <u>all</u> 11 units.

This differs from the practice called <u>multi-part pricing</u>, under which the firm would sell the first 10 units at the original $100 and then sell only the 11th unit at $99, the 12th unit at $98, and so on. Instead, the firm applies the new, lower P to <u>all</u> units sold, and not merely to a <u>part</u> of them.

TABLE VI

(A) Marginal Revenue -- Sloping D

Price (P)	Quantity Demanded (Qd)	Total Revenue (TR)	Marginal Revenue (MR)
$100	10	$1,000	$--
99	11	1,089	89
98	12	1,176	87
97	13	1,261	85
96	14	1,344	83
95	15	1,425	81
94	16	1,504	79

(B) Marginal Revenue -- Horizontal D

Price (P)	Quantity Demanded (Qd)	Total Revenue (TR)	Marginal Revenue (MR)
$100	1	$100	$---
100	2	200	100
100	3	300	100
100	4	400	100
100	5	500	100
100	6	600	100
100	7	700	100

This brings us to an important associated characteristic of the MR for a downward sloping D: at every selling P, the <u>MR is less</u> than the corresponding P. This, too, can be seen in Table VI (A): at a P of $99, MR is only $89; at a P of $98, the MR is only $87;

344

and so on. This characteristic tendency is likewise attributed to TR growing at a diminishing rate when D is elastic, that is, the "spoiling-of-the-market" effect noted above. We can graphically illustrate these characteristic features of MR in its relation to TR in Figure 37, panel A.

MR for the Horizontal D

So far, our discussion of the MR schedule is relevant only to the case of imperfect competition (IC), not to perfect competition (PC). The reason is that only in IC do we find downward-sloping demand schedules which do not exist in PC, where D schedules are necessarily horizontal. Under IC, demand schedules facing the firm characteristically slope downward because of product differentiation, as we saw in our discussion of Figure 34.

Mathematically, the MR derived from a horizontal D is calculated in the same way as for a sloping D (see Table VI (B)). But whereas MR is always less than P in the case of the sloping D, MR is always equal to P in the case of horizontal D schedules. For every unit sold there is only one P, the market P. Thus, since the horizontal D of the PC firm is its "price line," it is also its MR schedule. This characteristic coincidence of MR and P under perfect competition is illustrated by the P and MR schedules in Table VI (B) and in Figure 37, panel B.

Determining Maximum-Profit P and Q

We now approach the climax of the textbook case in favor of the PC firm and against the IC firm. At this stage of the analysis both types of firms are asked to determine their maximum-profit price and quantity by means of "marrying," so to speak, their respective MC and MR schedules. That is to say, they are both asked to apply a special method of determining that unique P and Q combination at which total profits will be a maximum, such that any other P and Q would yield less than maximum total profits. At its heart this method involves the juxtaposition of the MC and MR schedules relevant to the PC and IC firms, respectively. Let us first examine the case of the PC firm.

345

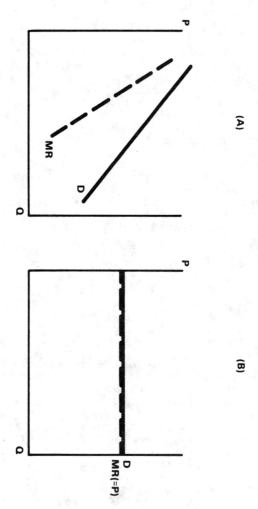

FIGURE 37:
MARGINAL REVENUE CURVES

(A)

(B)

346

How the Price-Taker Maximizes

How does the atomistic price-taker in PC determine his maximum-profit P and Q? According to the textbooks, we must look for that unique combination of P and Q at which MC equals MR—that is, graphically speaking, the intersection point of MC with MR. This special meeting place of MC and MR points out that particular price (P) and output (Q) which will maximize the firm's profits. This intersection point, where MC equals MR, is readily seen in Figure 38, panel A: it points both to the P (i.e., $100) along the horizontal D, and to the Q (vertically downwards, the quantity X). (Remember, for the price-taker and his horizontal D, the market P represents his MR, too). In this case, then, a P of $100 and a Q amounting to X are the unique pair of P and Q that maximizes total profits. Any other P and Q would be less than maximizing under the given MC and MR conditions. Why? Let us see.

A simple, logical process of elimination enables us to see why only that pair of P and Q at which MC equals MR brings maximum profits. If we look at panel A in Figure 38, we notice that the market has already given our price-taker the price at which he must sell; it remains for him only to find that unique quantity which will maximize his total profits. And we find this special Q at the output X that is indicated by the intersection point of MC with MR: only output X can maximize total profits; any other Q will bring less than maximum profits.

For example, if the price-taker produces more than X, MC will increase and exceed MR; this means that the extra costs of producing the additional units would be greater than the extra sales revenue and would, therefore, detract from total profits. Conversely, if the firm produces less than X, the MC is being exceeded by the MR, which means that the firm can still add to its total profits by producing more. Only when it reaches output X will the firm discover that its MC has finally caught up with its MR so that no more profits can be added by producing still more.

Balancing Costs vs. Benefits

To put it another way: it always pays the price-taker to produce more so long as MR exceeds MC, and to produce less when MR is exceeded by MC. That is

347

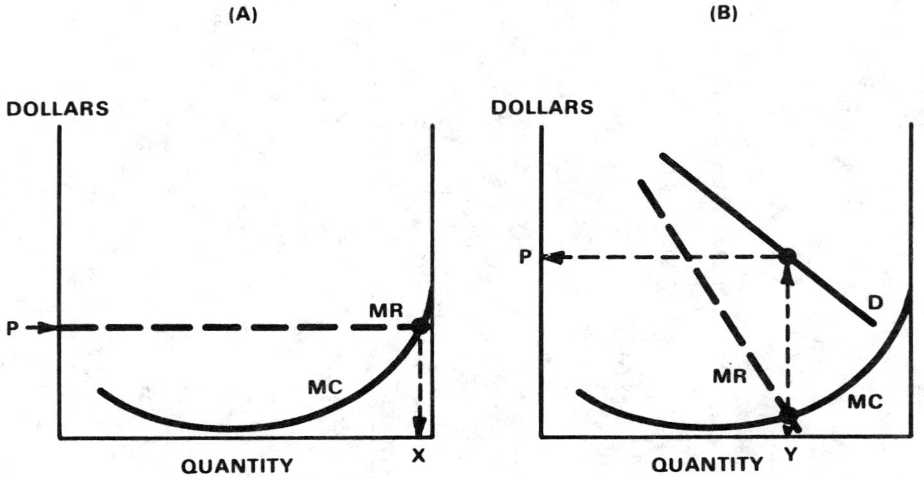

FIGURE 38:
PROFIT MAXIMIZATION

348

to say, so long as MR is greater than MC, additional profits can be earned by producing more, even though MC is continuing to rise: this rise in MC is merely slowing down the increments of increase in total profits but is not stopping total profits from growing. (Indeed, total profits continue to increase, albeit at a diminishing rate.) Similarly, so long as MR is being exceeded by MC, it means that the hitherto earned batch of profits is being eaten up by the excess of MC over MR. This excess of MC over MR is the signal that the firm is producing too much.

Actually, this principle by which the firm balances MR against MC is merely a special case of a general principle: It pays to put out extra effort or sacrifice (MC) so long as the extra benefits or gain (MR) exceeds it. The only difference between the application of this principle to (a) the firm, and to (b) human action in general, is that in the former case it is easier to quantify or assign numerical values to MC and MR, whereas in the latter case it is not possible to quantify the subjective valuations attached to extra sacrifices and extra benefits.

Price-Taker Is a Quantity Adjuster

At this point it is relevant to note that the PC firm is not only a price-taker but is also a quantity-adjuster. That is to say, once he is given the market P, he need only adjust his quantity of output to that rate which is indicated by the intersection of MC and MR and which will, therefore, maximize his profits.

For example, if on a given day the market price rises--say, from P_1 to P_2 in Figure 39--this causes a rise in marginal revenue schedule from MR_1 to MR_2 and a new intersection point with the unchanged MC schedule. This in turn indicates a new (higher) rate of output (to Y) that would maximize profits. Conversely, if the market price decreases--say, from P_1 to P_3 --the new intersection point of MR with MC indicates a reduction in output to the rate of Z. In summary, rising market prices enable output to expand into the higher MC ranges, whereas falling prices drive output down into lower MC ranges.

349

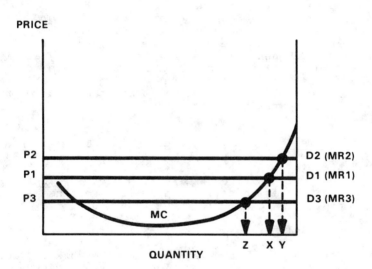

FIGURE 39:
PRICE-TAKER AS QUANTITY-ADJUSTER.

How IC Firms Maximize Profits

In contrast to the price-taker in the PC model, how does the firm in the IC market structure--monopoly, oligopoly, or monopolistic competition--maximize its profits? In the textbooks, the answer is straightforward: apply the same profit-maximizing principle. That is, look for the intersection of MC with MR, since only that P and Q which make MC and MR equal can maximize profits. Precisely this has been done in Figure 38, panel B. But notice some differences due to the sloping demand schedule characteristic of IC firms, to wit.

The downward-sloping demand schedule of the IC firm as we saw in Figure 37, panel A, generates a still greater downward slope in the MR schedule. For this reason we get a different intersection point for MC and MR, even though the MC schedule is the same in both cases: The intersection will characteristically occur at a point that is lower and leftward along the MC curve (see Figure 38). It is from this differently located junction of MC and MR that we now read off that unique P and Q combination that maximizes profits for the IC firm. When we do this, we find that the MC:MR intersection points to the smaller output of Y and the higher price than in panel A (remember, price is always read off the demand schedule).

Voilà! Less Q, Higher P

It is here that we have the textbook answer to our original conundrum--that the atomistic price-taker characteristically produces more and at a lower price compared to the IC firm whose Q is typically smaller and its P higher. Ostensibly, the key to the puzzle is the downward slope of the demand schedule characteristic of the IC market structure! If only the IC firm were not facing a sloping D schedule--that is, if it instead had a horizontal D curve--it, too, would produce as much as the PC firm and at as low a price. Only the sloping D induces it to retreat to the smaller Q and the higher P for its maximum profits; any lower P and greater Q would only cause a drop in total profits. Let us now proceed to raise a sticky question: To what extent is the sloping D really the key to the puzzle?

IV. Taking Stock of "Perfect Competition"

How are we to evaluate this textbook case in favor of the PC model? First, we will examine the PC model on its own terms to see if it really holds up as a superior model of competition. How realistic is "perfect competition" as a model or standard for real-world competition? How desirable is the PC model, even if it were possible to implement? Then we will swing over to the IC model and see if things there are really as inferior as they are made out to be. Let us now briefly review the realism of the four basic assumptions underlying the PC model.

Is Perfect Competition Realistic?

It should be clear by now that the PC model starts right off with three strikes against it by assuming the triad of product homogeneity, atomism of firm size, and perfect knowledge. All three are patently unrealistic conditions, yet the PC model brushes this handicap under the rug. It is like saying a person could fly merely by assuming that he already had wings! How does one get wings in the first place? How do we achieve homogeneity, atomism, and omniscience to start with?

Illusions of Perfect Knowledge

Omniscience? Perfect knowledge? How does this apply to real life? Knowledge or information are scarce resources because the means of acquiring them, and of overcoming ignorance in general, are themselves scarce and therefore costly to acquire: the time, effort, and money required for searching, trial-and-error experience, and learning.

Worst of all, the world does not stand still--it is in constant flux; demand schedules shift, techniques of production become obsolete through the introduction of new and better ones, and the supply and quality of resources alternately worsen or improve. The result is constant change in demand, supply, and prices--change that makes them unpredictable. As soon as we learn a given fact, so soon is it likely to become obsolete. At best we can expect only to acquire that amount of information which will hopefully maximize the likelihood of non-regretful decisions. For everyone to possess perfect

352

knowledge, however, you would have to make the world
stand still and remain changeless until everyone could
obtain all the information he needed to make non-
regretful decisions. That is, only in a static world
would perfect knowledge be possible.

Homogeneity vs. Nature

Homogeneity of product? This goes entirely
against the natural tendency of human beings to differentiate and distinguish themselves simply because they
are differentiated by birth. Whether it is by creating
different products or rendering individuated services,
each of us naturally seeks to individualize his personality and talents in some self-satisfying way. Hence,
it is unreasonable to expect differentiated human beings
to produce naturally a flow of undifferentiated (homogeneous) goods and services. The only way you can get
homogeneity of product is first to produce homogeneous
people. Short of that, you would have to impose a
dictatorship to compel people to produce homogeneous
results.

Atomism vs. Productivity

How about atomism of firm size? Theoretically,
the smallest irreducible size of the firm is the individual producer, working on his own homestead. Offhand,
it is difficult to object per se to such individual
farmers, craftsmen, industrial artisans, and self-
employed professionals as the basis of a household
economy. But an individualist economy does not necessarily imply homogeneity of product instead of differentiation. Indeed, given the natural tendency for human
differentiation, it is more reasonable to expect
differentiation rather than homogeneity of product in a
household economy!

Furthermore, history tells us that, when given
the chance, man would just as soon give up his household
economy and participate in the social division of labor
in order to enjoy its multitude of benefits: the
economies of large-scale production and their associated
lower costs and prices, the greater supply of human
talents that can be pooled in one locale, and the
greater variety of goods and services available in one
market. Again, the only way you might get a universal
reversion to one-man household economies would be by
totalitarian force.

353

An Inner Inconsistency

This brings us to an embarrasing inconsistency immanent in the PC assumptions--specifically, between atomism and homogeneity. It can be argued that the two key requirements of homogeneity and atomism are not necessarily mutually compatible. Thus, it does not necessarily follow that product homogeneity is more compatible with endless numbers of atomistic firms than is product differentiation. Indeed, on the basis of both logic and history, quite the contrary can be argued: It is standardization of product that could reasonably be associated with massive concentration of production within a few giant firms (i.e., oligopoly), whereas differentiation of product would naturally be associated with the host of atomistically small, independent producers, each turning out his more-or-less individualized product.

For one thing, standardized products are technically more easily adapted to large-scale mass production methods. (The Industrial Revolution proved that.) Add to this the economic attraction of lower unit costs and prices permitted by large-scale production. Hence, there is the undoubted attraction of concentrating production in a relatively few large-scale plants. In contrast, differentiation of product necessarily implies separate small plants or workships for each separate craftsman; and since there is no conceivable limit to the number of different products man can create, there is no assignable limit to the number of firms or workshops that would be established, except the limit posed by scarcity of resources. Thus, atomism does not necessarily mean homogeneity of product; the PC model is stood on its head.

Free Entry Makes Sense

What's left? It's free entry--freedom to compete--at last something we can accept as a reasonable way to achieve maximum production and exchange, and hence maximum consumers' welfare. But, as we saw in Chapter X (on consumers' sovereignty), the free-market system also features freedom of entry. Why push for fantastic perfect competition, with its triple chimera of homogeneity, atomism, and perfect knowledge? If free entry is desirable, then the free-market model would seem to be a more reasonable objective than impossible PC.

354

No Real Competition in PC!

This brings us to another serious flaw in PC. Where, oh where, is there any _real_ competition in this "perfectly competitive" model? Where is there even a whiff of rivalrous behavior in this world of passive quantity-adjusters? For example, where is there any _price competition_? As a matter of fact, the PC model precludes any incentive to engage in competitive pricing since each price-taker is a mere quantity-adjuster. Where is there any _non-price_ or _quality_ competition through product differentiation? There is none of that, either; it is homogeneity which rules the roost. The only rivalrous dimension in the whole of PC is _free entry_. But as we have just seen, free entry is by no means unique to the PC model. More important, however, free entry under PC becomes a meaningless feature: Firms are free to enter into only _passive_, _non-competitive_ production as mere quantity-adjusters! So again it must be asked: Where is there any _real_ competition in PC?

This is a real embarrassment! After all, how can anyone sensibly hold PC up as a model of competition when, by definition, it is totally barren of any real competition for the consumer's dollar? Thus, the free-entry condition provides only a delusive dimension of rivalry: PC firms are free to produce only homogeneous products. Indeed, as we will soon see, every attempt to compete by means of _product differentiation_ or _cost-cutting_ innovations proves to be futile--which is enough to kill off any incentive to compete in the first place. We will now see why.

Competition in the Real World

In the _real world_, as distinguished from the passive world of PC, competition only superficially takes place in terms of lower price and better quality. Underlying both price and quality competition is _innovation_--those seminal activities that bring about (a) the product _differentiation_ that enables the conquering of markets, and (b) the _cost-cutting_ that enables firms to reduce prices without squeezing profit margins (see Chapter IV). Indeed, we will now see why _only in the real world_ would it be reasonable to expect such innovation to occur, and why it is unreasonable to expect any innovation under PC.

By means of product differentiation, firms seek to tap new markets by filling gaps in market demand-- demand to satisfy wants or demand for new means. As long as people's tastes blossom and develop in endless variety and sophistication, and as long as people are naturally inclined to keep up with the Joneses, the market will continue to reveal "gaps" of unsatisfied demand which entrepreneurs will seek to fill. But none of this will happen automatically: only the alert firms, and the ones that command sufficient capital funds, will be able to capitalize on the untapped gaps in market demand.

Instantaneous Imitation of Product

In contrast, the PC model offers only homogeneity of product. We must now ask: What would happen in PC if a maverick firm, having spotted an untapped gap in market demand, decides to innovate--by producing a new product, improving on an existing one, or modifying it with a new style or design? Such innovation could enable this firm to increase it sales, grow in size, and increase its share of the market. However, given the magical assumptions of PC, such advantages would be extremely short-lived: perfect knowledge, mobile factors of production, and the firms' ability to instantaneously imitate any innovation would immediately erase any advantage to the innovator. Right on the heels of the innovator, all other firms would instantaneously duplicate the innovator's feat in order to recoup their lost shares of the market. As a consequence, innovators would soon realize that, given the likelihood of instantaneous imitation by rivals, it would be utterly foolish to innovate in the first place. Why bother?!

We can now also see why the PC model, which precludes product differentiation, is so unreal. In the real world it would take at least some time before any or all rivals could catch up with the innovator: resources are not so mobile as in PC; nor does every firm have personnel as talented or creative as the innovator's. Indeed, we can now see that the PC assumption of instantaneous imitation implies that every firm has equally talented personnel. Only this equality assures that what any one PC firm can do, every other firm can do as well, and instantaneously. In PC, homogeneity of product implies homogeneity of personnel!

Instantaneous Imitation of Technique

A similar threat of instantaneous duplication by rivals hangs over the PC firm if it dares to innovate new cost-cutting techniques. Why on earth would a firm introduce a new technique of production in the first place if rival firms can duplicate this feat in a jiffy? We can now see the real reason why, when faced with a horizontal D schedule, it would be foolish for the firm to sell below the market price. The reason is not simply that the firm is taking the easy way out by passively "taking" the market price; it is a bit more complicated than that.

First of all, selling below the market price means that, as a result of its price-cut, the firm's profit margin will be squeezed. True, this underpricing of product is silly if you are in PC and you are free to "take" the higher market price and still be able to sell all that you produce. So long as you are motivated to maximize your profits and wealth, so long will you prefer to sell at a higher price than at a lower price, ceteris paribus. Therefore, it makes no sense to squeeze your profit margin if you don't have to. But what if you can introduce a cost-cutting technique and cut your selling price without squeezing the profit margin? And what if you alone are able to cut costs while your rivals cannot, so that you can cut your price without cutting your profit rate while your rivals cannot do so? This possibility is diagrammed in Figure 40.

Unit Cost or AC Schedule

The first thing to note in Figure 40 is the average cost (AC) curve introduced in panel B. Based on observed date, the AC schedule shows the varied cost-per-unit of output incurred at different rates of production. At very low rates of production--say, in the OX range--the AC is above the minimum unit costs that occur in the large XY range of productive capacity. Only when the plant is operating at these higher rates of capacity--in the XY range--can it enjoy the minimum unit costs. Then, at the very high rates of production, in the approximately 85-100 percent of capacity range (YZ), unit costs again rise above minimum costs. The reasons for this are several-fold: overtime rates of pay; costs of repair and maintenance of overburdened equipment; and drop in productivity due to newly hired workers.

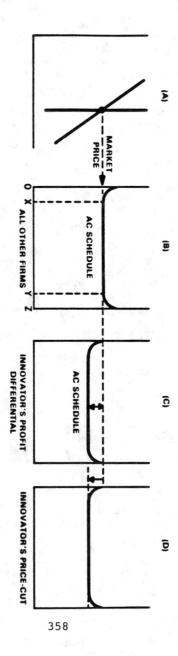

FIGURE 40:
INNOVATIVE COST-CUTTING AND PROFIT DIFFERENTIALS.

The next thing to note in panel B of Figure 40 is that the current market price just covers the minimum points of the AC curve. Since textbooks usually include a "normal" rate of profit in the AC schedule, this means that firms are able to earn a normal profit when their AC is covered by the going market price. (The reader should be aware that this inclusion of profit in the AC schedule differs from the treatment in Chapter IX. This difference of treatment is still an unresolved question in the technical literature. Here we adhere to the orthodox treatment, unless otherwise specified.)

This tangency of market price and minimum AC represents a state of equilibrium. If market price were to fall below AC, losses would begin to replace profits, firms would begin to exit from the industry, and the reduced supply would tend to drive prices back up again. The restored price level would then make it once again profitable to enter the industry. If, on the other hand, prices were to rise above the original level, the extra profits would attract new firms whose entry would increase supply and drive prices back down, thus reducing profits to their former rate.

Source of Differential Profits

Now, in panel C we can see the initial positive impact on the innovator's profits of his newly intro-duced cost-cutting technique. The new technique of production enables the innovator's AC schedule to drop; this means a lower unit cost of production. Since market price is still the same as before, the inno-vator's lower AC automatically increases the spread between selling price and AC. Thus our cost-cutting innovator enjoys initial differential profits--a higher profit rate than his rivals'.

He now has two basic choices: (a) continue to enjoy the full margin of differential profits, while leaving his selling price the same as his rivals' (panel C); or (b) reduce his selling price to where it just covers his minimum AC (panel D). The first option would generate an accumulation of profits and increase his wealth, while the second option could enable him to underprice his rivals and drive them out of business. (A very important byproduct of this rivalry between our innovator and the laggards is the lower price enjoyed by consumers). Since his rivals cannot match his lower price without suffering drastic losses, they lose

359

customers to the innovator. But then our innovator
would have to expand his productive capacity in order to
supply the increased demand for his product.

Whence will our innovator obtain additional
funds to invest in new plant and equipment? He can, of
course, borrow from the money and capital markets; but
he now also has a new source of investment funds: the
differential profits associated with choice (a) above.
However, the innovator, in line with much of U.S. experience, could decide upon a combination of both (a)
and (b), enjoying part of the financial benefits accruing from (a) and part of the competitive benefits
accruing from (b).

Instantaneous vs. Delayed Ajustments

Whichever course our innovator undertakes as a
consequence of his initial differential profits, the
fact remains that these profits can arise only so long
as none or very few of his rivals can duplicate his
cost-cutting feat, and so long as there is a sufficient
time-lag between his innovative advance and his rivals'
catching up to him. In real-world competition, significant differential profits are possible precisely because
firms are not equally capable of innovative advances and
cannot instantaneously imitate the innovator's feat. In
the PC model, however, all firms are required to be
equally capable in every dimension of competitive behavior. Ironically, as a consequence, no real-world
competition would actually take place. Why compete when
there is no advantage to it?

In the real world, by contrast, firms do have
incentive to innovate precisely because the inequality
of talents and creativity, on the one hand, and the
time-lags involved in catching up to the innovator, on
the other, may be sufficient to bring pioneer profits to
firms able to innovate. By the same token, the laggard
firms, in order to catch up, are desperately driven to
at least imitate the innovator, if not to innovate on
their own. Otherwise, they must resign themselves to a
secondary position in the industry. In the process of
imitation, the imitating firms may resort to luring away
key personnel from the innovator, intensive market research, product planning, and research and development.
Such catch-up efforts thus give an ironic twist to
real -world rivalry among firms: to the extent that
laggards intensify their imitation of the innovator--for

example, in style or design--to that extent a tendency
to homogeneity asserts itself and offsets the tendency
to differentiate products.

Homogeneity of Firms, Too

All of this helps bring home another important
implication of the PC model already noted above: The
logical concomitant of homogeneity of product is the
homogeneity of firms! The personnel of firms themselves
must be as homogeneous as the products they produce.
The talents embodied in each firm must be equally know-
ledgeable and creative in order to be able to achieve
instantaneous imitation of a rival's innovation. It is
as though the goddess of egalitarianism had descended
upon the world and redistributed the differentiated
talents of the world in order to create an even distribution of them. Hence the motto, "Anything you can do,
we can do!" appropriately describes what homogeneity of
product in PC really implies.

Is Perfect Competition Desirable?

Let us grant that no one really wants a reincarnation of the PC model under real-world conditions, and
that proponents of the PC model merely want us to
approximate it--by promoting tendencies toward homogeneity, atomism, perfect knowledge, and free entry.
After all, aren't these, in themselves, desirable characteristics for a competitive economy?

Well, to start, what about the desirability of
homogeneity? This characteristic must be ruled out
simply on the logical grounds that it makes no sense to
desire something that either (a) is impossible to
achieve (given the axiom of human differentiation) or
(b) is achievable only by undesirable means (i.e.,
totalitarianism). Atomism of firms must be disqualified
on virtually the same grounds. Furthermore, as we have
argued, atomism is more compatible with product differentiation than with homogeneity.

Perfect knowledge, too, must be rejected on the
grounds of impossibility. This is not to imply the
people will not prefer more knowledge to less knowledge,
but only that personal circumstances and subjective preferences of each individual--the degree of urgency and

361

motivation, and the availability of means—can determine the extent to which a person pursues greater knowledge.

Finally, we are again left with free entry as the only realistic and the only desirable goal in PC. We have already noted that free entry implies essentially the same thing as free competition in the free-market model in Chapter X: the absence of artificial barriers to new or existing firms that want to enter into competition in the given industry. But, as we have stressed, free entry is the only realistic element in PC; the rest of it—homogeneity, atomism, and perfect knowledge—must be abandoned as unrealistic goals.

Free Entry Means Free Market

If free competition is the most we can ask for in the real world, and the free market assures maximum free competition, it is reasonable to ask: Why bother with the impossible PC model when the free-market model —which is not impossible!—will suffice? Why saddle ourselves with the chimera of product homogeneity, atomistic firms, and perfect knowledge if the only necessary condition is free-market competition?

To repeat: the only one of the four basic assumptions of the PC model that can serve as a real-world starting point for creating more elastic D schedules is free entry; the only thing it requires is the removal of artificial impediments to free competition. In contrast, the other three assumptions cannot serve as starting points because they are impossible; nor can they serve as end results because they are either beyond human capability (e.g., perfect knowledge) or desirability(e.g., homogeneity, atomism).

Sloping Demand the Achilles' Heel

Let us now swing back to the much discredited IC firm, which is alleged to produce less Q at a higher P than the PC firm, and therefore is regarded less satisfactory than the imaginary PC firm. What is the single apparent cause of this inferiority? Technically speaking, as noted above, it is the sloping demand schedule. Everything else in the textbook argument seems OK—that is, since the marginal cost schedule is assumed to be the same as that of the PC firm, the Achilles' heel must be the sloping D.

362

If the sloping demand schedule automatically condemns the IC firm, it is proper to ask: What causes this slope in the first place? The answer is: product differentiation--the absence of very close substitutes. This even includes monopoly--open or closed--since its being the only firm in its field naturally differentiates it from all firms. Except for the closed monopoly, however, differentiation of product is, as we have noted, a byproduct of the natural differentiation of human beings--consumers having varied tastes and preference-scales, and producers having differentiated ability to cater to consumers' wants. Thus the indictment of the IC firm basically implies a denial of natural human variation--as though demand schedules in the real world could be anything but sloping!

Producing Less for a Higher Price

Is there any way of saving the IC firm from the curse of its sloping demand schedule, which alone induces it to produce a smaller Q at a higher P? One obvious way out would seem to be this: Let the firm settle for less than maximum profits! That is to say, let it produce more Q and sell at a lower P; for example, more than the amount Y in Figure 38, panel B; then drop the P in order to sell this greater Q. But this raises the obvious question: Why should the IC firm be forced to seek less than maximum profits? Does it not have the same right as the atomistic PC firm to seek maximum profits? It certainly does--but only by means of producing less and selling at a higher P. This question, in turn, brings up the more fundamental issue: Does not every firm have the right to produce as much or as little as it wishes?

For example, does Clint Eastwood have the right to ask for a higher salary than, say, Robert Redford--or vice versa? Does either of them have the right to make only one picture a year, if he wishes, instead of two or three? Does anyone have the right to compel them to make more movies for less pay per movie? Does the farmer have the right to sell less corn at a higher price per ear? Does the electrical worker have the right to ask for a shorter work week and a higher rate of pay per hour? Is there anyone working a forty-hour week who cannot be accused of preferring this to working fifty hours at less per hour?

363

Common law tradition has it that everyone has the natural right to produce as much or as little as he wishes, which includes working a shorter work week while asking for a higher price for his service. But he does not have the right--at least in a truly free society, with individual rights of self-sovereignty--to force others to pay a higher price for less work. Unfortunately, this principle is being widely violated; leading examples are (a) trade-union strike actions to reduce working hours and increase wage rates, and (b) legally enforced farm acreage restrictions to reduce supply for higher farm prices.

Bogey of "Artificial Scarcity"

The less-Q, higher-P indictment of the IC firm is part of a general line of attack which holds that any firm that dares to produce less Q than it can is guilty of "contriving artificial scarcity." This makes no more sense than to say that any of us who dares to rest from work or even sleep too much would also be guilty of "contriving artificial scarcity" by being less productive than otherwise.

More seriously, however, we need only recall that scarcity is a natural condition that is prior to man's productivity. Anything useful that man produces, no matter how great or small, can only help alleviate the scarcity of goods; it certainly cannot create "artificial" scarcity! It is totally irrelevant, therefore, that an oligopolist or any other real-world firm can produce more than they do: so long as they produce anything at all, they reduce scarcity, not create it! Yes, there is a way to create artificial scarcity, and that is to forcibly prevent or restrain a person from producing goods--for instance, by artificial legal barriers to entry of the type discussed in Chapter X (e.g., licenses or permits required by government), threats and violence by a Mafia gang, by trade union and agricultural restrictionism, as noted above.

If we grant the IC firm every free man's right to produce as much or as little as it wishes, and to charge whatever price it feels its product is worth (or whatever price the buyer is willing to pay), we must then ask: What grounds do proponents of the PC model really have for condemning the IC firm? If the IC firm does have the natural right to maximize its profits and to produce less Q at a higher P, on what grounds can we reject the IC firm?

Bogey of "Market Power"

A favorite ploy of opponents of the IC firm is the bugbear about "market power." What is this market power? In essence, it refers to one of two things: (a) the IC firm's ability to raise its price without fear of losing all its customers, a fear that haunts the price-taker under PC; (b) the ability of large companies to "administer prices." In the first case, "market power" merely refers to possession of a sloping D! Only a sloping D enables the firm to hold onto some of its customers even when it raises its P. Presumably, sloping D schedules must be outlawed! But enough has already been said about sloping D curves versus horizontal ones. Let us, instead, move on to the concept of "administered prices."

What Are "Administered Prices"?

The concept of "administered prices" (AP hereafter) implies that the large firm has an unrivaled power to raise its P at will--presumably in virtual defiance of the law of demand and supply! That is to say, the mere posting of its selling price by the firm suffices to realize this price in the market place. In the past 30 years or so, the concept of AP has cropped up whenever the general price level in the economy spurted upward--in association with charges that the big corporations were to blame for "too high" prices and "inflation."

This is not the place to get into the true causes of price inflation. Suffice it to note that, other things being equal, the primary inducement to raising the firm's P is to increase its TR (not decrease it). This implies that the firm believes it has an inelastic D schedule (Chapter VII): only an inelastic D will enable the firm to increase its TR by a price hike. That is, if the firm had an elastic D instead, the price hike would only cause its TR to drop and it would therefore have to rescind its price hike.

365

All Firms Are Price-Takers!

Two conclusions follow. One is that the bugbear about AP can only have relevance to firms possessing inelastic rather than elastic D schedules. The issue then becomes this: Does the big firm--or any firm--have the natural right to raise its P in order to increase its TR? We have argued the affirmative. More important is the second conclusion: After all is said and done, in the real world all firms turn out to be price-takers no less effectively than in the PC model.

For instance, no real-world firm really has the "power" to suspend the law of demand and supply--that is, to avoid ending up with a surplus for overpricing its product, or to avoid less-than-maximum profits by underpricing its product and realizing a shortage. Sooner or later, after trial-and-error searching for the market-clearing price, every real-world firm finds itself eventually having to "take" the market price that actually clears its supply. Thus real-world firms are "price-takers" no less than firms in pure competition, the only difference being this: PC firms "take" their P from the market right from the start (they have perfect knowledge!), whereas real firms "take" their P only after trial-and-error search in the market. Irony of ironies: real firms are, in an ultimate sense, price-takers, too!

What Firms Can or Cannot Do

To be sure, in the real world every firm is free to sell or not to sell at the going market price. For example, it is free to withhold some of its product if it believes this will cause a shortage and a rise in market price. But this "power" to withhold supply can in no way force the buyer to pay that higher price. The buyer is always free not to buy if he thinks the price is too high. The only "power" possessed by any firm is the right to post its selling price--merely to ask for whatever price it wants--that's all! In no way can it compel any buyer to pay that price.

Thus we see that so long as the firm: (a) must seek the market-clearing price in order to avoid over-pricing or underpricing its product and to maximize its profits, and (b) does not have the power to force buyers to pay its asking price, then so long must the firm-- even the ugly "giant" oligopolist--be viewed as a price-

366

taker rather than a price-<u>controller</u>. So long as the <u>market</u> demand can upset any price posted by the firm, we must conclude that it is market demand and not the firm that <u>ultimately</u> determines selling prices. In the absence of perfect knowledge, real-world price-takers have to grope and <u>search</u> for their profit-maximizing price instead of getting it automatically and instantaneously as in the unreal world of pure competition. In the real world, there is no way for the firm to avoid subservience to the market as the <u>ultimate</u> determiner of its selling price. Hence, since all real-world firms are necessarily price-takers, the PC model no longer has a monopoly on price-takers!

No Empirical Basis

What remains, then, of the case against the IC firm? On the one hand, the PC ideal stands shattered as an unrealistic and undesirable objective. Its horizontal D schedule is a pure heuristic device, unfit for human existence. Its free-entry requirement is not unique to PC, since it is also a basic tenet of the free-market model (Chapter X). Its price-taker, once he is deprived of his magical "perfect knowledge," turns out to be no more of a price-taker than any real-world firm. On the other hand, the IC firm does possess the natural right to seek maximum profits and to produce as much or as little as it wishes.

There is still another embarrassment for the PC model: the lack of any <u>empirical</u> basis for the charge that the IC firm actually produces less and charges more for its product than does the tiniest of PC firms. Indeed, reality is quite the reverse. For technological and economic reasons, the large-size IC firm is generally able to outproduce and underprice the puny PC firm.

Blowing the Whistle

This brings us to the most humiliating embarrassment of all for the PC model; the diagrammatic pyrotechnics of the textbooks, in effect, amount to a hoax being played on the reader. The hoax takes the form of the casual but inadmissable assumption that <u>both</u> the PC and IC firms have the <u>same</u> MC curves! (Panels A and B in Figure 38 remain true to this assumption.) There is hardly a text that does not assume that <u>both</u> the atomistic price-taker and the giant oligopolist have

367

the _same_ cost schedules. One prominent text even goes so far as to show the puny PC firm with _lower_ average cost (AC) and MC curves than the giant oligopolist! This glib assumption, of course, totally contradicts reality.

If we appeal to reality instead of diagrammatic hocus-pocus, we find that, except for cases where technology does not permit, the _larger_ firm is generally able to produce at lower costs rather than the smaller firm (see the following Figure 41). The reason lies in its special ability to capture the _economies_ of large-scale production which are technically and economically foreclosed to the undersized firm.

Thus, in practice, it is the IC firm--not the PC firm--which produces greater quantities at lower costs and prices. Instead of the untenable juxtaposition shown in Figure 33, it is much more reasonable to present the comparison depicted in Figure 41. Here, the PC firm has an extremely high cost and price level because of its puny size and scale of operations. In gross contrast, the oligopolist, with his large-scale economies, shows a relatively massive Q at a significantly lower cost and price. This is much closer to reality! As Joseph A. Schumpeter once put it, writing a script on market competition that omits both rivalrous product differentiation and competitive cost-cutting is "like _Hamlet_ without the Danish prince"![3]

V. Competition Is Good -- For Whom?

As we close this chapter, we come full circle--we return to the assertion that competition is a good thing. This raises the question: _For whom_ specifically is competition supposed to be beneficial? For the _consumer_? If so, in what way can competition benefit the consumer? Is competition also beneficial for the competing _firms_? If so, in what way?

Competition Benefits Consumers

Take the _consumer_ first. The consumer is always better off when he can buy at a lower P than at a higher

---

[3]Joseph A. Schumpeter, _Capitalism, Socialism, and Democracy_ (3rd ed., New York: Harper & Brothers, 1950), p. 86.

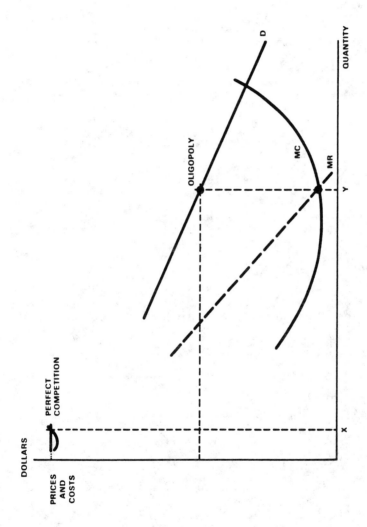

FIGURE 41:
OLIGOPOLIST PRODUCES MORE AT LOWER PRICE.

369

P, other things being the same. Under which conditions will price be under pressure to drop? When demand is decreased or supply is increased, as we saw in Chapter VIII. However, only the supply aspect interests us here, since consumers would prefer to have more supply to less, other things being equal. Hence, the question becomes this: How can we optimize the conditions under which supply can be increased? The answer has already been given in Chapter X: Only free or open markets are capable of maximizing the opportunities to engage in production and exchange. A similar line of reasoning applies to non-price competition via product differentiation. Here, too, only free markets provide optimal conditions of entry into rivalrous production and exchange.

A Mixed Blessing for Firms

Now, how about the firm? How does competition benefit it? From the firm's viewpoint, unlike that of the consumer's, competition under a profit-and-loss system is not an unmixed blessing! Whereas consumers stand only to gain from competition that drives costs and prices down and increases quality of product, firms must either gain or lose as the result of competition.

As we saw in Chapter X, the free market puts constant pressure on the firm to cater successfully to the consumer as the only way to earn profits and avoid losses. Firms are able to retain their hold on consumers' demand only via product differentiation or cost- and price-reductions. Failure to do so brings losses and possible banishment from the market. Furthermore, the more investors and stockholders prefer to invest in profitable firms (rather than in loss-ridden firms), the more will firms be under the gun to earn profits and avoid losses.

Competition Is War!

Ironically, the same free-market competition that is an unmixed blessing for the "sovereign" consumer can drive firms to run screaming for shelter. History reveals that every now and then some firms have sent up the cry, "Competition is war, and war is hell!" More than one firm has run to government to secure its protection from the fateful verdict of consumers' dollar ballots and competition from rivals at home and abroad.

Whether government protection takes the form of subsidy, bailout, tariff, price-fixing, so-called "regulation," or guaranteed market, it can only serve to undermine the degree of consumers' sovereignty in the market.[4]

The reason is that in a truly free market in which government refrains from tinkering with or hampering market competition, the only proper "protection" for the firm is to cater successfully to the consumer. The consumers' dollar ballots are so powerful ultimately that we must alter our conception of market competition: that which superficially appears to be "rivalry" among firms is actually an indirect manifestation of the consumers' fateful balloting. For example, if firm A outstrips firm B in the market place, and firm B closes down or shrinks in size, it is not firm A that is ultimately to blame for B's fate. Blame must fall ultimately on the consumers who showed overwhelming preference for A over B. Thus, when firms cry "Competition is hell!" they are really paying indirect tribute to the fateful power of the consumers' dollar ballots.

Summary

At the start, in Figure 33 we met the classic thesis that the PC firm outperforms the IC firm by producing more Q at a lower P than the bigger IC firm. We then explored the two paths that lead to this thesis; one path took us through the horizontal D schedule, the other went through the process of profit-maximizing by means of MC and MR. Things came to a head in Figure 38 which contains the curvilinear latticework that incriminates the IC firm merely because it has a sloping D schedule.

Finally, in denouement, we see that the case against the IC firm amounts to intellectual sleight-of-hand; after all, it is not the sloping D schedule that

---

[4]There is historical evidence that business leaders in major industries, including the railroads, have sought federal protection against competition, at least since the 1880's, via the Interstate Commerce Act and other so-called "regulation". For example, see Gabriel Kolko's two works, Railroads and Regulation, 1877-1916 (Princeton: Princeton University Press, 1965) and The Triumph of Conservatism (New York: The Free Press, 1963).

does in the IC firm so much as it is the oversight concerning the <u>cost</u> <u>curves</u>. However, none of this critique of the PC model should be construed as a whitewash of the big corporation. There <u>is</u> a case to be made against certain tendencies in corporate behavior, but it has little to do with atomism or sloping D schedules; it has more to do with business' tendency to run to government for protection whenever the going gets rough in competition at home and abroad.

FOR FURTHER READING

I. Introductory Works

Alchian, Armen A. and Allen, William R. Exchange and Production. 2nd ed., Belmont, CA: Wadsworth Publishing Co., 1977.

Dolan, Edwin G. Basic Microeconomics. 2nd ed., Hinsdale: Dryden Press, 1980.

Greaves, Bettina B. (ed.). Free Market Economics: A Basic Reader. Irvington-on-Hudson: Foundation for Economic Education, 1975.

Gwartney, James D. and Stroup, Richard. Microeconomics: Private and Public Choice. 3rd ed., New York: Academic Press, 1982.

Hazlitt, Henry. Economics In One Lesson. New York: Arlington House Publishers.

Heyne, Paul T. and Johnson, Thomas. Toward Understanding Micro-Economics. Chicago: Science Research Associates, 1976.

Jevons, Marshall. Murder at the Margin (novel). Glen Ridge, N.J.: Thomas Horton and Daughters, 1978.

Lee, Dwight R. and McKnown, Robert F. Economics In Our Time. 2nd ed., Chicago: Science Research Associates, 1983.

McKenzie, Richard B. and Tullock, Gordon. The New World of Economics. 3rd ed., Homewood, Ill.: Richard D. Irwin, Inc., 1981.

Sowell, Thomas. Markets and Minorities. New York: Basic Books, Inc., 1981.

II. Current Issues and Policies

Allen, William R. Midnight Economist. Playboy Press, 1981.

Friedman, Milton. There's No Such Thing As a Free Lunch. LaSalle, Ill.: Open Court, 1975.

McKenzie, Richard B. Economic Issues In Public Policies. New York: McGraw-Hill Book Co., 1980.

North, Douglass C. and Miller, Roger LeRoy. The Economics of Public Issues. 6th ed., New York: Harper and Row, 1983.

Williams, Walter E. America: A Minority Viewpoint. Stanford: Hoover Institution Press, 1982.

III. Economic Growth, Capitalism, and Living Standards

Chamberlain, John. The Enterprising Americans. New York: Harper and Row, Colophon Books, 1963.

Chamberlain, John. The Roots of Capitalism. Indianapolis: Liberty Press, 1976.

Hartwell, R. M. The Industrial Revolution and Economic Growth. London: Methuen and Co., 1971.

Hartwell, R. M., et al. The Long Debate on Poverty. London: Institute of Economic Affairs, 1972.

Hayek, Friedrich A. (ed.) Capitalism and the Historians. London: Routledge and Kegan Paul, Ltd., 1954.

Hayek, Friedrich A. The Constitution of Liberty. Chicago: Henry Regnery Co., Gateway Edition, 1972.

Hazlitt, Henry. The Conquest of Poverty. New Rochelle: Arlington House, 1973.

Jacobs, Jane. The Economy of Cities. New York: Vintage Books, 1970.

Jewkes, John, Sawers, David, and Stillerman, David. The Sources of Invention. 2nd ed., New York: W. W. Norton and Co., 1969.

Landes, David S. The Unbound Prometheus. London: Cambridge University Press, 1969.

Novak, Michael. The Spirit of Democratic Capitalism. New York: Simon and Schuster, Touchstone Books, 1982.

Nutter, G. Warren. Political Economy and Freedom. Indianapolis: Liberty Press, 1983.

Puth, Robert C. American Economic History. Chicago: Dryden Press, 1982.

Rand, Ayn. Capitalism, The Unknown Ideal. New York: New American Library, 1967.

Rougier, Louis. The Genius of the West. Los Angeles: Nash Publishing, 1971.

Smith, Adam. The Wealth of Nations. 2 vols., Glasgow ed. Indianapolis: Liberty Press, 1981.

Snyder, Carl. Capitalism the Creator. New York: The Macmillan Co., 1940.

Sowell, Thomas. Ethnic America. New York: Basic Books, Inc., 1981.

IV. Market Process and Competition

Alchian, Armen A. Economic Forces At Work. Indianapolis: Liberty Press, 1977.

Backman, Jules. Advertising and Competition. New York: New York University Press, 1967.

Backman, Jules. Pricing: Policies and Practices. New York: National Industrial Conference Board, 1961.

Brozen, Yale (ed.). Advertising and Society. New York: New York University Press, 1974.

Brozen, Yale (ed.). The Competitive Economy. Morristown: General Learning Press, 1975.

Brozen, Yale. Concentration, Mergers, and Public Policy. New York: Macmillan Publishing Co., 1982.

Chalk, Alfred F. "Mandeville's Fable of the Bees: A Reappraisal." Southern Economic Journal, XXXIII, No. 1 (July 1966).

Chambers, Raymond J. Accounting, Evaluation and Economic Behavior. Englewood Cliffs: Prentice-Hall, Inc., 1966.

Goldschmid, Harvey J., Mann, H. Michael and Weston, J. Fred (eds.). Industrial Concentration: The New Learning. Boston: Little, Brown and Co., 1974.

375

Hayek, Friedrich A. Individualism and Economic Order. Chicago: Henry Regnery Co., Gateway Edition, 1972.

Hutt, William H. A Rehabilitation of Say's Law. Athens, Ohio: Ohio University Press, 1974.

Hutt, William H. The Theory of Collective Bargaining. Glencoe, Ill.: The Free Press, 1954.

Hutt, William H. The Theory of Idle Resources. 2nd ed., Indianapolis: Liberty Press, 1977.

Kirzner, Israel M. Competition and Entrepreneurship. Chicago: University of Chicago Press, 1973.

Kirzner, Israel M. Market Theory and the Price System. Princeton: D. Van Nostrand Co., 1963.

Kirzner, Israel M. Perception, Opportunity and Profit. Chicago: University of Chicago Press, 1979.

Kirzner, Israel M., et al. The Prime Mover of Progress. London: Institute of Economic Affairs, 1980.

Knight, Frank H. Risk, Uncertainty and Profit. Chicago: University of Chicago Press, 1971.

Mandeville, Bernard. The Fable of the Bees. 2 vols., London: Oxford University Press, 1966.

McGee, John S. In Defense of Concentration. New York: Praeger Publishers, 1971.

O'Driscoll, Jr., Gerald P. Economics as a Coordination Problem: The Contributions of F. A. Hayek. New York: New York University Press, 1977.

Rosenberg, Nathan. "Mandeville and Laissez-Faire." Journal of the History of Ideas. XXIV (April-June, 1963).

Sowell, Thomas. Knowledge and Decisions. New York: Basic Books, Inc., 1980.

Vernon, John M. Market Structure and Industrial Performance. Boston: Allyn and Bacon, Inc., 1972.

V. Government Interventionism

Armentano, Dominick T. Antitrust and Monopoly. New York: John Wiley and Sons, 1982.

Boarman, Patrick M. Union Monopolies and Antitrust Restraints. Washington, D. C.: Labor Policy Associates, 1963.

Bradley, Philip D. (ed.). The Public Stake In Union Power. Charlottesville: University Press of Virginia, 1959.

Brookes, Warren T. The Economy In Mind. New York: Universe Books, 1982.

Chickering, A. Lawrence (ed.). The Politics of Planning. San Francisco: Institute for Contemporary Studies, 1976.

Cornuelle, Richard. De-Managing America. New York: Vintage Books, 1976.

Davidson, James D. The Squeeze. New York: Summit Books, 1980.

Fleming, Harold. Ten Thousand Commandments. Irvington-on-Hudson: Foundation for Economic Education, 1951.

Friedman, Milton. Capitalism and Freedom. Chicago: University of Chicago Press, 1962.

Friedman, Milton and Friedman, Rose. Freedom to Choose. New York: Harcourt Brace Jovanovich, 1980.

Hayek, Friedrich A., et al. Rent Control: A Popular Paradox. Vancouver: Fraser Institute, 1975.

Kolko, Gabriel. Railroads and Regulation, 1877 - 1916. Princeton: Princeton University Press, 1965.

Kolko, Gabriel. The Triumph of Conservatism, 1900-1916. New York: The Free Press, 1963.

McKenzie, Richard B. Bound to Be Free. Stanford: Hoover Institution Press, 1982.

Mises, Ludwig von. A Critique of Interventionism. New Rochelle: Arlington House, 1977.

Oppenheimer, Franz. The State. New York: Free Life Editions, 1975.

Orr, Daniel. Property, Markets, and Government Intervention. Pacific Palisades: Goodyear Publishing Co., 1976.

Petro, Sylvester.   The Labor Policy of the Free Society. New York: Ronald Press Co., 1957.

Reynolds, Morgan O.   Power and Privilege: Labor Unions In America. New York: Universe Books, 1984.

Rothbard, Murray N.   For A New Liberty.   Revised edition, New York: Collier Books, 1978.

Rothbard, Murray N. Power and Market. New York: New York University Press, 1977.

Schmidt, Emerson P.   Union Power and the Public Interest. Los Angeles: Nash Publishing, 1973.

Templeton, Kenneth S., Jr. (ed.). The Politicization of Society. Indianapolis: Liberty Press, 1979.

Wooldridge, William. Uncle Sam the Monopoly Man. New Rochelle: Arlington House, 1970.

VI. Perspectives on Socialism

Elliott, John E. (ed.). Marx and Engels on Economics, Politics, and Society. Santa Monica: Goodyear Publishing Co., 1981.

Flew, Antony. The Politics of Procrustes. Buffalo: Prometheus Books, 1981.

Foundation for Economic Education. Cliches of Socialism. Irvington-on-Hudson: Foundation for Economic Education, 1970.

Gray, Alexander. The Socialist Tradition: Moses to Lenin. London: Longmans, Green and Co., 1946.

Hayek, Friedrich A. (ed.). Collectivist Economic Planning. London: Routledge and Kegan Paul, Ltd., 1935.

Hayek, Friedrich A. The Road to Serfdom. Chicago: University of Chicago Press, Phoenix Books, 1944.

Hazlitt, Henry. Time Will Run Back (a novel). New Rochelle: Arlington House, 1966.

Hoff, Trygve J. B. Economic Calculation in the Socialist Society. Indianapolis: Liberty Press, 1981.

Mises, Ludwig von. The Anti-Capitalist Mentality. Princeton: D. Van Nostrand Co., 1956.

Mises, Ludwig von. Bureaucracy. New Haven: Yale University Press, 1944.

Mises, Ludwig von. Socialism. Indianapolis: Liberty Press, 1981.

Nove, Alec. The Economics of Feasible Socialism. London: George Allen & Unwin, 1983.

Roberts, Paul Craig and Stephenson, Matthew A. Marx's Theory of Exchange, Alienation and Crisis. Stanford: Hoover Institution Press, 1973.

Schoeck, Helmut. Envy. New York: Harcourt, Brace and World, Inc., 1970.

VII. Third World Aspects

Bauer, Peter T. Dissent on Development. London: Weidenfeld and Nicolson, 1971.

Bauer, Peter T. Equality, the Third World, and Economic Delusion. Cambridge, Mass: Harvard University Press, 1981.

Berger, Peter L. "Underdevelopment Revisited." Commentary, Vol. 78, No. 1 (July 1984).

Brunner, Karl (ed.) The First World and the Third World. Rochester: University of Rochester, 1978.

Sowell, Thomas. The Economics and Politics of Race. New York: William Morrow and Co., 1983.

VIII. Perspectives In Austrian Economics

Boehm-Bawerk, Eugen von. Capital and Interest. South Holland, Ill.: Libertarian Press, 1959.

Boehm-Bawerk, Eugen von. Shorter Classics. South Holland, Ill.: Libertarian Press, 1962.

Dolan, Edwin G. (ed.). The Foundations of Modern Austrian Economics. New York: New York University Press, 1976.

Kauder, Emil. A History of Marginal Utility Theory. Princeton: Princeton University Press, 1965.

Kirzner, Israel M. (ed.). Method, Process, and Austrian Economics. Lexington, Mass.: D. C. Heath and Co., 1982.

Lachmann, Ludwig M. Capital, Expectations, and the Market Process. (edited by Walter E. Grinder). New York: New York University Press, 1977.

Mises, Ludwig von. Human Action. 3rd revised edition, Chicago: Henry Regnery Co., 1966.

Moss, Laurence S. (ed.). The Economics of Ludwig von Mises. New York: New York University Press, 1976.

Rothbard, Murray N. Man, Economy, and State. New York: New York University Press, 1978.

Spadaro, Louis M. (ed.). New Directions In Austrian Economics. New York: New York University Press, 1978.

IX. Morals and Politics

Acton, H. B. The Morals of Markets. London: Longman, 1971.

Block, Walter. Defending the Undefendable. New York: Fleet Press Corp., 1976.

Hazlitt, Henry. The Foundations of Morality. Princeton: D. Van Nostrand Co., 1964.

Hospers, John. Human Conduct. 2nd ed., New York: Harcourt Brace Jovanovich, 1982.

Rothbard, Murray N. The Ethics of Liberty. Atlantic Highlands, N. J.: Humanities Press, 1982.

X. Methodological Issues

Hayek, Friedrich A. The Counter-Revolution of Science. Glencoe: The Free Press, 1955.

Hayek, Friedrich A. Studies In Philosophy, Politics and Economics. New York: Simon and Schuster, Clarion Books, 1969.

Kirzner, Israel M. The Economic Point of View. New York: New York University Press, 1976.

Mises, Ludwig von. Epistemological Problems of Economics. Princeton: D. Van Nostrand Co., 1960.

Mises, Ludwig von. Theory and History. New Haven: Yale University Press, 1957.

Mises, Ludwig von. The Ultimate Foundation of Economic Science. New York: New York University Press, 1978.

Schoeck, Helmut and Wiggins, James W. (eds.) Scientism and Values. Princeton: D. Van Nostrand Co.

INDEX

Abundance   9, 12, 83
AC: Average costs   See: Costs
Adjustments, by firms   199-206
Administered prices   267, 331, 365-67
Agriculture   166-68, 326, 364
Alchian, A. A.   81, 103, 230n, 287
Allen, W. R.   81, 103, 230n, 287
Altruism   105-13
Annuity   262-63
Anti-trust laws   319
AP   See: Administered prices
Arbitrage   43-44
Asceticism   12-13, 318
Assaying   47
Atomistic firms   324, 336, 353-54
Autistic exchange   101-102

Banks, commercial   25
Barriers to entry   See: Entry
Barter   14, 37-38, 40-45, 111
Bastiat, F.   33
Beg, borrow, or steal   2-4
Bergen, Edgar   110
Black markets   210
Boehm-Bawerk, E. von   90-92, 93-94, 238-39, 268
Borrowing   2-4
Bottlenecks   204
Broadway hit shows   210-12

Calculation, economic   See: Economic
Capacity of production   203-204
Capital
    accumulation   See: Investment
    consumption   See: Depreciation
    gain   263-64
    goods   60, 62-63, 67, 251, 307
    loss   263-64
    markets   251, 256, 294
    value   261-64
Capitalism   279-312
Capitalist production   65-66, 307
Capp, Al   9
Cartels   162, 174-75, 371n

384

385

Ex-post   95, 98-99
Ex-post supply   See: Supply

Fallacy of composition   3
FC: Fixed costs   See: Costs
Fiat money   57
Financial assets   53, 66, 68
Financial intermediaries   294
Firms   17-25, 60
    as discounters   243, 252-53, 256
    as income-generators   xix, 18-21, 74-78
    as intermediaries   20, 22, 73-74
    centrality of   xix, xxii
Fischer, Bobby   327
Fixed costs   See: Costs
Force 111   See also: Coercion
Form-utility   61
Foy, J. E.   312
Fraud   100
Free competition   See: Free market
Freedoms   See: Human rights
Free enterprise   311
Free entry   354, 355   See also: Free market
Free market   xiii-xv, xxv, 179-80, 207, 272,
    279-318, 323, 325, 362, 370-72
Free trade   34, 299
Future goods   240
Futurity of decisions   260-66

Galbraith, J. K.   xxvi, 312-18
Garden of Eden   9, 12, 83
Geographic variation   36-37
Getting by   1-8
Goethe, J. W. von   xii
Gold, as money   39-40, 45, 55, 57
Goodman, J. C.   xiii-n
Government   5-7
    borrowing   7
    and competition   292-93, 299-303
    and monopoly   292-93
Gray, A.   31
Groseclose, E.   39n, 49
Growth, economic   59-78

Haines, W. W.   39n, 47, 48, 55
Hamlet   95, 96, 368

Market-price system, outlined   xxi-xxiv
Market rate of interest   See: Interest
Market research   124, 135, 295
Market stability   xxii-xxiii
Market structure   See: Competition
Mark Twain   106-108
Marx, Karl   30n
Marxism   235, 266-67, 269
    See also: Labor theory of value
Matching problem   279-85
Maximization   xx, 94-102, 138-39, 194, 239
MC: Marginal costs   See: Costs
McCarthy, Charlie   110
McGee, J. S.   328n
McKenzie, R. B.   xviii-n
McNulty, P. J.   320n
Means   11, 12
    and ends   261, 316-18
    limited   9-10, 12, 15
    of production   11
Medium of exchange   See: Money
Menger, C.   268
Mercantilism   299, 302
Methodological individualism   102-105
Methods of production   See: Technology
Minimum losss   See: Loss
Minimum reservation price   182-83, 184
Mises, L. von   xx, 33n, 103, 239-40
Mismatch   See: Matching
Mobility, of resources   322
MOE: Medium of exchange   See: Money
Money   25-27, 38-58   See also: Cash balances
    abstract   54-57
    debasement   48-49, 52
    definition   45, 54
    fiat   57
    forms of   39-40, 45
    government role   48-49, 54-58
    inflation   226
    market origin   47, 49-52, 57-58
    medium of exchange   40, 45-47, 56-57
    metallic   46-47
    paper   57
    proper   50, 57-58
    silver   39-40, 45, 55, 57
    store of value   52   See also: Cash balances
    substitutes   57
    unit of account   54-57
    value of   51-52, 57, 237, 259
    weight nature of   55

Moneylender   236-37, 241, 252, 256
Monopolistic competition   331
Monopoly   292-93, 327-29
    closed   292-93, 328, 329
    open   328-29
    public utilities   292
Montaigne dogma   33, 35
Morality   xiii-xiv, 110-11, 176, 311
Morrison, H.   212
Motivation   94-95, 105
MR: Marginal revenue
MU: Marginal utility
Multipart pricing   344

National income   See: Income
National interest   104
Necessities   See: Needs
Needs   85-87
Neurotic   108
New money   25-27
Next time around   199, 201, 205
Non-price determinants of demand   118-24, 125-26
Non-profit firms   207, 209-212
Non-specific resources   276
Non-violence   34   See also: Morality
Normal rate of profit   xxv, 359
Novak, M.   xv-n

Oil, demand for   162
Oligopoly   329-31, 332
OPEC   188-90
Open markets   See: Free market
Oppenheimer, F.   4, 6-7
Opportunity cost   See: Costs
Optimal decisions   208
Out-of-pocket costs   See: Costs
Overhead costs   See: Costs, fixed
Over-pricing   186-87, 253
Over-production   196
Overtime pay   204

P: Price(s)
Pain and pleasure   108
Paradox of value   88-89
Payments-in-kind   41, 42
PC: Perfect competition
Percentage approach (elasticity of demand)   177-78

Profit (continued)
    entrepreneurial   256-59
    inflationary   256-57, 259
    maximization   176, 334, 340-51, 363
    normal rate   xxv, 359
    perspectives on   235
    squeeze   146
    under socialism   290-91
Profiteering   172, 173-74, 176, 193, 203, 205, 210-12, 227-29
Property rights   xxv, 303-11
Protectionism   207, 302-303, 370-72
PSP: Planned sales period
Public goods   284-85
Public utilities   See: Monopoly
Purchasing power of money   See: Money, value of
Pure interest   See: Interest

Q: Quantity; Quantities
Qd: Quantity demanded
Qd versus TR   154
Qs: Quantity supplied
Quality of life   86
Quantity-adjuster   349-50
Quantity demanded   117-24
Quantity supplied   182   See also: Supply
Queuing   210

Radford, R. A.   40n
Redistribution   109-11
Regret   98-101
Representation   104-105, 288
Research and development   71
Reservation prices   182-83, 184
Resources   See: Means
Resting on laurels   199-200
Revealed preference   85
Risk   206
Roberts, P. C.   14n, 30n
Robinson Crusoe   See: Crusoe
Rose Bowl   209-10
Rothbard, M. N.   xiv-n, xvii-n, xxiii-n, xxiv-n, xxvi-n, 39n, 58n, 84, 310n
Rush, Tom   97
Russell, Nipsy   75